Walking Tours of America

Walking Tours of America

Mini-Tours on Foot in Major Cities

With an Introduction by Wayne Barrett
**Developed by the
Kinney Shoe Corporation
in cooperation with
the President's Council on
Physical Fitness and Sports**
Edited by Louise Feinsot

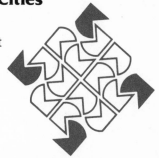

COLLIER BOOKS
A Division of Macmillan Publishing Co., Inc.
New York

COLLIER MACMILLAN PUBLISHERS
London

Macmillan Publishing Co., Inc.
866 Third Avenue, New York, N.Y. 10022
Collier Macmillan Canada, Ltd.

Library of Congress Cataloging in Publication Data
Main entry under title:
Walking tours of America.
    1. United States—Description and travel—
1960–   —Tours.   2. Walking—United States.
I. Feinsot, Louise.
E158.W34   1979   917.3′04′926   79-12127
ISBN 0-02-097250-4

First Printing 1979

Printed in the United States of America

CONTENTS

If all Americans would simply walk more, I am convinced that we would have a happier and healthier populace. Walking is a far more effective exercise than many people imagine, and it also is a good way to establish that intimate contact with the people and things around us that too often is missing from modern life.

Because it is a relatively "painless" exercise, there is a tendency to underrate the physical fitness benefits of walking. That is unfortunate. Done properly, walking can tone flabby muscles, burn up excess calories, improve circulation and respiration, and dissipate tensions. The secret is to walk briskly and purposefully for at least two or three miles at a time.

Walking requires a slightly greater investment of time than do some more strenuous activities, such as running or swimming, but it also has many advantages. It is not a seasonal activity, nearly everyone can do it, no lessons or special equipment are needed, and experience indicates that walking is habit-forming.

So, the next time somebody suggests that you "take a walk," take them up on it. You may learn some things about both your body and your neighborhood that you never knew before.

The Walk America tours have been planned to add scenic and historic interest to the simple pleasures of walking. I am pleased to recommend them to you.

C. Carson Conrad
Executive Director
THE PRESIDENT'S COUNCIL ON
PHYSICAL FITNESS AND SPORTS

*He who does not walk the land
is not a true citizen of his country.*

Come, Americans, take a walk in America! Whether it be in the cool corridors of the Pacific north woods, or a stroll along a magic bend of the Mississippi, or a history-steeped meander in Pennsylvania, or up through the canyons of Wall Street, or to reconnoiter some beachhead in California or Florida . . . America is yours for the walking.

Walking in America offers hidden splendors and surprises. No other country extends to the walker so much diversity, contrast, tranquility, and natural hospitality—plus the simple, wonderful freedom to explore.

The boundary lines between our states are invisible; they exist for constitutional purposes only. They present no obstacles to those traversing the land. Indeed, they are recognized as "welcome signs" inviting our citizens—and the citizens of the world—to come walk in all directions.

And yet, compared to other lands where walking is a leisurely sophisticated pastime with countless dedicated followers, Americans generally have not developed the gentle art of walking. Over the years, poets, medical authorities, and lovers in all nations have come to understand the multi-advantages of walking. Ancient Greek philosophers taught their disciples while walking. Walking alone can be one of life's unique, private experiences; walking with companions affords a joyous social occasion.

Kinney Shoe Corporation, together with a distinguished company of walking tour experts, proudly invites the American public to take a special walk this year, in any one of our carefully crafted walking tours coast-to-coast, and continue walking throughout the years—just for the health of it.

Kinney's *Walking Tours of America* is a celebration of American terrain by Americans—and a new kind of guidebook to help our foreign guests to also savor this land and its people.

We believe these documented, cultivated walks—offering a judicious balance between the bounties of nature and the lure of America's modern metropolitan centers—will inspire countless miles of personal fulfillment, an appreciation of scenery and historic points of interest, and positive reflections on the worth of contemporary America.

America today is an endless adventure for the walking enthusiast. Both individuals and families can reap the harvest of discovery—as their footsteps lead them to new levels of enlightenment, physical invigoration, and visual feasts.

It is our hope that these *Walking Tours of America* will arouse the dormant curiosity and vigor of many millions of Americans.

The season of walking is at hand. Let ours be the generation that got America walking again.

Walk tall, America!

Cameron I. Anderson
President
Kinney Shoe Corporation

ACKNOWLEDGMENTS

The preparation of the materials in this book took the better part of two years. It involved many dedicated and cooperative people all across America, to whom we wish to express our sincere appreciation.

We are particularly grateful to Kinney Shoe Corporation for commissioning the 60 tours in this book as part of its Walking Tours of America program—a national public service project designed to encourage Americans to start walking again—and to the President's Council on Physical Fitness and Sports for its cooperation and especially to C. Carson Conrad, executive director, for his enthusiastic participation in this effort.

Special thanks go to Kinney executives Cameron I. Anderson, president, John K. Aneser, vice president of marketing communications, and Robin Burke, managing director of public relations, and to Richard L. Anderson (Kinney's president when the project began, now senior executive vice president, F. W. Woolworth Co.) who recognized the merit and importance of this ambitious program and gave it their complete support.

We are indebted to Robert Bagar, creative director, and Louise Feinsot, vice president at Ruder & Finn, Inc., for planning the Walking Tours of America program and for carrying it forward with professional skill combined with a special brand of missionary zeal. Other members of the team who played a vital role in the production of the tours include: Alisa Zamir and Ulrich Ruchti of Ruder & Finn Design for creating the exciting graphic-design elements employed in the Walking Tours program; Patricia Luciani and Jessica Miller for assisting in the overall coordination of the program and for painstaking editing of all the copy; Marilu Lopez and Jo Ann Owen for meticulously preparing the walking tour maps; and the 21 writers for producing the lively and easy-to-follow text of the book.

We are indebted, too, to the following individuals who freely gave of their valuable time to assist the writers in researching and checking the accuracy of the walking tours: Paul Kneeland of the *Boston Globe;* Michael Frucci of the Cape Cod Chamber of Commerce; Jack Stovkis of the Paterson Division of Economic Development; Alice Brown of the Historical Society of Princeton; Kathy Shays of Princeton University; Justin J. Murphy of the Downtown Lower Manhattan Association; Jack MacBean of the New York Convention and Visitors Bureau; Helen Hoffman of the Bucks County Historical–Tourist Commission; Jeanne Fox of the Greater Pittsburgh Chamber of Commerce; Barbara Burns of the Pittsburgh Convention and Visitors Bureau; Janet Fuhrman of the Philadelphia Convention and Visitors Bureau; Mrs. John J. O'Malley of the Newport Chamber of Commerce; Peg Sinclair of the Alexandria Tourist Council; Austin Kenny and Joan Allen of the Washington Area Convention and Visitors Bureau; Alice Sinkevitch and Mary Sue Mohnke of the Chicago School of Architecture Foundation; Sandy Guettler of the Illinois Department of Business and Economic Development; Pat Shymanski of the Historic Pullman Foundation; Dennis Anderson, City Manager of Woodstock, Illinois; Catherine Barker of the Frank Lloyd Wright Home and Studio Foundation; Sandy Adams of the Columbus Visitors Center; Karen Stewart of the Metro Detroit Convention and Visitors Bureau; Joan Behles of the Minneapolis Convention and Tourism Commission; Steve Karbon of the St. Paul area Chamber of Commerce; Chuck Boyd of the Kansas City Convention and Visitors Bureau; Frank Carrell of the Cleveland Convention and Visitors Bureau; Virginia Haberman of the Greater Milwaukee Convention and Visitors Bureau; James Zeder of the Birmingham–Bloomfield Chamber of Commerce; Nancy Brennan of the San Antonio Convention and Visitors Bureau; Dale Young of the Greater Houston Convention and Visitors Council; John Marshall of the Fort Worth Chamber of Commerce; Wes Young of the Dallas Convention and Visitors Bureau; Jim Barton of Virginia Beach, Virginia; Gloria Salcedo of the Greater New Orleans Tourist and Convention Commission; Susan Davis of the Charleston County Park, Recreation and Tourist Commission; Phil Halpern of the Miami Beach Tourist Development Authority; and Margaret McPherson of the Atlanta Convention and Visitors Bureau.

Finally, we wish to thank the American public for its responsiveness to the Walking Tours of America program. Thousands of letters sent to Kinney Shoe Corporation requesting copies of the tours, which were published first in brochure form, confirmed our belief that given interesting places to walk, Americans would indeed take to their feet and begin walking again—for fitness, for pleasure, and as a way of "discovering America."

INTRODUCTION

Wayne Barrett

It's been said that in historic Annapolis, Maryland, a wise pedestrian always keeps one eye on the ground. That's because in some places old sidewalks have been heaved up by tree roots and worn down by the tread of two centuries. George Washington walked here on business and pleasure, as did other founding fathers and their ladies. They did not let buckled bricks and cobbles trip them up or an occasional puddle dampen their ardor for walking. Neither should you. With the aid of the descriptive tours and maps in this volume, you can chart a course to suit your fancy—through historic quarters and modern shopping plazas, along busy thoroughfares and scenic waterfronts, and into a dazzling array of gardens, galleries, and museums.

This Baedeker for city strolling, encompassing some sixty walks in urban America, came about, fittingly, through the efforts of a shoe company—Kinney Shoe Corporation—in cooperation with the President's Council on Physical Fitness and Sports. The project was conceived to be a public service—and so it is. Nowhere will you find Kinney promoting the walking tours in a self-serving way. If the shoe industry benefits from them, it will only be because we sedentary Americans decide to walk more and ride less—and thus will need to be better shod.

Before the automobile swept us off our feet, we were a determined nation of walkers. It was nothing for students to walk several miles to school. Nor was it out of the ordinary for a 19th-century American to set out across-country on foot. With knapsack, gun, and dog, "well moccasined" John James Audubon would walk several hundred miles in quest of portrait commissions. Like other naturalists, he enjoyed walking, waxing poetic at nature's wonders—"the gambols of the fawns around their dams," for example.

A more recent observer of nature, Donald Culross Peattie,

was no less eloquent in recounting "the joys of circumambulating city streets." But in order to enjoy city walking to the fullest, he said, you had to like people: "For a whistling boy must be your bird song, girls' faces your wayside flowers, the flow and roar of the street your clattering, swirling streams, and tall buildings your sun-smitten crags. And by night you have the spattered office lights above for your winking constellations."

Henry David Thoreau, who had many things to say about the virtues of walking, admitted that he came to town "to hear some of the gossip . . . as refreshing in its way as the rustle of leaves and the peeping of frogs. As I walked in the woods to see the birds and squirrels, so I walked in the village to see the men and boys." A well-known ornithologist of today is always on the lookout for birds—even when he comes to Manhattan, companions say. Walking softly, he squints upward into a forest of skyscrapers, scanning for a wayward osprey, perhaps.

City sidewalks were made for walking, of course. And for rubbernecking. You can dawdle along, stopping at your leisure to gaze and ponder, lingering at some new discovery such as a gargoyle hidden in the carved stonework of an old building. No more will you have to be satisfied with a fleeting glimpse from an automobile or crowded tour bus. Only on your feet can you truly appreciate that the skyscraper was born in Chicago's Loop; that San Francisco boasts a Civil War landmark—Fort Point; that the center of the Brooklyn Bridge is the place to stand for a breathtaking view of Manhattan. In these pages you are invited to take a vicarious walk through the nation's first zoo—in Philadelphia; stand in the shadow of San Antonio's Alamo, where Davy Crockett fell; retrace the footsteps (painted on the sidewalks) of Boston's patriots. New Orleans tempts with a moonlight stroll through the French Quarter down to the levee. Chances are you will stride along to the strains of Dixieland welling up from Bourbon Street.

Some of us like to whistle or sing while we walk; but unless our rendition of "Indian Love Call" or "The World Is Waiting for the Sunrise" is especially noteworthy, we are liable to be the target of stern looks or even be hissed off the street. Robert Louis Stevenson, an enthusiastic walker in his day, remarked that "you would be astonished if I were to tell you all the grave and learned heads who have confessed to me that, when on walking tours, they sang—and sang very ill."

As a rule, the musical walker tends to be a loner, whether he can carry a tune or not. Stevenson felt strongly that "to be properly enjoyed, a walking tour should be gone upon alone . . . because freedom is of the essence; because you should be able to stop and go on, and follow this way or that, as the freak takes you; and because you must have your own pace, and neither trot alongside a champion walker, nor mince in time with a girl." In other words, your thoughts should be company enough. Or as Stevenson put it: "There should be no cackle of voices at your elbow, to jar on the meditative silence of the morning."

To walk as the freak takes you—that is, whimsically and without apparent purpose—permits the mind also to wander. How many inspired ideas, scientific solutions, and wise decisions have been born in the course of a walk? Poets the stripe of Keats, Shelley, and Wordsworth doubtless conceived many of their memorable passages while afoot. Where else but on an aimless ramble to feel the west wind, thou breath of autumn's being, to hear a nightingale in such an ecstasy, to see a crowd, a host, of golden daffodils? It was on such a walk that Samuel Taylor Coleridge framed "The Rime of the Ancient Mariner." American authors like O. Henry, James T. Farrell, and Sinclair Lewis prowled the Bowery, the South Side, and Main Street to find settings for their stories. Street people filled the sketch pads of John Sloan, one of the founders of the Ashcan School of painting. Reginald Marsh, dubbed the "pictorial poet-laureate of the sidewalks of New York" in the 1930s, was uncomfortable anywhere else. Vermont was "too damn green" to suit him.

Today's walker is more likely to carry a camera instead of a sketch pad, a tape recorder instead of a notebook. But to many, the best way to record the pleasures of a stroll is with the mind, employing the senses to preserve the sights and sounds of a special time and place. Memorable walks are often the results of circumstances beyond our control—like the blackouts experienced in New York and other cities a few years ago. Strikes, blizzards, and gasoline shortages have forced people to rediscover that walking is still the most dependable mode of transportation. Indeed, the frontiers of North America were first breached by men on foot—Daniel Boone, Alexander Mackenzie, John Chapman (Johnny Appleseed), Meriwether Lewis and William Clark, Jedediah Smith, Marcus Whitman and his wife

Narcissa, and countless more settlers, trappers, soldiers, gold-seekers. In that number too were walkers enthralled by the boundless beauty of the continent. Such a one was John Muir. In 1867, when he was 29, he set out on a jaunt of a 1,000 miles, from Louisville to the Gulf of Mexico, pushing through "the wildest, leafiest, and least trodden way I could find." His self-appointed mission was to study plants—"to get acquainted with as many of them as possible." Settlers along the way, suspicious of strangers since the Civil War, found his story hard to believe; often he was refused food and lodging. "Traveled today more than forty miles without dinner or supper," he jotted down in his journal. "No family would receive me. . . . Went hungry to bed and awoke with a sore stomach—sore, I suppose, from its walls rubbing on each other without anything to grind." In his pack he carried little more than a few clothes, the New Testament, and a copy of Robert Burns' poems.

Although it is doubtful that today's long-distance walker could be better motivated, he or she is certainly better equipped. Taking advantage of compact, lightweight materials, a person can carry a kitchen as well as a bed on his back.

City walkers have no need for these accessories, of course, for theirs is not primarily a test of endurance. Intent on pleasure, they may interrupt their walk at any time to placate the appetite. At hand are restaurants of abundant variety—Cookie's in Provincetown, Forepaugh's in St. Paul, Kresge Court Cafeteria in Detroit, to name a few mentioned in these pages. Thirsty? Pause for free tastes at Milwaukee breweries and Sonoma wineries. Tired? Relax on a hand-hewn bench in a redwoods grove near Santa Cruz, or sit on the grass in Lafayette Square, across from the White House. Fatigued walkers in hilly San Francisco, noted columnist Herb Caen, "can lean against it."

It is not the energy expended but the time spent that most concerns us in this age of rush and ride. Even on the golf course the rush is on. Electric carts that whisk players from tee to green have eliminated the major attraction of the sport—a ramble through scenic countryside. To the Scots who invented the game, the act of striking a dimpled ball would never have been satisfactory without the exhilaration of an 18-hole walk—usually about 7,000 yards if you keep out of the rough. But, alas, for purists golf today is too often a race against time instead of the means for healthful exercise. The overweight businessman in a hurry chooses to ride between swings instead of following the example of Shakespeare's sweating Falstaff, who "lards the lean earth as he walks along." And helps his heart in the process, doctors would add.

Thomas Jefferson, whose opinions are widely respected, declared, "Of all exercises walking is best." Others who took long walks before and after entering the White House included Abraham Lincoln at Springfield, Woodrow Wilson at Princeton, and Dwight Eisenhower on the golf course. Jimmy Carter's inaugural walk down Pennsylvania Avenue made headlines. Harry Truman enjoyed a morning constitutional, brisking along at a two-step-per-second clip. Panting reporters trailed in his wake trying to match the Presidential pace.

Few could match the zeal for walking of Supreme Court Justice William O. Douglas. In 1954 he and a few hardy followers walked the entire length of the C&O Canal—180 miles—to protest a proposal to build a parkway along the route. Douglas became a dedicated walker after suffering from polio in childhood. He recalled how, as a 14-year-old testing his recovery, it felt to hike 40 miles in the Cascades: "I was proud of my legs. They were so tired they felt numb. But they never failed. They did not cry out in anguish nor did they ache. The plop, plop of my feet sounded far away, remote, impersonal. . . . I was an automaton that had been set out for a course and never missed a beat."

An orthopedic surgeon, M. Beckett Howorth, echoed the automatic nature of walking, calling it "a beautiful performance worthy of Pavlova." His description of the act of walking has a poetic lilt:

> The front of the thighs contract
> but a fraction of a second in a rippling movement,
> when swinging the leg forward.
> The muscles in front of the ankles contract
> similarly, preventing the foot from dragging
> just before the heel strikes.
> As the heel strikes,
> all the thigh and ankle muscles contract
> together, stabilizing the knee and ankle
> until the weight is stressed forward
> by the calf.

The muscles of the hips swing
the thigh forward, then stabilize it.
Trunk muscles become involved,
as well as the flank, back, and the chest.
Arms and shoulders,
the abdominal area, which probably need tightening,
the muscles of the ribs, which expand
the chest and lungs when breathing,
also come into play.
They all participate in the beautiful choreography
of the simple act of walking.

One action stimulates another,
and the blood, heart, lungs, and nerves
all get into the act.
Nerves send messages to the muscles,
and the sense of position to the central nervous system.
In fact, while taking a walk,
most of the muscles, organs, and tissues
become involved.
This is the reason that walking
is such good exercise.

It is self-evident that walking is good for you. But what sets it
apart from high-intensity forms of exercise is its fail-safe character. Unlike running or swimming or playing tennis, walking is all
but impossible to overdo. Walkers seldom suffer orthopedic ail-
ments common to jogging—muscle strains, heel bruises, shin
splints, sprains of the knee and ankle joints. A blister, at most, is
the only penalty a walker is likely to pay, and that is usually due
to shoe problems. True, after several hours of brisk walking you
may experience fatigue, but as heart specialist Dr. Paul Dudley
White noted, it is a "remarkably enjoyable" feeling. "A pleasant
fatigue of the muscles has time and again given me mental
repose, peaceful sleep, and a sense of equanimity."
    It is equally true that walking is the most social of all exer-
cises. In jogging and calisthenics the participant grimaces rather
than smiles, suggesting that it's serious business to work up a
sweat. The walker, on the other hand, is typically loose and
relaxed, with even the most taciturn likely to nod agreeably or
wish you a good morning. Walking, therefore, by its open and

communicative nature, is essentially a friendly act. Sitting behind a steering wheel, enclosed by a barrier of metal and glass, may not be; in fact, it may be harmful to your health both physically and mentally. Any bumper-to-bumper rush hour offers abundant proof of mounting tensions, with the public display of bad manners a common occurrence. A sane walker, however, would never force anyone off the sidewalk; and it is unthinkable that a walker would scream obscenities at another for cutting into his lane. English philosopher Bertrand Russell was convinced that unhappy businessmen "would increase their happiness more by walking six miles every day than by any conceivable change of philosophy." Writer Hal Borland enlarges on that perspective: "Walking can shrink the biggest of us, give us that sense of proportion which we all need on occasion. In an automobile you feel that miles are of no consequence and that all hills are low. In an airplane you lose your sense of both time and distance. In both cases you feel that you, not the machine, have altered reality. But on foot you soon learn how high is a hill and how long is a mile."

An advertising slogan a generation ago put an arbitrary value on that distance by proclaiming, "I'd walk a mile for a Camel." Today a smoker concerned about his health would be more likely to forswear tobacco and walk a mile or more for his heart. A few years ago physical-fitness researchers at Wake Forest University conducted tests that indicated that walking helps your heart as much as some strenuous exercises. Walking rapidly was found to be more effective than jogging slowly. The intake of oxygen increased by as much as 28 percent and pulmonary circulation increased 15 percent.

By extending the oxygen capacity of the heart and lungs, the risk of heart attack is lessened. Walking, which Dr. White called "the simplest and least expensive form of exercise," helps ease the heart's burden of pumping 18,000 gallons of blood through your 100,000-mile circulatory system every 24 hours. Standing on two legs instead of four, erect humans must overcome the pull of gravity to force blood to the heart and brain. Leg and trunk muscles activated by walking serve as a "second heart," rhythmically contracting and releasing to force blood up through the veins.

No one understood the beneficial aspects of walking more than historian George Macaulay Trevelyan. "I have two doctors," he said, "my left leg and my right." He believed that "an honest day's walk for whatever distance" gave a man "his reward in the repossession of his soul." Such exercise, quipped Plato more than 2,000 years earlier, "would almost cure a guilty conscience." To their select company—the professor roaming the grounds at Cambridge and the philosopher sauntering in his Athenian olive grove—add the voice of a mail carrier on his appointed rounds. "Walking is good for you," asserted John Fuller in Studs Terkel's book *Working*. "It keeps you active. You more or less feel better." One reason is that regular walking helps keep a body trim. You seldom see a fat mailman. Especially one who totes a 35-pound bag ten miles or more a day.

Trying to lose weight is one of America's favorite pastimes. We gulp magic pills, follow fad diets, and devour books that tell us how to think off the pounds. The results are often disappointing. Perhaps we should pay attention to an ancient remedy, one prescribed by Hippocrates, the father of medicine. Walk, he advised. Walk morning and night.

He was right. An hour's brisk walk—say, at 3 or 4 miles an hour—will burn up as much as 400 calories. Nine hours of walking later you will have shed a pound. And had fun doing it. Don't worry that walking will make you ravenous and spoil your fun. It won't. According to nutritionist Dr. Jean Mayer, moderate exercise actually suppresses the appetite slightly. Confirmation comes from studies like that at the University of California at Irvine. There Dr. Grant Gwinup put a group of 11 obese women on a year-long regimen of walking, with no diet restrictions. The women, up to 60 percent overweight, found that if they walked more than half an hour a day they lost weight— from 10 to 38 pounds each.

Other studies show that people who sit all day, like bus drivers, tend toward fat. And they have more coronary problems than less-sedentary workers.

"Sitting is a national disease," declared C. Carson Conrad, Executive Director of the President's Council on Physical Fitness and Sports. "TVs, cars, and sedentary occupations are contributing to American sedentariness. When you sit for prolonged periods, body fluids settle in the lower extremities. Many older people have swollen ankles and feet because of a pattern of sititus. People who are sedentary age faster, look older, and actually feel older. Sedentary living results in a decrease of muscular strength, muscular endurance, flexibility, and cardiorespiratory endurance. Sitting causes muscles to weaken and to fatten up.

The average American bottoms have increased in size up to an inch per generation, and this is partly due to increased sitting. Sitting for long periods is bad for your heart in that it tends to weaken the heart and lungs, rendering them less capable of withstanding stress. Regular brisk walking as opposed to sedentariness increases the capacity of the heart, blood vessels, and lungs."

A century earlier Thoreau had made a similar, if more caustic, observation. "I think that I cannot preserve my health and spirits," he wrote, "unless I spend four hours a day at least,—and it is commonly more than that,—sauntering through the woods and over the hills and fields. . . . When sometimes I am reminded that the mechanics and shopkeepers stay in their shops not only all the forenoon, but all the afternoon too, sitting with crossed legs, so many of them,—as if the legs were made to sit upon, and not to stand or walk upon,—I think that they deserve some credit for not having all committed suicide long ago."

A walking companion, Ralph Waldo Emerson, reasoned that it was "the best of humanity that goes out to walk." But he alleged that few men properly knew how. He listed these qualifications: "endurance, plain clothes, old shoes, an eye for Nature, good humor, vast curiosity, good speech, good silence, and nothing too much." Walking, he said, was "one of the secrets for dodging old age," and he recommended it to people growing old against their will.

The advice is still sound. Although he and his crony Thoreau might look down their blue noses at city walkers, the benefits to be gained make the effort worthwhile. Despite drawbacks such as noise and pollution, there are pleasant oases— like the Dumbarton Oaks gardens in Georgetown, for instance—that reward the pedestrian. Walkers may also take encouragement from the trend to ban cars from some city streets.

"Walking is as natural as breathing," stated Paul Dudley White. And almost as necessary. It is important that we, comfortably cradled in our automobiles, do not forget how. For should there be another energy crisis—a not unlikely prospect, experts say—we shall be forced to get reacquainted with our feet. What better way to stay in shape for such an eventuality than to try some of the tours in this book? We might discover that we've been missing something good. We might learn, as naturalist John Burroughs suggested, of "our need to cultivate the art" of walking. He believed that "it would tend to soften the national manners, to teach us the meaning of leisure, to acquaint us with the charms of the open air, to strengthen and foster the tie between the race and the land." His challenge remains, finding new expression in these walking tours of America.

Walking the Northeast

MASSACHUSETTS

BOSTON, THE HISTORIC HUB
Edwards Park

Writers on Boston papers have an affinity for the word "Hub" to describe their city. It fits a crammed headline, and synthesizes the Boston attitude. Hub of what? you ask. Of Massachusetts? Of New England? No, explains the Bostonian with quiet self-assurance, of the Universe.

Touring the Hub is like having a date with a queen—demanding as well as rewarding. You may get a peep at the crown jewels, but you mustn't take liberties. Here are some rules of protocol. Choose late spring or early fall, for the Hub is sticky in summer and often snowbound in winter. Sunday is a good day to walk. Streets are empty and vistas open up before you. Some restaurants may not be open, so check first.

For years Boston has had a well-tested walking tour, the Freedom Trail. It leads you through the maze of "downtown," from one historic site to another, linking about sixteen of them to give you the feel of the Boston of Paul Revere's day—a sea-going town of cobbled streets and gracious red brick houses. It shows you where the cause of liberty was voiced, where the young sparks of rebellion were fanned to fire, where Patriot heroes met and hurled defiance at King George, where British troops marched from their billets to battle this new cause. The Freedom Trail is a well-planned journey along our road toward independence. You will follow it some of the way, cross it, reverse it, and if you're up to it, add to it.

Boston Common
If you drive to where you will start your walking tour, go to the underground garage at Boston Common, that ancient peo-

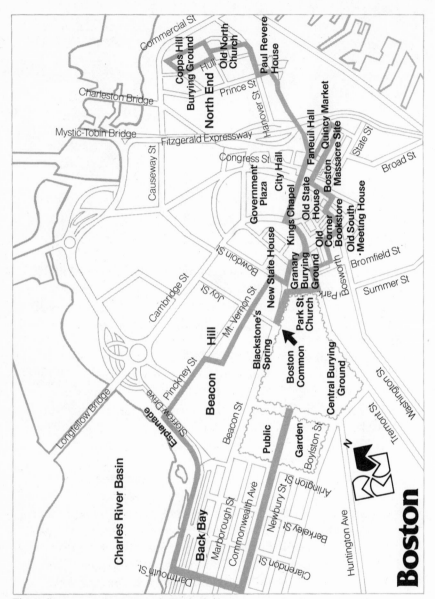

This walking tour is approximately 5 miles long.

ple's park where cows can still be kept (but are not). When the garage was excavated, human bones were uncovered. Planners hadn't realized that early settlers were put to rest here even before the Central Burying Ground (where artist Gilbert Stuart lies, among others) was established.

On the Beacon Street side of the Common (north), near Joy Street, stands a memorial to Blackstone's Spring, the water source for William Blackstone who dwelt on the banks of the Charles River in the 1620s on the peninsula that the Indians called Shawmut. This memorial is your starting point.

Walk east on Beacon Street, with the edge of the Common on your right. You pass solid, bay-windowed houses of Federalist style, some with blue-tinted glass, once grand residences, now often clubs and associations. In one woman's club a visiting speaker was forced to admit that she came from Iowa. "My dear," said her Boston hostess, "in Boston we pronounce it 'Ohio.' "

Freedom Trail

Pass the splendid gold-domed New State House, built in 1795, but still "new" to Bostonians because they have an older one which you will soon see. Swing right on Park Street and descend to the Park Street Church with its soaring white steeple. It stands on the corner of Tremont Street—"Brimstone Corner," so named because gunpowder was once stored in the church basement. Turn left on Tremont—named for the three peaks that once marked Beacon Hill and have long since been shaved away for landfill—and beside the church you'll find the Old Granary Burying Ground where such notables as Paul Revere, Sam Adams and John Hancock lie. If you're a headstone buff, you'll find some very old ones, but rubbings aren't allowed.

Opposite the burying ground, small streets lead downhill to Washington Street. Take any one of them and note the varied shops along the way. If you go down Bosworth, however, you'll come to the Province Steps, an old stone staircase that simply marks the end of one small street. Nothing more charmingly reminds you that Boston was designed for people, not cars.

However you reach Washington Street, you're within a pebble's throw of the Old South Meeting House on the corner of Milk Street. Like many New England churches, it served as a political forum as well as house of worship. From here, in December, 1773, activists who had been fighting Britain's tax on tea took off toward the waterfront for the Boston Tea Party. Their route is marked, but is less rewarding than the Freedom Trail. Later, by car, you may want to visit the replica of the tea ship, *Beaver,* moored in Fort Point Channel.

From Old South, walk to your right along Washington Street past the Old Corner Bookstore. Gathered here are those names you remember from high school English—Emerson, Thoreau, Longfellow, Whittier, and on and on. The fine old building, dating from 1712, is now maintained by the *Boston Globe.*

The Old State House now comes into sight on the east side of Washington Street. It was built in 1713, and the colonial government had its headquarters here until the Declaration of Independence was read from its balcony. Varied exhibits inside depict the city's maritime history, the great fire of the 1870s and include Revolutionary War memorabilia. More interesting, really, is the early Georgian architecture and the layout—assembly room on one side of the graceful spiral staircase, the Royal Governor's chamber on the other.

Leaving by the side door, turn left and pause at the next street corner to gaze at the cobbled ring in the pavement that marks the site of the so-called Boston Massacre of 1770. This was where a handful of British soldiers, badgered beyond all patience by a mob pelting them with rock-filled snowballs, finally fired and killed five people. Boston leaders, quick to see the propaganda value of the sad event, blew it into a sort of preview of revolution. But lawyer John Adams, ever the champion of justice, braved the hatred of his fellow citizens by successfully defending the British officer in charge.

Faneuil Hall and Quincy Market

You are now firmly upon the Freedom Trail. Its distinctive brown markers and painted footsteps on the sidewalk (sometimes they wear away or are snow-buried) will guide you straight to Faneuil Hall, an imposing colonial building with a wonderful gilded grasshopper weathervane that has been its trademark since 1742 when Peter Faneuil—the name is French Huguenot—built this combined market and meeting hall. Revolutionary ideas flashed back and forth here in the 1700s, and the tradition persists.

The actual market is now in the next block east—Quincy Market—and you should forsake the Trail here to wander through this Greek Revival building, and perhaps take a lunch break. Every kind of shop and stall crams the covered sidewalk, and Bostonians of all stations crowd them and eat at the sidewalk tables. There is an endless variety of ethnic foods being hawked from the crowded stalls and you have a choice as broad as your imagination. In fact, the sidewalks facing Faneuil Hall and Quincy Market to the northeast are still clogged with the parked pushcarts of marketmen noisily selling fish, fresh vegetables, fruit and scores of articles as well as foods, all dispensed with great flair—a whistle for the pretty woman, a wink for her escort, a "freebie" for the children, and a broad grin for all. If you take a short side trip east toward the harbor you'll enjoy the open-air delights of Marine Park. From here you can watch harbor activity.

The North End

Pick up the Freedom Trail markers back at Faneuil Hall. You need it to navigate to and through Boston's North End. This old section, now the city's Little Italy, lies beyond the confusing concrete complex of overpasses that form the Fitzgerald Expressway. Only the Trail knows how to get across this mess. Stick with it and you'll emerge on narrow streets which used to echo to the tread of British regulars who were billeted in the North End. After you take a short, well-marked detour from Hanover to North Street, Paul Revere's House, the oldest house in Boston, stands before you.

Revere was an authentic hero of the Revolution, carrying messages from colony to colony in the spare time that he seized from his job as silversmith and *pater familias* (married twice, he sired 16 children). His famous midnight ride was actually one of his easier assignments.

In Paul Revere Mall, next stop on the Trail, rises the Old North Church where Revere's signal lanterns—"two if by sea"—were hung on that epochal night of April 18, 1775, when the redcoats set out for Lexington and Concord. Revere's statue stands in front. On a pleasant day you will find the benches filled with the neighborhood residents discussing, arguing, laughing, dreaming in the sun, sometimes playing *boccie*. Note the other church that faces Revere's statue, the only remaining one in Boston designed by Charles Bulfinch, whose graceful architecture marks so much of late-18th-century New England.

Follow the Freedom Trail to Copps Hill Burying Ground

for a fine view across the harbor to Charlestown, Bunker Hill Monument and the frigate *Constitution* ("Old Ironsides"). It was from here that British guns pounded colonial breastworks on Breed's Hill, where the battle was actually fought, setting fire to much of Charlestown in the process. Little of the battlefield remains, thanks to years of development. There is a fine diorama at Bunker Hill Monument, and you may want to make a side trip over to Charlestown to see this and also go aboard the splendidly restored old ship. The Freedom Trail will lead you back from the North End and safely across the expressway. At Faneuil Hall, cut across Adams Square, in front of the building, and the new malls toward the City Hall and Government Plaza. This gives you a glimpse of what city planners have done with this complex old city that outgrew its original boundaries decades, even centuries ago.

City Hall and Government Plaza

The plaza is an 8-acre expanse, planned by I. M. Pei, that was opened by the clearing away of old Scollay Square with its shoddy shops and bars and Old Howard burlesque theater, dear to generations of adventurous Harvard students. On the plaza rise new government buildings dominated by City Hall, a controversial contemporary structure designed by Kallmann, McKinnell & Knowles. It's a remarkable building, and if you have time you may want to take one of the regular tours through it. If not, cross the plaza slowly, noting the fountains, the steps, the strangely "un-Boston" appearance, yet remembering that it's become a grand place for protests, as ever-protesting Bostonians will agree.

Keeping the new government office buildings on your right, cross Pemberton Square and pick up the end of Tremont Street once more. You will now pass King's Chapel, so named because it was originally Church of England before following its inclinations and becoming Unitarian. Its burying ground dates back to the very beginnings of the town, 1630.

Turn right at the start of Beacon Street, leaving the famous Parker House, home of those rolls, on the corner to your left. You are now climbing back toward the New State House, but before you reach it, veer off on Bowdoin Street, to the right, and then turn left on Mount Vernon. This will take you right under the State House, over Beacon Hill, and straight to Louisburg Square, home of Boston's Brahmins. Here lovely Federal town houses face a tiny enclosed park to which only residents have keys. On Christmas Eve, shades are raised and curtains pulled aside welcomingly while carolers and bell ringers stroll from house to house. Unfortunately, so many sightseers move about, too, that the effect loses some of its charm.

Leave the square by Pinckney Street, which meets its western side. Go downhill to cross Charles Street with its interesting international shops, and head for the river. A footwalk takes you across the rushing traffic of Storrow Drive and on to the Esplanade. Turn left here and walk upstream beside the broad Charles River. You will see small sailboats racing and single sculls slipping past from the Union Boat Club. Children play along the shore. It's a happy walk to Dartmouth Street's footbridge.

Back Bay

There you cross back again and walk through a little of the Back Bay. This was indeed a bay—but very shallow—until the landfill from Beacon Hill was dumped into it in order to provide the overcrowded Boston peninsula with more bedrooms. It is now well over a century old, and its streets are famous as the addresses of "good" old families, their clubs and shops. Beacon Street is said to be old and rich, Marlborough old and poor, Commonwealth Avenue new and rich, and Newbury new and poor. Today, all of them are young—at least their inhabitants are—for the Back Bay is a huge dormitory for students. And Newbury is a street of smart and expensive shops.

Turn left on any of these, but end up by strolling along the tree-shaded mall down the center of Commonwealth Avenue. You will pass the statues of Boston greats—Robert Treat Paine, signer of the Declaration of Independence, William Lloyd Garrison, who thundered against slavery in the Park Street Church, and after you cross Arlington Street and enter the Public Gardens, George Washington is there to greet you.

The Public Gardens are a delight in spring with the flower beds winking in the sunlight and swan boats drifting on the lagoon. Keep to the central path, cross Charles Street again, and you are back on the Common with the garage ahead of you.

You'll be tired, for you've done close to 5 miles. But you'll never forget the Hub and the panorama of American history that you have just walked your way through.

CAPE COD – PROVINCETOWN
Roy Bongartz

Besides the spectacular stretch of surf and sand along the 40 miles of the Cape Cod National Seashore, where walkers and beachcombers hardly need any sort of marked path to find their way, there are many delightful tours to be made on foot just inland. These include strolls through old fishing ports, along nature trails and into woods and swamps. Here are three of the best walking routes the Cape has to offer.

Provincetown
The first walk takes you along the waterfront of Provincetown, jam-packed and lively at the height of summer but returning to its charm as a year-round fishing center the rest of the year. At the very end of U.S. 6, 60 miles from the beginning of the Cape at Sagamore, the town's main thoroughfare, Commercial Street, takes walkers to most points of interest.

Start at the intersection of Cook and Commercial to see the exhibitions of painting and sculpture at the Art Association and Museum. Open daily from June–Sept., 11 to 5 and 8 to 10; Sunday from 2 to 5. Adults 75 cents, children and senior citizens free. Provincetown has been as famous for its artists' colony as for its seafood. Continuing along Commercial Street, you pass old sea captains' houses with the widow's watch on top. At Center Street you'll want to browse in the Heritage Museum, displaying marine artifacts and antique fire equipment. Open daily 10 to 9 June–Oct.; adults $1, children under 12, free.

Nearby, also on Commercial, is the Fo'c's'le, with its carved sign swinging in the wind, a saloon with rustic benches and sawdust on the floor. It's the best place to meet the locals and to share an icy stein of beer. Just beyond is the heart of town, MacMillan Wharf, named for a hometown Arctic explorer.

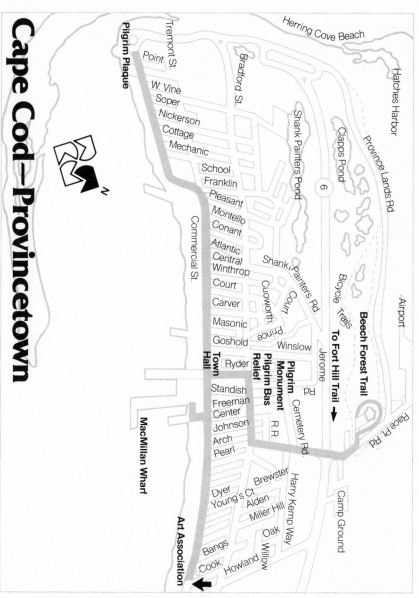

Cape Cod—Provincetown

The Provincetown walk is approximately 1¼ miles.
The Red Maple Swamp walk is approximately 1½ miles.
The Beech Forest Trail walk is approximately 1 mile.

Here scores of fishing boats crowd in upon the pier every morning to unload their catches.

A few steps farther along, behind the town hall, is a great bronze bas-relief depicting the first landing of the Pilgrims on November 17, 1620. They stayed in P-town for five weeks before departing for Plymouth Rock. Above rises the 252-foot-high Pilgrim Monument—you may climb an easy ramp to its top for a spectacular view of the great sweeping tip of the Cape. A first-rate historical museum is open along with the monument, with every sort of salty local memorabilia: a captain's parlor behind glass, patchwork quilts and sexy ships' figureheads of buxom damsels. Open daily year-round 9 to 5 except mid-June through mid-Sept., 9 to 9; adults 75 cents, children 25 cents.

Continue on Commercial Street past the scores of snack bars and souvenir shops. For a taste of real Portuguese cooking, including the best squid stew in New England, stop in at Cookie's restaurant. A final historic point marks the end of this walk. The Pilgrim Plaque, where the town reaches out to sea, designates that famous landing place at the beginning of Commercial Street. From here return to the town center, and you have but a quick drive or an easy hike to the start of the second walking tour—a woodsy environment just out of town called the Beech Forest Trail.

Beech Forest Trail

One of eight nature trails within the 27,000 acres of Cape Cod National Seashore, the Beech Forest Trail is an easy stroll of just a mile in length. It starts from a parking lot on Race Point Road ½ mile from U.S. 6, and consists of two loops, one around a pond and the other circling a wood. As you start out you see the great Province Lands sand dunes rising in all directions covering most of the land between the town and the sea to the north. Climbing up and in through some of these dunes can give an unexpectedly private and isolated sensation—your own personal desert.

On the trail again a middle layer of plant life, bushes of blueberry, bayberry, and beach plum, reaches up for sunlight among taller trees and along the shore of the pond. As the path reaches deeper into the forest, the pines take over—six different species. They have a population of woodpeckers, whose insistent tapping is often heard. Along the way you'll also see sassafras trees with their mitten-shaped leaves. Tea is sometimes still made from the roots.

The wood takes its name from the American beech, which proliferates in one "climax" part of the trail. A bit farther along the tree tops become shorter as greater exposure to the sea winds cuts down total growth. Cribbage-board patterns in an oak trunk are the work of the yellow-bellied sapsucker, woodpeckers who tap their way into the sap flow. Also note the variety of plants that cover the forest floor—lily-of-the-valley with its tiny white flowers, exquisite lady's slippers, ferns, mosses, and, of course, poison ivy.

At one point on the trail a vast dune seems to be attacking the woods, moving inexorably upon all that grows. Plantings of beach grass on dunes were once done to save the town itself from destruction caused by blowing sand; unchecked, this, in time, would wipe out the forest. As you move along the sandy path you may come upon traces of deer, fox, raccoons, skunks, woodchucks and weasels who share the shadowy undergrowth with other smaller animals. If you come along very early in the morning you are quite likely to spot some of them. The pond, too, has its own kinds of life: turtles, frogs and many water bugs.

The Red Maple Swamp

A surprisingly different environment awaits you some 25 miles upcape on U.S. 6 at Eastham along the Fort Hill Trail through the Red Maple Swamp. Most of the walk is over duckboards that take you in perfect comfort over soggy marsh and reaches of shallow still water. The 1½-mile tour starts from the Fort Hill parking lot on Governor Prence Road, 1½ miles from the main highway. Here you will see the Captain Edward Penniman house, an exceptional example of Victorian architecture dating from 1867, built by a whaling captain. Note the tremendous gateway made from a whale jawbone.

As you start out on the trail, look down from a rise to Nauset Marsh, home of many birds—pheasants, herons, rails, an occasional marsh hawk, and a rare peregrine falcon, as well as the ubiquitous gulls. Farther along, Indian Rock has shallow troughs cut into it by prehistoric Indians to use in making tools.

Proceed down a slope for the best part of this walk as the well-hidden boardwalk takes you into the mysteries of the jungly swampland. The cool silence and the still blackness of the water make you think you've found a Louisiana bayou. A drop of water from a vine-covered, gnarled red maple makes perfect moving circles on the mirrorlike water. The sweep of boardwalk is greenish with mossy growth, and lichens hang from branches in stringy lengths like Spanish moss. At a curve, a bench invites you to sit and look up at the sky of the outside world, which seems very far away.

Emerging from the swamp, the trail takes you back to the parking lot, crosses the road and leads you around the Penniman house through a sweet green meadow to the site of Fort Hill, once an Indian outpost, which commands a magnificent view of the sea coast and provides a capital picnic spot.

RHODE ISLAND

CLIFF WALK, NEWPORT
Roy Bongartz

The Cliff Walk is a fabulous pathway winding for 3½ miles along the sea front, edging the lawns and formal gardens of great fabled mansions of the rich in Newport, Rhode Island. On one side you can watch the surf crashing against steep rocks, and on the other you'll discover a "Land of Oz"—of castles and palaces. Some are stark and fortresslike; others are laced with Victorian fancy. Several are open to the public so that after your hike you can stop and see the treasures within: priceless furnishings, tapestries, china, paintings and structural details from everywhere on earth.

A Public Way

The public way along these cliffs was established by fishermen as early as 1640, and the citizens of Newport have exercised the right ever since. A century ago when the mansions (always called "cottages") were built, their owners—among them the aristocracy known as the "400 families"—objected to strangers on their land. But whenever a fence went up, it was pulled down and the offending householder taken to court for blocking the public way. In 1913, Newport's mayor led a parade of demonstrators to tear down an obstructing fence. Since then the owners have merely tried, on some of their properties, to shield themselves from view by hedges or rose arbors. At Marble House, a Chinese tea house sits at the cliff edge with the walk leading through a tunnel underneath it.

The starting point for your tour is Cliff Walk Manor, the hotel and restaurant on Memorial Boulevard. Most of the path is paved with asphalt, and the sections the sea had washed away

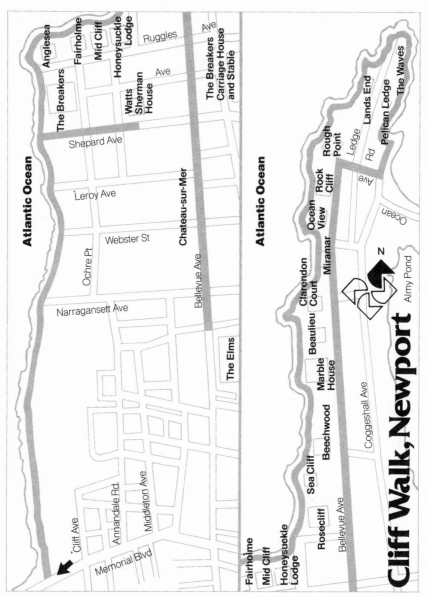

Cliff Walk, Newport

Atlantic Ocean

Anglesea
Fairholme
Mid Cliff
Honeysuckle Lodge
The Breakers
Watts Sherman House
Ruggles Ave
Ave
The Breakers Carriage House and Stable
Shepard Ave
Leroy Ave
Ochre Pt
Webster St
Chateau-sur-Mer
Bellevue Ave
Narragansett Ave
The Elms
Cliff Ave
Annandale Rd
Middleton Ave
Memorial Blvd

Atlantic Ocean

Fairholme
Mid Cliff
Honeysuckle Lodge
Rosecliff
Sea Cliff
Beechwood
Marble House
Beaulieu Court
Clarendon Court
Miramar
Ocean View
Rock Cliff
Rough Point
Ledge
Lands End
Pelican Ledge
The Waves
Rd
Ave
Ocean
Coggeshall Ave
Bellevue Ave
Almy Pond
N

This walking tour is approximately 3 miles long.

have been solidly repaired within the past few years by the Army Corps of Engineers. Along the way are fine grassy knolls atop the rocky heights, creating perfect picnic spots. On Sundays, hundreds of strollers enliven the scene, which has changed little over most of a century—white triangles of sailboats and orange dots of lobster-pot buoys in the blue-gray sea off Newport Beach, and the fairyland of great houses rising on the landward side.

Although these vast houses of 50 to 100 rooms are rarely used by just one family anymore, there are still some exceptions. Most have been well maintained in later conversions to schools, colleges, and luxury apartments. The walk and its adjoining beaches and coves make perfect places to study, and you'll see many students propped up against boulders with books and sandwiches or candy bars.

The Breakers

Among the most notable of the more than two dozen mansions you will pass is the Breakers, owned by the Preservation Society of Newport County and open to the public. Dating from 1895, it is a famed monument to American architecture, built for Cornelius Vanderbilt by Richard Morris Hunt. There is also a marvelous children's playhouse on the grounds. The carriage house and stable has a major collection of American horse-drawn coaches and buggies. At first glance the great structure may remind you of some ornate Mediterranean railroad station. There is a tunnel leading from outdoors into the coal cellar, which is large enough for a team of horses to pass through, and the place is piped for both running rainwater and salt water.

Stately Mansions

A short departure now from Cliff Walk—perhaps to be saved for the return stroll—takes you up Shepard Avenue past a medieval-style English manor, the Watts Sherman House, designed in 1874 by Stanford White and presently used as a church home. Then go to the ornate Chateau-sur-Mer, open to visitors. It was built in 1852 for a tycoon in the China trade, William S. Wetmore, and has Newport's first great French-style ballroom complete with gold threaded draperies, magnificent chandeliers and exquisite marble fireplaces. A delightful Victorian toy museum is also open. On the lawn a feeling of peace surrounds a memorial earth-mound sculpture made several years ago by the New England artist Richard Fleischner.

On Cliff Walk, once again, you'll pass Anglesea, a rambling cottage with a slate roof; Fairholme, the Robert R. Young home; Mid Cliff, the former Perle Mesta partying center; and the sizable Queen Anne cottage, Honeysuckle Lodge. Then you'll come to still another great masterpiece, Rosecliff, also the work of Stanford White. This, too, is open to visitors. Of gleaming white terra-cotta, it was copied from the Grand Trianon in Versailles and makes for one of the most spectacular interior visits in the city.

A rare newcomer to the walk is Sea Cliff, only 25 years old, the work of architect Frederic Rhinelander King, who also built the Trinity Church Parish House on Spring Street in the center of town. Beechwood is still another of the mansions open to visitors. Once owned by Mrs. William Astor, it, too, has an ornate ballroom with intricately painted angel figures on the ceiling and a view that looks out to sea. The work was done by a large company of craftsmen brought over from Italy, who camped in the basement while the building was under construction in 1851 and 1852.

You are welcome to visit Marble House, next along the walk. The overwhelming lavishness of this fantastic Victorian cottage is apparent from the Gold Ballroom, where the gilt could put the Hollywood of the 1920s to shame. Designed by Richard Morris Hunt for William K. Vanderbilt, it was completed in 1892 and holds what seems to be acres of marble, gilt wood, fanciful murals, and other rococo works. Mrs. Vanderbilt's bedroom is walled in peach damask, and the dining room contains the only solid bronze furniture known of in the United States. The Vanderbilts, after they opened the great house, threw only one big party. Then they promptly divorced and closed the house.

Beaulieu, with its fine mansard roof, is the former home of John Jacob Astor and, later, Cornelius Vanderbilt III. Clarendon Court is in 18th-century English style. Next come the stately wings of Miramar, built in 1915 by architect Horace Trumbauer for the Wideners of Philadelphia. Legends from American history abound in these old places. Ocean View, for example, went up in 1866 for Ogden Mills, son of the famous '49er and financier Darius Ogden Mills. Rock Cliff, dating from 1869, was the property of the longtime defender of the America's Cup, Harold S. Vanderbilt.

Toward the end of the walk, as you go by formidable wire fences around Doris Duke's house, Rough Point, where barking mastiffs patrol the grounds and snarl at your passage, there may be a chill wind off the sea. Perhaps you'll encounter and nod a greeting to a fellow stroller, a determined-looking woman in tweed suit and knit stockings, who returns a proper "Good afternoon, lovely day for walking!" as she taps the end of a hawthorn stick into the path in rhythmic accompaniment to her pace.

As you hike around Land's End, you come into view of the Waves, the spectacular home of architect John Russell Pope, who designed the Jefferson Memorial, the National Gallery of Art in Washington and the National Archives Building. He built the Waves for himself in 1927. The last home on the walk, Senator Claiborne Pell's, is a wood-shingled Cape Codder called Pelican Ledge. Senator Pell designed this cottage in 1950. You'll come to the end of the walk just before Bailey's Beach, the last exclusive holdout of Newport aristocracy.

You may choose to return the way you came, viewing all these hard-to-believe extravagances from a somewhat different angle, or you might prefer a straight walk down Bellevue Avenue, just inland from Cliff Walk. Here still another visit awaits you at the Elms, at the corner of Dixon Street. An 18th-century French-styled estate with formal gardens, fountains, and statuary, it makes a striking scene on summer nights when the grounds are illuminated.

Whichever way you choose to do the length of the walk, you will not be quite the same afterwards. Be warned that your own house or apartment is going to seem tiny and plain. The visual memory that stays with you may grow a bit faint over the months until this shoreline of make-believe appears only as a dream. But to bring it to life again, summer or winter, all it takes is another trip to Newport.

Hammersmith Farm

An added attraction when visiting Newport is Hammersmith Farm, set on 50 rolling acres overlooking Narragansett Bay. Try to arrange for time to tour the only working farm in the City of Newport; it served as a summer White House from

1961 to 1963, and where the wedding reception of Senator and Mrs. John F. Kennedy was held. Follow the signs in Newport for Ocean Drive and Fort Adams State Park. The farm is adjacent to Fort Adams.

The schedule for all mansions is: April, the Breakers, Marble House, and Rosecliff, daily 10 to 5; other mansions weekends 10 to 5; May through October, all mansions open daily 10 to 5, plus first two weekends in November, 10 to 5. From July through mid-September many of the mansions are open evenings until 8. Check for more specific information at (401) 847-1000. Admission at the Breakers is $2.50, adults; $1.25, children ages 6–15. At most other mansions, $2, adults; $1, children ages 6–15. For information on combination tickets, ask at any mansion or call (401) 847-1000.

Walking
the
East

NEW YORK

UPPER FIFTH AVENUE: MANSIONS, MUSEUMS, AND CENTRAL PARK
Karen Cure

If there's any section of Manhattan that seems designed to silence those who would cast aspersions on New York, it's the 2½-mile stretch of Fifth Avenue above 59th Street. Between the turn of the century and the time the stock market crashed, the avenue was the scene of almost constant construction as some of the richest people in America put up castles, townhouses, mansions, and other home-sweet-homes of French and Italian Renaissance, François I, Louis XIII, neo-Federal, neo-Grecian, and Gothic inspiration. The ornamentation—elegant marble columns and voluted capitals, delicate wrought-iron railings and doorways, French windows with leaded panes, elaborate cornices, porticos, balconies, entablatures and roof balustrades—is everything. On the west side of this great boulevard you'll see the eastern boundary of Central Park, New York's great green lung. A walk in the area is always pleasant, because when you've had your fill of craning your neck, you can plop yourself down on a park bench under the trees or go in for the kind of gentle stroll which Frederick Law Olmsted and Calvert Vaux had in mind when they designed the park in the early 1860s. The "pestilential spot where rank vegetation and miasmic odors taint every breath of air" described by a contemporary—a shantytown where more than 5,000 squatters raised pigs—has given way to a rolling tract of greenness that is laced with paths for biking, walking, and horseback riding and spotted with playgrounds and athletic facilities. Any summer afternoon, bicyclers will be whizzing by, kids will be squealing in the playgrounds, mothers will be out taking the air with their youngsters in strollers, and vendors will be hawking hot dogs and cold drinks.

From 103rd Street to 88th Street

Along the way there are also some incredible museums—
among them the Museum of the City of New York at 103rd
Street where you'll start your tour. Housed in a red-brick
Georgian-style building, it is more reminiscent of the University
of Virginia than concrete New York. Inside, you'll find fine exhibits on the city's history, plus wonderful toy and doll collections. (10 to 5 Tuesday through Saturday, 1 to 5 Sunday and
holidays; free.)

At 1130 Fifth, at 94th, Willard Straight's elegant 1914 neo-
Georgian mansion now houses the changing exhibits of the International Center of Photography. (11 to 5 Tuesday through
Sunday; admission $1 for adults, 50 cents for students, free to
children under 8 and senior citizens.) Between 93rd and 92nd,
housed partly in a Gothic Renaissance-style mansion built
around 1900 for the Felix Warburg family, is the Jewish Museum, the U.S.'s main repository of Judaica. (11 to 6 on Sunday, 12 to 5 Monday through Thursday; admission $1.75 for
adults, $1 for students.)

At 2 East 91st Street, in the heart of the area known as
Carnegie Hill, the Cooper-Hewitt Museum—a branch of the
Smithsonian entirely devoted to design and filled with samples
of fabrics, wallpapers and other beautifully designed objects
from all civilizations—holds forth in the former chateau of Andrew Carnegie. The Cooper-Hewitt is open 10 to 9 on Tuesday, 10 to 5 Wednesday through Saturday, noon to 5 on Sunday. Admission is $1.50 for adults and $1 for senior citizens;
children under 12 enter free—as does everybody between 5
and 9 on Tuesday.

Carnegie built the house after he had sold his own steel
company to U.S. Steel to become one of the richest men in the
world; the site was occupied by squatters before the building
went up in 1901. Most people thought that Carnegie was a little
daft to move so far up Fifth Avenue; the super-rich of the day
were living in the 70s. But soon Carnegie was joined by other
industrialists and philanthropists as they built some of the most
beautiful mansions in the city. Like that of Otto Kahn—the
German-born banker's son who launched the period of the
Metropolitan Opera's greatest success and brought avant-garde
companies like Diaghilev's Russian Ballet to the U.S.—most are
occupied by institutions (in this case, the Convent of the Sacred

Heart, 1 East 91st Street). Equally elegant are the Duchesne
Residence School, formerly the James A. Burden residence, at
7 East 91st, and the John Henry Hammond House at 9 East
91st Street. Hammond, husband to Emily Vanderbilt Sloane
(heiress to the Sloane and Vanderbilt fortunes), was also Benny
Goodman's father-in-law.

Just two blocks south between 88th and 89th streets
there's the Solomon R. Guggenheim Museum, the famous
Frank Lloyd Wright-designed circular mass where modern
paintings are hung along the outside wall of a ¼-mile-long spiral
ramp; the central space ranks among the world's great modern
interiors. The Guggenheim is open daily except Monday from
11 to 5, and on Tuesday until 8. Admission is $1.50 for adults,
75 cents for students with ID and visitors over 62; children
under 7 are free, as are all admissions on Tuesday evening between 5 and 8.

The Middle 80s

Munsey's Magazine, long defunct, called Fifth Avenue's
millionaire row "the Grand Canal of Mammon"—and as you
keep walking you'll see why. Retired capitalist William Starr
Miller lived at 1048 Fifth Avenue (at 86th Street) in a dignified
two-story slate-roofed palace reminiscent of those red-brick
limestone-roofed establishments in the 16th-century Place des
Vosges in Paris. His daughter, Edith Starr Miller, wife of Sir Al-
meric Hugh Paget, Baron Queenborough, divided her time between stays there and at the couple's provincial French chateau
in Newport, Rhode Island. Grace Wilson Vanderbilt, a leader of
society in both cities, and, according to *The New York Times,*
one of the last remaining links between society in regal pre-
World War I days and that of the more democratic post-World
War II era, bought the house in 1944. She was the widow of
Cornelius Vanderbilt III. The building is now the Yivo Institute
for Jewish Research.

Between 84th and 85th streets,1033 Fifth Avenue, now
owned by the Government of Iran, was originally a property of
the Edward Payson Hatch family, whose fortune had been
amassed while Hatch was with the Wilcox & Gibbs Sewing
Machine Company. Number 1030—a 13-story apartment building—was constructed in 1924–25 for Louis Gordon Hamers-
ley, a philanthropist and real estate investor who divided his

Upper Fifth Avenue: Mansions

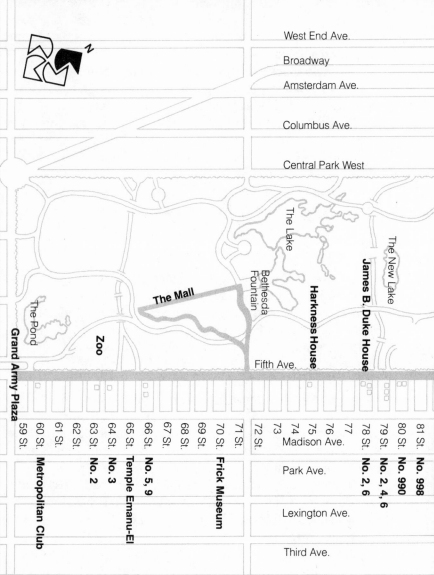

West End Ave.

Broadway

Amsterdam Ave.

Columbus Ave.

Central Park West

The Lake

The New Lake

James B. Duke House

Harkness House

Bethesda
Fountain

The Mall

The Pond

Zoo

Grand Army Plaza

Fifth Ave.

59 St.
60 St.
61 St.
62 St.
63 St.
64 St.
65 St.
66 St.
67 St.
68 St.
69 St.
70 St.
71 St.
72 St.
73
74
75
76
77
78 St.
79 St.
80 St.
81 St.

Madison Ave.

Metropolitan Club

No. 2

No. 3

Temple Emanu-El

No. 5, 9

Frick Museum

Park Ave.

No. 2, 6

No. 2, 4, 6

No. 990

No. 998

Lexington Ave.

Third Ave.

Museums and Central Park

Central Park

The Reservoir

105 St.		
104 St.		
103 St.	**Museum of**	
102 St.	**The City of N.Y.**	
101 St.		
100 St.		
99 St.		
98 St.		
97 St.		
96 St.		
95 St.		
94 St.	**Int'l Center of**	
93 St.	**Photography**	
92 St.	**Jewish Museum**	
91 St.	**No. 7, 9**	
90 St.	**Cooper Hewitt**	
89 St.	**Museum**	
88 St.	**Guggenheim Museum**	
87 St.		
86 St.	**Miller Mansion**	
85 St.		
84 St.	**No. 1033, 1030**	

This walking tour is approximately 4 miles one way.

time between Southampton, Palm Beach, and New York City, and owned a speedboat, *Cigarette Jr.*, famous for the record it set on the run from New York to Albany.

Between 83rd and 84th streets, 1026 Fifth Avenue, which with numbers 1027 and 1028 is now owned by the Marymount School, belonged first to banker's widow Mary Macy Kingsland and then to Dunlevy Milbank, a leading New York philanthropist. Number 1027 was first the property of banker and broker George Crawford Clark and then of Herbert Lee Pratt, chairman of the Socony-Vacuum Oil Company, second-largest oil firm in the U.S. at the time. Number 1028 was originally built for Jonathan Thorne in 1901–1903; Thorne descended from an old New York family that had traditionally worked in leather goods.

The Stupendous Metropolitan

Of all the public buildings on the avenue, the biggest is the Metropolitan Museum of Art, one of the world's most spectacular museums (at 82nd Street). Split into some 15 separate units and housed in 236 galleries that occupy 4 city blocks, its collections contain over 2,000 European paintings, 3,000 European drawings, a million prints, 3,000 American paintings and statues, 4,000 musical instruments and 4,000 objects of medieval art; about a fourth will be on display at any given time. Audio-tape tours, which you can rent for $2 from the Main Audio Guide Desk on the Main Floor to your left as you enter the museum, and at several other locations around the museum, will fill you in on what you're seeing; the "Director's Choice" tour covers some of the collections' high points. Or you can just pick up a map at the Information Booth at the center of the Great Hall on the Main Floor, where you enter, and wander as you please.

Downstairs on the ground floor, be sure to take in the Costume Institute—where spectacular costume exhibits are designed around special themes and change each year. Upstairs, again, stop at the tranquil Medieval Sculpture Hall, a cavernous space fronted by an intricate wrought-iron choir screen crafted in the late 17th century, and at the marvel-filled Egyptian galleries, where you'll see linen sheets woven thousands of years ago. The Temple of Dendur, a 5th-century B.C. Egyptian temple, reconstructed stone by stone in the new Sackler Wing, is stupendous—as is the Lehman Pavilion, a series of rooms and galleries built around a lovely central courtyard and filled with paintings and drawings, Gothic tapestries, faïence from Persia, bronzes of the Renaissance, Venetian glass, and much more. On the second floor, take in the musical instruments. The collection includes three Stradivarius violins, as well as elaborately decorated keyboard instruments and the first pianoforte ever made. Hire the special audio machine, and you can hear what they sound like. The museum's Rembrandts—33 of them, including the celebrated *Aristotle with a Bust of Homer,* the most expensive painting in the world when it was acquired in 1961—are also on the second floor, along with Van Gogh's *Sunflowers,* Turner's *Grand Canal,* John Constable's *Salisbury Cathedral,* and works by Manet, Monet, Renoir, Degas, Seurat, and Gauguin, among others. You may well want to save your visit to the museum for another day. It's open on Tuesday from 10 to 8:45, Wednesday through Saturday from 10 to 4:45, and on Sunday from 11 to 4:45 (closed Monday). There is a voluntary admission fee ("pay what you wish but you must pay something") for all except members, senior citizens, and children under 12 accompanied by an adult, for whom admission is free.

The Lower 80s

Across the street, 1014 Fifth Avenue, now Goethe House, was occupied by James Francis Aloysius Clark, a banker and stockbroker, member of the New York and Boston stock exchanges. Gallery hours are 11–5 on Friday and Saturday; 11–7 Tuesday through Thursday. Free.

Meanwhile, 991 Fifth Avenue between 80th and 81st Streets (now the headquarters of the American-Irish Historical Society) was owned successively by Mary A. King, by Mr. and Mrs. David Crawford Clark (James Francis Aloysius Clark's brother) and by William Ellis Corey, who had worked his way up through the steel mills from a $15-a-week laboratory assistantship to the presidency of the United States Steel Corporation; his second marriage in 1907 to musical comedy star Mabelle Gilman had tongues wagging around the world.

East 80th Street, one of the earliest blocks in the area to be settled, was always associated with the Woolworth family. Frank W. Woolworth, who began the chain of five-and-dimes, built at 990 Fifth Avenue (northeast corner of 80th Street), and then between 1911 and 1916 commissioned architect C.P.H.

Gilbert to build three houses for his daughters and their hus-
bands on the south side of the street. The handsome residence
at 2 East 80th (formerly the Blessed Trinity Convent House)
was built for Edna Woolworth and her stockbroker husband
Franklyn Laws Hutton; their daughter, Barbara Hutton, in-
herited a $42 million fortune that has prompted people to call
her the richest woman in the world. Her sister Jessie Woolworth
and her husband James P. Donahue, married in 1912, lived at
number 6. His music-loving sister-in-law Helena lived at
number 4 with her husband.

The 70s
    If anything, the mansions in the 70s are yet more splendid
than those you've seen so far. In 1879, banker and real estate
developer Henry Cook had purchased the entire block between
78th and 79th and Fifth and Madison for about $500,000 (the
price of some apartments in the area today), but no development began until the 1890s. The fine François I mansion at 2
East 79th Street, now the Ukrainian Institute of America's headquarters, was built originally for Isaac D. Fletcher, a Maine-born
industrialist and art collector who bequeathed a major portion of
his estate to the Metropolitan Museum of Art. A later occupant,
Harry Sinclair, had started out as a pharmacist, but changed his
career. Thinking that oil might be more profitable, he ended up
founding the Sinclair Oil Corporation, getting involved in the
Teapot Dome scandals, serving a prison sentence for contempt
of court, and holding the position of chairman of the board of
Atlantic Richfield. In the course of things, he also owned the St.
Louis Browns and Zer, 1923's Kentucky Derby winner. Sub-
sequently, Augustus van Horn Stuyvesant and his sister Ann,
the last direct descendants of New York's early governor Peter
Stuyvesant, bought the house. Augustus, a bachelor who never
pursued any career, lived as a recluse and went out only for
daily constitutionals in his neighborhood.
    You can go inside, where there are often special exhibits,
Tuesday through Sunday from 2 until 6. Free.
    East 78th Street, one of the blocks most evocative of the
early years of Upper East Side elegance, is presided over by the
James B. Duke house at 1 East 78th Street (now NYU's Institute of Fine Art). Designed by Horace Trumbauer for the tobacco magnate, it is the only freestanding building in a block of
townhouses and attached mansions, and seems even more im-

portant as a result. Duke, a self-made man, was born in North Carolina, and grew up learning to cultivate, cure, and sell tobacco. He began the so-called Tobacco War between the Duke firm, producer of nearly half U.S. cigarettes at the time, and other major tobacco companies, a competition which ended with a huge merger. The resultant fortune built Duke University in Durham, North Carolina, and provided Duke's daughter Doris with the wherewithal to lead an elegant life in Newport. Oliver Payne, who was principal among the capitalists who played an important role in Duke's tobacco interests, was uncle to Payne Whitney, Duke's next-door neighbor at 972 Fifth Avenue (now a division of the French Embassy). Whitney, who had married the daughter of John Hay, Secretary of State to Presidents McKinley and Roosevelt, was well known for his racing and breeding stables on Long Island and in Kentucky, while Mrs. Whitney was a major Metropolitan Museum donor and their daughter Joan Payson, more recently, owned the New York Mets until her death. With 973 Fifth Avenue (commissioned by Henry Cook, who died before its completion), 972 Fifth Avenue was designed by the noted firm McKim, Mead & White, which also executed the apartment house at 998 Fifth Avenue. The firm, one of the most famous and productive in the history of American architecture, gained its most considerable notoriety after the 1906 murder of Stanford White on the summer roof garden of the old Madison Square Garden, by an insanely jealous Harry Thaw, whose wife White had courted before her marriage. McKim, deeply disturbed by the incident, retired from practice the next year and died in 1909.

Moving down Fifth still farther, you'll encounter the Edward Harkness house at 1 East 75th Street, built in 1907 for a son of one of the six original partners of the Standard Oil Company, and the ornate James Stillman House (now the Lycée Français) at 9 East 72nd.

A Detour into the Park

If you're curious to see what lies beyond the wall on the west side of Fifth Avenue, turn right at 72nd Street through the park entrance gates. At the children's playground (on your left), turn right. Following either path at the fork, you'll come to Conservatory Pond, where, most days, you can watch Sunday sailors with their giant motorized model boats. Backtrack, then follow the main road as it curves and bear roughly straight

ahead—along the walkways, or, on summer afternoons and
weekends the rest of the year, when the park is closed to vehicular traffic, along the park road itself. Trees are everywhere;
Frederick Law Olmsted and Calvert Vaux intended to one-up
Mother Nature when they drew up the plans for the landscape.
Ahead of you to your right is the Bethesda Fountain, a wonderful creation overlooking the lake, with a shoreline as irregular as
if it had always been there. The rowboats you see can be rented
at the Loeb Boat House at the east end of the lake between 9
and 5 daily ($2 the first hour, 50 cents for each quarter hour
thereafter; $10 deposit required).

To your left as you face the fountain is the famous bridge,
reproduced countless times in engravings; beyond it you can
see the tall buildings of Central Park West, the Fifth Avenue of
Manhattan's West Side, as full of apartment buildings as grand
as the mansions of Fifth Avenue. Across the road from the fountain, you'll see the mall reaching southward beyond a band
shell where orchestras play on summer evenings. To find out
what's on, you can call 755-4100. Walk down the tree-lined
alleyway to the end, then bear northward again along the curving paths to your right and retrace your steps to 72nd Street.

An Elegant Museum and a Few More Mansions
The Frick Collection, one of the high points of any visit to
New York, gives you the chance to see how this other half lived
in their fabulous palaces. Installed in a mansion at 1 East 70th
Street, the former home of Pittsburgh industrialist Henry Clay
Frick, this museum has thick carpets, elegantly polished floors,
lofty ceilings covered with scroll-worked moldings. You won't
recognize very many of the paintings in the collection, which is
mostly European work, but the quality is such that each piece
may touch you in a way you've never been touched before.
The collection is never too large to overwhelm you, but at the
same time it's substantial enough that you'll want to stay a long
time, and then come back soon. The Frick is open from 10 to 6
Tuesday through Saturday, and from 1 to 6 on Sunday,
September through May; from 10 to 6 Wednesday through
Saturday, and from 1 to 6 on Sunday, from June through August. Closed Monday year-round, and on Tuesday during the
summer. Children under 10 are not admitted; youngsters under
16 must be accompanied by an adult. Admission is $1 for adults

and 50 cents for senior citizens Tuesday through Saturday, $2 for all on Sunday.

The 60s

Leaving the Frick and continuing southward down the avenue, you'll come to the Charles Scribner residence at 9 East 66th (now Poland's U.N. mission); the Temple Emanu-El, at 65th Street, the largest Reform synagogue in the U.S. (10–5 Sunday to Thursday, 10–4:15 Friday, 12:15–5 on Saturday); the Margaret Shepard house at 5 East 66th (now the Lotos Club); the Edward Berwind House at 2 East 64th Street, built by a man who was the largest owner of coal mines in the world at that time and now being remodeled as posh cooperative apartments; the Mrs. Marshall Orme Wilson house, now the New India House, at 3 East 64th; and the Metropolitan Club at 1 East 60th Street, built by McKim, Mead & White for J.P. Morgan and his cronies.

At Grand Army Plaza, where your walk ends, you can head down Fifth to 58th for a foray into the toy wonderland that is FAO Schwarz; stop at the celebrated, old, and beautiful Plaza Hotel for high tea in the Palm Court; walk northward into Central Park and visit the Central Park Zoo, and have a snack or a meal at the Zoo cafeteria; head westward following the paths that run roughly parallel to the Transverse Road for a visit to the quaint old carousel; or just sit in the plaza, New York's only public urban plaza for people, and watch the city go by. After your respite, you'll be ready to stroll farther down Fifth Avenue—shopping as you go—or head westward across Central Park South, and then up Central Park West for a lovely and quite different view of the city.

Special Events

The Museum of the City of New York sponsors regular "Mansions of Fifth Avenue" walking tours (April through October). Phone 534-1672 for details. Also look into special events at the Metropolitan Museum of Art (535-7710) and at the Frick (288-0700). Check *Cue, New York* or *The New Yorker* magazines for information on special events in the park and special exhibitions at the museums.

LITERARY GREENWICH VILLAGE
Karen Cure

When you look at a list of the famous writers who have called Greenwich Village home, you almost think you're seeing the table of contents from a high school literature text: James Fenimore Cooper, Washington Irving, Edgar Allan Poe, Henry James, Edith Wharton, Mark Twain, Bret Harte, Frank Norris, Willa Cather, Edna St. Vincent Millay, John Dos Passos, e.e. cummings, Edmund Wilson, James Agee, Edward Albee— to name only a few of the best-known. When writer Alfred Kazin called New York City "the single most important factor in American writing," he probably should have said Greenwich Village. Every house in this tiny area, bounded on the north by 14th Street and on the south by Houston Street, has a story to tell. Some have several.

That, together with the diminutive houses in every imaginable architectural style, the infinitesimal boutiques peddling everything from water pipes to kitchenware, the coffee shops like the old Caffe Reggio (119 MacDougal Street between Minetta Lane and Bleecker), the restaurants, and the cozy, almost small-town ambiance of parts of this corner of the great metropolis make it a perfect spot for a walk.

The tour you'll soon begin takes in some of the highlights of the Village's literary past and of its lively present—but only the highlights. Every narrow, crooked street you cross will tempt you to go off and explore. When that happens, make a mental note of the location—and go back later. That most of the streets started off as cow paths means that this part of the city is a maze—even to the natives. It's all too easy to get lost.

Washington Square
Start at Astor Place (a stop on the East Side IRT local trains). It was in the Great Hall at Cooper Union (founded in 1859 by the inventor and philanthropist who manufactured the first U.S. steam engine) that Abraham Lincoln made the "Right Makes Might" speech that won him the nomination for the Presidency. Nearby, James Fenimore Cooper rented 6 St. Mark's Place, which is now the St. Mark's Baths. Just south of Astor Place on Lafayette Street, you'll come to Colonnade Row, a series of houses built in 1836 with identical columns across the facade; Washington Irving lived there when the build-

ings opened. The Astor Library across the street, now the home of the Public Theater, which produces some of the most innovative plays on the U.S. dramatic scene, provided the nucleus of the present-day New York Public Library. Some 100,000 volumes were available without charge—which was revolutionary at the time. Turn west on Astor Place, walk south on Broadway, then turn west and cross Washington Place. Henry James was born at 21 Washington Place between Greene Street and Washington Square East. The Brown Building was actually the site of the March 25, 1911, Triangle Shirtwaist Company fire where some 146 young people, mostly newly arrived immigrants, were killed: supervisors had locked the ninth-floor exit doors and the single fire escape proved grossly inadequate. Walk north on Washington Square East and just half a block from where it becomes University Place, turn west into Washington Mews. This cobblestoned lane with its two rows of converted stables and carriage houses, where no cars are permitted, makes you feel the city is 1,000 miles away. John Dos Passos rented a room (between numbers 14 and 15), from Elaine Orr Cummings in 1922; Sherwood Anderson often stayed with a friend at number 54; and, just to the north, around the corner in an apartment at One Fifth Avenue, the poet Sara Teasdale committed suicide in 1933 by taking all the barbiturates which had been prescribed to help her sleep.

Walk down Fifth Avenue to the Arch. Designed by architect Stanford White (murdered by a former sweetheart's husband in 1906), it ranks with the Arc de Triomphe in Paris as one of the world's finest triumphal arches; mobilist Alexander Calder's father, Alexander Stirling Calder, sculpted the civilian statue of Washington you see there, and the pianist Paderewski liked it so well he played a benefit performance there.

Back in 1916, John Sloan, father of the Ashcan School of painting, together with a group of other bohemians, forced the door of the staircase on the right side of the arch one cold winter's night, lit a fire in a beanpot, illuminated some Japanese lanterns, spread out a picnic—and read poems, fired pistols, and otherwise celebrated the independence of the state of "New Bohemia" until the constabulary also made its way up the staircase and put an end to the hijinks.

Many years earlier, Washington Square—first a marshland,

a colonial hunting ground, a municipal potters' field on which
some 10,000 early Americans were buried, and a favorite duel-
ing ground—was even livelier. In the early 1800s, public hang-
ings drew merrymakers by the hundred, and at the park's dedication in 1828 at a mammoth public picnic, the assembled
throngs consumed two oxen, 200 hams and a quarter-mile of
barreled beer. Within the next couple of years, the entire south
side of the square was built up with now-demolished Greek Revival houses, similar to those in the row of red brick structures
you can see now on the north side east of Fifth Avenue. Edith
Wharton lived at number 7 in 1882 after she and her mother
returned from a European trip that followed her father's death;
number 3 has been home to Elaine Orr, later the wife of
e.e. cummings, and Edmund Wilson and John Dos Passos, who
wrote *Manhattan Transfer* while living there. Henry James, who
made Washington Square famous in the novel by that name,
spent time at number 19, west of Fifth Avenue, the home (no
longer standing) of his grandmother.

New York University
    Today, Washington Square serves as a campus for stu-
dents at New York University, a private institution which, since
its founding in 1831 by Albert Gallatin, has numbered Thomas
Wolfe and Samuel F. B. Morse among its professors. If you
stroll through the square, you'll see the students throwing Fris-
bees, chatting, picking at their guitars, and playing chess.
    Particularly remarkable is the striking red-sandstone Bobst
Library, designed by Philip Johnson and Richard Foster and
located on the south side of the square. Don't miss the interior
of this building with its central atrium, rising the full 12 floors.
Just across LaGuardia Place, also on Washington Square
South, is Loeb Student Center, which occupies the site of the
boarding house known as the "House of Genius" for the array
of writers who supposedly lodged there—Theodore Dreiser,
Stephen Crane, O. Henry, Frank Norris, Willa Cather, and
Eugene O'Neill, among others (though only Frank Norris' stay
had been verified) before its demolition in 1948.
    The Judson Church, on the corner of Washington Square
South and Thompson Street, was, like the Arch, designed by
Stanford White; its stained glass windows are by John La Farge.
Judson Hall, a graduate-student dormitory at number 53, was a
hotel when Edward Arlington Robinson stayed there in 1906.

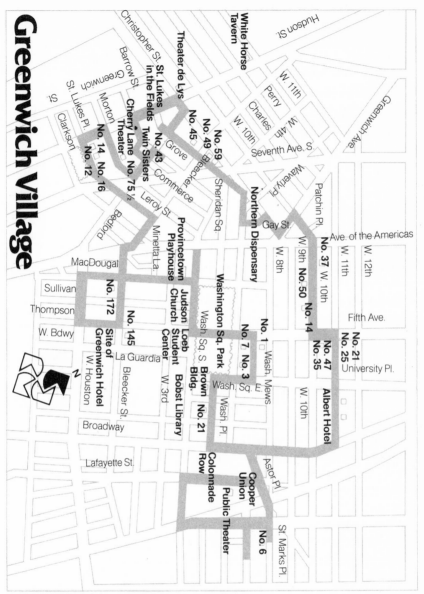

Greenwich Village

Hudson St.

White Horse Tavern

W. 11th
Perry
Charles
W. 4th
W. 10th

Seventh Ave. S.

Christopher St.

Theater de Lys

St. Lukes in the Fields

Greenwich

Barrow St.

No. 59

No. 49

No. 45

Bleecker

Grove

St. Lukes Pl.

Clarkson

St. Lukes

St.

Cherry Lane Theater

No. 43

Twin Sisters

No. 75½

Commerce

Morton

Bedford

No. 14

No. 16

No. 12

Leroy St.

Sheridan Sq.

Minetta La.

Northern Dispensary

Waverly Pl.

Gay St.

Patchin Pl.

W. 8th

W. 9th

No. 37

No. 50

W. 10th

W. 11th

Greenwich Ave.

Ave. of the Americas

W. 12th

Fifth Ave.

No. 21

No. 25

University Pl.

No. 14

No. 47

No. 35

Albert Hotel

W. 10th

Provincetown Playhouse

Judson Loeb Student Center

Washington Sq. Park

Wash. Sq. S.

No. 7

No. 3

No. 1

Wash. Mews

Wash. Sq. E.

Church

Bobst Library

Brown Bldg.

No. 21

Wash. Pl.

MacDougal

Sullivan

Thompson

W. Bdwy

No. 172

No. 145

Site of Greenwich Hotel

La Guardia

W. 3rd

W. Houston

Bleecker St.

Broadway

Lafayette St.

Colonnade Row

Cooper Union

Public Theater

Astor Pl.

St. Marks Pl.

No. 6

N

This walking tour is approximately 4 miles round trip.

From Washington Square South, continue west on West 4th Street (a continuation of Washington Square South). John Barrymore lived at number 132, and, at a former café at number 148, Al Jolson was discovered and Norma Shearer worked as a hat-check girl. Backtrack next to MacDougal Street and turn south. The Provincetown Playhouse, Eugene O'Neill's theater, is at number 133; revivals are occasionally held. Numbers 127 and 131—little Federal houses built for Aaron Burr in 1829—are among the oldest in the city. Burr's ghost reportedly haunts the Café Bizarre around the corner at 106 West 3rd Street.

A block south on MacDougal, you'll spot Minetta Lane. Both Minetta Street and Minetta Lane were named after Minetta Brook, which meanders throughout the area—all underground nowadays. Villagers swear to hearing its gurgling on quiet nights—but then there are few of those in these parts. *The Reader's Digest* was born at One Minetta Lane in 1922, with a press run of 5,000 copies. Continuing on MacDougal, you'll come to Bleeker. The San Remo, a famous restaurant which used to occupy the corner, was one favorite haunt of the beat generation of writers, including Gregory Corso (born at 190 Bleecker); William Styron (who had come to New York in 1947 to work as a junior editor at McGraw-Hill, a job from which he was fired for flying a paper airplane into his supervisor's office); William Burroughs; Allen Ginsberg; and Jack Kerouac. When one of the bartenders beat up one of the guests, the nearly 400 regulars all moved en masse to a bar in Sheridan Square—and the San Remo was never quite the same again. Turn east onto Bleecker.

Nearby at 172 Bleecker Street, James Agee had a floor-through apartment on the top floor of a red-brick building from 1941 to 1951. Theodore Dreiser paid a quarter a night to stay at what was then the Greenwich Hotel, on the corner of Thompson and Bleecker, when he first arrived in New York in 1895; James Fenimore Cooper had lived across the street at 145 Bleecker—with wife, four Swiss servants, and a French tiger cat named Coquelicot—a half-century earlier when the block was called Carroll Place. That Mrs. Cooper had considered the house (picked out for them by their friend Samuel F. B. Morse) "too magnificent" is hard to believe when you see it now.

Meander Through the Maze

Turn south onto Thompson Street, west on Houston, north on MacDougal, west along Bleecker across the Avenue of the Americas, and then left onto Leroy Street. Just past Bedford Street, across Seventh Avenue, you'll come to St. Luke's Place—which ranks as one of the city's loveliest blocks because of all the ginkgo trees (pollution-resistant as well as pretty) and the handsome Italianate houses. In 1922, three different writers lived there simultaneously: Marianne Moore, red-headed and reed-slender, who stayed at number 14 from 1918 to 1929 and had the reputation for knowing everything about everything; Theodore Dreiser, who lived on the parlor floor at number 16; and Sherwood Anderson, who briefly called number 12 his home (the same house which in 1931 was the home of the ill-fated Starr Faithful, who went out to do some shopping one June morning and was found washed ashore, strangled, on a Long Island beach two days later). Anderson had never before met Dreiser, but wanted to introduce himself; time and time again he'd walk over, then lose his nerve before ringing the bell. When, one day, Dreiser happened to open the door while Anderson was there—and shut it as soon as he found out who was facing him—Anderson spent a long day making the rounds of the Village saloons before he found out that Dreiser had simply been embarrassed. At number 6, the mayor's lamps point out the former residence of the swinging New York City Mayor Jimmy Walker; such lamps were put up in front of every mayoral residence before Gracie Mansion provided the city's chief executive with a permanent home.

From here, go north on Hudson, then east on Morton Street—a typical Village street full of doglegs, tiny houses, and changing facades. Then turn north onto Bedford Street. John Barrymore probably lived at 9½-foot-wide number 75½, as did Edna St. Vincent Millay briefly after her marriage to Eugen Boissevain; this house is also, supposedly, the narrowest house in the city, while number 77, next door, is generally considered the oldest. Walk north until you get to Barrow Street, then turn east. Up at number 43, Joseph Wood Krutch and Mark Van Doren shared an apartment in an old three-story brick house. Backtracking towards Bedford again, turn south, then west on Commerce. The Cherry Lane Theater, on your left, has hosted

American premieres of plays by Albee (who wrote *The Zoo Story* on the wobbly kitchen table at 238 West 4th Street), Beckett, and Ionesco. On your right, opposite the Cherry Lane Theater, you'll see "the Twin Sisters," two identical houses built for a sea captain who said his daughters couldn't live together under the same roof. Turn west back onto Barrow, then north up Hudson Street. Not far from Barrow you'll spot St. Luke's in the Fields, built in 1821, occupying the block bounded by Christopher, Barrow, Greenwich, and Hudson streets. Its first vestryman was Clement Clarke Moore, author of *Visit from St. Nicholas.* There's a lovely garden; ask the caretaker to let you in. Number 487 Hudson Street, one of several circa-1825 Federal houses that now belong to St. Luke's, was home to Bret Harte, author of the *Tales of Roaring Camp* and *The Outcasts of Poker Flat.*

A Theater, a Mews, and a Club

Continue northward to Christopher and turn right. It was in the Theatre de Lys that Kurt Weill's *Threepenny Opera* ran for nine years with Weill's wife Lotte Lenya as its star. On Bedford Street, to your right, there are said to be more Federal-style houses than anywhere else in the city. Follow Bedford to Grove, turn west, then start looking for Grove Court, a tiny, secluded mews built as laborers' quarters in 1854, known then as Mixed Ale Alley, and now converted into triplexes. Leaving there, you should turn east on Grove. Built in 1830 and remodeled in 1870, number 45 on Grove Street was home to Hart Crane late in 1919. Across Bleecker Street at 49 Grove, Gore Vidal, Louis Auchincloss, William Styron, and James Jones, among others, gathered in the home of Vance Bourjaily in the '50s; during the same period some other writers, including Dylan Thomas, would hang out at the White Horse Tavern at Hudson and 11th Streets.

The literary history doesn't end there. Thomas Paine died in the back room at what is now 59 Grove Street nearly two centuries earlier. He had been living elsewhere, getting sicker all the time, and finally beseeched a friend to move him and take care of him.

Stay on Grove Street as you cross Sheridan Square. Close to the spot where Grove Street becomes Waverly Place, you're at the Northern Dispensary, built in 1831 and still looking much as it did in 1837 when Edgar Allan Poe was treated there for a head cold (free). Turn right onto Waverly Place.

Gay Street, which you'll soon cross, was the center of a small black neighborhood in the latter half of the 19th century; in the 1920s it was lined by speakeasies. Ruth McKenny, who lived at number 14, wrote a play about the area, and about her sister Eileen (*My Sister Eileen*). Mary McCarthy lived at number 18. Turn right onto Christopher Street, then left onto Greenwich Avenue, then right onto 10th. Walking straight, you'll come to Patchin Place, on your left. Poet e.e. cummings lived at number 4 from 1923 until his death in 1962. The houses were built in the middle of the 19th century to house workers of the then-elegant Brevoort Hotel on Fifth Avenue.

From here, walk east on 10th Street. Hart Crane lived in the five-story brick house at 54 West 10th Street in 1917; Edward Albee in the carriage house at number 50 during the '60s; Sinclair Lewis and Dorothy Thompson across the street in number 37 after their marriage in 1928; and Mark Twain in the handsome house at number 14 in 1900. He spent his days receiving visitors from a huge carved Italian bed, propped up against pillows piled at the foot end so that he could enjoy the view of the headboard, or dressed up in white serge, his white hair flowing, promenading the streets enjoying being recognized. On the corner of Fifth and 10th Street, a plaque used to commemorate Willa Cather's stay at the Grosvenor Hotel, at 35 Fifth Avenue, now the Samuel Rubin International Hall, an NYU dorm. Turn north on Fifth.

The Salmagundi Club, formed in 1871 "for the promotion of social intercourse among artists" and named for Washington Irving's satire magazine, occupies a brownstone mansion (one of the last of the grand ones) at 47 Fifth Avenue. Heading eastward on East 11th Street, you'll come on 21 East 11th, home of Edith Wharton's sister-in-law Mary Cadwalader Jones, with whom Henry James often stayed while in New York; Hart Crane stayed at what used to be a cheap rooming house (now remodeled and quite lovely) at 25 East 11th. Thomas Wolfe lodged in room 2220 at the former Albert Hotel at University Place and 11th Street (now apartments) when he came to New York to write plays and teach at New York University.

From here, bear south on Broadway to Astor Place and you're back at your starting point.

FROM CITY HALL MANHATTAN TO CITY HALL BROOKLYN
C. Ray Smith

"Others will see the shipping of Manhattan north and west, and the heights of Brooklyn to the south and east. Others will see the islands large and small. . . . A hundred years hence, or ever so many hundred years hence, others will see them. . . ."
(Walt Whitman: "Crossing Brooklyn Ferry")

A walk across the Brooklyn Bridge—from City Hall, Manhattan to Borough Hall, Brooklyn—fulfills Walt Whitman's prophecy of over 100 years ago. Today we still see the ships of Manhattan and the harbor islands as we stroll across the Brooklyn Bridge. But this majestic feat of engineering has transformed Whitman's ferry view into a soaring bird's-eye view from high above the swift currents of the East River.

When Whitman wrote his poem in 1856, the Brooklyn ferry was the only connection between Manhattan island and Brooklyn. The two boroughs were then separate cities. Designer-engineer John Augustus Roebling dreamed of connecting the two cities by roadways and a pedestrian promenade which would "allow people of leisure and old and young to stroll over the bridge on fine days." The Brooklyn Bridge, opened in 1883, is the fulfillment of his dream. The marvel of its silvery webs of steel cable—the delicate tracery of Roebling's most daring invention—suspend the bridge for nearly 1,600 feet. For years the Brooklyn Bridge was the longest suspension bridge in the world.

City Hall Park, Manhattan
Start your walk on the Manhattan side of the bridge at City Hall Park. It was here that the Declaration of Independence was read to General Washington and his troops on July 9, 1776. Here, at the foot of City Hall Park to the southwest, you can see the brownstone portico of St. Paul's Chapel, where Washington worshipped during his Presidency. Inside, you'll find Washington's pew with the Great Seal above it. The pink, blue, cream, and gold rococo-Georgian interior is hung with glittering Waterford chandeliers. Opened in 1766, it is the oldest church in Manhattan.

Now stroll a block north on Broadway—the longest street in Manhattan—to the Woolworth Building, once the world's

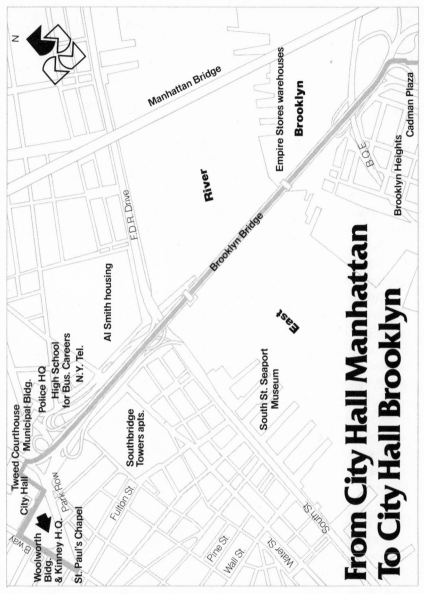

From City Hall Manhattan To City Hall Brooklyn

This Walking Tour is Approximately 2 Miles Long.

tallest at 60 stories and 792 feet high. It is still considered one of
the strongest upward-thrusting skyscrapers. Look in at the
sumptuous Gothic lobby with its mosaic ceiling of gold, blue,
and green, its creamy marble pilasters, and its sculpted gilt-
bronze decorations with high Gothic detailing. You'll see why it
was called "the cathedral of commerce" when it opened in
1913.

Next cross over to City Hall at the north of the park. You'll
find a handsome white limestone structure with a Georgian
cupola and clock. City Hall has been the seat of New York City
government since 1811. Look inside at its rotunda with twin
spiral stairs, fluted columns and coffered dome; it is one of the
most elegant classic spaces in the city. You can visit the upstairs
rooms Monday through Friday from 10 to 4. At the head
of the stairs you'll find the Governors Room, decorated with
fine carving, lined with portraits by John Trumbull and filled
with Federal furniture. You may also see the City Council
Chamber on the east of the building and the Board of Estimate
Chamber on the northwest corner—superb spaces with semi-
circular ends, white benches and dark wood handrails; with
blue, white and gold furnishings and beautiful mid-Victorian
crystal chandeliers.

The Brooklyn Bridge

Now you are ready for the truly exhilarating course. Walk
toward the Brooklyn Bridge, which is clearly visible as you exit
from City Hall. Veer slightly to the north, past the statue of
Horace Greeley outside the notoriously costly but handsome
Tweed Court House, which was built under the graftsmanship
of the infamous "Boss" Tweed. You'll be facing the elaborately
sculpted Surrogates Court building with its rich gold marble
entry court in high Beaux-Arts style. Turn right past the great
arch of the Municipal Building and, at the first traffic light on
Park Row, cross to the island approach to the bridge.

You are now beginning your walk across the Brooklyn
Bridge. And it's free—you *cannot* buy the bridge, no matter
what anyone says—although the walk used to cost a penny
when it was first opened. In the beginning your walk will seem
merely a stroll down the middle of a divided highway—on land
with traffic whizzing by in both directions. But soon the pathway
begins to rise up above the surrounding buildings. Ahead you'll
see the great gold-brown masonry towers of the bridge with their

pointed Gothic arches topped by heavy flat cornices—a seemingly odd combination until we recall that the designer grew up in Mühlhausen, Germany, among Gothic churches and walled fortifications.

As you proceed, cast your mind back to the time before this first bridge to cross the East River was built, and recall a New York skyline on which Trinity Church, now dwarfed at the top of Wall Street, was the tallest structure for miles. Imagine how gigantic the bridge must have looked as its towers were a-building and its roadway soared up to more than three times the height of the surrounding buildings. Then you will feel the genius of Roebling's vision when he dreamed of Brooklyn Bridge.

As you walk along, you will pass the more modern civic buildings on the north: the tall white Municipal Building topped with a gilded statue of *Civic Fame;* the red-brick and cream-pilastered Roman Catholic Church of St. Andrew; and the red-brick Police Headquarters building (the only civic government building not in gray masonry). On the next block is the plum-brick High School for Business Careers, with its cylindrical turrets at each corner. All of these buildings are a city government parade in themselves.

As you gaze out over the Manhattan waterfront, the masts and rigging of the sailing ships in the South Street Seaport Museum come into view. You are high above the low-lying early-19th-century buildings that were instantly dwarfed when the bridge was built.

Mount the steps to the wood promenade of the bridge and turn back to look at the spectacular Manhattan skyline: you'll be able to see the pyramid and lantern atop the Bank of the Manhattan Company building on Wall Street, the art deco spire of the American International Group building on Pine Street, and the twin aluminum towers of the World Trade Center—all of which now dwarf the Brooklyn Bridge.

Soon you are out over the East River and amid the vast expanses of air, wind, and horizon. To the north spanning the river is the Manhattan Bridge of 1909, with trains crossing it from time to time. (Trains originally crossed the Brooklyn Bridge on each side of the promenade.) Farther north you catch glimpses of the Empire State Building and the gilded pyramid of the New York Life Insurance Company building. But it is to the south that the view really widens out: in the harbor you'll see the

Coast Guard base on Governors Island, and on the horizon, the high point of the harbor on Staten Island, where the Verrazano Bridge—now the longest suspension bridge in the world—spans the Narrows to Brooklyn.

As you forge ahead, you begin to be enmeshed by the supporting cables that, along with the diagonal cables from the towers, create silver fishnets on both sides. Below is the boat traffic on the river—tugs and barges, freighters and tankers, and, to the south, ferries plying the harbor to the islands.

Soon you'll approach the Manhattan-side tower of the bridge—with its topstone dated 1875, the year the towers were completed—where the promenade rises eight more steps to a broad observation platform. From there you have another dazzling view of the Manhattan skyline through the cables. Plaques celebrate the designers and engineers of the bridge. Roebling's son, Colonel Washington Augustus Roebling (1837–1926), was injured during an underwater inspection of this tower's foundations and was crippled for the rest of his life. He devoted the next 14 years to completing his father's vision, directing construction from his nearby home.

Now you are on the slope to the center of the bridge's span—135 feet above mean high water and above the curve of the suspension cables—with a clear, breathtaking view to both north and south. At the middle of the bridge, where old street lights along the promenade recall the days of old New York, you can see the Statue of Liberty south in the wide harbor. Her inspiring copper-green image is still a towering symbol of the city and of our country. Gulls circle overhead and the East River below is sometimes white-capped.

The Brooklyn Side

From the middle of the bridge, the Brooklyn shore and skyline come more and more into view. On the right, or south, are the piers and waterfront warehouses of Brooklyn with the Brooklyn-Queens Expressway stretching out beyond them. The expressway is a brilliant urban planning concept—its roadways are on two levels and the "Esplanade" pedestrian plaza of Brooklyn Heights is above them.

At the tower of the bridge on the Brooklyn side, John Roebling was injured in 1869 during a preliminary survey and died soon after from tetanus. He never saw his bridge rise.

Below to the left on the Brooklyn shore are the romantic-looking, metal-shuttered, brick Empire Stores warehouses with their star-ended tie rods, and, to the south, you can see the low-scaled residential streets of Brooklyn Heights.

Cadman Plaza Park
The whir of the traffic subsides as you descend from the wooden promenade to a landlike concrete walkway. When you come to the steps at the end of the bridge, go down to the street and turn right, continue uphill, and swing into the park called Cadman Plaza. Here sycamore trees, evergreen hedges, and granite blocks of paving make a broad urban mall where children scamper and play.

Follow the rise to the center of the mall and read the dedication on the Brooklyn War Memorial—a large gray-stone monument flanked by huge statues. As you amble along you can catch glimpses of the charming 19th-century townhouses in Brooklyn Heights through the modern towers of Cadman Plaza housing on the right. Cross Tillary Street and look at the rich Romanesque gray-stone carvings, towers, and turrets of the main Brooklyn post office on the left. At Johnson Street, which crosses Cadman Plaza, you will find a statue of Henry Ward Beecher (1813–1887)—"the great apostle of the Brotherhood of Man."

Beyond is a full view of the classic Brooklyn Borough Hall—an 1848 Georgian building with a tall flight of steps to its portico which is topped by an elongated cupola. Mount the steps and enter the two-story "rotunda" with its natural stone fluted columns and old bell. On the third floor you can see a mid-Victorian courtroom with dark wood columns. Compare it with the Board of Estimate Chamber you saw in Manhattan's City Hall where you began your tour. And, finally, return to Cadman Plaza and pause at the vista of the Manhattan Bridge's tower—so different in steel from the masonry towers of the Brooklyn Bridge—and beyond the Empire State building—still the symbol of New York's brilliant skyline parade.

Brooklyn Heights and Atlantic Avenue
Incurable explorers can wander through the streets of Brooklyn Heights with its restaurants on Montague Street (one is called Capulet's), its lavish townhouses, and the Esplanade at the river's edge overlooking the spectacular skyline of Manhattan. Maps on numerous lampposts outline a landmark trail. Or

you can continue to Atlantic Avenue, where a center of shops and restaurants offers some of the best Middle Eastern food in the city.

Public Transportation back to City Hall.
At Borough Hall, the total distance you will have walked from City Hall Manhattan is 2 miles. For those who need to rest weary feet, public transportation back to Manhattan is downstairs in the Municipal Building behind Borough Hall. It can take you to Chinatown for a refreshing Chinese meal and another special tour.

Return via Brooklyn Bridge
For those who thrive on skyline vistas, the return to Manhattan over the Brooklyn Bridge promenade is perhaps even more sensational than the trip in the easterly direction. With the sun in the west and the buildings backlighted, you will see an almost completely new panorama. And you can appreciate more fully Herman Melville's words: "There now is your insular city of the Manhattoes, belted round by wharves as Indian isles by coral reefs—commerce surrounds it with her surf."

MANHATTAN'S WALL STREET FROM RIVER TO RIVER
C. Ray Smith

The Street and the Wall
No street in America shares the present of today's big city business with the historical significance of its past as Wall Street does. The Street, bastion of our banking community, was also the line of actual defense for the first European settlers on Manhattan island. As you walk along Wall you can tour the skyscraper canyon of finance and retrace the line of "the Wall"—a 5-foot-high log palisade—built by the Dutch of New Amsterdam in 1653 as a bulwark against attack by land.

In addition, Wall Street makes a triangle with that natural treasure of the city, its splendid harbor, which from the beginning has made New York a vital trading post and center of commerce. For the first three centuries of our nation, the harbor served as the principal water defense and gateway to our country. From river to river a walk along Wall unfolds the commercial foundation of shipping and finance that gave New York a lead over American cities from the earliest days.

At the East River, brick and granite warehouses recreate the scene of the harbor in the early 19th century. At the Hudson River you can visually retrace your steps and also see the full panorama of the harbor from a breathtaking 20th-century viewing platform. (You can do it in reverse too, but the sun may be in your eyes as you walk down Wall.)

South Street Seaport Museum

The best time to begin your walk is around 10:30 A.M. Begin at Fulton Street (there is a Broadway IRT stop at Fulton and William Streets) and walk east on the north side, downhill toward the river and the silvery web of the Brooklyn Bridge. At Water Street, you'll see the copper-green lighthouse that signals the South Street Seaport Museum and historic district—a building-scape of low brick and cast-iron warehouses.

If you look across Fulton Street, you'll see the tall masts and rigging of a vast sailing ship rising above the shops and steep roofs of Schermerhorn Row. You may well feel that you are back at the New York harbor of 1811.

Be sure to take in the museum's ship-model displays and printing exhibition—a tribute to the area's former role as a printing center—at 207–211 Water Street, and stop at the Visitors Center, 16 Fulton Street, and other seaport shops, which are open from 11–6. Roam through the Fulton Market of handcrafts and food stalls and past the adjoining Fulton Fish Market, which faces the river and Pier 17, and on to the Seaport Museum's Pier 16. Here, in the smell of the salt air and under the circling gulls, eight ships are moored—schooners, fishing sloops, a ferry, and the Ambrose Light ship. Four are ready to be boarded—free, except for the four-masted square-rigger bark *Peking,* the largest sailing vessel ever built (admission is $2.50 and worth it). From May to September the schooner *Pioneer* will take you on a three-hour sail in the harbor for the truest taste of the early salt (reservations recommended).

Seafood

You may already have a hankering for lunch, if you started in the morning, and this is where you'll find the freshest seafood

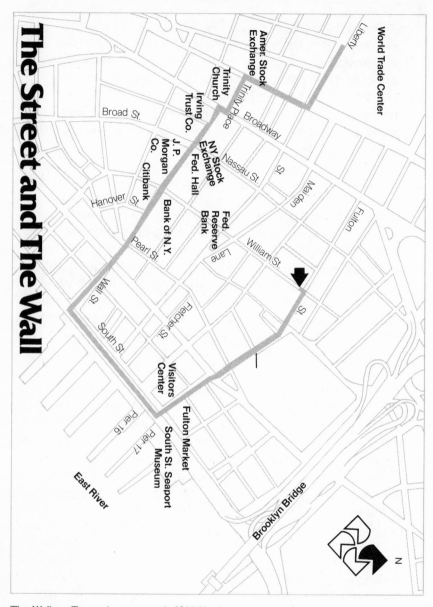

The Street and The Wall

- World Trade Center
- Liberty
- Amer. Stock Exchange
- Trinity Church
- Broadway
- Trinity Place
- Broad St.
- Irving Trust Co.
- NY Stock Exchange
- Fed. Hall
- Nassau St.
- J. P. Morgan Co.
- Citibank
- Hanover St.
- Bank of N.Y.
- Fed. Reserve Bank
- Maiden Lane
- Fulton
- Pearl St.
- Lane
- William St.
- St.
- Wall St.
- Fletcher St.
- South St.
- Visitors Center
- Pier 16
- Fulton Market
- Pier 17
- South St. Seaport Museum
- East River
- Brooklyn Bridge
- N

This Walking Tour is Approximately 2¾ Miles Long.

in town. At the corner of Fulton and South Streets, you can mount the stairs to the old seafood house Sweet's (usually without a line at noon), which has been serving lunches and dinners since 1845 in a virtually untouched old New York atmosphere—with riverboat Gothic gingerbread over the windows. You can also amble over for more modest meals at Sloppy Louie's on South Street or on-the-run meals at the stalls in the Fulton Market and on the Seaport's Pier 16.

The Waterfront

After lunch, stroll down South Street five short blocks (away from the Brooklyn Bridge), passing the old warehouses and printing plants—reminders of the area's early days as a printing center—and the boats berthed along the river. If you look up Fletcher Street you can catch a glimpse of the glistening aluminum twin towers of the World Trade Center. On the pier across from Maiden Lane are the inflated bubbles of the Wall Street Racquet Club, and up Maiden Lane is the fortified Neo-Renaissance palace of the Federal Reserve Bank of New York.

Wall Street

When you turn right into Wall Street, you'll see the spire of Trinity Church guarding the canyon of banks and investment houses. As one crusty old banker said, "Trinity Church points a velvet-looking but admonishing finger to heaven as a reminder to the financial community that it is being watched." Along the street the successive monuments reveal the aspirations of the giants of finance and the ways in which they used buildings to symbolize financial power and prestige.

Cross over to the south side of Wall and look up at the sky-scraper tops. A Greek temple is on top of 52 Wall, a Roman monument with a copper-green winged victory atop 48 Wall, and a pyramid with a Gothic lantern on 40 Wall. These are relics of an age when buildings aimed for importance by mimicking models of the past and stretched themselves out tall with numerous undifferentiated floors in the middle.

Continue on Wall to Pearl Street where the Dutch wall began, running from river to river (for the water line originally came up to Pearl Street).

Cross north to 74 Wall—the Williamsburgh Savings Bank—where a plaque commemorates the home of Edward Livingston, U.S. Secretary of State from 1831 to 1833.

Go a few steps farther west and you'll pass by 59–63 Wall—the brown-and-buff-brick private banking house of Brown Brothers Harriman, which has been on that site since 1833. The main entrance is a pleasant, domed classic rotunda.

At Hanover Street you can see the angled pattern of narrow, crooked streets—all that survives from the Dutch days, a distinct contrast to the familiar grid pattern of streets elsewhere in the city.

At 55 Wall, you'll find the Citibank building, the lower portion of which was designed in 1842 by Isaiah Rogers as the Merchants Exchange. Go over to see what the original interior looked like: a magnificent trading hall with a coffered ceiling, barrel vaults and central gilded dome. The building was expanded in 1907 by the turn-of-the-century architectural firm of McKim, Mead & White.

When you come out of 55 Wall, look up at the top of 52 Wall opposite and you'll be delighted by the little Greek temple perched on top of it.

Wander across Wall to number 48, the headquarters of the Bank of New York, founded in 1784 by Alexander Hamilton. A double stair leads to the 1927 Georgian banking floor above.

As you move along to the corner of Wall and William Streets, a bronze plaque locates one of the bastions of the Dutch wall. Look north up William (from that bastion where cannons and sentries once kept watch), and you'll see today's headquarters of the Chase Manhattan Bank and, beyond, the fortress of the Federal Reserve Bank again. Farther on the skyline, you can see the towers of the Municipal Building with its 25-foot gilded statue of *Civic Fame* and the Federal Court building with its gilded pyramid and Gothic lantern. Wander a bit south on William Street and you'll have another view of the Roman monument on top of 48 Wall. You can also see the Georgian cupola of red brick and fluted columns atop the National Bank of North America at 44 Wall.

Continue walking past 40 Wall, the 72-story, 925-foot-high skyscraper built by the former Bank of the Manhattan Company. Designed in 1929, its pyramidal crown and Gothic lantern are landmarks on the street. Look back toward the East River for a skyline view of Brooklyn Heights beyond. High above Wall on the south side between Hanover and Pearl you'll see the brown and buff French-topped tower with lacy ironwork on the Brown Brothers Harriman building you passed at 59–63 Wall.

Ahead at the corner of Broad Street is 23 Wall, the headquarters of the J. P. Morgan & Company financial empire. On the Wall Street facade are the scars of a 1920 explosion by a political terrorist. If you enter the corner doorway you'll discover a main banking hall of grand dimensions—130 feet by 90 feet by 30 feet high—with a conspicuously grand chandelier—16 feet high by 12 feet in diameter, weighing about 2 tons.

New York Stock Exchange

Next, proceed across Broad Street to number 8, the New York Stock Exchange with its Corinthian-columned portico and sculpted pediment. Inside you'll find the hub of the financial community and one of the great classic spaces in the city. People are standing, walking, gesticulating amid a buzz of buying and selling, and the noise level in this cavernous space is astonishingly high—signboards tick over numbers, ticker-tape machines spew out tape, and telephones flash. You can see the activity by entering at 20 Broad on business days from 10 to 4. And although from the visitors gallery you may wonder how our economic system thrives in the midst of such apparent chaos, frequent tours provide reassuring clarification.

Federal Hall

Walk back to the north side of Wall and the top of Broad where the statue of George Washington by sculptor J(ohn) Q(uincy) A(dams) Ward stands in front of the national memorial, Federal Hall. Here, on the site of the city's second City Hall (1699–1812), which also served as the first capitol of the United States, George Washington took the oath of office as President in 1789. The Doric-columned structure, built in 1842 by Town & Davis, is a simplified version of the Parthenon and considered the best example of New York's Greek Revival period. Inside, unexpectedly, you'll discover a rotunda with a graceful dome of gold, white, and pale-blue decoration. Exhibits recount Washington's inauguration and other colonial and Federal events in New York. (Open 9–4:30, Sunday through Friday.)

Continue along Wall to the west, past the Bankers Trust

Company building at 16 Wall, which rises 39 stories and 542 feet with a stepped pyramid on top. Inside you'll find a dark, richly-paneled 1930s banking hall.

Next look across the south side of Wall at number 1, the Irving Trust Company building. Finished in 1932 and rising 51 stories to a height of 650 feet, it is a splendid example of the Art Deco style by architects Voorhees, Gmelin & Walker. Enter the flamboyant "Red Room" with its blazing red-to-orange and gold mosaics to see one of the best and most dazzling 1930s-style interiors in the city.

A plaque on 1 Wall locates the site of the "Land Gate" in the Dutch palisade through which early settlers could see up Broadway to the northernmost portion of Manhattan. Today you can see the towers of the Woolworth, Chrysler, and Empire State buildings, landmarks on the city skyline.

Trinity Church

Now you arrive at the ever-present symbol of Wall Street— Trinity Church, the first English parish in New York, established around 1700. This is the third church on the site. It was designed by Richard Upjohn and completed in 1846. The parish has enormous landholdings from the original grant from Queen Anne in 1705, stretching from Fulton to Christopher Streets and from Broadway west to the Hudson River. Through the sculpted bronze doors, designed by Richard Morris Hunt, is a Gothic Revival foyer under an elaborately carved wood organ loft. The delicate stone tracery of the church itself—in a muted sandstone color—offsets the off-white plaster of the vaulting.

Then stroll through the cemetery on the north side (Alexander Hamilton and Robert Fulton are buried on the south), and behind the church descend the stair, exiting onto Trinity Place through "The Cherub Gate" from Christopher Wren's London church of St. Mary-le-Bow. (A plaque tells more.)

American Stock Exchange

Across the street you can see the American Stock Exchange, New York's second major stock exchange, in bustling action. The visitors entry is located at 78 Trinity Place and open from 9:45 to 3 on business days. Note the plaque on the north corner of the exchange that details its history. Look back at the Wall Street skyline to see the stepped pyramid atop the Bankers Trust Building.

Proceed north on Trinity Place to where the modern build-ings begin. Across Broadway you'll see the sleek black Marine Midland Bank Building, designed by Skidmore, Owings & Mer-rill in 1967, with its corner-balanced orange-red cube sculpture by Isamu Noguchi. And across Liberty Street you come to One Liberty Plaza, another black sheathed structure by Skidmore, Owings & Mer-rill. Built for U.S. Steel Corporation, the building's major tenant is the brokerage house of Merrill, Lynch, Pierce, Fenner & Smith.

World Trade Center
Finally, to see the ultimate breath-catcher in New York, cross Liberty Street and go west to the southern or downtown tower of the World Trade Center, called World Trade Center Number 2, where King Kong showed his size. Take the escala-tor to the upper level of the lobby, where a ticket booth pro-vides admission to the 107th-floor enclosed observation deck and to the 110th-floor open-air "rooftop promenade." Arrived at by rocketlike elevator in slightly over one minute, these ob-servatories—more than ¼ mile in the sky—have a visibility of over 50 miles on clear days. Here you can sit with a snack, tea, or coffee and trace the route of your walk along the Wall from the early 19th century to your 20th-century viewing platform. Here you can see the full panorama of New York Harbor as it could not be seen before our century. (Admission: adults, $1.70; children 6–12, 85 cents; children under 6, free; senior citizens, $1.25. Open 9:30 to 9:30 daily.)

Refreshment
If you cannot move from all this intake of information, many World Trade Center restaurants—with much variety of location, atmosphere, and price—provide refreshing places to recollect your tour.

Return
Subways come together in the base of the World Trade Center to take you back—to prepare for yet another day and another New York walk that will further enrich your eye, your mind, and your soul.

NEW JERSEY

PATRICIAN PRINCETON
Mark A. Stuart

Patrician Princeton, the quiet lady dressed simply as Cynthia Gooding describes her, by a designer no one else has rediscovered.

Literate Princeton, where the ghosts of F. Scott Fitzgerald and Thomas Mann and John O'Hara haunt the tap rooms and the libraries . . . where half a dozen writers on today's bestseller lists sit behind their barricades pecking away at tomorrow's blockbusters.

Historic Princeton, where Washington and Woodrow Wilson and Grover Cleveland are spoken of as casually as if they had just been seen around town . . . where the home of a signer of the Declaration of Independence is the governor's mansion.

Princeton, architect's fantasy, where Victorian splendor is as common as the tract houses that dominate the California landscape.

If you walk briskly from site to interesting site in other towns, in Princeton you amble. Walk too quickly, and you'll miss a significant piece of sculpture, a President's home, the national Capitol in 1783. In Princeton, unlike too many other towns, the most interesting walks are in and around the busiest shopping areas. Here history meets commerce, and commerce gives way.

There is, of course, the town's anchor, the university. Some would call it Princeton's reason for being, but they'd be wrong. Princeton was the way it is before the university grew, but the school does give the town its inevitable cachet.

The university is so large, so scattered, that it has the aura

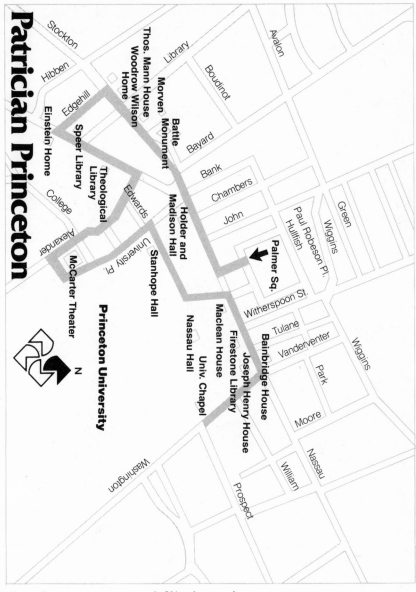

Patrician Princeton

This walking tour is approximately 2½ miles round trip.

of Oxford or Cambridge. To take it all in would require a separate walk. Fortunately, the casual walker can discover historic Princeton—town and gown—together.

We begin at Palmer Square, the central point, across the main street—Nassau Street—from the oldest part of the university. The square has an inn, a tiny green, a playhouse that's really a movie theater, a post office and a collection of shops that will keep you enthralled for hours.

Palmer Square

Palmer Square has the look of history. In reality it was the work of Edgar Palmer, a clever entrepreneur and benefactor of the university, and was designed in 1936 to look as if Thomas Jefferson had been the planner.

Before we push on, let's stop at the Nassau Inn, a Palmer reproduction also built in 1936. The original building can be traced back to 1757. Go into the Yankee Doodle Tap Room, and imagine what it must have been like to hear the whispered gossip of the Continental Congress here.

Across Nassau Street from the east side of Palmer Square one can see the great open face of the university with Nassau Hall set back from the street. Restrain the impulse to rush over, for we'll be back, and turn right on Nassau Street.

Walk past the church, built in 1868, and look for a park bench, the one on which you'll see an elderly man reading a limp copy of *The New York Times.* Don't worry, he's always there, day and night, winter and summer, rain or shine. Sculpted by Seward Johnson, he's made of bronze, no matter how lifelike he looks, and so is the paper he's reading. Look at the headlines. They scream of the resignation of Richard M. Nixon as President of the United States. You can read the whole story, in bronze. That's Princeton whimsy.

Princeton bustles on weekends. People come from miles around to shop, to stare, to sightsee. The best time for a walk is when school's in session because the town is alive with teachers and scholars. But try the middle of the week, when classes are crammed. That way the shops won't be so crowded.

Residential Princeton

The west end of Nassau Street is seldom crowded, even when school's in session. Cross Nassau Street at Bayard Lane, where Nassau becomes Stockton Street. By the time you reach

Battle Monument, a large classic work depicting General Washington, Gen. Hugh Mercer, and a drummer boy, you'll be in residential Princeton. The monument, the design of Frederick MacMonnies, has been a bone of contention since it was dedicated in 1922. Some in town hate it; others tolerate it. A truce has been drawn; hardly anyone speaks of it anymore.

Behind the monument and to your right is Morven, the ancestral home of Richard Stockton, patriot, and member of that select group of men who drew up the Declaration of Independence in Philadelphia. It is now the official residence of the Governor of New Jersey. It isn't a large, imposing place and you'll pass it by if you are looking for something grand. It's modest enough so that former Gov. Richard J. Hughes, who had ten children, complained that it was too small for his family.

A few doors from Morven is another pleasant-looking home. Here Thomas Mann lived and worked on three of his novels: *Lotte in Weimar, The Transposed Head,* and *Joseph the Provider.*

Charles Steadman was the 19th-century builder most responsible for the way Princeton looks today. His dignified, clapboard Greek Revival houses are easily recognized and highly prized by today's residents.

The pale-yellow Steadman house and its large tudor neighbor on the west side of Library Place were both homes (at various times) of Woodrow Wilson when he was a faculty member at Princeton. Further west along Stockton Street is Lowrie House, once the home of Paul Tulane, founder of Tulane University in New Orleans, now the home of the president of Princeton University.

As you walk south on Edgehill Street you'll lose yourself in one of America's quaintest, most prestigious residential areas. The homes date from every period—colonial to contemporary. Solidity, grace, charm, and a certain disdain for privacy are characteristic. These homes enjoy looking at each other.

The home where Einstein lived, 112 Mercer Street, is a white Steadman clapboard house like so many in Princeton. The home is near enough to the Institute for Advanced Study so that the great man could have enjoyed a stimulating walk, yet close enough to the homes around it so that neighbors could have heard the old man playing his violin.

Past Einstein's home on Mercer Street is the Princeton Theological Seminary, a separate institution from the university.

An agreement reached in 1811 led to the location of the seminary in Princeton. The Speer Library and Alexander Hall (or "Old Seminary"), at the corner of Mercer and Alexander and now used as a dormitory, are both parts of the seminary.

Battle Road boasts the home of David Lilienthal, guiding spirit of that great New Deal project the Tennessee Valley Authority. Still an active engineer, Lilienthal now plumps coast to coast in town after town for the return to water power as energy-saver.

The University

The university is still the town's hub, and a return walk along Mercer Street should take in part of the campus. Turn right along the east side of Alexander Street, and two blocks along, stop at the McCarter Theatre, home of one of the great national repertory companies and a university center for the performing arts. From here head back towards Mercer on University Place.

Wander among these attractive examples of collegiate Gothic like Holder and Madison Halls at the corner of University Place. They have the solidity, the form and grace that remind you of the great European universities.

The litany of building names speaks of Princeton past, home to great minds and important government leaders— Stanhope Hall, now the center for guided tours of the school, Blair Tower, Witherspoon Hall, Murray-Dodge Hall, the University Chapel, the Woolworth Center, Seventy-Nine Hall. The crown of the campus, just opposite Palmer Square, is Nassau Hall.

A little history is in order. The university, then known as the College of New Jersey, came to Princeton in 1756 from Newark for the climate, the official records say. The move may have had more to do with the fact that Princeton was willing to hand out 1,000 English pounds, 10 cleared acres of campus, and 200 wooded acres for firewood.

Princeton had been a tavern town on the King's Highway. The traffic from Philadelphia to New York, passing through the town, never failed to stop for refreshments. To this roisterous spot, then, came the straightlaced Presbyterians who ran the college. Until Woodrow Wilson, every president of Princeton had been a Presbyterian minister, and Wilson was a Virginia minister's son.

Nassau Hall was always the hub of the university. The original structure was opened in 1756 and was the largest building in the colonies. Nassau Hall was disfigured during the Revolution, bombarded by cannonballs, and used as a barracks by both sides. In 1802, during peacetime, a fire almost destroyed the hall. Another more devastating fire in 1855 resulted in a rebuilding that gave the structure its present lines.

It was here that the Continental Congress met in 1783, and Princeton was for a time capital of the new United States. The news of the signing of the peace with England was received in this building. The hall is open for visitors from 9 to 5 weekdays. It is shown by Orange Key guides as part of a tour of the campus.

Around Nassau Hall are the other fine historic buildings that have served the college since Revolutionary days—Maclean House, Joseph Henry House, from which one of the earliest telegraphs was strung by the famous physicist from his home to his office. Built in the late 1800s, Alexander Hall, a magnificent Romanesque structure, dominates the campus behind Nassau Hall. This Alexander Hall is affiliated with the university, not the seminary.

Refreshing Princeton

Because it's a university town, Princeton offers many good eating and drinking establishments. You can dine at Lahiere's, with its French menu, on Witherspoon Street. Directly across the street is the less formal atmosphere at the Alchemist & Barrister's. The Nassau Inn has three restaurants, and the Rusty Scupper on lower Alexander Street is part of a chain of informal places that offers an unusual menu.

Princeton will delight those who enjoy gracious living in an informal attitude. People smile and greet you on the streets as if they were old friends, or as if they were fearful they had met you at a cocktail party or a faculty tea and had forgotten your name. Life may speed up as megalopolis sweeps down from New York and up from Philadelphia, but Princeton clings to the old gracious ways and will fight tooth and nail any attempt at change.

PATERSON, ALEXANDER HAMILTON'S DREAM
Mark A. Stuart

Paterson, America's first great industrial city, began as an idea at a picnic.

Marching his Continental Army from Paramus to Morristown on July 10, 1778, Gen. George Washington stopped to eat beside the Great Falls of the Passaic River and to admire the second largest waterfall east of the Mississippi. With him were two aides, the Marquis de Lafayette and Col. Alexander Hamilton.

The general marveled at the spectacle. The shrewd Hamilton, however, saw something else in the cascading torrent 77 feet high and 280 feet wide—power. Power to drive the wheels that would make the new country industrially, as well as politically, independent.

Thirteen years later in 1791, Hamilton, by then Secretary of the Treasury, submitted his famous "Report on Manufactures" to Congress. It suggested the need for a huge industrial drive toward independence to begin in a city. Where? Why, the spot Hamilton had first seen, of course—Paterson, New Jersey.

Two years of scheming and maneuvering resulted in the creation in 1791 of the Society for Establishing Usefull Manufactures (SUM), a private investment group that included Hamilton—of course—that acquired large tracts of land near the falls. SUM asked Pierre L'Enfant, planner of Washington, D.C., to design a water raceway system that would power the plants invited to locate in this great city devoted to industry. L'Enfant's plans were rejected because they were too expensive and too elaborate. Peter Colt, then treasurer of the state of Connecticut, was hired to design the present system. The raceways can still be seen today in downtown Paterson.

For a private corporation, SUM was given enormous power by the state legislature. Its property was exempt from all state and local taxes. How this exemption was engineered was Hamilton's secret. But the city, after all, was named for the governor of the state, William Paterson.

SUM was dogged by mismanagement almost from the start. It remained a property owner until 1945, but it never became the dominant manufacturing goliath that Hamilton dreamed it would.

Yet from the plants built along the raceways came the first

Colt Repeating Revolver (1835), the gun that helped tame the West; the Rogers Locomotive, the engines that drew the first transcontinental trains; John Holland's first practical submarine (1878); and the Wright motor that powered Lindbergh's *Spirit of St. Louis* to Paris. The falls and their raceways also helped create a booming silk industry that gave Paterson its reputation as the silk city of the world in the early 1900s.

The great old factories have suffered decay, but they haven't disappeared. They have become part of a latter-day Paterson renaissance. Some have undergone extensive renovation and become schools and offices. Others are in the process of being converted into studios, boutiques, restaurants, lofts for artists and residences for young people seeking an opportunity to live in spacious apartments—one is even a museum and cultural art center.

The Great Falls

The area around the Great Falls where we begin our walk has been a National Historic Landmark District since 1976. The falls have been a National Natural Landmark since 1969.

The Great Falls, easily accessible by auto from Interstate 80, Main Street exit, are about a quarter of a mile away. The best vantage point to see the falls from is Overlook Park, facing the falls at McBride Avenue Extension and Spruce Street. There is ample parking here.

The ideal time to see the falls is during or after a rain. The Passaic River plunges over the precipice, its hurtling waters raising a mist that climbs higher than the roofs of the tallest buildings nearby. There is no roar, more like a loud hiss; it's soothing, not deafening like Niagara's. The rushing waters, the mist, and the quiet of Great Falls Park have inspired poets like Allen Ginsberg, who grew up in Paterson, to use the city as a basis for his famous long narrative poem about the American dream. William Carlos Williams, who practiced medicine in Rutherford, some 10 miles away, felt that the city was symbolized by the falls.

Garret Mountain

Leaving the falls, walk downhill on Spruce Street. Looming in front of you is Garret Mountain, which dominates the city's skyline. You'll be able to see it from almost anywhere in Paterson. An observation tower jutting into the sky atop the moun-

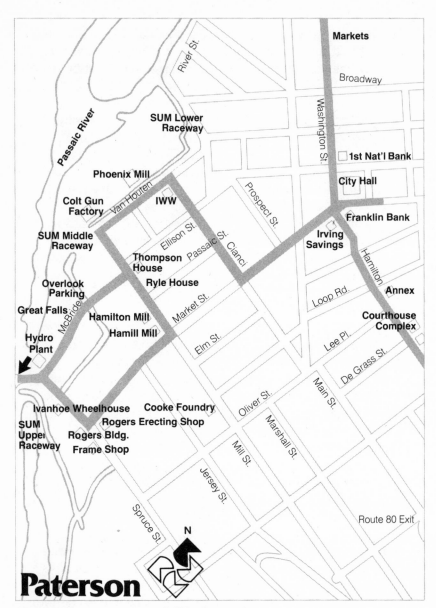

Paterson

This walking tour is approximately 2½ miles round trip.

tain hovers over Lambert Castle, built by a millionaire silk mill owner. The mountain and castle are worth a visit. There are trails offering a breathtaking panorama that stretches all the way to the New York skyline. Inside the castle, the Passaic County Historical Society maintains a historical museum and is in the process of restoring the Victorian interior.

The tower and castle are a brisk 2-mile walk from the center of the city, and the trail is steep. It is usually a separate walking tour.

Hamilton's Dream

We're in the heart of industrial Paterson as we descend the Spruce Street hill. Blocks on blocks of old red-brick factory buildings fill the streets, giving the area the appearance of a crowded ghost town. Appearances are deceiving. Not only are some of the factories humming, others are in the process of being converted.

Some of Hamilton's dream of industrial might came true in the early 1800s. Spruce Street had the Ivanhoe Wheelhouse, power center for a complex of ten paper mills. The wheelhouse is being restored. Just down the street is the complex known as the Rogers Locomotive Works. Remember the famous Civil War locomotives, the *General* and the *Texas,* and the famous Golden Spike ceremony with engine number 119 at Promonitory Point, Utah, joining the Union and Central Pacific Railroads, the nation's first transcontinental link? Those engines, and thousands more, were made at the Rogers plant and neighboring Danforth-Cooke and Grant locomotive factories.

The Rogers Erecting Shop, at the corner of Spruce and Market, where the locomotives were assembled, is being restored as the planned home of the New Paterson Museum. In addition to the museum, the building will house private offices. While work is going on, there is an exciting photographic and multi-media exhibit displayed on the ground floor.

Walking east on Market Street one block to Mill Street you'll pass the vacant lots where once stood the Grant and Danforth-Cooke locomotive works and a covey of mills, some dating back to 1793. Beneath some of the mills, and visible from the street, are the middle and lower raceways—water diverted from the falls to turn the wheels that powered the factories. The lower raceway can be seen on Van Houten Street running parallel with the sidewalk, and sometimes right under the factories. At the corner of Mill and Van Houten streets is the Colt Gun Factory, approachable only through an iron gate in front of a complex of small, scattered buildings just below the raceway. Also on Van Houten is the largest of the mills, the Phoenix Mill, built in 1816 and still in use.

Neighborly Neighbors

But factories aren't all we see in the area. Throughout this neighborhood, once known as the Dublin section because this is where the Irish immigrants originally settled, we find the two- and three-story homes of the millworkers that date back to the 1830s. Some are in disrepair, yet many reflect the concern of the current immigrants who live in them. Some are freshly shingled, siding newly installed. The architecture reflects the working-class nature of the area. The ethnic blend now provides the warmth and charm.

Just across Mill Street, where McBride Avenue spills down from the falls, are two of the oldest homes in the city. The John Ryle House, built in the 1830s, was home of the man who is known as the father of Paterson's silk industry. Right next door is the Benjamin Thompson House, built in 1835. SUM sold Ben Thompson the land for his house in 1833 for $500.

Among these houses, whispers of unions and anarchy first were spread. At Van Houten and Cianci Street is the building that housed the Industrial Workers of the World, the feared and maligned Wobblies—the anarchist group whose leaders organized the devastating silk strike of 1911–1913. One of the unfortunate effects of this strike was that it played a role in the start of the textile industry's moving south. The corner building, now the Question Mark Bar, was once the Nags Head Bar. It was here that Haywood, leader of the IWW and later convicted of the Haymarket Bombing in Chicago, held the meetings in support of the strike.

The City Mix

Cianci Street has been the heart of Paterson's Little Italy; it is now slowly changing its ethnic composition. In this bustling area you'll find food delicacies and specialty goods from half a dozen foreign countries, as well as newspapers and magazines from all over the world.

Walking east on Market Street we come into the center of the city. In addition to the shopping on Main Street, you'll find many examples of the classical architecture so widely used at the turn of the century for both public and private buildings. City Hall is its finest example. This massive, square-block building was finished in 1896 and destroyed six years later in the Great Fire of 1902 that leveled parts of downtown. The building was rebuilt from the original plans of the architects, Carrere and Hastings, who also built Washington's Old Congressional Office Building, New York City's main Public Library and other notable buildings. City Hall Annex at 137A Ellison Street, another fine classical example, was one of the first buildings designed by Owings who later became a partner in the famous architectural firm of Skidmore, Owings and Merrill.

City Hall is surrounded by other fine examples of classical and Beaux-Arts architecture: the First National Bank Building, also the work of Carrere and Hastings, on the corner of Washington Street; the Franklin Bank; and the L'Enfant Building at 1 Hamilton Street.

After a short walk north on Washington Street from City Hall, we cross Broadway into the lower Main Street mall and the heart of one of the city's two great indoor-outdoor food markets, bursting with exotic goodies from foreign lands. The air is filled in summer with vendors hawking their delicacies, competing for customers with songs.

In the reverse direction from City Hall, we walk down Hamilton Street toward the county courthouse complex. The old courthouse building at Hamilton and DeGrasse was finished in 1903. It's typically classical. The modern addition was completed in 1971. At Hamilton Street and the new Loop Road is the city's prize architectural piece. The former post office, now the courthouse annex, is one of the two pure examples of Flemish Renaissance architecture still standing in this country. Look at its crenelated lines and its gables, and remember that it was modeled after Butcher's Hall in Haarlem, Holland.

Exciting Rejuvenation

Paterson, once America's premier industrial city, fell on hard times immediately after World War II. The mills had gone south; the suburban shopping centers had challenged Main Street; many of the middle-class families who were the backbone of the city's cultural and business life had moved to the suburbs. Paterson, slowly, is making its comeback in the '70s. Renewal has rebuilt the center of the city. New business is moving in. It's still the county seat, and retains the attention of those who are in public life.

The heart of the city, its pulse, its arms always wide open for the newcomer from other lands—as it was from the time of the Revolution—is still there. The city center is filled with many interesting small specialty shops reflecting the multi-ethnic population of this vibrant city. And better still, young people are beginning to recognize the value of living in an urban center with its superior transportation facilities. They are flocking back to the city as home-ownership and rentals in the suburbs grow more expensive. The old red-brick factories are beckoning, much as they did in New York's SoHo district, for rehabilitation into apartments. As the word spreads, Paterson is rejuvenating.

WASHINGTON, D.C.

THE MALL AND CAPITOL HILL
Wayne Barrett

Mind-boggling describes this walk. Surrounding you are vast
treasure-troves of historic relics, priceless masterpieces, rare
documents, countless objects of man and nature through the
ages. Beyond are the marbled halls of government where de-
mocracy lives. Be forewarned, as you join some 15 million annually who leave their footprints on the Mall, that an arresting
exhibit or collection may rob you of time. Reconnoiter, then,
the daunting scene and promise to return and return. The
Smithsonian museums alone catalog some 70 million items; so
even if you live as long as an Old Testament patriarch, there will
always be something new to see.

South Side of the Mall
Something new and grand is the National Air and Space
Museum, where your tour begins. Park underground (entrance
on 7th Street), then ascend into a capacious airdrome of glass
and Tennessee marble spanning 3 city blocks. Rockets reach for
the 90-foot-high ceiling, and squadrons of famous planes hang
from sky hooks. Suspended in time are the Wright Brothers'
Flyer and Lindbergh's *Spirit of St. Louis.* From Goddard's embryo rocket (launched in 1926), you leap into the space age
with John Glenn's *Friendship 7,* the scorched *Apollo 11* com-
mand module, a chunk of the moon. And there it is—a lunar-
scape of football-field dimensions painted by Robert McCall.
Across the corridor you are dazzled by Eric Sloan's panorama of
vaulting sky over the Grand Canyon. Tugging at you for attention are walk-in exhibits, films, models, animated dioramas,
even a touch of whimsy—the Rube Goldberg-like Lunacycle

Washington: The Mall and Capitol Hill

House where Lincoln died

Nat'l Portrait and Fine Arts Galleries

History and Technology

Natural History

Freer

Victorian Garden

Arts and Industries

Smithsonian

The Mall

Hirshhorn

Archives

N.A.S.M.

Independence Ave.

Madison Dr.

Jefferson Dr.

Nat'l Gallery

East Bldg.

Grant Memorial

Botanic Garden

House Office Bldgs.

Library of Congress

Supreme Court

Senate Office Bldg.

Folger Library

African Art

U.S. Capitol

Ford's

F.B.I. Bldg.

10th St.

9th St.

7th St.

6th St.

5th St.

4th St.

3rd St.

2nd St.

1st St.

Constitution Ave.

C St.

D St.

E St.

F St.

North Capitol

Delaware Ave.

1st St.

2nd St.

3rd St.

C St.

Union Station

N

This walking tour is approximately 5 miles long.

spinning its many wheels as it is "pedaled about in all directions."

You take the hint and continue on your way. Across the street the cylindrical Hirshhorn Museum looms like a huge concrete doughnut. Ride escalators to rings of galleries and treat your eyes to a smorgasbord of American painting. Here is something for a variety of tastes, from Academician and Ashcan to Op and Pop. Sculpture abounds inside and out, ranging from small, evocative caricatures by Daumier to welded slabs of iron. From the Hirshhorn courtyard, walk through the tunnel under Jefferson Drive to the terraced Sculpture Garden, setting for Rodin's *Burghers of Calais*.

In the summertime, hurdy-gurdy music lures you up the street to a spinning kaleidoscope of color and sound. Opposite the carousel, in the Arts and Industries Building, you are greeted by resounding whumps, rattles, clangs, and tootles of an orchestrion. Here you step back in time to 1876, when crowds thronged the Centennial Exhibition in Philadelphia to gape at shiny machines with slapping belts and marvel at ornate showcases filled with false teeth and other essentials. Costumed docents' "sales talks" lend authentic flavor.

Stroll behind the building to the Victorian Garden. Pause to aim your camera at "a most picturesque subject"—the adjacent red sandstone Smithsonian Castle, completed in 1855. Barn owls, once banned, again reside in its crenelated towers. Designed by James Renwick—who also planned St. Patrick's Cathedral in New York City—the building, used mainly for offices, has an information center for visitors. As you enter, notice the tomb of James Smithson, the English eccentric who willed that his fortune—105 bags of gold—found "an establishment for the increase and diffusion of knowledge among men." That bequest is echoed in the nearby Freer Gallery of Art, a collection of Oriental treasures. This Florentine Renaissance palace also boasts works by American painters, notably Whistler, friend of donor Charles Lang Freer. Take note of the famous Peacock Room and seek out the portrait of Whistler's father.

North Side of the Mall

The Mall's vast lawn sweeps from the Washington Monument to the Capitol—the way L'Enfant planned it. Nothing impedes your view (except, perhaps, a schoolboy's kite). It was not always thus. At various times the Mall has been a swamp, a

Civil War encampment, the site of the Pennsylvania Railroad
Station. All of that is gone, as well as endless lines of automobiles; broad walkways of crushed stone replace busy
streets of a few years ago.

After your walk across the green lawn, you enter the Museum of History and Technology, and the first thing you see is
the patched Star-Spangled Banner that flew over Fort McHenry
"through the perilous night." In the center the Foucault Pendu-
lum swings as the earth turns. Awaiting your inspection are
George Washington's uniform and First Ladies' gowns, Whitney's cotton gin, Bell's telephone, Ford's Model T, and the
Southern Railway's old No. 1401. The big locomotive is wired
for sound; its chuffs are so realistic that one visitor pulled a little
boy back from the track.

One is also inclined to keep his distance from the African
bush elephant, menacingly mounted in the rotunda of the Museum of Natural History, the next stop as you proceed on your
tour. In this domed building skeletons abound in closets and
out. You will find tableaux and dioramas of the Stone Age,
showcases of gems—including the Hope diamond—and a 92-
foot fiberglass blue whale.

Archives, Ford's, and the Arts

Cross Constitution Avenue to the National Archives. There
the Constitution itself is displayed along with the Declaration of
Independence and the Bill of Rights. Continue north to the new
FBI Building, offering frequent guided tours. A few more steps
up 10th Street takes you to the restored Ford's Theatre. Here,
on the evening of April 14, 1865, John Wilkes Booth shot
Abraham Lincoln. On view in the basement museum is the assassin's derringer. Across the street, in the unpretentious Petersen House, is where Lincoln died.

Five weeks earlier the President had celebrated his second
inaugural ball in the Old Patent Office Building, a few blocks
away. Rivaling the Capitol and White House in age and beauty,
the Greek Revival structure now houses the Smithsonian's National Portrait Gallery and the National Collection of Fine Arts.
Here more than in any other museum, perhaps, you catch the
nation's spirit—in the varied scenes of America, her moods, her
character, her people. You meet the likenesses of Pocahontas,
Mary McLeod Bethune, Mark Twain, George Gershwin in a
revealing self-portrait. In the same building is food for the body

as well as the soul; you'll find quality fare at the "Patent Pending" cafeteria, opening onto the courtyard.

Refreshed, hie yourself back to the Mall, to the monumental National Gallery of Art. Since founder Andrew Mellon planned that there should never be an admission fee, consider your visit to this princely realm as priceless. From the great rotunda, its soaring columns ringing a fountain, proceed through a maze of exhibition rooms where you confront the masters—Leonardo da Vinci, Raphael, Vermeer, Cézanne, Monet, Van Gogh. Offered are guided and taped tours, free Sunday evening concerts in the East Garden Court, and—if you're a serious artist—an easel and permission to copy a painting. The gallery's modern East Building is the newest showcase on the Mall. This architectural triumph with a beautiful faceted glass roof and dramatic open spaces was designed by I. M. Pei. It houses many never-before-shown works of art and provides much needed space for the gallery's expanding collections.

Capitol Hill

Jenkins Hill was, noted city planner Pierre L'Enfant, "a pedestal waiting for a monument." In time that was supplied by amateur architect Dr. William Thornton, whose design George Washington praised for its "Grandeur, Simplicity and Convenience." On September 18, 1793, the President, in Daniel Webster's words, "heads a short procession over naked fields, he crosses yonder stream on a fallen tree, he ascends to the top of this eminence . . . and here he performed the appointed duty of the day." Silver trowel in hand, Washington laid the cornerstone.

You approach the gleaming Capitol mindful of the nation's heritage. "Here, sir, the people govern," spoke Alexander Hamilton. Before you assault the banks of steps on the terraced west front—or circle to the less demanding east front—pause to gather strength at the Union Square reflecting pool and at the imposing Grant Memorial by sculptor Henry Shrady. From this west-side vantage point, charge onward and upward to heights where Presidents take the oath of office, then pass through massive bronze doors into the Rotunda. Here, beneath the dome's swirling fresco by Brumidi, silent throngs have filed past flag-draped catafalques, paying final respects to Lincoln, Kennedy, Humphrey.

Guided tours leave from the Rotunda every few minutes,

or you can go it alone. In Statuary Hall, the old House chamber, a plaque in the floor marks where John Quincy Adams collapsed and later died. At that spot can be heard a whisper from across the room. A "national Valhalla," the chamber is ringed with statues of notable citizens from the states—Ethan Allen, Sam Houston, William Jennings Bryan, Robert M. LaFollette, Huey Long, among many others. In the adjoining Hall of Columns a bronze of Will Rogers stands "where I can keep my eye on Congress."

Below the Rotunda you'll find the Crypt, planned for Washington's tomb but famed for the "Three Ladies in a Bathtub"—a marble monument of suffragettes Elizabeth Cady Stanton, Susan B. Anthony and Lucretia Mott.

The small Senate rotunda designed by Benjamin Latrobe is a reminder of the War of 1812. Instead of reconstructing the stairs the British burned, he replaced them with a handsome circular balustrade and marble columns with tobacco-leaf capitals. The old Senate chamber, "built with uncommon solidarity," survived the blaze. Now restored to its former brilliance, the place evokes momentous occasions. Stand and close your eyes and hear, if you will, the thundering declaration of Daniel Webster: "Liberty and Union, now and forever, one and inseparable!"

Between sessions visitors are admitted to the galleries in the House and Senate chambers. Visit your Congressman for a pass, taking the free subway connecting the Capitol and Congressional office buildings. (Passes aren't required for conducted group tours.)

If time permits, detour northward past the Senate Office Buildings to Romanesque Union Station fronted by a sculpture-embellished fountain celebrating Columbus's discovery of the New World. From recent renovations has emerged a spacious National Visitor Center, an alternate place to begin this tour if you arrive by train or Metro's rapid-rail system (a subway station is nearby).

Proceed to 316 A Street NE and discover a rich display at the Museum of African Art. Now turn the corner and head for designer Cass Gilbert's "building of dignity and importance"— the Supreme Court. Your guided tour includes views of two elliptical staircases, spiraling through five floors, and a leisurely look at the rose-hued courtroom. When the Court is hearing cases, visitors check cameras and line up for scarce seats.

"Oyez! Oyez! Oyez!" chants the Marshal of the Court. The gavel falls, and robed Justices take their places—"nine black beetles in the Temple of Karnak," an anonymous member quipped.

Like a character in *Henry VI* "wishing his foot were equal with his eye," you next pay a call on the Bard at the Folger Shakespeare Library. With a bow to Puck in marble, step back into Elizabethan times. Here, in a richly paneled gallery, you see among the many trappings models of the Globe playhouse.

Cross 2nd Street to the Library of Congress, Victorian queen of the Hill. Her multi-million volumes grew from a few thousand books purchased from Thomas Jefferson after the British burned the original collection. Among the treasures guarded here is Jefferson's original draft of the Declaration of Independence. From the visitor's gallery you are treated to a bird's-eye view of the Main Reading Room crowned by its spectacular golden dome. As you leave the building head west.

The last leg of your long walk takes you down Independence Avenue. At the southwest approach to the Capitol pause to view the Botanic Garden's dazzling display of orchids. After that delightful pause you'll find the rest of the way back is all downhill.

FROM THE WHITE HOUSE TO THE MONUMENTS
Wayne Barrett

Consider this a Presidential tour. It is a walk—and a bus ride—through almost two centuries of American history, with stops at symbolic mileposts: a towering obelisk, a brooding statue, an eternal flame. Past melds into present as you pause before historic old buildings standing their ground against modern intrusions. Near the White House, open spaces still survive; there is grass enough yet for cattle to graze—as President Taft's cow Pauline once did. Now, however, you see office workers with brown bags assembling on the green every noontime, surrounded by pigeons waiting for leftovers. You look up as joggers thud by, running in place while waiting for a light to change. You may see pickets shouldering signs and pacing along the piked iron fence in front of the White House.

"I wonder who lives there?" a Senator once wisecracked to Calvin Coolidge. "Nobody," the President replied. "They just come and go." And so they do, as the Constitution provides. But the imprints of the Presidents remain, as you will discover on this tour.

The "President's Palace"

The line forms on East Executive Avenue, where loudspeakers hidden in shrubbery give visitors a recorded preview of their White House tour. East Gate opens at 10 Tuesday through Saturday, closes at noon. From late May through Labor Day the hours are from 10 to 1. (You can beat the crowd by joining the VIP tour at 8; contact your Congressman for details.)

Calling at the President's House is a time-honored tradition, although the practice is more controlled now than, say, during Andrew Jackson's inaugural, when followers in muddy boots made a shambles of the mansion. "Ladies fainted, men were seen with bloody noses," an observer wrote. During the Civil War, throngs dogged Lincoln's footsteps, even "interrupting the President on his way to meals." Charles Dickens, a visitor in 1842, noted that when he rang the bell and no one answered, he "walked without further ceremony through the rooms."

Often the President was present to greet visitors. Coolidge boasted that he once "shook hands with nineteen hundred in thirty-four minutes." Expect no such fringe benefits today. Although the President may well be on the premises, his Oval Office and the first family's second-floor quarters are off-limits to the public. You are ushered through five state rooms on the first floor and out the North Portico in about 15 minutes. But brief as it is, you will have trod a stage of history rivaled by few others.

You first enter the East Room, or—as architect James Hoban labeled it—"the Public Audience Chamber." For John and Abigail Adams it was something else. The unfinished room, wrote the resourceful Mrs. Adams, "I make a drying-room of, to hang up the clothes in." Hanging there now is Gilbert Stuart's full-length portrait of George Washington, the only object dating to 1800, when the house was first occupied. Dolley Madison

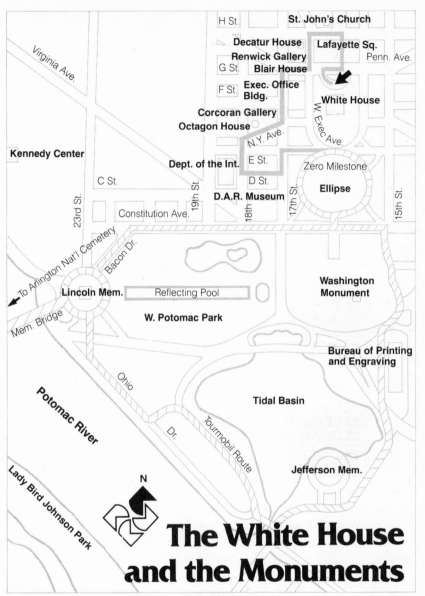

The White House and the Monuments

The walking portion of this tour is approximately 1½ miles.

saved the painting from British arsonists in 1814. The East Room today frequently serves as a salon; here Pablo Casals and Vladimir Horowitz have played for Presidents. In this room, several times touched by sorrow, Lincoln lay in state, as he had dreamed he would. His presence remains, haunting the White House. Professed Theodore Roosevelt: "I see him in the different rooms and in the halls."

Moved by that spirit, perhaps, you enter Hoban's "Common Dining Room," now known as the Green Room. Although Thomas Jefferson took his meals there, it was used mainly as a parlor, where gentlemen played whist and sipped brandy. Now step into the oval Blue Room, where bay windows overlooking the South Grounds of the White House offer an unimpeded view of the Jefferson Memorial. On satin-covered walls hang portraits of the first seven Presidents. Cupid has reigned in this elegant reception room on several occasions, the most notable in 1886, when Grover Cleveland wedded Frances Folsom.

From that redolent atmosphere, turn next to the dazzling Red Room, a Christmas package of cerise silk bordered in gold filigree. Indeed, it is a Christmas room, where orphans receive gifts, following a tradition started by Andrew Jackson. The spirit of giving might also have been present on the night of March 3, 1877, when Rutherford B. Hayes was secretly administered the oath of office there, thus ending the Presidential aspirations of his opponent Samuel J. Tilden, in America's most disputed election.

During the Hayes administration, "water flowed like wine," as the First Lady (nicknamed Lemonade Lucy) forbade the serving of alcoholic beverages, even at state dinners. That has since changed, as has the size of the State Dining Room, your next stop. Enlarged in 1902, the spacious white chamber, glittering with gilt, has accommodated the world's most famous persons. There John F. Kennedy welcomed Nobel Prize recipients, "the most extraordinary collection of talent . . . that has ever been gathered together at the White House, with the possible exception of when Thomas Jefferson dined alone." Before you leave, take note of the inscription on the mantel. John Adams wrote these words to his wife on his second night at the mansion: "I Pray Heaven to Bestow The Best of Blessings on THIS HOUSE and on All that shall hereafter Inhabit it. May none but Honest and Wise Men ever rule under This Roof."

Lafayette Square

Cross Pennsylvania Avenue to the 7-acre park opposite the White House. The imposing equestrian statue in the center glorifies Andrew Jackson, not—as might be expected—the Marquis de Lafayette. His memorial stands at the corner of Pennsylvania and Madison Place, a silent sentinel poised above passing parades. Statues at the other corners of the square honor Revolutionary War generals Rochambeau, Kosciuszko and Steuben. Follow brick paths to the north side of the park to see, at 16th and H streets, the second-oldest building on the square— St. John's Church, "the Church of Presidents." Benjamin Latrobe designed it and was its first organist. Soon after, he built a three-story house on the square (748 Jackson Place) for Commodore Stephen Decatur, remembered for his ringing declaration: ". . . our country, right or wrong." Mortally wounded in a duel, he died in the parlor downstairs. Docents of the National Trust for Historic Preservation guide you through Decatur House (Monday–Friday, 10 to 2; Saturday and Sunday, noon to 4; admission $1.50). You'll see why Henry Clay, who moved there in 1817, described it as "the best private dwelling in the City."

The tidy townhouses on Jackson Place evoke a 19th-century ambiance despite Federal office buildings looming at their back doors. Saved from the wrecker's ball was Blair House, around the corner on Pennsylvania Avenue. Harry Truman's residence while the White House was being remodeled, it was the scene of a shoot-out in 1950, when two gunmen attempted to assassinate the President.

Gallery-hopping to the Ellipse

"Dedicated to Art." That inscription in stone above the main entrance welcomes you to the Smithsonian's Renwick Gallery, at the corner of 17th and Pennsylvania Avenue. Showplace for crafts and decorative arts, its rooms—particularly the Grand Salon—are masterpieces of Victorian decor.

Continue south on 17th past the flamboyant Old Executive Office Building, which Truman affectionately dubbed "the greatest monstrosity in America." Cross New York Avenue to the Corcoran Gallery. Climb its grand staircase to view exhibits mostly modern and American. Another imposing stairway is but a block distant, in Octagon House. Maintained as a museum by the American Institute of Architects—whose headquarters over-shadow the misnamed six-sided house—the building's main at-traction may be its ghosts. Two daughters of owner John Tay-loe, a friend of George Washington's, mysteriously plunged down the stairs to their deaths. Screams are still heard, it is said; and the bell lantern in the stairwell sways on its long chain. Another disembodied visitor may be Dolley Madison, trailing a scent of lilacs. She lived here with President Madison after the British burned the White House. Ironically, it was here that he signed the Treaty of Ghent, ending the War of 1812.

Proceed down 18th Street to the Department of the Inte-rior, where you'll find American Indian arts and crafts on dis-play. Now cross to 1776 D Street and see, in the DAR Museum and State Rooms, art and memorabilia from the Revolutionary War period. Swing back on 17th Street and head for the Ellipse, the circular park lawn south of the White House and site of the National Christmas Tree. Near the Zero Milestone—the point where distances from Washington are measured—rest your feet and wait for the bus.

Riding to the Monuments

Boarding pass in hand (adults, $2.75; children under 11, $1.40), relax as the articulated Tourmobile bends around corners and pulls to a stop near the Washington Monument. For a 10-cent fee, ride the elevator 500 feet to the top and experi-ence a bird's-eye view of Pierre L'Enfant's grand design.

Back on the bus, you continue on 15th Street to the Bureau of Printing and Engraving, where you can see how to make a dollar. No samples. Cruising past cherry trees fringing the Tidal Basin, the Tourmobile deposits you next at the serene Jefferson Memorial. A classic colonnade rings the standing bronze—19 feet high—of the third President. Chiseled in stone at the base of the dome is his credo: "I have sworn upon the altar of God eternal hostility against every form of tyranny over the mind of man."

Ride on, past the playing fields in West Potomac Park, to the Lincoln Memorial, most beloved of our national shrines. Some 60 million visitors have climbed its marble steps. In a Greek temple designed by Henry Bacon, a heroic Lincoln sits enthroned on a 10-foot pedestal. To sculptor Daniel Chester French, the memorial "tells you just what manner of man you are come to pay homage to; his simplicity, his grandeur and his power." Through the years men and women have come here to find solace, to renew strength: Marian Anderson in 1939, Martin Luther King in pursuit of his dream, a troubled Richard Nixon. Lincoln's words—his Gettysburg and Second Inaugural addresses—are inscribed on the walls, compelling you to read and ponder. Now turn from these and gaze, as he does, out over the Reflecting Pool, mirroring the Washington Monument beyond. In winter, skaters skim over the ice.

At this juncture you may board a shuttle bus (extra fare) to Kennedy Center or continue on to Arlington National Cemetery via the Tourmobile. The latter route takes you across the Potomac. From Memorial Bridge you may glimpse to the northwest Theodore Roosevelt Island, sanctuary for wildlife. Ahead, along the George Washington Memorial Parkway in Virginia, is Lady Bird Johnson Park, where millions of daffodils bloom in the spring.

Cool breezes waft through Arlington House (also known as the Custis-Lee Mansion), built by George Washington Parke Custis. His son-in-law Robert E. Lee called it home until the Civil War transformed the plantation into a burying ground. The mansion, high on a hill, commands a sweeping view. Fittingly, L'Enfant's tomb, engraved with his masterful plan, overlooks the city he envisioned.

Below Arlington House is John F. Kennedy's grave, marked by its perpetual flame. Nearby lies his martyred brother Robert. Just north of the cemetery stands the Netherlands Carillon, its chiming floating over the hillsides. In the same area—and worth the walk to see it—is the Marine Corps War Memorial, depicting the flag-raising on Iwo Jima.

The winding drive through the cemetery takes you to the Tomb of the Unknown Soldier. Here white-gloved sentries from the army's Old Guard stand vigil. If your schedule permits, time your visit so that you may see the ceremonial changing of the guard; perhaps you'll hear in the distance a bugler sounding taps.

The ride back to the Ellipse affords you another view of much of what you have seen. That is a bonus, an encore for a memorable performance.

GEORGETOWN AND EMBASSY ROW
Wayne Barrett

Treat this tour as you would a menu. Select from it rather than try to sample all of it; otherwise, you will be running instead of walking. However, if your appetite for the posh and picturesque is insatiable, make this a two-day movable feast, enjoying Georgetown one day and Embassy Row the next. Begin at the oldest-known building in the District of Columbia, arriving at the M Street location via Metrobus (any of several numbered in the 30s).

Old Stone House and the C & O Canal
The Federal City was not yet a gleam in the eye of Pierre L'Enfant when Christopher Layman began building his modest stone dwelling in 1764 on Bridge Street (today's M Street). Its no-nonsense construction—shop and kitchen on the first floor, plain living quarters above—evokes an era of brawn and bustle, when Georgetown was a busy port. Down rolling roads, long since paved over, rumbled hogsheads of Maryland tobacco destined for the England of George II—after whom, incidentally, the town was named. National Park Service attendants in 18th-century garb describe how life was in the Old Stone House (open 9:30 to 5, Wednesday through Sunday); and if you ask, they will tell you there's nothing to substantiate the legend that George Washington and L'Enfant used the building as their headquarters while planning the nation's capital.

After a turn through the tidy garden, stroll east on M, through the historic heart of Georgetown, to 30th; then head south a block to the C & O Canal. There the mule-drawn barge *Canal Clipper* takes summer sojourners on lazy trips into the past; joggers and bicyclists share the towpath. Browse through the Foundry, its chic shops cast from an old mold. Proceed west on cobblestoned Towpath Lane past tiny canal cottages to Thomas Jefferson Street, a reminder that the author of the Declaration of Independence lived here while serving as Washington's Secretary of State. Jefferson's house, however, no longer stands. Continue on to 31st Street where the shops of Canal Square beckon; the complex was imaginatively converted from an old warehouse.

On your meandering walk through Georgetown you'll discover a dazzling variety of goods and goodies—hometown crafts, high-priced imports, baubles galore, fresh truffles and choice wines, "Hot Diggity Dogs" (no preservatives), waiters on roller skates (La Niçoise). Dodging traffic, bear left on M Street and join the parade of shoppers. Note the clean Federalist lines of City Tavern, a private club, built in 1796—John Adams, among others, dined here. Double back to Wisconsin Avenue and, after running the gamut of more enticing restaurants and boutiques, head west on N Street.

J.F.K.'s House and Georgetown University

A pleasant walk past Smith Row, the handsome Federal townhouses on the north side of the street, leads you to 3307 N, the three-story brick house built in 1812 by William Marbury, who figured in the landmark Supreme Court case Marbury vs. Madison. John F. Kennedy bought the house for his wife Jacqueline when daughter Caroline was born. Soon after, they moved to larger quarters—the White House. Farther up the block is Cox's Row, a string of Federal houses built by Georgetown mayor Colonel John Cox. Despite muddy roads, he "would saunter downtown in silk stockings and pumps, not getting a spot upon himself." Perhaps Lafayette, a guest of the mayor's in 1824, fared as well.

While savoring the good old days, swing one block south to 34th and Prospect for a glimpse of Halcyon House, built by Benjamin Stoddert in the late 19th century "after the manner of some of the elegant homes I have seen in Philadelphia." Equally evocative of the neighborhood is Quality Hill. Built of brick imported from England in 1799, it stands assured at 3425 Prospect Street. The house called Prospect—at 3500—dates from 1788, when prospects for Georgetown never looked brighter. Once the home of Secretary of Defense James Forrestal, it has on occasion served as a guest house for foreign VIP's.

Returning to N Street via 36th, you'll see the classical simplicity of Holy Trinity Church, which served as a hospital during the Civil War. Half a century older is the adjacent convent, which housed the first Roman Catholic Church in Washington. Towering over it and all else in the vicinity are the Gothic spires of Georgetown University. At the foot of N Street are stone stairs you can climb to reach the campus. In front of Romanesque Healy Building, a gray, granite fortress built in 1877, you will encounter a seated figure in bronze, founder John Carroll, who was named archbishop in 1808. Student pranksters have

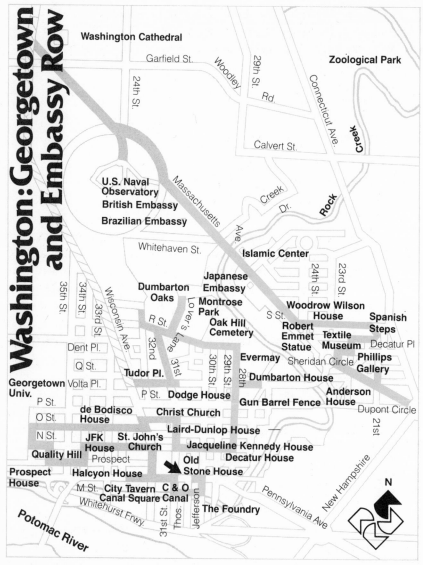

Washington: Georgetown and Embassy Row

Washington Cathedral

Garfield St.

Woodley

29th St.

Zoological Park

Connecticut Ave.

Creek

Calvert St.

24th St.

Massachusetts

Creek

Dr.

Rock

Ave.

U.S. Naval Observatory

British Embassy

Brazilian Embassy

Whitehaven St.

Islamic Center

Japanese Embassy

24th St.

23rd St.

Dumbarton Oaks

Montrose Park

Oak Hill Cemetery

Woodrow Wilson House

S St.

Spanish Steps

35th St.

34th St.

33rd St.

Wisconsin Ave.

R St.

Lover's Lane

32nd

31st

Robert Emmet Statue

Textile Museum

Decatur Pl

Dent Pl.

Evermay

Sheridan Circle

Phillips Gallery

Q St.

Tudor Pl.

30th St.

29th St.

28th

Dumbarton House

Georgetown Univ.

Volta Pl.

P St.

P St.

Dodge House

Anderson House

Dupont Circle

de Bodisco House

Christ Church

Gun Barrel Fence

O St.

N St.

JFK House

St. John's Church

Laird-Dunlop House

Jacqueline Kennedy House

Decatur House

21st

Quality Hill

Prospect

Old Stone House

New Hampshire

N

Prospect House

Halcyon House

M St.

City Tavern

C & O Canal

Canal Square

Whitehurst Frwy.

31st St.

Thos.

Jefferson

The Foundry

Pennsylvania Ave

Potomac River

The Georgetown walk is approximately 4 miles, and Embassy Row is approximately 3½ miles. The bus route is not included in mileage.

placed jack-o'lanterns on the archbishop's head and commodes under his chair. But he endures, as does his architectural contemporary, the red-brick Old North Building, completed in 1795.

O Street Churches, N Street Homes

Leaving the university through the main gate, walk eastward on O Street to 3322, scene of a June-and-January marriage in 1841. With Henry Clay, Daniel Webster and other notables in attendance, Russian Ambassador Baron Alexander de Bodisco took a bride 47 years his junior. He vowed that 16-year-old Harriet Beall Williams "might find some one younger and better looking, but no one who would love her better." Farther down O Street stands St. John's Church, the genesis of its design attributed to Dr. William Thornton, architect of the Capitol. Continue on—but mind the jog at Wisconsin Avenue—to Christ Church at 31st and O. This beautifully situated mini-cathedral with Gothic tower and gables was built in 1885.

Return again to N Street, via 31st, this time exploring eastward. Note the Victorian trim of the Wheatley houses (3041-45) and the arched windows of the Laird-Dunlop House at 3014, once the home of Robert Todd Lincoln. A boundary stone in the garden marks the northeast corner of the original town. Across the street, at 3017 N, the widowed Mrs. Kennedy sought seclusion. Sorrow had in 1820 cast its pall on another N Street house (2812) just two blocks away. Here retreated the wife of Commodore Stephen Decatur, killed in a duel.

Rock of Dumbarton

North of the old boundary, on the high ground, sprawled the 795-acre land grant of Scotsman Ninian Beall. He dubbed it Rock of Dumbarton, after his birthplace on the River Clyde. As you turn up 28th Street to explore the tract, look for the gun-barrel fence that locksmith Reuben Daws made from old muskets. The fence is just around the corner at 2803-11 P Street. Continue up 28th to the distinctive Dodge House, a classic in pastel, at the corner of Q Street. Now turn right for a unique treat—the opportunity to view a Georgetown home from within as well as from the outside.

The iron gate swings open at Dumbarton House, 2715 Q, from 9 till noon Monday through Saturday (closed July and August). The Colonial Dames of America, who own the mansion, show it with pride. Among its antique furnishings is Martha Washington's desk. The house, once known as Bellevue, bears the stamp of Benjamin Latrobe's genius; he remodeled it in 1805. A few years later Dolley Madison found it a temporary haven when fleeing from the burning White House. In 1915 the house stood in the way of progress—the construction of Q Street—and it was moved up the hill to its present location. Leave a contribution if you wish (there is no admission fee), and return to 28th Street, continuing north past the Evermay estate. That magnificent Georgian manor was built in the 1790s after owner Samuel Davidson sold the federal government a parcel of swampy land that became the site of the White House and Lafayette Square.

Follow 28th around the bend at Oak Hill Cemetery to R Street, the crest of your uphill walk. Stroll along the rim of Montrose Park and, if the mood moves you, down Lovers Lane. But don't tarry, for the best is yet to be. If you have timed it right— between the hours of 2 and 5—you will enter into what may be "the last great garden created in America," or anywhere else, for that matter. Encompassing 16 terraced acres, the Renaissance Gardens of Dumbarton Oaks open grandly before you, brick footpaths winding from one self-contained stage to another. A veil of water where songbirds splash covers a cartouche of mosaic called the Pebble Garden; spring gold cascades down Forsythia Hill; in a "secret" garden camellias bloom, and you delight in your discovery. You meander down boxwood alleys, pause before spouting dolphins, rest on a bench while pondering a great spreading beech. Reluctantly you leave the rose garden and the Orangery, retracing your steps to R Street. Around the corner on 32nd, you are admitted (no charge) through Georgian doors and vestibule to space-age wings of glass and marble that showcase pre-Columbian gold and jade and Byzantine art objects. In the contrasting Music Room adjoining the main house are beautiful Renaissance furnishings and art. This was the setting in 1947 for Igor Stravinsky performing his *Dumbarton Oaks Concerto*. In 1944 the Dumbarton Oaks Conference was held here, leading to the drafting of the United Nations charter. Four years earlier Mr. and Mrs. Robert Woods Bliss had given Dumbarton Oaks to Harvard University as a home for the humanities. Note that Harvard, adhering to academia's calendar, closes garden and collections to the public from July 1 to Labor Day.

Doubling back toward the garden entrance, cross R Street and walk south on 31st to Q Street. Now look back up the hill to Tudor Place sitting in splendid isolation. The house was designed by William Thornton for Thomas Peter, Georgetown's first mayor, and his bride Martha Parke Custis, granddaughter of Martha Washington. Spared alteration and the ravages of encroachment, it remains a faithful testament to Georgetown's rich past. Now proceed to the frenetic present, westward to Wisconsin Avenue, where you will board a northbound bus.

Washington Cathedral and the U.S. Naval Observatory

You alight at Massachusetts Avenue. Washington Cathedral rises before you, crowning the highest point in the city. In size and grandeur it rivals the great churches at Rheims and Chartres. You will note, as have others, that the Gothic structure is unfinished, although work began in 1907. But to complete a building of this magnitude in less than a century would be rushing things. You should not rush, either. Enjoy its rare book library (boasting a first-edition King James Bible), the walled Bishop's Garden, and the Herb Cottage, where you can buy something nice to take home. Guided tours lasting less than an hour begin at 10, Monday through Saturday.

A 10-minute walk down Massachusetts Avenue takes you to the U.S. Naval Observatory, where afternoon and night tours are offered, the latter (by reservation) affording views of the moon through a 26-inch refractor telescope. Sharing the parklike grounds is the Vice President's House. Departing from the 34th Street gate, you next head southward into Washington's gilded yesteryear.

Embassy Row

Down dappled sidewalks, past manicured lawns and gardens, you gaze upon stately pleasure domes where tycoons once held court. Today the occupants are largely foreign diplomats. Welcoming you with his famous V-for-Victory sign is Winston Churchill in bronze, standing tall in front of the British Embassy. You march on, past Brazil's big glass box to more traditional modes across Rock Creek. On the east side of the street rises the minaret of the Islamic Mosque, a mosaic of gold, turquoise and white. Before entering the carpeted chamber, remove your shoes. Opposite the mosque is the Japanese Embassy, which offers tours by appointment during summer and fall months. Of special interest is the tea house in the garden.

Continue past the embassies of Venezuela, Zambia and Paraguay to a small plot bounded by Massachusetts Avenue, 24th Street and S Street. Here stands Ireland's martyred Robert Emmet. The bronze statue was accepted for the American people in 1917 by President Woodrow Wilson. The house where Wilson died is but a few steps away, at 2340 S Street. Now a property of the National Trust for Historic Preservation, the house received World War I leaders David Lloyd George and Georges Clemenceau. For a small admission fee, docents guide you through rooms of memories. The building next door houses the Textile Museum (open 10 to 5, Tuesday through Saturday). Oriental rugs and exotic tapestries delight the eye. Exhibits change frequently.

At the end of the block you will find not 22nd Street but flights of stone stairs flanking a fountain. Descend the Spanish Steps to Decatur Place and circle past a cluster of embassies, one of them Franklin D. Roosevelt's former house at 2131 R Street, before returning to Massachusetts Avenue. Your course is south, but first take a moment to admire Gutzon Borglum's equestrian bronze of General Philip Sheridan in the circle that bears his name. Just around the corner at 21st Street you will find the Phillips Collection, mostly modern but also distinguished by choice Impressionists and earlier paintings. On late Sunday afternoons the Renaissance Revival hall features free concerts. Nor does it cost you to tour Anderson House, an opulent neighbor at 2118 Massachusetts Avenue. Open afternoons (2 to 4) Tuesday through Sunday, it is the showplace home of the Society of Cincinnati. Back on the street, head toward Dupont Circle, graced by Daniel Chester French's marble fountain. In this urban oasis rest your tired feet and reflect on your accomplishment—a walk through storied neighborhoods firmly established in the national heritage. You have seen the past that was prologue evinced in a thousand ways: a President's wooden-shafted golf clubs, weathered brick, the timeless C & O Canal. Savor your triumphal march before you re-enter the reality of today.

VIRGINIA

OLD TOWN ALEXANDRIA
Wayne Barrett

This is George Washington's town. As a "braw laddie" of 17, he helped survey it in 1749 and later, as a dashing young officer, drilled Virginia militia in Market Square. He served as a town trustee, was a member of the volunteer fire company, owned stock in the bank, picked up his mail at the Apothecary Shop. He worshiped at Christ Church, lodged with merchant friends William Ramsay and John Carlyle, dined and danced with Martha at Gadsby's Tavern. Here, on the Fourth of July, 1793, President Washington proffered a toast: "Prosperity to the Town of Alexandria." Today visitors to Old Town raise their glasses to his memory and walk in his footsteps.

Ramsay House and Market Square
Resist the urge to wander—you'll save lots of back-tracking—and head straight for Ramsay House Visitors Center in the heart of Old Town. The clapboard structure, dating to 1724, was the home of Scottish merchant William Ramsay, "first projector and founder of this promising city." He was also the town's postmaster and only Lord Mayor. After admiring house and garden, take 13 minutes to view the color film on Alexandria, gather pamphlets and maps, and ask for your honorary citizen certificate—it entitles you to free street parking for 72 hours. From Alexandria's oldest house, proceed to the grandest just up the block—John Carlyle's Georgian mansion. In its paneled council room General Edward Braddock, with aide Washington, heard royal governors advocate taxing the colonies to support the campaign against the French and Indians in the Ohio Valley. Thus, the specter of taxation without represen-

Old Town Alexandria

Oronoco St.

Princess St.

Queen St.

Cameron St.

King St.

Prince St.

Duke St.

Wolfe St.

Wilkes St.

Patrick St.

Alfred St.

Columbus St.

Washington St.

St. Asaph St.

Pitt St.

Royal St.

S. Fairfax St.

Lee St.

Union St.

Hallowell School

Lee's Boyhood Home

Edmund Jennings Lee House

Lee-Fendell House

Light-Horse Harry Lee House

Lloyd House

Christ Church

G. Washington House

Court House

Yeaton-Fairfax House

flounder

Friendship Fire Co.

Lyceum Bicentennial Center

Confederate Memorial

Stabler-Leadbeater Apothecary Shop

Gadsby's Tavern

Market Sq.

Carlyle House

Bank of Alexandria

Torpedo Factory

Ramsay House— Visitors Center

Gentry Row

Athenaeum

Captains Row

Lafayette House

Dulany House

Presbyterian Meeting House

Craik House

"flounder" houses

N

Potomac River

This walking tour is approximately 2 miles round trip.

tation—*cause célèbre* of the American Revolution—first became a corporeal issue, Virginians argue, in Carlyle House.

Stroll past the bank, chartered in 1792, and cross to Market Square, an open plaza of brick and greenery with fountain and pool for a centerpiece. Underground are two levels of parking. On Washington's birthday and other occasions you'll hear the skirl of pipes, the rattle of drums, fifes tweedling "Yankee Doodle"; you'll see soldiers in regimental garb dress ranks and smartly pass in review. Here yeomen in homespun once shouldered muskets and churned the dust as 22-year-old Lt. Col. George Washington barked commands. In colonial times the square was common ground for tradesmen, farmers, waterfront roisterers; a place for fairs, cockfights, electioneering around hogsheads of rum.

Stabler-Leadbeater Apothecary Shop

Effective in getting out the vote, rum also was used to bolster a soldier's resolve and, if need be, anesthetize his wound. Washington purchased 16½ gallons of rum at Ramsay's store before he led his troops into the wilderness. Martha Washington depended on the Stabler-Leadbeater Apothecary Shop for remedies, once requesting "Mr. Stabler to send by bearer a quart bottle of his best castor oil and a bill for it." Located across the square on South Fairfax Street, the old drug store opened the same year the bank did, and remained in business until 1933—141 years. Now a museum (free admission), it boasts an unrivaled collection of hand-blown glass bottles— many still retain original gold-leaf labels—and mahogany chests with compartments for leeches. The old clock on the wall once had wooden works and kept good time. Customers included the Senate's famous oratorical triumvirate of Henry Clay, Daniel Webster, and John C. Calhoun. U.S. Army Col. Robert E. Lee was in the shop when he was summoned to Harpers Ferry, where John Brown had seized the arsenal. Pharmacist Edward Stabler dispensed books as well as medicines, serving as librarian of Alexandria's subscription library. Dues: $4 per year; nonmembers could "hire" books.

Old Presbyterian Meeting House and Flounders

Continue south on Fairfax to the Presbyterian "Dissenting Church" built by John Carlyle in 1774. The parishioners were "rebellious scoundrels," an English visitor noted, the service a "political discourse instead of religious lectures." In December of 1799 the bell of the Meeting House tolled for Washington; and the funeral sermon was preached here, "the walking being bad to the Episcopal Church." Lightning struck the steeple in 1835, and fire gutted the building. The church was rebuilt on the original foundations, beside the burial ground. Here lie Carlyle, Dr. James Craik—Washington's physician and "compatriot in arms"—and an Unknown Soldier of the American Revolution. Nearby is the old manse—used now for church offices—one of Alexandria's distinctive flounder houses. A house evenly divided, its tallest side is windowless—as one side of a flounder (the fish) is sightless. Such a structure needed only a matching half to complete the peaked-roof design of a conventional colonial house. Perhaps lack of materials or scarcity of skilled workmen explains the origin of flounders. Walk around the block to Lee Street, and you'll see two of them. Turn up Duke Street and stroll past Dr. Craik's four-story dwelling, where Washington was often a guest.

Cobblestones and Damn the Torpedoes

Double back on Fairfax and bear right at the 200 block of Prince Street, known as Gentry Row. One of the handsome 18th-century houses belonged to George William Fairfax, whose wife Sally inspired Washington to "profess myself a votary of love." Another resident of the block was Dr. Elisha Cullen Dick, Alexandria's health officer. Devoted to the arts, he resorted to verse when penning a dinner invitation:

> If you can eat a good fat duck,
> Come up with us and take pot luck. . . .
> The day 'tho wet, the streets 'tho muddy,
> To keep out the cold, we'll have some toddy.
> And if perchance you should get sick,
> You'll have at hand, Yours, E. C. Dick.

He, with Dr. Craik, was in attendance at Washington's last illness and opposed the excessive bleeding of the patient. At the moment of death he stopped the clock.

A pleasing anomaly in this tasteful Georgian enclave is the Greek Revival athenaeum. Built as a bank in 1850, it served as a church after the Civil War, and is now the Gallery of the Northern Virginia Fine Arts Association (free admission).

Pavement gives way to cobblestones—legend says they
were laid by Hessian prisoners—on Captains Row, the 100
block of Prince Street. From here, barely a stone's throw to the
docks, a master could see his ship swinging at anchor. His
house, snug against its neighbors and nudging the sidewalk,
often served as storehouse as well as dwelling. Turn north on
Union Street, past dockside warehouses crammed with imports
and crowded with customers. Directly ahead, across King
Street, sprawls the Torpedo Factory, where explosives were
manufactured during World Wars I and II. Nazi war records
were also stored here. Today the battle cry might well be
"Damn the torpedoes and on with the arts!" Beating swords
into plowshares, a phalanx of painters, sculptors, printmakers,
potters, engravers, a variety of artisans and crafters, even a
scrimshaw artist, have set up shops on several floors. You are
free to wander in, watch them work, and perhaps buy something.

Gadsby's Tavern

Walk west on King Street and run the gamut of quaint restaurants and shops with names like Cafe Rembrandt, Pewter
Place, the Wharf (seafood), the Tiny Dwelling (dolls), Colonial
Heritage (gifts). Turn up Lee Street—known as Water Street
before General Robert E. Lee's time—and duck into cobblestoned alleys (Ramsay and Swift) young Washington and Lee
explored. Proceed west on Cameron past City Hall, a century-
old brick structure crowned with a classic clock tower and spire.
There once stood the original courthouse, pillory and whipping
post close by. In July 1774, the old chamber heard Washington
read fellow trustee George Mason's Fairfax Resolves, one of
which declared: "All men are by nature born equally free and independent"—words that Thomas Jefferson would echo two
years later in drafting the Declaration of Independence. Follow
Washington and Mason across Royal Street to Gadsby's Tavern, once again offering sustenance to the wayfarer. You may
want to dip a pewter spoon into a steaming bowl from the
stockpot, perhaps sample Miss Cory's pecan pie. Let your imagination range free. Glasses clink across the room, and in the
mists of time you see John Paul Jones welcoming the young
Marquis de Lafayette and a soldier of fortune who calls himself
Baron de Kalb. The door swings open for Benjamin Franklin
and John Adams. There is Burr and Hamilton—at different

tables, of course—and that "withered little apple-John," James Madison. A young lawyer from Maryland is announced—Francis Scott Key.

Dating to the 1770s, the tavern has worn a succession of names—Mason's Ordinary, Fountain Tavern, Bunch of Grapes, and others. It became famous as Gadsby's after an ambitious English boniface by that name leased it in 1796. By that time the property included the adjoining City Hotel, built several years earlier. It is now a museum (Monday–Saturday, 10 to 5, Sunday, noon to 5; Adults $1, Children 50 cents) owned by the city. In the grand ballroom Washington and his lady, wigged and powdered, danced the minuet while musicians played from a balcony. Today's room is a replica of the original, sold to New York's Metropolitan Museum of Art in 1917. Hotel and tavern, ravaged by years of neglect, were then being used as tenements; and they might have been razed had not Alexandria American Legion Post No. 24 acquired them and paved the way for restoration.

By the turn of the 19th century, Alexandria had no less than 34 inns. Even so, a traveler to this busy port—then a part of the District of Columbia—might find lodging hard to come by. George Washington found it advantageous to build a small townhouse about a block from Gadsby's, at 508 Cameron. His place ultimately fell into disrepair and was torn down in 1855. It was rebuilt 95 years later from a crude sketch that a neighbor made "for posterity." Continue to the 600 block for a sidewalk glimpse of two houses owned by famous families. At 607 Cameron resided Thomas, ninth Lord Fairfax, namesake of the lord proprietor who controlled more than 5 million acres between the Potomac and Rappahannock. Next door stands the first Alexandria home of Revolutionary War hero Gen. Henry (Light-Horse Harry) Lee, who eulogized Washington as "first in war, first in peace, and first in the hearts of his countrymen."

Lee Corner

After detouring to the 500 block of Queen Street for a glance at another flounder, proceed up St. Asaph Street to 607 Oronoco, the boyhood home of Robert E. Lee (Open daily; Adults $1, Children 50 cents). He attended Hallowell School next door before leaving for West Point. When the house was owned by Col. William Fitzhugh, George Washington slept there—as witness his diary: ". . . went to Alex's and lodged myself at Mr. Fitzhugh's." Visitors to the Lee-Fendall House (Adults $1, Children 50 cents) on the corner included Washington and Robert E. Lee's father, Light-Horse Harry, who once owned the lot. His stepfather-in-law Philip Richard Fendall built the house. He was married thrice—all to Lees. Cross Washington Street for a closer look at the Edmund Jennings Lee House and, two blocks south, the Lloyd House, both with Lee connections.

Christ Church and Friendship

Walk a block to Columbus Street to enter Christ Church. Welcoming communicants for more than two centuries, this "Church in the Woods" was where Washington worshiped, "weather and roads permitting." He sat in pew No. 60, near the front. Robert E. Lee, who was confirmed here in 1854, had pew No. 46. In the graveyard, its headstones worn smooth by time, lies William Ramsay.

Two blocks west on Alfred Street is the Friendship Fire Company Museum (Adults 50 cents, Children free; Tuesday–Saturday, 10 to 4). Adorned with cupola, this charming 19th-century building houses the fire engine Washington ordered in 1774, while in Philadelphia at the Continental Congress.

Lyceum and Lafayette

Return to Washington and Prince Streets, and pause to admire in the intersection the Confederate Memorial of a sorrowing soldier. Now turn to the Lyceum, where John Quincy Adams once lectured that man's nature required three things—"one fixed house, one wedded wife, and a belief in God." Alexandria's cultural center before the Civil War, the Greek Revival building now serves as a state travel center and museum. After perusing exhibits, walk south to Duke Street and turn east for one block to Lafayette House. Here the French nobleman stayed in 1824. Imagine the crowd gathered to welcome him; then accompany him across the street to Dulany House. There on the steps he found a platform from which to greet the citizens. Many of them doubtless returned to Gadsby's, and you may wish to follow.

PENNSYLVANIA

DOWNTOWN PITTSBURGH
Lynn Detrick

Pittsburgh is a city of hilltops and valleys, tunnels and bridges. It's a city of many faces and contrasting moods. Jammed in the narrow peninsula of land known as "Downtown" are the skyscrapers that symbolize its corporate power. The United States Steel Building dominates them all. Pittsburgh houses the headquarters of 14 of the nation's largest corporations including Gulf Oil, Alcoa, Westinghouse, and Koppers, but its foundation is steel.

Pittsburgh also has a softer, more humane side apparent at Heinz Hall, the Scaife Gallery and the Pittsburgh Public Theatre. It is evident at the quiet churches nestled among the office towers or in the plazas, parks and squares that add breathing room to the grid of downtown streets. Pittsburgh's muscle is heavy industry; its beauty derives from its determined efforts to remake itself.

Photographs of Pittsburgh after World War II show the air so thick with soot and smog that street lights burned at noon. It was a grim, hard, dirty city. Generations of Pittsburghers, suffering a black and reeking sky, embraced a folklore that smoke was a good thing. Smoke pouring from the mills was an index of prosperity, and Pittsburgh from the earliest times has been a working town, a business town where profits and production count.

Yet in the postwar years when smoke threatened to suffocate its growth, the city's tremendous energy was concentrated on efforts to clean up and rebuild. Republican industrialists, financiers and businessmen led by Richard K. Mellon and Democratic political forces headed by David L. Lawrence effected stringent smoke control laws and collaborated in intelligent planning. Together they brought about change—change that is evident throughout the city—at Point State Park, Gateway Center, Mellon Square, Allegheny Center and the Civic Arena.

Point State Park

Let's begin our downtown walking tour where Pittsburgh began—at the point. British colonists recognized the strategic advantages of this land at the source of the Ohio River and began to build a fort here in 1754. They were driven from the site by the French who erected Fort Duquesne. This fort gave the French control of the Ohio Valley during the early years of the French and Indian War. The British overthrow of the French began in 1758 when General John Forbes marched his army of 6,000 westward from Carlisle to raid Fort Duquesne. The French, realizing they were hopelessly outnumbered, burned their fort and fled two days before Forbes arrived. Writing to the British Prime Minister William Pitt, Forbes suggested naming the point Pittsburgh in his honor.

The British built Fort Pitt, which became a center for trading and negotiating with the Indians. Only once—during an Indian attack in 1763—did it see military action. All that remains today of the British installation is the Block House, the oldest building in western Pennsylvania.

At Point State Park you can visit the Block House and the Fort Pitt Museum. The museum houses artifacts, models and life-size exhibits depicting colonial life. Films and live interpretative programs are scheduled periodically. Military history buffs will find detailed descriptions of battles and bastions. The Block House and museum are open from 10 to 4:30, Tuesday through Saturday and noon to 4:30 on Sunday. Block House admission is free. Museum admission is 75 cents; children under twelve and senior citizens are admitted free.

Take time to stroll along the park's broad walkways. The spectacular fountain that crowns the point sends a 200-foot column of water into the air. It is computer-controlled and fed by an underground river. Watch the river traffic: motorboats, cabin cruisers, and hardworking riverboats nudging coal-filled barges to Pittsburgh's steel mills and power plants. Pittsburgh's waterways were its early lifelines but have been a serious menace, too. On St. Patrick's Day, 1936, flood waters cresting at 46 feet inundated the lower city.

Look across the Allegheny River to Three Rivers Stadium. Here the Pittsburgh Pirates and Steelers play to demanding fans who remember the World Series of 1971 and Super Bowls IX and X.

The steep sides of Mt. Washington rise dramatically above the Monongahela River that borders the other side of the park. Cable cars of the Duquesne and Monongahela Inclines climb the mount regularly. Luxurious condominiums and apartments and some of the city's finest restaurants are perched on this magnificent hill. If you watch the sunset from the observation decks along Grandview Avenue atop Mt. Washington, the city's skyscraper center becomes indeed a Golden Triangle.

Gateway Center

As you leave Point State Park by the main walkway, you'll face an arc of skyscrapers. On the far right is the Westinghouse Building and next to it is the six-story building that houses both the city's dailies: the *Pittsburgh Press* and the *Pittsburgh Post-Gazette.* The *Post-Gazette* is a lineal descendent of Pittsburgh's first newspaper, the *Gazette,* founded in 1786. It was the first paper published west of the Alleghenies. The turquoise structure displaying the Commonwealth seal is the State Office Building. Other buildings include Bell Telephone, Gateway Towers with its 314 luxury apartments, and four Gateway Center office buildings. Gateway One houses KDKA-TV and Radio. A pioneer of radio communications, KDKA was the first station to announce election results on the air and to institute musical programming and radio advertising. This 23-acre area bordering the park was once a commercial wasteland. Its new vitality is evidence of Pittsburgh's aggressive urban redevelopment program, its "Renaissance," of the 1950s and '60s.

From the park walkway head to the left toward the golden facade of the Hilton Hotel to the corner of Liberty and Commonwealth. As you walk down Liberty, you'll soon be in the heart of Gateway Center and Equitable Plaza. Each spring during the Three Rivers Arts Festival this handsome plaza becomes an open-air gallery for painting, sculpture and photography. Local bands and dance ensembles perform as visitors saunter among crafts booths. Giant balloons and colorful banners top

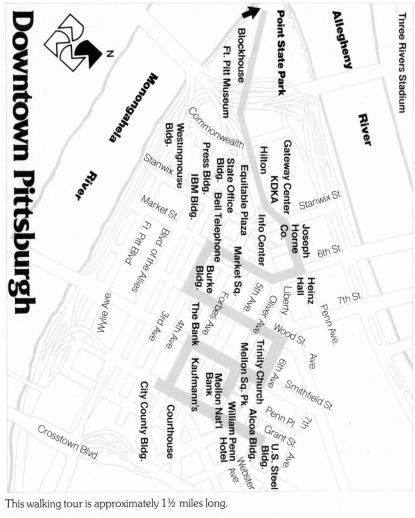

Downtown Pittsburgh

Three Rivers Stadium

Allegheny River

Point State Park

Blockhouse

Ft. Pitt Museum

Monongahela River

Commonwealth

Gateway Center Co.

Hilton

KDKA

Info Center

Joseph Horne

Heinz Hall

Stanwix St.

6th St.

7th St.

Penn Ave.

Equitable Plaza

State Office Bldg.

Bell Telephone

Market Sq.

5th Ave.

Liberty

Oliver Ave.

Wood St.

6th Ave.

Smithfield St.

Ave.

Press Bldg.

Burke Bldg.

Forbes Ave.

Trinity Church

Mellon Sq. Pk.

Alcoa Bldg.

Penn Pl.

7th

Westinghouse Bldg.

IBM Bldg.

The Bank

Mellon Nat'l Bank

William Penn Hotel

U.S. Steel Bldg.

Grant St. Ave.

Stanwix

Market St.

Kaufmann's

Webster Ave.

Blvd of the Allies

Ft. Pitt Blvd.

4th Ave

3rd Ave

Courthouse

City County Bldg.

Wylie Ave.

Crosstown Blvd.

N

This walking tour is approximately 1½ miles long.

the festivities. For further information call the Three Rivers Arts Festival at (412) 687-7014.

The Pittsburgh Convention and Visitors Bureau Information Center sits on the grassy patch where Liberty Avenue forks out to meet Stanwix Street. Stop here to collect free maps and pamphlets and a calendar of scheduled events.

As you leave the Information Center, bear to the left to the corner of Penn Avenue and Stanwix Street and proceed on Penn past the Joseph Horne Company, one of Pittsburgh's major department stores. Facing Horne's across Penn is the Jenkin's Arcade, an urban shopping mall that dates back to 1911.

Heinz Hall

On the corner of Penn and Sixth Street is the Steel City's showcase for the performing arts, Heinz Hall. Formerly the Penn Theater, it's now the home of the Pittsburgh Symphony, Pittsburgh Opera, Pittsburgh Ballet Theatre and Civic Light Opera. This baroque hall noted for its sumptuous interior and fine acoustics was financed primarily with funds from the Howard Heinz Foundation. Howard Heinz was the son of H. J. Heinz who began a modest food processing plant in Pittsburgh in 1869. (Tours of Heinz Hall on Monday, Wednesday, Friday at 12:30, with reservations; call 281-8185.)

Market Square

Turn right on 6th Street, and walk past Heinz Hall one block to Liberty Avenue. Cross Liberty to Market Street which angles sharply to the right. Stay on Market as it crosses Fifth Avenue until you reach Market Square. The grocery stores, fruit and fish markets that dot the square are a reminder that this was once the city's retail grocery center. The Original Oyster House is reputed to have the cheapest and biggest fish sandwich in town. Nicholas' stocks an impressive selection of coffees and teas. Although the recently added gas street lamps and brick-patterned streets create a nostalgic air, the square's real character derives from the lively after-work and nighttime crowds that frequent its pubs, discos and jazz clubs.

Burke Building and The Bank

After a leisurely exploration of the square continue on Market Street to Fourth Avenue and turn left. At 209 Fourth Avenue is the Burke Building, the city's first office building, which dates back to 1836. Designed by John Chislett, Pittsburgh's first important architect, it exemplifies the severe classicism of the Greek Revival architecture that once abounded in the city. Today the structure houses two restaurants, an antique shop and several offices.

Walk up Fourth Avenue one block to Wood Street where you'll see The Bank. Five antiquated buildings including an old bank have been uplifted, refurbished and transformed into a block-long mall of shops, cinemas and restaurants. Blackened exteriors have been sandblasted, and inside marble columns and stained-glass skylights have been restored. The original bank vault with its huge heavy door is the striking setting for a jewelry shop.

Oliver Plaza and Trinity Church

Continue down Wood past Forbes towards Fifth. The Pittsburgh National Bank Building dominates the corner of Wood and Fifth. Farther down Wood are the sleek towers of Oliver Plaza and the fashionable Hardy and Hayes and Hughes and Hatcher Stores. From the plaza you can see the mural of a giant steelworker over the entrance of 550 Wood Street. The Pittsburgh Press Club, the olest chartered press club in the nation, sits atop this building. It's a favorite meeting place for the city's press corps and broadcasting personalities.

When you turn right on Sixth Avenue you enter a block that has preserved an air of stately calm. Limousines glide silently up to the green-canopied entrance of the Duquesne Club. Pittsburgh's most prominent businessmen have for decades met regularly for luncheon at this exclusive club.

Perhaps the pervading calm of this area has lingered from earlier times when a cemetery of nearly 4000 graves filled the entire block. Soldiers from Fort Duquesne, Fort Pitt and Revolutionary battles are buried in the cemetery which still surrounds Trinity Cathedral and the adjacent First Presbyterian Church.

Mellon Square

The tempo seems to quicken as you reach the corner of Smithfield Street and Sixth Avenue. Up Sixth Avenue you can see the Alcoa Building whose 30 stories are sheathed in stamped aluminum panels. Everything from the window frames to the wiring, the water pipes to the lobby sculpture, is made of aluminum. The Alcoa Building towers over Mellon Square, an oasis of shrubs and fountains that is a lunchtime haven for officeworkers.

Mellon Square Park was built with funds from three Mellon family foundations and dedicated to the memory of Andrew W. and Richard B. Mellon. Their financial acumen and public spirit boosted the development of Pittsburgh's major industries. The chief interest of the brothers, however, was T. Mellon and Sons, which was incorporated in 1902 as Mellon National Bank. The imposing four-story granite structure to the south of the square is the bank's headquarters. Its huge bronze doors open into a main banking room distinguished by 60-foot Doric columns. On the uphill side of Mellon Square is the gracious William Penn Hotel. You might want to rest for a minute in the massive Victorian-style chairs in its ornate lobby. A hotel in the grand tradition, the William Penn reflects the charm and elegance of architectural fashion in the 1920s. Visitors accustomed to flatter terrains may be interested to note that the hotel's entrances are on three different levels.

Return to Smithfield Street and walk past Mellon Bank on your left and Sak's Fifth Avenue on the right. Cross Fifth Avenue and proceed down Smithfield in front of Kaufmann's Department Store. On the site across from Kaufmann's, Harry Davis and John P. Harris in 1905 opened the Nickelodeon, the country's first all-motion picture house. Pittsburgh was an early center for the film industry. The Warner brothers had their first headquarters here.

The Courthouse
Turn left and follow Forbes Avenue to Grant Street. Across the street to your right is the nine-story City County Building whose stately neoclassical architecture reflects its function as the seat of local government.

Adjacent to the City County Building is the Allegheny County Courthouse and Jail. This massive fortress reminiscent of the Southern French and Spanish Romanesque style was completed in 1888. Murals depicting the city's history deck the lobby, and exhibitions in the gallery can be viewed Monday through Friday, 8:30 to 4:30.

As you continue your walk on Grant Street look to the hill on your right for a glimpse of the Civic Arena. With its retractable roof, the structure cost $22 million to build. The first million was given by the late Edgar J. Kaufmann, former president of the department store and a key figure in Pittsburgh's "rebirth." The arena is the home of the Pittsburgh Penguins of the National Hockey League and hosts rock and pop concerts throughout the year. Each spring the Folk Festival, featuring costumed performances by more than two dozen local ethnic groups, is staged here. In the later 1800s thousands of European immigrants settled in Pittsburgh to work its mills and factories. The annual Folk Festival is just one of many celebrations saluting the city's ethnic diversity.

The last stop on our tour is the building you probably spotted first. Poking its head above the hills that encompass the city, the 64-story United States Steel Building is Pittsburgh's tallest structure. Its skeletal columns are made of a rusty-looking steel alloy, Cor-ten, which, as it oxidizes, forms a protective coating that halts further rusting. This giant stands a distance from the street lest it completely obscure the delicate Gothic church opposite it. There is no public observation deck, but if you're ready for refreshments, ride the elevator to the 62nd floor to Stouffer's Top of the Triangle Restaurant for a commanding view of Pittsburgh.

From this vantage point you can assess the topography that has given Pittsburgh its special character. You can see its neighborhoods scaling the hillsides and tucked in the valley. The downtown triangle that fans out from the point is relatively flat. Its surface has been reshaped, its most severe humps laboriously leveled. Pittsburgh's corporate and industrial powers are evident from this perspective, but its charm must be discovered below on foot.

PITTSBURGH'S OAKLAND
Mike Kalina

Oakland—about 3 miles from the heart of the Steel City—is one of Pittsburgh's most integrated and diversified neighborhoods. It's a mixture of styles and ethnic groups, the poor and the more affluent. Many of its once fine homes have been divided into tiny apartments to house students who attend Oakland's three colleges: the University of Pittsburgh, Carlow Col-

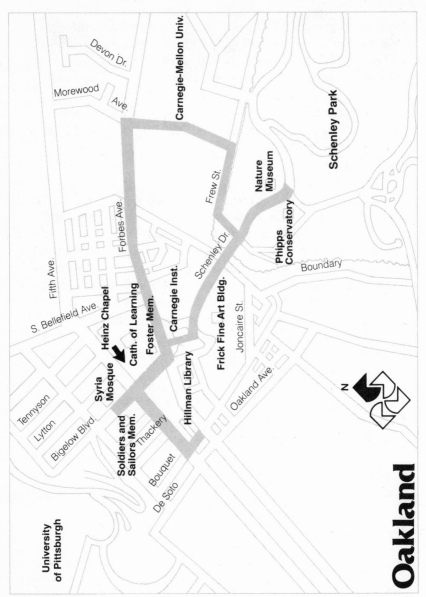

This walking tour is approximately 2 miles long.

lege, and Carnegie-Mellon University. But there are still numerous well-to-do residences and expensive condominiums. Its restaurants range from the Park Schenley with its French menu and elegant entrees to small Middle Eastern restaurants to the inevitable fast-food chains.

Oakland is dotted with imposing public and private buildings. Its cultural and educational attractions, including the world-renowned Carnegie Institute, have earned it the designation as Pittsburgh's Civic Center.

Oakland is also the site of the University Health Center of Pittsburgh which includes the University of Pittsburgh School of Medicine and six hospitals: Children's Hospital, Eye and Ear Hospital, Magee-Women's Hospital, Montefiore Hospital, Presbyterian-University Hospital and Western Psychiatric Institute and Clinic. Among the research advances that have focused international attention on this medical complex is the discovery of the polio vaccine by Dr. Jonas E. Salk.

Traffic congestion is a continuing woe in Oakland, and the best way to get around is on foot. Pedestrians have the right of way and frequently the upper hand on motorists.

University of Pittsburgh

A hub of much of Oakland's activity, the University of Pittsburgh campus is a logical starting point of our tour. In 1921 when the growing university was cramped for space, the chancellor startled the city with a proposal to build a 52-story skyscraper of classrooms and offices with a price tag of $10 million. The plan initially met strong opposition, but in 1926 work began on the world's tallest educational structure, the *Cathedral of Learning.* The completed tower has only 42 stories but cost approximately $32 million.

The main area of the cathedral's first floor, known as the Commons Room, resembles a medieval castle. Encircling the Commons Room are nineteen of what surely must be the nation's most handsome college classrooms, the Nationality Rooms. They were gifts to the university from Pittsburgh's ethnic groups and have been designed and furnished to reflect their heritages. You may wander through the rooms not in use during school hours or on Sunday afternoons. Guided tours are available Monday through Saturday, 9 to 5. On the periphery of the Commons Room is the Visitors' Center open weekdays, 9 to 5. A 35-minute narrated slide presentation, *The Story of the*

Nationality Rooms, is shown with advance reservations (624-6000). While you're in the cathedral, take the elevator to the 36th floor for a commanding view of the Oakland area.

Stephen Foster Memorial

Adjacent to the cathedral on the corner of Forbes Avenue and Bigelow Boulevard is the Stephen Foster Memorial. Many Pitt dramatic productions are staged in the small theater; the back rooms house about 10,000 pieces of memorabilia of this Pittsburgh-born composer. Stephen Foster, it has been said, "was the creator of the first distinctively American musical idiom, the singer of the commonplace, the elemental, the democratic." The wealth of tunes he left behind includes, *Oh! Susannah, My Old Kentucky Home, Jeanie with the Light Brown Hair,* and *Old Folks at Home.* The memorial is usually open Monday through Friday, 9 to 5, except university holidays. Admission is free.

Heinz Memorial Chapel

Across the stretch of lawn from the cathedral and the Stephen Foster Memorial is Heinz Chapel. Twenty-three stained glass windows composed of over 250,000 pieces of glass offer pictorial interpretations of faith, hope, justice, tolerance and wisdom and add warm beauty to this starkly elegant structure. The chapel is generally open weekdays, 9 to 4 and Sunday between 1:30 and 5:30. A hostess is usually on duty Tuesday through Friday.

Carnegie Institute

After your visit to the chapel, cross Forbes Avenue to Carnegie Institute. This extensive and impressive cultural center at 4400 Forbes Avenue includes the Museum of Art, the Museum of Natural History, the Carnegie Music Hall, and the Carnegie Library.

Andrew Carnegie was Pittsburgh's steelmaster extraordinaire. In 1890 he offered $1 million for the construction of a library. When it was opened in 1895, he enlarged his donation, giving additional funds for a museum, art gallery and technical school. Andrew Carnegie combined an enterprising imagination with an aristocratic notion of service. During his lifetime he distributed $350 million to charities and civic and cultural projects.

The Carnegie Library is just one of nearly 2,000 libraries he donated around the world.

Dinosaur skeletons, rare fossils, Egyptian mummies, American Indian artifacts, birds, insects, snakes and shells are among the seven million specimens in the Museum of Natural History. The three exhibit floors also include dioramas of wild animals in simulated natural settings and a marine hall. At the Information and Orientation Center you can listen to recorded lectures on natural history.

The world's largest pipe organ—8,600 pipes in all, including one that is 32 feet long and weighs 1,000 pounds—is in the Carnegie Music Hall.

The Carnegie Museum of Art has a distinctive collection of artwork housed in its new Scaife Gallery. The collection spans the period from the 14th century to the present, but recent acquisitions have emphasized the modern. Browsers can view paintings by Rembrandt, Goya, Van Gogh, Renoir, Monet, Matisse, and Miro as well as DuBuffet and Lichtenstein. The Bruce Gallery houses a beautifully displayed collection of furniture and accessories.

The museum gift shops are worth a visit, and if you're hungry, try the basement cafeteria for an inexpensive lunch, or eat in the Scaife Gallery cafeteria and look out on the plaza of dancing fountains. The Carnegie Institute is open Tuesday through Saturday from 10 to 5 and from 1 to 6 on Sunday. It is closed Monday and holidays. Admission is $1 for adults and 50 cents for children except Saturday when admission is free.

Carnegie-Mellon University

Continue up Forbes Avenue approximately one-fifth mile to the intersection of Forbes and Morewood Avenues and the campus of Carnegie-Mellon University (CMU). Another legacy of steelmaster Andrew Carnegie, it was known as Carnegie Institute of Technology until 1967 when it merged with the Mellon Institute to become Carnegie-Mellon University.

Turn right on the campus walkway and follow it to the end. CMU is spread on a 100-acre site bordering Schenley Park. Typically ranked as one of the nation's foremost engineering schools, it boasts an outstanding fine arts program. Noted actors and actresses such as Jack Klugman, George Peppard, Sada Thompson, and Arthur Kennedy have studied at its drama school.

Schenley Park

At the end of the campus walkway turn right onto Frew Street and follow it about 100 yards to Schenley Drive. To your left is Flagstaff Hill and Schenley Park—a perfect resting spot. The city's first park, a gift from Mary E. Schenley, is a popular retreat for students and residents with its grassy hills, hiking and jogging trails, bikeways, 18-hole golf course, seasonal ice-skating rink, and miniature golf course.

Phipps Conservatory

Across Schenley Drive cresting the hillside to your left is Phipps Conservatory. It was named for its benefactor Henry Phipps, an eagle-eyed manager and business associate of Andrew Carnegie. The conservatory houses more than 2½ acres of exotic and domestic trees, flowers and plants. Its orchid collection is particularly outstanding. Special flower shows are held in the spring, at Christmas and usually in the fall. The conservatory is open daily 9 to 5 for free browsing except during shows, when hours are extended and a nominal admission is charged.

The Schenley Park Nature Museum across the street from the conservatory features still-life nature exhibits, snakes and fish. It is free and open Monday through Saturday, 9 to 5, and Sunday, 1 to 5.

From the conservatory and nature museum walk back down the hill on Schenley Drive, across the bridge to the parking area bordering Carnegie Institute and Library. Bear to your left, passing in front of Pitt's Frick Fine Arts Building, Professional Quadrangle and the Hillman Library. In the sidewalk you'll see a brick tracing marking the location of the outfield wall of old Forbes Field, the original home of the Pittsburgh Pirates.

Syria Mosque

At the first light, cross Forbes Avenue and proceed on Bigelow one block, past the old Schenley Hotel, which is now the Pitt Student Union. Cross Fifth Avenue. On your right is the Pittsburgh Athletic Association and behind it the Syria Mosque. Opened in 1916, the mosque is representative of Arabic design. Its entrance is flanked by bronze sphinxes. Numerous concerts and rock shows are scheduled here regularly.

Soldiers and Sailors Memorial Hall

Across the street from the mosque is Soldiers and Sailors Memorial Hall, a public auditorium that also houses wartime memorabilia, most of it from the Civil War. The hall can be toured weekdays, 8 to 4, weekends and holidays, 1 to 4. Admission is free.

Return to Fifth Avenue and turn right. Walk approximately two blocks and turn left onto Bouquet Street. A right onto Forbes at the next intersection will take you into the heart of Oakland's business district. By making a left on Forbes you will return to our starting point.

HISTORIC PHILADELPHIA
George S. Bush

Some years ago, a local joker endowed with an ironic wit reminiscent of Ben Franklin's dreamed up a contest in which the grand prize was one day in Philadelphia and the loser had to spend a whole week. The fellow wasn't just being nasty. For many decades, the heart of the city had been the victim of terrible neglect, like a wonderful old grandfather clock that's allowed to run down and rust. But all this has since changed. Old Philadelphia, renewed and revitalized, now stands as one of the nation's true showplaces. There's enough to keep you entranced here, not only for a day or even a week, but for much longer, and this tour is merely a sampler.

For a preview, elevator up to William Penn's perch atop City Hall Tower. At the statue's feet there's an open-air observation deck that lets you look out over the city from an elevation of 537 feet—high enough for a nearly 50-mile horizon. The ride is free (9 to 4:30 weekdays, in summer also on weekends), and besides the splendid panorama you'll also get a good idea of where you'll be walking.

Almost directly beneath you stretches the refurbished downtown, with its sleek hotels and new business buildings and the stunning, glittering Gallery Mall, a shopping center that transports you straight into the 21st century. Beyond, toward the blue ribbon of the Delaware River, you'll see the open ex-

Historic Philadelphia

16th St.

15th St.

Broad St.

Juniper St.

Tourist Center

City Hall

N

Chestnut St.

Market St.

Filbert St.

Arch St.

13th St.

12th St.

11th St.

10th St.

9th St.

8th St.

7th St.

6th St.

Race St.

Chinatown Living Hist. Center

Chinese Afro-Amer.

Cultural Center Museum

Benjamin Franklin Grave

U.S. Mint

Franklin Bust

Betsy Ross House

Elfreth's Alley

Sanson St.

Walnut St.

Locust St.

Spruce St.

Pine St.

Lombard St.

Fritzwater St.

Bainbridge St.

South St.

Antique Row.

The Gallery

Jewelers Sq.

Norman Rockwell Museum

Penn Mutual Observation Deck

Independence Hall

Second Bk. of U.S.

Carpenters Hall

Independence Nat. Hist. Pk.

Independence Visitors Center

Liberty Bell Pavilion

Maritime Museum

Christ Church

Penn's Landing

←to Italian Market

5th St.

4th St.

3rd St.

2nd St.

Front St.

bus route

Society Hill

Head House Sq.

New Market

Historic ships

DelawareRiver

This walking tour is approximately 3 miles long.

panse of Independence National Historical Park with Independence Hall as its centerpiece. Immediately to the south of this historic preserve, your gaze sweeps over blocks upon blocks of beautiful colonial brickwork. That's "Society Hill," whose name has nothing to do with the social register, as most people think, but was derived from the Free Society of Friends, the Quakers, who settled here before the Revolution. This venerable quarter, snatched from the bulldozer jaws of urban renewal in the nick of time, is today the most successful restoration this side of Colonial Williamsburg. You'll love its near old-time streets—spruced up by young people with a penchant for nostalgia.

But these are only some of the highlights of your walk. Tucked away in the welter of the downtown streets are numerous other attractions you can't distinguish from your City Hall Tower vantage point. Before the day is out you'll be strolling past a most amazing concentration of jewelry stores and down a remarkable row of antique shops. And you'll even take a side trip by bus to the Italian Market, a slice of Mediterranean hustle and bustle transplanted to the southern outskirts of downtown.

A Quilt of Cultures

The Quakers and the Italians were not the only ones to claim Philadelphia as their own. Would you believe, there's a Chinatown? You'll pass it on your way from City Hall as you walk along Arch Street toward the city's historic enclave. Arch itself is hardly inspiring—it's a dreary reminder of what much of downtown was like before its latter-day face lift. But wonder of wonders, a miniaturized Mandarin palace, the Chinese Cultural Center, rises to intricate pagoda roofs: you can bet it will long survive the seedy shops nearby.

Farther down Arch, be sure to visit the Afro-American Museum which reflects our history strictly from the black perspective. It's open 10 to 5 Tuesday through Saturday, noon to 6 Sunday, closed Monday, and the admission is $1.50; under 12, 75 cents.

More conventional in its approach but unusual in its presentation is the Living History Center, which you'll come to next. By means of the latest multi-media techniques—multiple screens and sounds that engulf you—you can experience exciting moments from our past. The center's most impressive show is a drama projected on a 70-foot-high wrap-around screen.

Doors open at 9:30 on all weekdays except Monday, at 12:30 on Sunday, and the shows run at least until 5:30, with longer hours in summer. The charge is $3.50; under 18, $2, which includes admission to a terrace playground where youngsters can climb and ride on outsized replicas of toys from the olden days.

Coins by the Millions

You'll pass the Christ Church Burial Ground at the corner of 5th and Arch on your way to the U.S. Mint. Ben Franklin, along with four other signers of the Declaration of Independence, lies here. That the U.S. Mint was built but a few steps from the cemetery is probably a coincidence, but appropriate enough. Coinage was one of Franklin's major preoccupations, *Poor Richard* notwithstanding. The mint punches out up to 1.5 million coins per hour. You can watch, but not touch, from a glassed-in observation deck (Monday through Friday, 8:30 to 4; no charge).

Around the corner from the mint and behind a firehouse stands a real oddity, the "Penny Franklin," a bust artfully composed of 80,000 pennies contributed by school children.

Betsy Ross Stitched Here

You now arrive at the charming Betsy Ross House, where the Quaker seamstress lived and is presumed to have sewn the first 13 stars and stripes together. The house, built in 1760, is filled with period furniture. It's open daily 9 to 5, and 6 in summer; no charge.

Around the corner, on Elfreth's Alley, you'll find even more venerable homes. This cobblestone lane, lined with residences on both sides, dates back to 1702 and is believed to be the oldest street in America whose original houses are still lived in today.

A Maritime Detour Plus Society Hill

The accompanying map shows you how to get to Penn's Landing on the Delaware River. Unfortunately for Philadelphia walkers (but most fortunately for the city), you can't take the indicated route for granted. This section of downtown is still being razed and rebuilt, with construction sites shifting from month to month—so you'll just have to find your way.

Your ultimate destination is the wharf where the Spanish-American War battleship *Olympia* and the World War II guppy-class submarine U.S.S. *Becunia* are moored. One of the striking things about this combination exhibit is that the old battle-wagon—which served as Admiral Dewey's flagship in the Battle of Manila Bay—isn't really a whole lot bigger than the 50-year-more-recent submarine. You can tour both ships daily from 10 to 5, and in summer until 8 in the evening, for $2; children half price.

Now recross Delaware Avenue to explore Society Hill, whose stately Georgian homes have been restored to perfection—their red brick scrubbed and the wrought iron polished and everything adorned with joyously painted shutters. It's a delight every step of the way.

At the heart of Society Hill—on its gentle top, as it were—sits the long covered shed of Head House Square. Fire companies used the Head House as their headquarters and social club (to douse their own internal fires) as early as 1745. In the last few years, the adjoining block has been turned into the gourmet center of Society Hill. Eighteen historic buildings, complemented by contemporary glass towers, now form the New-Market development of eateries, drinkeries, entertaineries, exotic food shops, and fashion boutiques. Somewhat surprisingly, the historic nooks blend happily with the modern crannies.

Bicentennial Philadelphia

Now return to Christ Church at 2nd and Market where the signers of the Declaration of Independence prayed. Modest as this small house of worship may seem today, it shocked many early Philadelphians, who considered its spire too high, too obvious, and too garish. The simple interior of stained glass, set off against somber walls, houses the first bishop's chair in this country. The church also has a minister's bell, cast in 1711, that once hung in a tree and called the faithful to services (open daily from 9 to 4:30; closed Sunday and holidays except for worship).

As a general introduction to Independence National Historical Park, which you'll visit next, step into the Visitors Center. Every 45 minutes there's a film about the colonists' struggle for liberty. Like the other buildings in the park, the Visitors Center is open from 9 to 5 daily (later in summer) and admission is free.

Independence Hall is a must, of course, as is the new Liberty Bell Pavilion, which faces it across the walking mall of

Chestnut Street. Half-hour guided tours of the hall set out every 20 minutes, starting in the ground-floor courtroom and moving on to the Pennsylvania Assembly room where the 1775 Continental Congress met to name George Washington the new American Army's commander-in-chief.

Note the building directly south of Independence Hall. That's the Penn Mutual Tower. It has an enclosed observation deck on its 22nd floor, plus a theater and several interesting exhibit areas. If it's been too blustery a day for you to enjoy the open-air view from City Hall Tower, here's your chance to take in the bird's-eye perspective of Philadelphia.

Bangles and Baubles

On your trek west on 8th Street you'll be passing through Jewelers' Row, as the area between Chestnut and Walnut and 7th and 9th has come to be called. In these blocks some 300 dealers, silver platers, and silversmiths engage in their trades at discount prices, with mind-blowing displays of rings, chains, bracelets, watches, diamonds, sterling ware, gems, and assorted trinkets.

Italy on the Delaware

Now grab the 8th Street bus (No. 47, 45 cents), and ride south to Washington Street. Around the corner on northbound 9th, the utterly unbelievable Italian Market goes on and on for blocks in a melee of mouth-watering scents and sights: stores and sidewalk stalls with mountains of produce, seafood of all kinds, chest-high tubs of pickled goodies, burlap sacks of spices, old-country cheeses, and strings of sausages dangling from rafters.

You won't be able to carry everything you'll want to buy, but if your stomach is growling beyond control, lunch at the Villa di Roma (936 South 9th), where mussels à la marinara are a specialty and the house Chianti reasonably priced and solid.

Antiques to Star Wars

Return downtown by the 9th Street bus (again, 45 cents), and get off at Pine Street to explore "Antique Row." The 3 blocks of Pine between 9th and 12th are lined with retailers and wholesalers of Chippendale chairs and cigar-store Indians, Queen Anne settees and Chinese vases, brass fixtures and yesteryear's dolls—almost anything you can think of. Shopping hours are erratic, but most places post off-hour phone numbers for customers who can't wait to part with their cash.

Finally, if you still have the time and energy, continue on the No. 47 bus to 9th and Market Streets, and browse through the brand-new enclosed Gallery Mall with its four floors of 125 shops and restaurants. Here you can purchase anything from blue jeans to wicker chairs and in between nibble on egg rolls, quiche, or guacamole.

There's More

For information on the attractions shown on the map but not described in this book—like the Maritime Museum—stop by the Philadelphia Convention and Visitors Bureau, the domed modern pavilion at 1525 John F. Kennedy Boulevard near City Hall. If you've parked in the convenient underground garage at Arch and 16th, that's right on your way to City Hall Tower. In any case, you can't take all this in on just one walking tour, and you'll be coming back for more—if for nothing else than for the soft, mustard-splashed pretzels sold on the downtown Philadelphia streets. They are sure to keep you coming back!

PHILADELPHIA'S FAIRMOUNT PARK
George S. Bush

In the face of today's cost-of-living crunch, it almost seems a miracle that you may enjoy a rich folks' treasure trove—some 8,000 acres of manicured green, laced with winding creeks and graced by mansions and museums and some of the world's finest sculpture—all for a few modest admission fees, a little shoe leather, and a bus ticket.

This repository of culture and beauty, as well as just plain fun, is Fairmount Park, the largest city park in the world. Located along the banks of the Schuylkill River, it's less than one hour's walking time from downtown on the grandiose Benjamin Franklin Parkway.

You couldn't hope, of course, to cover all the attractions in detail on one excursion, nor to explore the whole vast park on

foot. With more than 100 miles of trails and bridle paths meandering through the preserve, even jogging wouldn't help.

To accommodate sightseers, the city has provided a special
"on-off" excursion bus—you can walk when you want to, and
ride when you get tired. Decked out to look like a trolley of old,
it cruises up the parkway and through Fairmount Park, making
22 stops enroute. The all-day, unlimited, on-and-off bus ticket
costs $1 (children, 50 cents), and it's a must-buy even if you hardly
use the colorful conveyance. With the ticket in hand you get
substantial discounts on all admissions, more than compensat-
ing for the initial outlay. The fees cited in this walking tour
reflect these discounts.

The trolley-bus does have one drawback. Its last round trip
leaves the Philadelphia Tourist Center on John F. Kennedy
Boulevard near City Hall (see map; phone 864-1976) at 4:45 in
the afternoon, so if you want to take in one of the top-notch
summer evening concerts in the park—from classic symphony
to pop and jazz—you'll have to rely on other transportation. But
during the day, every day of the week from April through October, there's a bus every 15 minutes, and that's also the
frequency with which it shows up at the successive stops.

Start Off in Victorian Splendor

Although the Academy of Fine Arts is not part of Fairmount
Park proper, you'll want to visit it first. Leave your car in the
garage at 16th and Arch ($3.50 all day). It's convenient to both
the tourist center and the academy.

What's so intriguing about the academy isn't just its brilliant
collection of 18th-century American art. The building itself is a
masterpiece of the Victorian era. Not that you'd have noticed a
few years ago when its splendors lay hidden under countless
layers of renovations like the features of a once beautiful
woman, since smothered in folds of fat. In celebration of the Bicentennial, however, the structure was stripped of its surplus
poundage. Its exquisite old wood was bared from beneath successive coats of paint, brass knobs and hinges were scraped and
polished to a spit-shine finish, and the ornate details in gilt and
polychrome so typical of the Victorian period were reproduced
to perfection.

In the upstairs galleries where archways repeat themselves
like reflections in an infinite mirror, paintings have been arranged for endless, easy viewing and the sculpture placed at

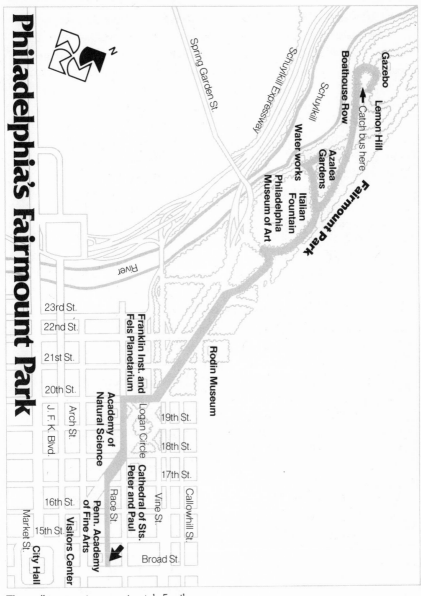

Philadelphia's Fairmount Park

Gazebo
Lemon Hill
Boathouse Row
Catch bus here
Schuylkill
Water works
Azalea Gardens
Italian Fountain
Philadelphia Museum of Art
Fairmount Park
Spring Garden St.
Schuylkill Expressway
River
Rodin Museum

N

Franklin Inst. and Fels Planetarium
Academy of Natural Science
Logan Circle
Cathedral of Sts. Peter and Paul
Penn. Academy of Fine Arts
Visitors Center
City Hall

23rd St.
22nd St.
21st St.
20th St.
J. F. K. Blvd.
Arch St.
16th St.
15th St.
Market St.

19th St.
18th St.
17th St.
Vine St.
Callowhill St.
Race St.
Broad St.

This walking tour is approximately 5 miles.

startling angles. Don't miss the "Lansdowne" portrait of George Washington by Gilbert Stuart. You've seen it in print—here it's for real. (Open 10 to 5 Tuesday through Saturday, 1 to 5 Sunday, guided weekday tours at 11 and 2. Admission $1, children half price.)

Gothic Ghosts and Prehistoric Monsters

Heading west on your trek up the elegant, spacious parkway, be sure to see the interior of the Cathedral of Saints Peter and Paul (open daily 9 to 4), whose design was based on the Church of San Carlo al Corso in Rome. Behind the cathedral's massive doors, the domed chamber echoes with your footsteps, and dark, mysterious corners hint at the presence of Gothic ghosts.

Then visit the Academy of Natural Sciences. Its centerpiece, flanked by other paleontological relics, is the leering skeleton of a 95-million-year-old dinosaur. As American museums go, its home isn't exactly a youngster either. The academy is the oldest natural science museum in the country, dating back to 1812. But it's far from musty. There are excellent dioramas of North American, Asian, and African wildlife, including some true marvels of taxidermy, such as a bobcat with its teeth clenched around a mouthful of quail.

If you have youngsters along, schedule your visit to coincide with one of the 30-minute "Eco-Shows" with live animals, usually staged twice a day (phone 299-1000 for hours). The show is included in the $1 admission; ages 13–17, 75 cents; children 5–12, 50 cents; 4 and under free. The museum is open daily from 10–4. Needless to say, here, as elsewhere on your park rounds, you'll have a better time on weekdays than on crowded weekends.

The Franklin Institute: Where Science Is Child's Play

You'll be tempted to spend the rest of the day at the Franklin Institute and Fels Planetarium, for this is a huge place. It better be—one of its exhibits is a Boeing 707 and *that's* only a small part of it.

Your kids can also climb into the cockpit of a fighter plane, ride in the cab of a gigantic steam locomotive that actually commutes on a short track in one of the halls, and pretend they're blood corpuscles and clamber through the throbbing chambers of a two-story-high heart. Most exhibits are to touch, experiment with, learn from by doing—almost all, that is, except a carefully shielded stage where man-made lightning bombards a toy house with sound effects worthy of a Frankenstein movie. The institute is open Monday–Saturday, 10 to 5, Sunday 12 to 5; astronomy shows are held in the planetarium daily. Admission to the museum is $2 for adults, $1.50 age 12 through college, $1.25 under 12. There's a small extra charge for the planetarium.

From Rodin to Warhol

Farther on along the parkway, sheathed in greenery, stands the tiny gem of a Grecian temple, the Rodin Museum, which houses the largest collection of that master sculptor's work outside of France. You enter through an archway that frames his famous *Thinker:* inside you can study the immortalized *Burghers of Calais,* intrude on the privacy of Adam and Eve, and delight in a nearly endless procession of Balzacs, one of Rodin's favorite subjects. Or you can rest—by now you'll need to—on a stone bench outside, beside a glittering pool, and strike a thinker's pose yourself. The hours are 9 to 5 daily. Admission is free, although a contribution is requested.

Now follow the flags of all nations that line the parkway to the Philadelphia Museum of Art, which seems to dwarf even the Franklin Institute. Its 200 galleries cover 10 acres. Its facade looms like that of the Parthenon in Athens.

Among its treasures you'll find everything from medieval arms and armor to Cambodian sculpture to work by Andy Warhol—and you can get an art lesson besides. In a special exhibit on style, you are taught how to examine color, brush stroke, line, and shape. The museum is open daily from 9 to 5. Adults pay $1; under 18, 50 cents. On Sunday from 9 to 1 you get in free.

Two Fancy Mansions and a Japanese Tea House

Now board the trolley-bus and ride the East River Drive, past Abraham Lincoln's monument to the Mount Pleasant Mansion which was bought in 1779 by Benedict Arnold for his bride. Although Arnold never got a chance to live there, he would have felt right at home—there are as many false doors as there are real ones, for the house was designed with spectacular symmetry (daily, except Wednesday, 10 to 5; admission 40 cents, children 20 cents).

The largest of the noble Fairmount Park houses is Straw-berry Mansion, another short hop by bus. Guides will explain the architecture of this basically Federal-style residence and its curious contents: a "bed and board," so called because it served both purposes; the significance of the various samplers adorning the walls; the screens used to shield ladies from the heat of the fireplace in order to preserve the wax they used to fill the small-pox pits in their faces. The attic is full of antique gadgets and toys, another plus for youngsters (daily, except Monday, 10 to 5; admission 40 cents, children 20 cents).

Another bus stop is the Japanese House. This authentic 17th-century scholar's home, with a thick cypress-bark roof, sits in the midst of a walled garden and is surrounded by a moat. In summer, the house is open daily for tea and tours (admission 25 cents, tea extra).

The First Zoo, Greatly Improved

Of course, you can get off the bus at every stop and walk, although you're likely to find the distances forbidding between most. At the Philadelphia Zoo, which dates back to 1874 and was the country's first such animal park, you'll get a chance to stretch your legs again. There's enough room here for 1,600 species, a baby animal nursery, an outdoor gorilla house, a snake house, a 2-acre children's zoo, and even a mile-long safari monorail. Open Monday to Friday, 9:30 to 5; Saturday and Sunday, 9:30 to 6. Basic admission costs $1.50; ages 2 to 11, 50 cents; under 2, free. Add 25 cents for the children's zoo, $1.25 for the monorail (kids 75 cents).

Gardens and River Views

There's yet more walking if you still have the energy. On the way back, get off the bus at the Lemon Hill stop and look for the pointed green cap of the Gazebo which offers a most pleasant perspective of the Schuylkill River through the trees. Then walk down the hill to Boathouse Row, a series of Victorian structures built of rich purple stone, originally designed for row-ing clubs and still used to house a medley of brightly painted boats.

When once again you come upon the statue of Lincoln, cross to the Azalea Gardens. They are at their best in May when 2,000 azaleas bloom among daffodils, rhododendron and flowering dogwood. Then, from the Italian Fountain, where four sprightly Pegasuses spout water from their hooves, head for the Fairmount Park Waterworks.

Waterworks in this lovely setting? Well, no longer. But the five acres around these waterworks were the beginning of the park, in 1815, which later grew with the city. The works, now defunct, provide the finest view of the river, an apt conclusion to your tour.

Concerts in the Dells

On the accompanying map, you'll note Robin Hood Dell East and Robin Hood Dell West, two grand amphitheaters, and you'll be passing both on the bus route. Evening concerts are held at both throughout the summer. Dell East offers jazz, pop, rock, and folk concerts at very reasonable ticket prices, while Dell West presents the Philadelphia Orchestra and such artists as Leonard Bernstein and Beverly Sills—and there's a good chance of getting in free. Half of the 15,000 tickets are given out without charge at the tourist center on the day of the performance. For schedules, check with the center.

BUCKS COUNTY'S TRANQUIL TOWPATH
George S. Bush

Less than 90 minutes by car from downtown Philadelphia—and not much more than that from New York City—lies one of the loveliest unspoiled walking trails in our country, the towpath of the Delaware Canal. For more than 100 years, from 1828 to 1931, this gentle grass trail on the canal's embankment had been the workaday route of mule teams. Harnessed to long ropes and coaxed and cussed along by their handlers, they towed coal barges down that calm waterway, constructed to parallel the tempestuous Delaware River on its Pennsylvania side. The barges slid leisurely from lock to lock under the heavy green canopies of shade trees and under tiny wooden bridges, all the way from Easton to Bristol, the canal's terminus on the outskirts of Philadelphia. Since then the narrow channel has lost none of its tranquil old-time charm. Yet surprisingly, despite its proximity to the East Coast megalopolis, it remains practically unknown and most of its towpath is rarely traveled.

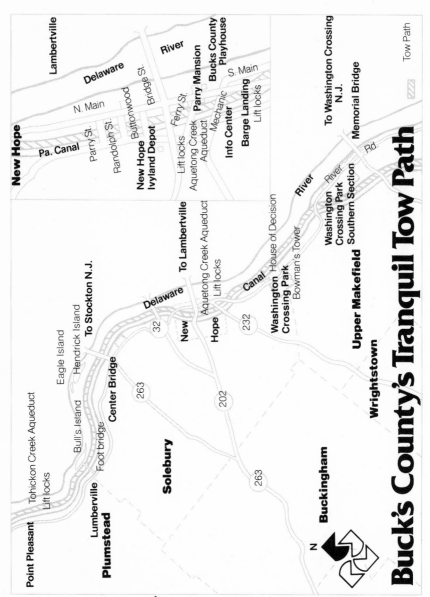

Buck's County's Tranquil Tow Path

The sections of this walking tour range in distance from 1.6 to 4.1 miles. The total distance of the tour is approximately 14½ miles.

How can that be? Well, because the canal and its towpath, now preserved as Theodore Roosevelt State Park, are 60 miles long but, together, only about 40 feet wide—and how are you ever going to show such a thin strip on a map?

So here's your chance to do some delightful strolling far from the noise and fumes and bustle of traffic. There are so few people around that everyone smiles and nods when meeting on this serene serpentine. Hard to believe, but true.

Of course, you won't have to walk the whole 60 miles in one trip, although you might well make a weekend hobby out of it until you've covered all of the canal, top to bottom or vice versa. The grassy path, level all the way and easy on the legs, is accessible at any number of spots from Pennsylvania Route 32. We'll just talk about the best stretches for you to stretch your legs on, ranging in length from 1.6 to 4.1 miles. Enjoy only one segment or string a couple together. Either way, you'll have a splendid outing.

Incidentally, to avoid backtracking, it's a good idea to team up with friends who are also driving. Park one of the cars at your planned destination, then drive the other to your starting point. At the end of the day, you pile into your destination car and drive off to pick up the automobile you left behind in the morning. That's known as a two-car shuttle, and it comes in handy on all kinds of one-way hikes.

A Most Pleasant Starting Point

It's only 1.7 miles from Point Pleasant to Lumberville. On your trek, you'll have the chance to walk on an aqueduct, a water channel built overhead to bridge land, a structure common in the days of ancient Rome but a rarity now. In this case, the Delaware Canal crosses the spectacular gorge of Tohickon Creek just before it empties into the Delaware River.

Then you'll pass some lift locks—you'll encounter these devices again and again on the canal. They are pools, enclosed by more or less watertight gates, in which the barges were raised on their way upstream and lowered on their way downstream so the canal itself could be level and without current. Of course, the locks are no longer in use, but kids love to pretend that they are working the rusty, crusty old cranks.

Below Point Pleasant you'll experience an unusual sensation—you'll almost feel as if you are walking on water. That's because the towpath here straddles a narrow embankment, with the river on your left and the canal on your right, and not a house or soul to be seen on either shore.

Perhaps you'll see a couple of canal canoeists (rentals available in Point Pleasant), but this is not likely except on weekends. At least not until you reach Lumberville, a somnolent settlement whose roadside marker was graffiti'd to read "Slumberville" and stayed that way for years. About 170 refugees from suburbia live here in fieldstone and brightly painted colonial homes that date back a century or two, nestled between the canal and the lush hillsides of the Delaware Valley.

The village boasts a unique feature—a walking bridge. This narrow span, on which even bicycling is barred, crosses the Delaware River to the public parklands of Bulls Island on the New Jersey side (camping permitted). Within a few steps of the bridge, in Lumberville, are three places to lodge if you're spending the night: the Black Bass Inn (antique and candlelight romantic) and the 1740 House (less antique but with a small swimming pool to make up for it), both right on the canal; and the Bridgeview House, a proud mansion that lets out gracious guest rooms.

In the Bucolic Boonies

The next segment—3.3 miles from the Lumberville lift locks to the highway bridge at Center Bridge—is devoid of settlements. Route 32, the "River Road," climbs out of sight up and away into the rhododendron-jungled hills. The towpath, meanwhile, after about a mile on the dike that separates river and canal, meanders through wondrous woods, past mossy ponds and sparkling brooks. About two-thirds along the way are some picnic tables, but most wanderers prefer to spread their lunches on the green.

Center Bridge also has a country hostelry, the Center Bridge Inn, with some newly fixed-up guest rooms. Downstairs is one of the favored local watering holes.

More Nostalgia and Such

From Center Bridge it's 3.2 miles to New Hope, the only village on the canal that regularly draws tourist crowds. Enroute you'll pass Phillips Mill, a cozy cluster of stone cottages whose oldest structure, once a grist mill, dates back to 1756. It's now the setting of a tea room—a nice spot to stop for refreshments.

Soon after that you'll enter New Hope. Charming small

(and not so small) homes, ranging from the traditional to the unconventional, now line the canal's banks. You practically walk through their gardens. As you approach the center of town, ducking under rattling bridges that carry New Hope's street traffic over the canal, the towpath turns into a lively promenade. On weekends every few feet some hopeful artist has an easel set up, and almost everyone carries a camera. Few scenes are more picturesque than this waterway, framed here by the ivied walls of period houses.

Most popular is the section between the Ferry and Mechanic Street bridges, both of which have stairs leading down to the towpath. Here again the canal goes through locks and crosses an aqueduct, this one over Aquetong Creek, whose glen cuts right through the village.

New Hope, which traces its history back to a William Penn deed of 1700, is justly (and profitably) proud of its quaintness and certainly makes the most of it. Part art colony, part tourist attraction, it keeps itself spruced up. Boutiques and galleries line its narrow streets and you'll want to go browsing.

A Splendid House Museum

A must on your New Hope tour, which will add no more than a half mile to your trek, is the Parry Mansion, maintained by the local historical society. There are 11 rooms, each furnished from a different period, spanning the 1770s to the turn of our century. The mansion is open most days from May through September during the usual daylight hours. Admission is: adults, $1.25; children, 50 cents.

Across Main Street from the Parry Mansion is the famous Bucks County Playhouse, and across Ferry Street, the Logan Inn, which serves good meals. For an unusual snack, amble up South Main to Gerenser's Exotic Ice Cream store, which sells undreamed-of flavors. And down South Main is the Information Center, where you can find out all sorts of things about New Hope. Most important, it has rest rooms. (For general information on the whole area, contact the Bucks County Historical-Tourist Commission, One Oxford Valley, Suite 410, Langhorne, Pennsylvania 19047.)

The Trail of 1776

Continue south along the towpath from New Hope, and you'll come upon a place that lives on in history—the river banks where George Washington crossed the Delaware on Christmas night of 1776 to wallop the Hessians at Trenton. It was a master stroke. The Redcoats, having celebrated with abandon, were too drunk to put up much of a fight.

Next, 1.6 miles south of New Hope, you can visit the Thompson-Neely House, the "House of Decision," where Washington and his adjutant James Monroe, then a mere lieutenant, planned the attack. The 1702 farmhouse, beautifully restored and authentically furnished, is open daily except on major holidays from 9 to 4:30. You pay 50 cents (under 12, free), and this also gets you into the Old Ferry Inn farther down in the lower section of Washington Crossing Park.

Meanwhile, you might want to take a detour across Route 32 to see a reconstructed grist mill. From there climb straight up Bowman's Hill—a 20-minute scramble—to the fortresslike tower on top that marks the spot from which Washington's scouts peered across the river to make sure there were no enemy troops waiting with muskets loaded and rarin' to practice their marksmanship. The tower is not open, but the view is available to all.

The attack was finally launched about 3 miles downriver (4.1 miles along the towpath) in what is now the southern section of Washington Crossing Park at Washington Crossing, Pennsylvania. It is here in the Memorial Building that you'll find a copy of the famed Emanuel Leutze painting of *Washington Crossing the Delaware.* An appropriately dramatic narration accompanies your inspection, and there's also a film. Nearby, within a few yards of where Washington embarked, is the McConkey Ferry Inn, which you can visit with the House of Decision ticket.

Interestingly enough, a plaque on the inn states that Washington crossed the Delaware a number of times that night—which would seem to indicate that his soldiers were none too happy about D-daying it on Christmas Eve and that he had to shuttle back and forth, making sure that everybody climbed aboard. Luckily, the Delaware doesn't get jammed with ice the way Leutze shows it in his paintings—but then the German artist had never been in America and did the canvas from his imagination.

Side-trip Adventures

When you tire of walking, you can take a couple of nice, easy trips out of New Hope. One is the hour-long ride into the interior of Bucks County on the New Hope & Ivyland Railroad (several afternoon departures on weekends from March through November, and also on weekdays July and August). The other is an hour-long barge excursion on the Delaware Canal. Call (215) 862-2842 for the prices and the April-through-October schedule.

Walking the South

VIRGINIA

NATURE TRAILS NEAR NORFOLK
G. S. Bush

You'll find it hard to believe that near sprawling metropolitan Norfolk and almost next door to the bustling boardwalks of Virginia Beach, you can stroll through a wonderful wilderness, far removed from the smells and noise of traffic. This unique preserve—unique not only because of its big-city location but for its remarkable ecology—is Virginia's Seashore State Park, whose 2,800 acres, off U.S. 60, gird Cape Henry on the Chesapeake Bay shoreline and range inland to the swampy banks of Broad Bay.

How to Get There
To get there from Norfolk, take 264 to 44 (Virginia Beach Expressway) or Virginia Beach Boulevard south to Pacific Avenue. Turn left on Pacific—Pacific becomes U.S. 60 West. Continue on Route 60 for about 6 miles until you see the entrance marked Seashore State Park Natural Area on your left.

A Hikers' Paradise
What makes this such a hikers' paradise is that here, in a region where winter is no stranger, you can explore forest and marshlands lush with semi-tropical vegetation: cypresses draped with Spanish moss, live oaks, water lilies, even orchids. Along some stretches, you'd think you are in Florida. Yet more astounding is the discovery that all this exotic flora exists side by side with oak and hickory, holly and maple.

And Seashore State Park isn't the only nature reservation where one can walk through true wilderness without going off on a long trip. Another fine preserve, with equally unusual ad-

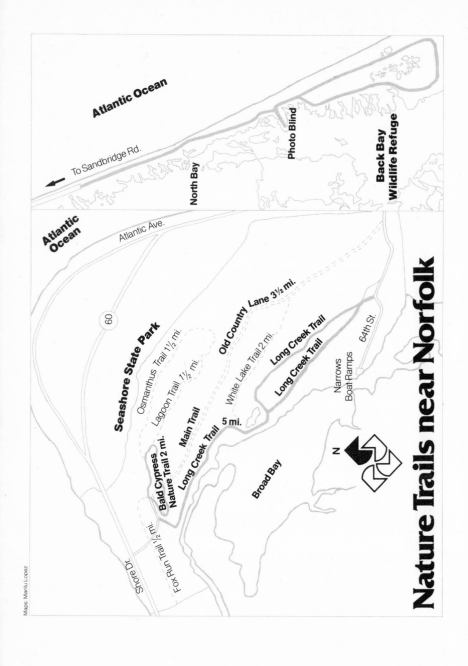

Nature Trails near Norfolk

Atlantic Ocean

To Sandbridge Rd.

North Bay

Photo Blind

Back Bay
Wildlife Refuge

Atlantic
Ocean

Atlantic Ave.

60

Seashore State Park

Osmanthus Trail 1½ mi.

Lagoon Trail 1½ mi.

Old Country Lane 3½ mi.

White Lake Trail 2 mi.

Long Creek Trail

Long Creek Trail

Main Trail

Long Creek Trail

5 mi.

Bald Cypress
Nature Trail 2 mi.

Fox Run Trail 1½ mi.

Shore Dr.

Broad Bay

Narrows
Boat Ramps

64th St.

N

Maps: Marilu Lopez

ventures, lies but 15 miles south of the park—the Back Bay National Wildlife Refuge, which every fall attracts around 125,000 migratory birds, among them huge formations of lovely, sparkling-white geese.

You don't have to be husky backpackers to enjoy either area. Both offer easy, gentle trails of varying length, from ½-mile samplers to all-day excursions. For that matter, the longest trails aren't always the most interesting, although, of course, there's an extra-special joy in penetrating deeply into the wilds.

Seashore State Park alone has more than 30 miles of trails—more than enough for three days of easy hiking. Priority should be given to the self-guiding Bald Cypress Trail, a 2-mile loop (or about an hour's leisurely walk), which passes through several distinct ecological zones.

A Desert Ecology

First you'll find yourself in an arid, semi-desert belt—land that was sand dunes a few thousand years ago. Cape Henry is steadily pushing out into the sea, and as the cape slowly expands, sea oats and dune grasses yield to plants that can survive in sandy soil: yucca and cactus—yes, here in Virginia—the kinds that store precious water. In this region, you're likely to spook some cottontail rabbits, and you'll see skinks (small lizards), tiger beetles, mantises, and possibly a hog-nosed snake, a totally harmless species.

Keep your eye open for tiny pits, about 4 inches across, in the sandy, dry ground. They are ant-lion traps, built by a clever bug that dines on ants. The ant lion hides out in the sand at the bottom of the pit, and when an ant comes tumbling down the side, quickly grabs it with lobersterlike claws. Capture an ant, toss it into one of these pits, and watch carefully: ant lions move very rapidly and are not much larger than their prey.

The Environment Changes—Cypresses Abound

As you proceed along the trail, away from the shore, the country gets scrubbier, with lots of huckleberry (i.e., wild blueberry) bushes all around, and thickets of sassafras, prickly ash, and wax myrtle. Then, suddenly, the surroundings change. You cross a little wooden footbridge, and before you know it you're in a primeval forest of bald cypresses, whose warped "knees" are anchored in dark, still ponds. The cypresses are the oldest living things in the park, some dating back more than 500 years.

The Indians, who once lived and hunted here and picked the huckleberries, used the cypresses' soft moss drapery for towels and diapers, and carved the cypress trunks into dugout canoes.

How Did Pickerel Get Here?
Surprisingly, pickerel and other freshwater fish live in the ponds; you might see some flashing through the water. How they got here was a mystery to naturalists who first examined this area, for the ponds are spring-fed and not connected to any streams. Finally, somebody figured out that herons and other shorebirds must have carried fish eggs on their feet when they came here from other hunting grounds.

Salt Marshes Come to Life at Low Tide
To see the salt marshes that border Broad Bay, you must take the Long Creek Trail, from Fox Run Trail to the southern end of the park, a round trip of about 10 miles. Along this trail, you'll find black fiddler crabs by the hundreds scurrying in the water channels between the clumps of marshgrass. Periwinkle snails feed on the greenery, and at low tide you'll discover whole communities of mussels and oysters. In summer, the marsh hums with dragonflies, their wings aglitter.

Seashore Park: Lovely at Every Season
Indeed, each season has its own special joys. Spring is marked by the new fragrance of shadbush, sweetbay, dogwood, and jasmine. In May, lady slipper orchids start to bloom, followed by foxglove, sourwood, and the sweet pepper bush. As summer progresses, goldenrod appears and the huckleberries darken, and in autumn partridgeberries speckle the underbrush red. As leaves drop from the hardwoods, perching birds become easier to spot: cardinals (usually on the lower branches), mockingbirds, brown thrashers. Then, in winter, with the hardwoods bare, you begin to see all the new plant life that has taken root under the old trees; for instance, there are sturdy young water oaks that remain green right into the New Year. And everywhere there are carpets of true moss, punctuated here and there by resurrection ferns, which often look dead in the dry weather of summer but glow in bright green with winter rains.

The Back Bay Wildlife Refuge

Autumn and winter are the best seasons to explore the Back Bay Wildlife Refuge. The bird migration starts here in mid-October with the advent of black, white, and gray Canada geese. Toward December, the population begins to peak as some 20,000 snow geese fly in from yet farther north. Meanwhile, coots and ducks of all kinds—pintails, canvasbacks, mergansers—start dropping in, reaching their greatest concentration in late December and January. Eventually, the refuge harbors so many birds that its grasslands are covered with them when they browse, and the sky is all but blotted out, and the air reverberates with their flapping and honking when they take to wing.

A 3.2-mile dike road, no longer open to vehicular traffic, extends into the reservation (open daylight to dark). You get there by driving south on Route 615 and turning east on Sandbridge Road (Route 629). As you approach the shore, there'll be signs pointing you to the refuge.

Naturally, you don't have to walk through the whole refuge to observe the birds. Hike in as far as you like and then turn back. In fact, if you want to stroll a little piece, branch off on the first trail you reach—about ¼ mile from the entrance. At the end of this trail, on the bay, is a photo blind where you can hide and wait for birds to come close.

Keep in mind that geese, particularly, are most active early and late in the day, when they scout for new feeding areas. At the height of the day, they tend to stay down and snooze most of the time. This is especially so when the moon is bright, for then they do most of their flying at night. So keep track of the calendar, and schedule your walk here around a new-moon period.

SOUTH CAROLINA

HISTORIC CHARLESTON
G. S. Bush

Here's one of the ironies of history: if the Confederacy had won the Civil War, Charleston wouldn't be the delightful old city it is today. But with the South defeated and its economy destroyed, Charleston—whose rich port had rivaled those of New York and Philadelphia—was left destitute. For decades there was no money to raze old buildings and replace them with new ones, and that's how Charleston became a living museum for the antebellum days.

It's a city for leisurely browsing. At a fast pace, the details would elude you—the intricate ironwork of the balconies and garden gates, the ornamentation chiseled into stone, the plaques that once identified houses in case of fire (each insurance company had its own fire crew that only looked after the company's customers). Indeed, you might even miss Charleston's most telling preservation symbol: the blunt heads of turnbuckles which were used to pull split walls back together after the earthquake of 1886. You'll see those "earthquake bolts," as Charlestonians call them, in the facades of many homes.

You'll not be able to enter most houses, only admire them from outside and envy their occupants—Rainbow Row, for instance, on East Bay Street, and the splendid Simmons-Edward House and Sword Gate House on Legare Street; they are identified on the map. Gardens are another matter. It's a gracious old Charleston tradition to leave the garden gate open to welcome passersby to enjoy the blooms and greenery within. And often they are open. As one sign reads:

> If you would have a mind at peace
> A heart that cannot harden

Walk in this gate that's open wide
Upon a friendly garden.

The Elfe House—a Restored 1760s Home

But to begin your tour you can visit a home, and one of the most interesting at that. Park in the lot on Queen Street located behind the Mills Hyatt House (the lovely lobby of this famed hotel is well worth a look) and head for the Thomas Elfe Workshop. Don't be confused by the name. It's actually a private home built around 1760 by Thomas Elfe, the most renowned furniture maker of that period, to live in and presumably work in.

Ordinarily in a historic house like this you'll encounter ropes across doorways and warnings not to touch anything. Not so here. Betty and Francis Brenner, an energetic retired couple who restored the house a few years ago, let you walk anywhere you like, touch anything you like, and even ask you to sit down in exact reproductions of its original chairs while they explain Elfe's remarkable workmanship. The house is open weekdays 10 to 5, Saturdays 10 to 1, and the admission is $1.50.

Catercorner from the Elfe Workshop you'll see the French Huguenot Church, which has an interesting story. The Huguenots worked plantations upriver and came to town in boats. To keep them from being stranded, services were always scheduled according to the tides. Across the street from the church is the Dock Street Theatre, on the site of one of the first playhouses in North America and the 1809 Planter's Hotel. Both phases have been preserved in the structure's renovation so that, most curiously, you walk into the theater auditorium through a hotel lobby (daily 10 to 4, free). Then take a short side trip down cobblestoned Chalmers Street to drop in at the Old Slave Mart, which was used as a slave auction market prior to the Civil War. It's now a small museum of African and American Black culture (daily 10 to 5, Sundays 2 to 5; admission $1, children 35 cents).

The Hunley Museum

At 50 Broad Street, on the corner of Church, the Hunley Museum is easy to spot in summer by the pink glow of crepe myrtle in its front yard. This 1797 building, which originally housed a bank, is now the repository of the first submarine that saw action. This tiny Confederate warship, fashioned from a steam boiler and with a primitive torpedo attached to a spar in its prow, blew up a Union sloop in 1864, then sank in Charleston harbor alongside its prey. You can inspect the reproduction of the *Hunley,* together with related exhibits, from 10 to 5 weekdays, 1 to 5 Sundays; admission is free.

Catfish Row

Keep your eyes open as you proceed down Church Street. You'll be passing a courtyard lined with "Charleston single houses." That's Catfish Row, made famous by DuBose Heyward, who used it as the setting of his *Porgy.* The Heyward-Washington House, just beyond Catfish Row, did not belong to the author, however. This 1772 Georgian mansion was the home of Thomas Heyward, one of the signers of the Declaration of Independence, and George Washington really slept there: it was leased to him in 1791. The house is filled with authentic Charleston furniture throughout, and has a lovely garden and a separate kitchen house (also refurbished) in back. It's open daily 10 to 5. Admission is $1.75; under 16, 50 cents.

But before you go in, take a good look across the street. Here is a row of three perfect "Charleston single houses." This unique architectural style was developed to provide natural air conditioning: the front doesn't face the street but looks sideways into a garden, in the direction of the prevailing winds. Cooled slightly by the greenery, the breeze then blows through the house, which is only one room wide. A refreshing idea, and most charming.

Opulent Mansions Overlooking the Harbor

The next home you'll visit is a grandiose example of this type—really a double-wide. It's the Edmondston-Alston House, at 21 East Battery Street, whose windows on the East Battery overlook the blue expanse of Charleston's harbor. The Alston family bought the place in 1838 and fixed it up in Greek Revival fashion; moreover, they were insatiable collectors and apparently hung on to everything that ever crossed their threshold. They turned the house into a treasure trove of opulent furniture, silver, china, paintings. When you enter, be sure to buy $3 combination tickets that also include admission to the Nathaniel Russell House later on this tour (both houses open 10 to 5 weekdays, 2 to 5 Sundays).

Historic Charleston

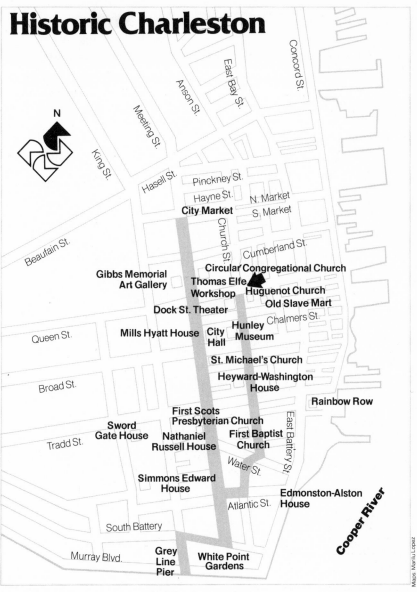

This walking tour is approximately 2¼ miles round trip.

Maps: Marilu Lopez

Charleston Harbor—Where the Civil War Began

But before you continue your walk toward the Russell mansion, take time out to explore the harbor that played such an important role in our history. At the foot of King Street, right next to the White Point Gardens of the Battery, is the Grey Line Pier where you can board the stern-wheeler *Charles Towne Belle* for 2-hour cruises; there are up to five departures daily, depending on the season (adults, $3.50; children, $2). You'll steam past Fort Sumter, target of the cannon shot that started the Civil War; past Fort Moultrie, where South Carolinians repulsed the British Fleet in 1776; through the U.S. Navy base, with its submarines, minesweepers, and destroyers; and along today's bustling commercial port—a fascinating sight, but you'll have to imagine the era when countless sailing ships called here to fill their holds with rice and cotton.

That's when Nathaniel Russell made his fortune, and as you'll see when you reach his house on Meeting Street, he was no piker. In the year 1800, when a dollar a day was generous pay, he sank $80,000 into the place. An astonishing flying staircase spirals without support from the entrance hall (in one place the plaster has been replaced by glass so you can examine the stairs' construction), and Russell's opulent rooms are all different shapes, some elliptical, others oblong, rectangular, square, and each filled with priceless furnishings.

Now from the sublime to the eccentric.

City Hall

In most towns you wouldn't waste time on City Hall, but Charleston's has a portrait gallery on its second floor (open only weekdays during office hours). Among the pictures—Jackson, Monroe, Calhoun, etc.—is also one of Washington with his horse, and this one deserves a closer look. When John Trumbull painted it, he originally had Princeton, New Jersey, in the background. The city fathers of Charleston insisted that he wipe out Princeton and paint in Charleston, which made the artist mad. He did as asked, but he delicately raised the horse's tail over Charleston.

You can see another historical oddity in the churchyard of St. Michael's—across Broad Street from City Hall. When Mary Ann Luyton died in 1770, her husband didn't have money for a gravestone, so he marked her eternal resting place with the family bedstead. Made of cypress, it's still there today.

The City Market

Your itinerary—check the map for other points of interest—ends at the City Market, whose sheds date back to 1809. Today, most of it is occupied by craft shops and antique shops and a funky flea market, although in one area fresh produce is still sold. But the best part of today's market is the "Market Square" next door—a gaily decorated hall, whose walls are lined with snackeries serving soups, pizza, crepes, salads. You take your stuff to the tables in the center and munch away.

GEORGIA

ATLANTA'S PEACHTREE STREET
Diane C. Thomas

In Margaret Mitchell's enduring portrait of the Old South, *Gone with the Wind,* Aunt Pittypat and Scarlett and Rhett Butler lived on Peachtree Street. This street was "the" fashionable address for countless prominent real-life Atlantans until well past the turn of the century.

Serving first as Atlanta's most exclusive residential corridor and evolving into a sought-after commercial and retailing address, Peachtree is one of the most famous streets in the South. Like the rest of Atlanta and the South, it juxtaposes the old and the new. This walk through the center of Atlanta takes you through much of the city's early history as well as its spectacular recent development.

Zero Mile Post—Underground Atlanta
To begin our walk at the beginning of Atlanta, it is necessary to start a little to the east of Peachtree Street—under the Central Avenue Viaduct in Underground Atlanta.

A 25-cent admission charge admits you to this area that was once Old Atlanta, now a maze of boutiques, restaurants and "museums" with a turn-of-the-century motif. Here you will find the Zero Mile Post, driven into the ground in 1837 to mark a point judged most convenient for the branching of railroads in northern Georgia and creating an upland community in the wilderness appropriately called "Terminus."

In 1847, the booming railroad town it had become was officially chartered as Atlanta.

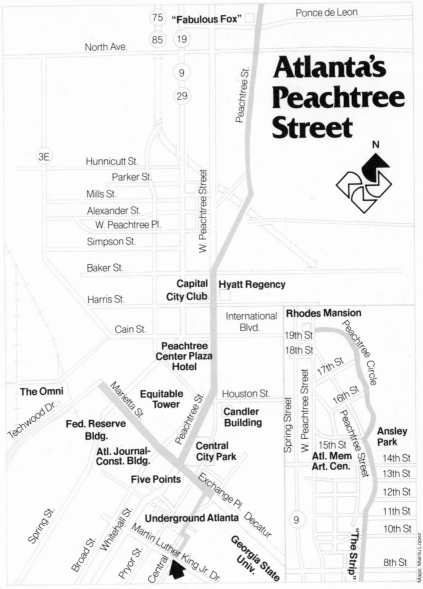

Atlanta's Peachtree Street

75 "Fabulous Fox"   Ponce de Leon

85 19

North Ave.

9

29

N

3E

Hunnicutt St.

Parker St.

Mills St.

Alexander St.

W. Peachtree Pl.

Simpson St.

Baker St.

Capital   Hyatt Regency
City Club

Harris St.   International   Rhodes Mansion
Blvd.
19th St

Cain St.   18th St

Peachtree   17th St
Center Plaza
Hotel   16th St

The Omni   Equitable   Houston St.
Tower
Fed. Reserve   Candler   Ansley
Bldg.   Building   Park
Atl. Journal-   Central   15th St   14th St
Const. Bldg.   City Park   Atl. Mem
Art. Cen.   13th St
Five Points
12th St

Underground Atlanta   11th St

10th St
Georgia State
Univ.   8th St

Peachtree St.

W. Peachtree Street

Marietta St.

Techwood Dr.

Peachtree St.

Exchange Pl.

Spring St.

Broad St.

Whitehall St.

Pryor St.

Central

Martin Luther King Jr. Dr.

Decatur

Spring Street

W. Peachtree Street

Peachtree Circle

Peachtree Street

"The Strip"

9

Maps: Marilu Lopez

This walking tour is approximately 5 miles long.

Five Points

Climb the stairs to Central Avenue, thread your way around construction for Atlanta's new subway system, turn right, and walk north. To your right, you will see Georgia State University. The yellow-brick building—a converted parking garage—was where this urban university got its start just over 30 years ago. Turn left in front of it onto Exchange Place. Head up the hill, to the west. On your right, you will pass Central City Park. This plot of valuable downtown property was purchased for the City of Atlanta in the early 1970s by an anonymous donor. It has become a favored luncheon spot for downtown office workers and the site of many noontime concerts and entertainments.

Cross the street, and you arrive at Five Points, the historical center of Atlanta. In the town's earliest days, this convergence of streets was the site of an artesian well and a popular meeting place for the citizenry. Today it is the heart of the city's thriving business and financial district.

Omni International

From here, you can walk 6 blocks west on Marietta Street to the Omni International complex at the southwest corner of Marietta and Techwood. On the left, you will pass the Atlanta *Journal-Constitution* Building, which houses both the city's daily newspapers, and next to it, the imposing marble Federal Reserve Building, erected in the early 1970s. The 101 Marietta Street building is another Atlanta landmark, with its striking glass facade.

At Omni International—a breathtaking 15-story covered "megastructure"—you may take a turn on the indoor ice rink, stop at one of several restaurants, browse in the international bazaar, and shop at such elegant emporia as the Houses of Hermes and Lanvin, Pucci, the Brothers Christie Fur Salon, the Arnold Gallery, and Rizzoli Bookstore. The complex also includes a hotel and two office buildings. It is contiguous to the Omni Coliseum, home of the Hawks and the Flames, and to the Georgia World Congress Center convention facility.

After touring Omni International, retrace your steps to Five Points and turn north on Peachtree Street.

The Candler Building

On your left, you will pass the Equitable tower. Its fountain is a gathering place for noontime girl watchers.

On your right, where Houston Street (pronounce it "house-ton") crosses Peachtree, a fine example of one of the city's earliest "skyscrapers" is the 17-story Candler Building.

Built in 1904 by Asa G. Candler, founder of the Coca-Cola Company, it was recently renovated and rents as prestige downtown office space. Carvings of noted figures from the arts and sciences, including Shakespeare, Wagner, Michelangelo and Raphael, embellish the external marble panels. Marble portraits of Candler's parents and other persons judged important to the South—"Uncle Remus" creator Joel Chandler Harris and poet Sidney Lanier among them—are found in niches in the lobby's ornamental frieze.

Peachtree Center

Proceeding north on Peachtree Street, look up 72 stories to the top of the Peachtree Center Plaza Hotel on the southwest corner of Peachtree and Cain Streets. (The latter is more frequently referred to now as "International Boulevard.") Designed by internationally famous Atlanta architect John Portman and completed in 1975, the Plaza is the tallest hotel in the world. The ground-floor lobby features an interior lake, and an exterior elevator, affording a magnificent view, carries visitors to a revolving restaurant at the top.

Continuing up Peachtree Street, you will pass on your right and left several coordinated white office towers. Also designed by Portman, they comprise the Peachtree Center complex, which includes, in addition to the office buildings, a shopping gallery, outdoor cafe, restaurants, and a dinner theater.

On the northwest corner of Peachtree and Harris Streets is the Capital City Club. Founded in 1883, it is Atlanta's oldest private club. Its current headquarters was completed in 1911.

In the next block, on the right, is architect John Portman's other Atlanta hotel, the Hyatt Regency. The structure, which has been widely imitated, was the first to feature the now familiar soaring interior courtyard. When the hotel first opened in 1967, its tunnellike entranceway was nicknamed "profanity corner" by the local press after the thousands of astounded sightseers who passed through looked up 22 stories to the hotel's distinctive blue bubble top, and said, "----!"

Like the Plaza, the Regency is topped by a revolving restaurant. The brown glass cylinder to the southeast is a recent addition.

A little farther north on Peachtree Street, bear right at the small triangular park. To your right, you will see the graceful spires of the Church of the Sacred Heart. On your left you will pass First Methodist Church. Behind it you can see the Peachtree Summit glass office building, a striking example of the juxtaposition of the old and new coexisting peaceably.

The "Fabulous Fox"

At the intersection of Peachtree and Ponce de Leon, on the northwest corner, stands the Fox Theater, referred to from its opening day as the "Fabulous Fox."

Originally begun as a Masonic Temple and completed in 1929 for use as a motion-picture theater, it seats 4,500 in an interior designed as a lavish imitation of a Moorish courtyard, replete with minarets, colonnades, a midnight-blue "sky" with "stars" and even puffy white clouds that float by on a revolving drum (not currently operational).

In the early '70s, the Fox was purchased by Southern Bell Telephone Company, which intended to raze it as part of its prospective headquarters site until the building became the target of a preservation campaign. Today it serves as a splendid addition to Atlanta's auditoria.

The Georgian Terrace Hotel across the street was completed in 1911 and for years served as the "home" of Metropolitan Opera stars during the weeks the Met performed at the Fox. The adjacent Ponce de Leon Apartments were completed in 1913 and boasted Atlanta's first penthouse.

The Strip

The rambling rose-colored mansion you glimpse on your left at 848 Peachtree Street, almost entirely obscured by a red-brick office building, was built in 1892 for a local railroad president. Today it functions as the headquarters for a variety of nonprofit public service organizations under the name of "Metanoia"—Greek word for changing direction.

The intersection of Peachtree and 10th streets is the center of "The Strip." Known after the Civil War as "Tight Squeeze," it was a forest camp for hoboes and criminals and it was said to be "a tight squeeze to get through it with your life." Later, as Atlanta's residential district moved northward, "Tight Squeeze" became a fine neighborhood commercial center of shops, restaurants and theaters. After World War II, when Atlanta's suburbs began to grow, the area began to decline. In the early '70s, largely because of the proximity of then inexpensive apartment housing, it functioned as the center of Atlanta's hippie community. They named it "The Strip."

With the passing of the hippies, much of the area was abandoned. It is now being reclaimed to provide shops and services for Midtown and Ansley Park, two fine old nearby residential areas which have recently undergone restoration.

The complex of white buildings to the northeast of 14th Street is Colony Square, a "micropolis" consisting of offices, shops, a hotel, apartments, and condominiums. Built by Atlanta developer Jim Cushman, it was designed by Jova/Daniels/Bushbee, the architectural firm responsible for the "look" of Underground Atlanta.

Ansley Park

At the northwest corner of Peachtree and 15th streets, you will see Atlanta Memorial Arts Center, which houses the High Museum of Art, the Atlanta Symphony, and the Alliance Theater.

To your left is Ansley Park. First developed in 1904, many of the city's finest homes are in it. The neighborhood began to attract restorationists in the mid-1960s and is today the proud address of many of the city's young professionals. The Georgia Governor's Mansion was in Ansley Park until 1967, when it was replaced by a newer structure on West Paces Ferry Road.

For a closer look at the homes of Ansley Park, turn off Peachtree Street and follow Peachtree Circle.

Rhodes Hall

Where Peachtree Circle rejoins Peachtree Street, on the northwest corner, is the imposing gray stone Rhodes Mansion, its turrets and battlements inspired by Rhineland castles. Completed in 1905, it was the home of a prominent local furniture dealer. Now part of the Georgia Department of Archives and History, it is open from 8 until 4:30. Its fine interior detailing is worth examining, and its employees may be able to answer questions that have been raised by your walking tour on the history of Atlanta and its famous Peachtree Street.

Return via Marta Bus

Peachtree Street continues northward to Buckhead—an elegant residential community—and beyond, but at this point our walking tour concludes. At the sign in front of Rhodes Hall, you can catch one of the striped buses of the Metropolitan Atlanta Rapid Transit Authority (MARTA) for a quick and inexpensive ride back to town. Debark on Walton Street, go a block east to Central City Park, and retrace your steps to Central Avenue and Underground Atlanta, where it all began.

FLORIDA

MIAMI: FROM KEY BISCAYNE TO FAIRCHILD GARDEN
G. S. Bush

Don't just take Miami lying down—there's lots more here than lounge chairs lined up against wall-to-wall hotels. For instance, you can stride for miles along a beach that's so secluded you might encounter skinny-dippers. Then there's Vizcaya, a multimillionaire's dream house, now a museum where you can stroll through extravagant halls and stunning gardens like those you see in Italy. And for a window-shopping, people-watching promenade, you'll like Coconut Grove, Miami's own little Carmel-by-the-Sea, whose ambience blends the funky with the fashionable. Finally, you can explore a splendid park, the Fairchild Tropical Garden, 83 acres of floral exotica, of which most Gold Coast visitors have never even heard.

All this on a 15-mile arc around the blue Biscayne Bay, within freeway minutes of downtown.

Walk Along the Beach at Key Biscayne
Your beach walk takes you up the Atlantic shore of Key Biscayne, first of the keys that gird Florida's tip, and the first to have left its mark on history. John Cabot charted it in 1497, Ponce de Leon soon followed, and the island then became a pirate haven. It's said that some 26 tons of silver lie buried in its palmetto thickets. Not that you are likely to find Black Caesar's cache. Many other optimists have tried—and failed.

Leave your car at the southern point of the key, in Cape Florida State Park. Before you begin your walk, climb the 98-foot-high lighthouse, which was built of brick 132 years ago after raiding Indians burned its smaller wooden predecessor

The areas pictured on this map are not true to scale but are enlarged to show more detail.

Coconut Grove

Commodore Plaza

Fuller

S. Bayshore Drive

Parking

Grand Avenue

Blue Water Marine Supplies

Strawthings
Key West
Hand-Print Fashions

La Petite Patissierie
Monty Trainer's Village Inn
The Barnacle

Charles Avenue

Peacock Park

McFarlane Rd.

Coconut Grove Playhouse

Main Hwy.

N

5 mi.

Traffic Circle
Old Cutler Rd. (2nd Rd. off Circle)

Fairchild Tropical Garden

The Coconut Grove walk is approximately 2½ miles round trip.

The Fairchild Garden walk is approximately 1½ miles round trip.

U.S.I.

Rickenbacker Causeway

S. Miami Avenue

Mangroves

Marina

Vizcaya

Crandon Blvd.

Crandon Park

Parking
Miami Zoo

'acht Basin

Key Biscayne

Biscayne Bay

Atlantic Ocean

**Towers of
Key Biscayne**

Cape Fl. State Park

Miami:
From Key Biscayne
to Fairchild Gardens

Cape Florida

Lighthouse

The complete Crandon Park walk is 4 miles. The walk to the Miami Zoo
is 2½ miles. Buses are available to take you back to your car.

(open daily 9—4, 25 cents). The panorama is a stunner: in flat
Florida you rarely get this kind of view except from airplanes.
To the east, out at sea, you see the busy shipping lanes of the
Gulf Stream. To the west you look across the sprawling city of
Miami, right into the Everglades. To the north, Key Biscayne lies
at your feet, and you can trace the whole length of the beach
you'll walk. Beyond, the hotel skyline of Miami Beach huddles
on the horizon.

The first mile of your walk you'll be in the state park, its
beach backed by forest, sea grape, and feathery ferns. The next
mile takes you past the community of Key Biscayne, ushered in
by the Towers of Key Biscayne, the fanciest condominium in
these fancy parts. Then comes a string of hotels. Unlike those in
Miami Beach, they sit well back from the surf, leaving you
plenty of room for beachcombing. Among them is the Key Biscayne Hotel, scene of many top-level meetings during the
Nixon administration. You may recognize it by its cottages that
perch on the bluff above the beach—the second one you come
to is where Kissinger often stayed.

Crandon Park—The Miami Zoo

Beyond the hotels, you'll find yourself in Crandon Park, a
municipal recreation area that's crowded with suntan traffic on
weekends but nearly empty during the week. At its northern
end, the beach is shielded by mangroves; that's the corner popular with folks who insist on tans all over. To get back to where
you parked your car, round the beach here and cross the Rickenbacker Causeway to the bus stop at Crandon Marina. If,
however, 4 miles are too much for you, you can leave the
beach earlier, about 2½ miles from the lighthouse, and catch
the same bus in front of the Miami Zoo in Crandon Park.

The zoo is worth a detour in any case. Its special pride is
the rare aardvark, a most comical-looking creature that sucks up
ants with its vacuum-cleaner tongue. Altogether some 1,000
animals of 350 different species are on display, and if you happen to be taking the beach walk in the afternoon you might
want to time yourself to arrive at the zoo in time for the daily
3:30 feeding. The zoo is open 9:30 to 4:30; admission 50 cents.

On to Vizcaya—a Multimillionaire's Fantasy Home

Next, Vizcaya, for which you must drive back to the mainland; you turn left onto S. Miami Avenue right after you exit

from Rickenbacker Causeway then left again. Even as you enter the estate, you know that you're in for an extraordinary experience. Vizcaya's driveway winds through a mysterious tropical hardwood hammock of gumbo limbo, banyan trees, and ebony, overhung with vines, dappled with light and shadow. Then suddenly you're looking at the place that seems to have been lifted in one piece from 16th-century Tuscany.

Which, indeed, it almost was. The basic structure was built of native Florida limestone, cut on the site, but all its appurtenances came from abroad: the fawns and nymphs, the stairs and columns of marble, the gates from a Venetian *palazzo*, the Renaissance ceilings from Rome. The priceless furnishings are no less exquisite. James Deering, son of the founder of International Harvester, really splurged when he built this villa in 1914. Luckily he had good taste, or he could have ended up with a monstrosity.

There's even a limestone ship, out in the bay in front of the Great House: it's a copy of the famous stone barge—a sort of giant planter—that fronts the Villa Borromeo in Lake Maggiore. The gardens, too, are landscaped in the Italian manner, a maze of levels, vistas, fountains, and grottos, presided over by a Baroque *glorietta*, a gazebo-like structure, perfect for aristocratic trysting. Vizcaya is open daily from 9:30 to 5:30. The $3 admission (students, $1.50; children, $1) includes guided tours of the villa by volunteer guides. In the gardens, though, you may stroll on your own.

The Shops at Coconut Grove

While Vizcaya is out of this world—who nowadays could hire 1,000 workmen to build his vacation home?—the neat shopping district of Coconut Grove is strictly with it, a cornucopia of odds and ends no one truly needs but which are delightful to shop for: jewelry, crystal, pottery, paintings, bric-a-brac, fad foods, gorgeously wild-colored fabrics (Key West Handprint Fashions), French pastries (La Petite Patisserie), things made of straw (Straw Things, where else?)—in short, everything the affluent heart may desire.

The place to park for Coconut Grove is the Dinner Key Marina, about two miles south on Bayshore Drive from Vizcaya. Hundreds of craft of every style, size, and cost are moored here. Oceangoing cruisers, hosting lavish cocktail parties on their poop decks, look down on happy-go-lucky houseboats whose proprietors are more inclined to share potluck. When you walk from here into Coconut Grove, you can see one of the places where these boaters obtain their paraphernalia: the Blue Water Marine Supply store, which carries an intriguing array of merchandise like shipboard radios, radar units, compasses, boat shoes, water skis, lifebelts, fittings, fixtures.

Also, if you have the time, be sure to visit the Barnacle, an old homestead on the bay shore of Coconut Grove, deep in a gumbo limbo jungle. And, around the Coconut Grove Players Theatre corner, take a look down Charles Street with its original "Conch" cottages. These were the homes in the 1800s of the first Blacks on the Florida mainland; they came from the Bahamas to work at the Peacock Inn, the first of the Miami hotels and now long gone: it stood in Coconut Grove, not "on the Beach."

For lunch, try Monty Trainer's Village Inn, with specialties like gazpacho and Monterey Jack cheese dishes.

Fairchild Tropical Garden

Another 5 miles south—see map for route—and you're at the Fairchild Tropical Garden, a truly outstanding botanical preserve where you'll find palm trees from remote Pacific islands, breadfruit trees, parrot's flowers, and a rain forest. As if the plants in the park were not rare enough, there's a "Rare Plant House" for such esoterica as bat flowers from Malaya, wax palms from Borneo, and tree ferns from the West Indies.

The garden is open daily from 10 to 4:30; admission $2, under 16 free. If you're too tired by now to cover it all on foot— the developed walkway loop runs on for about 1½ miles—you can take a tram tour, which leaves from the gate every hour on the hour from 11 to 4. The ride takes about 40 minutes and costs $1.

LOUISIANA

NEW ORLEANS: THE FRENCH QUARTER
G. S. Bush

New Orleans is best when its lights begin to sparkle in the dusk
and the musicians get turned on. That's the time to lounge on
the lacy iron balcony of the Embers, sip a drink slowly, and let
yourself be steeped in the cacophony of Dixieland pulsing up at
you from the joints on Bourbon Street. This is the heartbeat of
the city, and here, at the corner of Bourbon and St. Peter in the
French Quarter, you feel it more profoundly than anywhere
else.

But much of the magic would elude you if you hadn't first
looked at the day face of the city and learned what makes this
old town tick: its past that reaches way back to the heyday of the
Spanish Empire. Jean Lafitte, the pirate, frequented its taverns.
Napoleon Bonaparte's supporters gathered in the French
Quarter—the Vieux Carré (Old Square), as it's still called—to
plot the emperor's return from Elba. Jim Bowie came through
en route to Texas, his "iron mistress," the famous Bowie knife,
snug by his side. Andrew Jackson stood in Jackson Square to
offer a *Te Deum* after the Battle of New Orleans. All the while,
of course, immense wealth found its way here, creating enclaves
of luxury and prompting a general predisposition for living as
high on the hog as one could reach.

On your exploration, you'll stroll the old streets of the
Vieux Carré, a unique alchemy of 19th-century Europe, ancient
Africa, and neon America. You'll also take a stern-wheeler tour
on the Mississippi, whose murky waters are the city's lifeblood.
If there's time left, you might catch a streetcar named St.
Charles Avenue Trolley (Desire is now a bus), and ride out to
the Garden District, a preserve of splendid mansions. Finally,

well after dark, you'll visit Preservation Hall, the shrine of jazz. As you can see, it'll be a busy, long day.

Begin at Brennan's

So start fairly early, and consider stoking up for your adventures by eating breakfast at Brennan's, an expensive tradition (from about $10 a person up) but in keeping with New Orleans' preoccupation with its palate: perhaps milk punch followed by oyster soup, veal grillades, grits, and flaming Creole cream cheese. An optimist's overture for lunch.

Catercorner from Brennan's, in the columned edifice that originally housed the Bank of Louisiana at 334 Royal Street, is the Tourist and Convention Bureau, where you can pick up helpful brochures. More long-ago banks are across the street: the Old Bank of the United States and the Old Louisiana State Bank, both now occupied by antiquaries as monied as these banks once were. The Manheim Galleries in the latter are particularly intriguing. A sign invites you to see the jade collection, largest on sale in the Western Hemisphere, about $3 million worth of vases and statuary in hues ranging from mint to apple-green to lavender (very rare), all delicately veined, carved and polished with Oriental skill. This visit tells you of New Orleans' richness and educated taste.

The Jazz Museum

Next comes its musical history. For that, you drop in at the Jazz Museum (10–5 Tuesday through Saturday; admission $1, children 50 cents). With Dixieland drumming from speakers in the background, you can examine a "family tree" that traces the descent of jazz from Africa through numerous ethnic marriages to its most recent offspring, like bop, rock, and the new disco beat. Displayed in wall cases are the instruments—grown beautiful with use and age—of jazz greats, Louis Armstrong's trumpet and Sidney Bechet's soprano sax among them.

Historic Homes—Survivors of the Fire of 1794

Around the block, on St. Louis, you can get your first indoor glimpse of the New Orleans life-style: the Hermann-Grima House, built in the 1820s (open daily except Wednesday 10–4, Sunday, 1–5; $1.50, students 75 cents). But there'll be more such interesting old homes along your route, and if you don't

New Orleans: The French Quarter

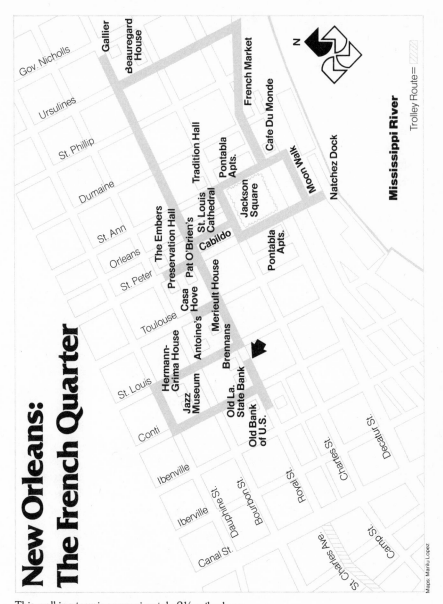

Maps: Marilú López

This walking tour is approximately 2½ miles long.

want to see all of them save your money for the others, especially the Gallier House.

Coming up next, however, when you turn back on Royal
after passing Antoine's famed restaurant, is the Merieult House,
which dates back to 1792 when New Orleans was still under
Spanish rule. The Merieult House, one of the few structures of
that period to survive (most of the city burned down in 1794),
contains the Historic New Orleans Collection of prints, paintings, and documents and houses the 1812 Louisiana Constitution (Tuesday through Saturday, 10–5; guided tours, $1; chil-
dren, 50 cents). Next door is the Pearl Factory, a store where
you can pick your own oyster out of a bucket for $6: you are
guaranteed at least one pearl. An inebriated customer recently
gulped two of the oysters, pearls and all, before he could be
stopped. He didn't even notice that they were pickled in for-
maldehyde.

Now take a detour on Toulouse to the Casa Hove, circa
1725, another survivor of the New Orleans conflagration.
Downstairs is a perfume shop that blends its own exotic scents;
upstairs are restored living quarters filled with priceless antiques
(weekdays 10–4:30; 50 cents).

Jackson Square

Cut through quaint Pirates Alley—a misnomer since it
wasn't there yet in freebooter days—to reach Jackson Square,
the grand concourse of the Vieux Carré. Originally the parade
ground of the Spaniards, it's now the site of a permanent show
by dozens of sidewalk artists: a delightful scene if you don't look
too closely at the paintings.

Jackson Square is flanked by the Pontalba buildings, magnificent row houses dating back to 1849, with shops and restaurants on the ground floors. At the head of the square stands St.
Louis Cathedral, the country's oldest, with fine stained-glass
windows. The present structure was built in 1794 after a hurri-
cane destroyed its predecessor, a 1722 parish church. Adjoining
the cathedral is the Cabildo, where the Spanish governors held
forth. Today it houses exhibits of the Louisiana State Museum,
including Napoleon's death mask (daily except Monday 9–5;
$1; under 12, 50 cents). Also nearby, on St. Anne, is Tradition
Hall, where you can sometimes catch an afternoon jazz concert.

Down to the Levee

The Mississippi levee rises at the lower end of Jackson Square. It is topped by the Moon Walk, a pedestrian promenade with a great view of the city and the port. You'll cross it to reach the dock at the Toulouse Street Wharf, where the *Natchez* picks up passengers for its two-hour cruises, several miles both upriver and downriver, and you've never seen so many ships flying so many different flags—freighters and tankers from Africa, South America, the Far East, and Europe, even the Iron Curtain countries. The *Natchez* leaves to the amplified sounds of a calliope and many blasts of its steamwhistle at 11:30 and 2:30 (a good, reasonably priced lunch is served aboard), and again at 7 for a dinner cruise. The cruise fare is $5.50; children 6 to 12 pay $2.25; under 6 free. For lunch, add $3.75 and $2 respectively.

After your boat excursion, walk through the French Market, now in the final stages of restoration as an area of shops, boutiques, eateries, and adjoining a vast vegetable and fruit shed that does a booming business. Stop at the Cafe du Monde for a New Orleans specialty, good any time of day: delicious French doughnuts (*beignets*) washed down with chicory coffee. The combination costs 70 cents.

Two Lovely, Well-Restored Homes

The Beauregard and Gallier houses, the two most interesting open houses, are next on your itinerary. Confederate General Beauregard roomed in the former when he returned, impoverished, from the Civil War; later it was the home of novelist Frances Parkinson Keys (daily 10—4; $1.25, children 75 cents). The Gallier House, lovingly restored and super-elegantly furnished, makes up in splendor what it lacks in glamorous history: if you only want to see one house, this is it (Monday through Friday 9—5; $2.50, children, $1).

A Ride on the St. Charles Trolley

Now, if it's not too late, take your side trip on the St. Charles Street Trolley, which you board at the corner of Canal and St. Charles. The complete round trip out to the University and River Bend areas takes better than an hour, a beautiful ride that will give you a perspective on the newer New Orleans. Or go only as far as the Garden District, with its fine homes, most of which were built just before and after the Civil War. The homes are not open to the public, but you'll enjoy them even from the outside. For each leg on the trolley you will need 30 cents per person. Be sure you have it in exact change—a sign of the times.

Back to the Quarter—Jam Session at Preservation Hall

As night falls, you should be back in the French Quarter, of course, at the corner of Bourbon and St. Peter. Pat O'Brien's Patio, the Vieux Carré's favorite watering hole, is across St. Peter from the Embers, as is Preservation Hall, a must for later. You'll gladly stand in line to pay your $1 donation, then jam into a tight little auditorium with wooden benches, smoky air, rapt faces, and probably tip-toe standing room only, to hear grizzled old jazz greats play. It may be your last chance: their generation is already of the past, and when the last one of them starts marching with the saints, there'll only be records left of the original, authentic Dixieland.

Walking the Southwest

TEXAS

DOWNTOWN DALLAS
G. S. Bush

Any tour of downtown Dallas is, perforce, part pilgrimage. For, no matter where you walk, you are almost bound to touch President John F. Kennedy's last mile, as he rode in triumphal procession down Commerce Street, then briefly right on Houston, then left on Elm—only to keep his date with an assassin's bullet at precisely 12:30 P.M. on November 22, 1963.

Until this fateful hour, while most Americans recognized Dallas as being in Texas, only a few knew more than that. The vast majority had no idea that it was one of the Southwest's largest cities, the market center of one of the country's most productive regions, and indeed one of the first official settlements in its state.

The First Homestead

The fellow who put Dallas on the map to start with, back in 1845, was one John Neely Bryan, who built himself a little log cabin here in the midst of the wide plains, and then proceeded to organize Dallas County, and put up the first post office and the first courthouse in what was then still wilderness. You'll see Bryan's primitive hand-built cabin, since deeded to the city with much of the land around it, when you start your walking tour on Elm Street, between Record and Market. There are several parking lots and garages in this area, so you shouldn't have a problem leaving your car.

Memorials and a Museum—In Honor of J. F. Kennedy

Directly south across Main Street from the weathered Bryan Cabin stands the Kennedy Memorial Cenotaph, a starkly simple quadrangle of native rock, the only structure in this block. Its walls, open to the sky, enclose a black marble slab that bears no inscription other than the slain President's name.

The John F. Kennedy Museum is only a block west of here, at Elm and Record. You'll probably be tempted to head immediately for the site of the assassination, but do stop at the museum first. Its 25-minute slide presentation covers all the events that preceded and followed the murder, and will help you orient yourself when you leave there to cross Houston Street—in effect retracing Lee Harvey Oswald's presumed steps to the Texas School Book Depository. (The John F. Kennedy Museum, whose exhibits also include a rifle like the one used by Oswald, and a model of the PT boat JFK skippered in World War II, is open daily 9 to 5, and into the evening in summer. The admission is $1.50; children under 5, free.)

Oswald aimed his Mauser from the fourth floor of the School Book Depository, the second window in from Houston Street. Walk down the grassy incline along the freeway access: President Kennedy's open-topped limousine had traveled about halfway to the overpass when he and Texas Governor John Connally were hit. Look up the embankment on the right. That's where, according to some reports, other shots were fired, and indeed you may remember a photograph of a policeman, his gun drawn, racing up that slope immediately after the shooting.

Finally, on this pilgrimage, see the JFK memorial obelisk on Dealey Plaza, which overlooks the assassination scene. The marker stands in a small garden on the west side of Houston Street, above the lawn between the freeway lanes.

The Adolphus Hotel
Now stroll back into the Dallas of today, following Main Street east, past downtown's spectacular high-rises to Akard Street, stretches of which have been turned into a most pleasant mall. At the corner of Commerce, you'll find the Adolphus Hotel, built by brewer Adolphus Busch shortly before World War I. It's undoubtedly the only hotel in the world with a beer bottle on its roof, a 40-foot-high cement replica that's somewhat out of character for this elegant turn-of-the-century edifice. Ornate stone scrollwork adorns the hostelry's walls, and its lobby, filled with heavy furnishings and elaborate chandeliers, reflects

the opulence of an era when paunches were honored as marks of affluence.

New and Adventurous Architecture

Three blocks south of here, you'll come upon the sweeping plazas of the Dallas Convention Center and the new City Hall. Fronting the Convention Center is Pioneer Park, where the city's earliest settlers lie buried, including the aforementioned John Neely Bryan, who died in 1877. The fact that Dallas was in the rebel realm is attested by a fine monument with statues of four Confederate heroes: Gen. Stonewall Jackson, Jefferson Davis, Gen. Robert E. Lee, and Gen. Albert S. Johnston.

The new City Hall, on the other hand, is hardly designed to promote nostalgia. It's bound to be one of the most unusual structures you ever saw. Parts of the building resemble an inverted pyramid: the upper floors, instead of being set back, are cantilevered successively over the lower stories, like a stairway turned upside down.

But adventurous architecture is a Texas specialty these days. Just look back toward downtown from the City Hall plaza. There's, for instance, the shiny metal-encased Republic National Bank Building, and beside it the Republic National Bank Tower with its needlelike steel spire. The Hyatt Regency has an adjacent 50-story revolving restaurant tower (Reunion Tower), and within the hotel is a 19-story atrium, with a waterfall cascading down to the hotel's ballroom level.

The Historical Perspective of Old City Park

When you see such futuristic fantasies, it's almost inconceivable that Dallas wasn't born a science-fiction city. To get a feeling of what it was like in its formative years, you must visit Old City Park. That's about a 20-minute walk south of downtown—good exercise, but not much else, for the intervening surroundings aren't anything special. So you might want to drive there (see map), and make it a separate walking tour after completing the downtown loop.

But, either way, you should go there. It's a wonderful park for a leisurely sightseeing promenade, and it will help you appreciate the city's newly acquired gloss in its historical perspective.

Downtown Dallas

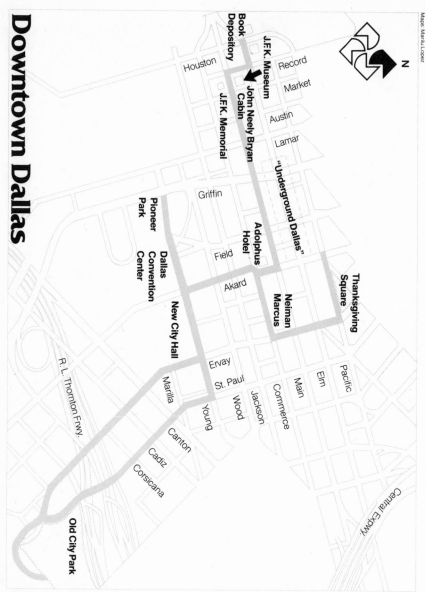

Maps: Marilú López

Book Depository

J.F.K. Museum

John Neely Bryan Cabin

J.F.K. Memorial

Houston

Record

Market

Austin

Lamar

"Underground Dallas"

Griffin

Adolphus Hotel

Field

Akard

Neiman Marcus

Thanksgiving Square

Pioneer Park

Dallas Convention Center

New City Hall

Ervay

St. Paul

Wood

Young

Marilla

Canton

Cadiz

Corsicana

Pacific

Elm

Main

Commerce

Jackson

R.L. Thornton Frwy.

Central Expwy.

Old City Park

N

This walking tour is approximately 3 miles round trip.

Old City Park is precisely what it says it is: the first public park Dallas ever had. Most important about it in the early days were its springs, now covered, which supplied the town with water. In fact, the first phone installed in Dallas had a line strung out to the park. When fire broke out, the park phone rang, and the man who looked after the springs was told to work his pumps extra hard.

Of course houses were mostly of wooden construction then, and that's what you'll see in the park, which has become an old-age home for venerable buildings rescued from all over the area by the Dallas County Heritage Society. Among them is an 1847 one-room log cabin, whose owner, a planter named Miller, made good in a hurry. By 1855, he'd started to build himself a fairly splendid antebellum mansion, which he appropriately called Millermore, although it still lacked a bathroom, and its "necessary" stood out in back. Millermore is the pride of the park, furnished with all the fancy paraphernalia of Victorian elegance (including "night vases"—the Victorians couldn't even get themselves to call them chamber pots). No less interesting is the simpler 1856 Gano House, in a style that was called a "dog-trot cabin"—two separate cabins connected by a breezeway, the "dog trot."

Altogether there are 16 buildings you can visit in the park, not only homes, but also a school, a church, a railroad depot, a small hotel that used to cater to traveling salesmen, and a doctor's office. Each building is staffed by a volunteer guide who explains what it's all about. That way you can get the benefit of authoritative information without having to join a rubberneck group on your stroll through the park.

To avoid school outings, come after 2. Or, if you show up earlier, eat your lunch—good Southern home cooking—at the Brent Place, one of the houses that's been turned into a small restaurant.

The park is open from 10 to 4 Tuesday through Friday, and from 1:30 to 4:40 on weekends. The admission is $1; children, 50 cents—a bargain indeed—but there's a store that may well part you from some more money, especially if you have kids. Among the wares sold here are expertly crafted toy replicas of the kind of furniture you've seen in the old homes— rope-strung trundle beds, miniature corner cupboards, tiny rugs, pillows, and quilts.

Back to Downtown

For more up-to-date shopping, you'll have to go back to downtown, where you'll pass the original Neiman Marcus store at the corner of Ervay and Commerce.

From there, continue north on Ervay to Dallas' newest park, Thanksgiving Square, a triangular island of tranquility in the midst of a busy city, yet of an ultramodern design that fits in with the surroundings. At one end of the park stands a 50-foot tower with three bronze bells that ring out at noon; at the other end, you'll see a spiral of white marble. Despite this structure's unprecedented shape, you'll sense immediately that it must be a chapel. Step inside, and you'll be bathed in the magic glow of its stained-glass ceiling.

"Underground Dallas"

On your way back to where you left your car at the start of the downtown loop, dip into "Underground Dallas," a new subterranean system of walking streets, lined with shops and restaurants, including some of the city's finest. There's at least one access stairway or escalator in every building along the route of this air-conditioned all-weather route. You might enter it from the Akard Street side of the First National Bank Building, and exit at One Main Place, from where, looking west, you once again see the Kennedy Cenotaph.

DALLAS—FAIR PARK AND NATURE TRAILS
G. S. Bush

Texas is many different lands—from its western deserts to the pine forests that border Arkansas and northern Louisiana, from the rugged Canada Breaks up in the Panhandle to the humid, bayou-drained coastal flats along the Gulf of Mexico. The diversity puzzles even native Texans, let alone newcomers, which is what most Texans are these days. A great place to sort it all out is the Dallas Museum of Natural History, which stands in Fair Park, about 3 miles east of downtown.

The Dallas Museum of Natural History

At that museum, the state's ecological realms are pictured in grand wildlife dioramas that blend foreground scenes—

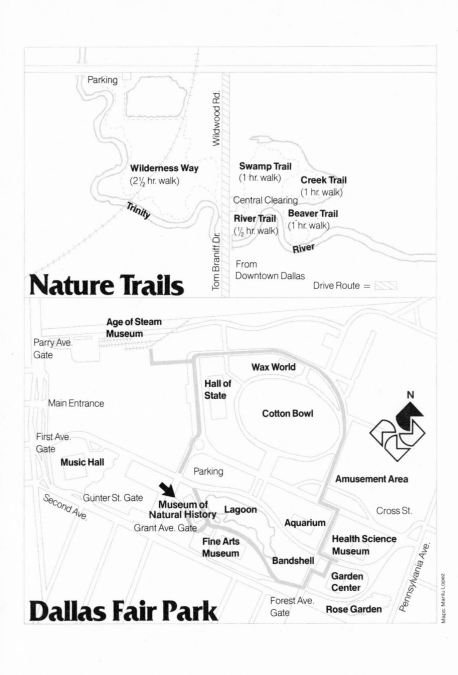

Nature Trails

Parking

Wildwood Rd.

Wilderness Way
(2½ hr. walk)

Trinity

Swamp Trail
(1 hr. walk)

Creek Trail
(1 hr. walk)

Central Clearing

River Trail
(½ hr. walk)

Beaver Trail
(1 hr. walk)

River

Tom Braniff Dr.

From
Downtown Dallas

Drive Route =

Dallas Fair Park

**Age of Steam
Museum**

Parry Ave.
Gate

Main Entrance

First Ave.
Gate

Music Hall

Second Ave.

Gunter St. Gate

**Museum of
Natural History**

Grant Ave. Gate

**Hall of
State**

Wax World

Cotton Bowl

N

Parking

Lagoon

**Fine Arts
Museum**

Bandshell

Amusement Area

Cross St.

Aquarium

**Health Science
Museum**

**Garden
Center**

Forest Ave.
Gate

Rose Garden

Pennsylvania Ave.

Maps: Marilu Lopez

whether they be of mountain lions in the western Guadelupes or of bisons in the central plains, or of elk and mule deer in the eastern woods—so artfully with background paintings you'd have to be completely bereft of imagination not to believe you've been transported to the real-life site.

The Museum of Natural History is where you begin the first round of this two-part walking tour. The first takes you through Fair Park, site of the annual State Fair in October, and of course the Cotton Bowl. This famed stadium sprawls at the center of the complex, and ranged around it are numerous museums, an aquarium, and some stunning gardens. Later, provided your legs haven't quit on you, there's a second hike: the nature trails of the Museum of Natural History, way over at the other end of town. So if you feel that Fair Park has been enough of an adventure for one day, be sure to explore those trails some other time. Few big cities have such easy access to wilderness right in their backyards.

Pick up the free guide book to the Nature Area as you enter the museum; then visit the outstanding Texas dioramas, which are displayed on the ground floor. You'd never guess that these exhibits were the first of their kind. The dioramas here were conceived in the 1930s and are still recognized as tops.

The second floor is devoted to birds, from egrets to eagles, an astounding collection. Still, you may feel let down at first glance, after the vivid wildlife scenes you've just seen. But don't be fooled by the fact that the birds are shown in plain glass cases, without special backgrounds. There's a sound reason for this lack of showmanship: related birds tend to resemble each other, and it's not until you can study them side by side that you can recognize the subtle differences.

The Fine Arts Museum
Next on your itinerary, along a path that passes a picturesque lagoon, is the Fine Arts Museum. It's particularly strong in American classics—Edward Hopper, Thomas Hart Benton, John Singer Sargent, Winslow Homer, Gilbert Stuart. Among the familiar paintings is the one of young George Washington being put on the spot after chopping down the cherry tree, and the Rembrandt Peale portrait of Washington as President.

But most fascinating of all is the museum's collection of ancient American art: the statuary, pottery, grotesque mummy masks, and exquisite gold work of early American Indian cultures, not only pre-Columbian but indeed from the pre-Christian era.

If you want to see these exhibits, don't take this tour on a Monday. The art museum, unlike the others, is closed that day. The rest of the time, its hours are 10 to 5 weekdays, 2 to 5 weekends, slightly shorter than those of the other museums.

The Garden Center

Now continue on the path, skirting the back of the band shell, to the Garden Center. There's a Texas-style—i.e., king-size—rose garden, but don't let that showpiece distract you from going into the building, too. There you'll find a glassed-in pavilion of overpowering lushness and beauty, filled with bromeliads, frangipani, exotic palms, all sorts of trees, shrubs, and flowers from as far away as Malaya. As you should expect in a jungle, it's hot and wet, but a sparkling little waterfall spills down into a pool in the midst of all this greenery, and the cascade's tinkling sounds help keep you relatively cool.

Health Science Museum and an Aquarium

Across the Fair Park Drive from here sits the Health Science Museum, also worth a visit and free like the other city museums, but keep an eye on the time, particularly if you are taking this tour on a Monday or Thursday. At 3 o'clock those afternoons it's feeding time in the tank that harbors the bulkiest resident of the Dallas Aquarium next door—a giant alligator-snapper turtle that's usually immobile, so still in fact that some people think it's an algae-coated rock. But about an hour before it's to be fed, an alarm seems to go off in its tiny head: it suddenly perks up, and that's a sight to behold.

History Recorded in Wax—the Age of Steam Museum

You'll want to circle the Cotton Bowl now, the amusement park to your right (open daily in summer; weekends in other seasons), and head for the Wax World, a wax museum of superior quality that features tableaux from the lives of our Presidents. So far, Carter hasn't made it, but everyone else is there. Recorded narrations explain the scenes—like John Adams taking his morning dip in the Potomac since the White House didn't yet have a tub—and it's well worth the admission price:

$2 for adults, $1.50 for students; $1 for ages six to 12. The hours are 10 to 6:30; noon to 6 on Sundays.

The next attraction on your route, the Age of Steam Museum, also is a commercial attraction ($1.50; children, 75 cents), but it's open only in summer and during the 17-day State Fair of Texas in October. Still, you don't have to go in to see its exhibits, at least from the outside: yesterday's parlor cars, Pullmans, and locomotives.

The Hall of State

Your last stop in Fair Park takes you back to Texas. It's the Hall of State, an imposing neoclassical edifice of the kind you wouldn't expect to find this side of Washington, D.C. This building is designed for special functions, but you can go in anyway and gawk. There's a pomp-and-circumstance hall, with a marble floor and huge murals on its walls—the kind of place that makes you whisper since the slightest sound reverberates. The hall's grand entrance is flanked by larger-than-life statues of Texas heroes, among them Sam Houston, who founded the Republic, and Colonel William B. Travis, the defender of the Alamo.

That's all for Fair Park. Now return to your car, and head out to the Houston Park Nature Area, about 10 miles northwest of downtown Dallas, via I-35, and state highways 183 and 114.

The Nature Trails

As you can see from the Nature Area map, you have your choice of five walks that range in duration from about half an hour to more than 2 hours, depending, of course, on how briskly you proceed: the times cited on the map assume that you'll stop wherever you find something interesting to see.

The trails' names pretty well tell you what they are about, except for the Beaver Trail. Under ordinary circumstances, you won't see beavers, only signs that they hang out here, such as tree trunks chewed at the base. To observe the animals, you'd have to wait quietly under cover until dusk, and even then you might not be in luck.

Probably the most interesting of the walks is the lower section of the Wilderness Way along the Trinity River. You don't have to do the whole trail to see this area—you can backtrack.

What you find there is true primeval forest. Peer under the deadwood of fallen trees, and you'll discover whole families of frogs, salamanders, and centipedes. Golden orb weavers string their shiny spiderwebs between tree limbs and weed stalks, and down at the river bank you can watch turtles coming up for air, herons waiting for lunch to swim by, and snakes sunning themselves. Don't worry: there have been no sightings of poisonous snakes.

The Swamp Trail is another fine experience, but not recommended for hayfever victims during pollen season. Along much of this trail, you'll be walking through a mysterious green tunnel formed by the densely intertwining branches of swamp privets. But have your binoculars handy for the open spaces, where you'll probably see wood ducks, as well as some very pretty and unusual species of sparrow. All trails are marked: white numbers refer to interest points, yellow numbers to plant identifications, and you'll find the explanations in the booklet you picked up at the Museum of Natural History.

FORT WORTH
G. S. Bush

On the freeway you can hustle from Fort Worth to Dallas in less than an hour, but where the good folks of Fort Worth are concerned, Dallas is way back there, somewhere in the unmentionable East. Their own city, however, that's the real West—and, what do you know, they're absolutely right. While Dallas got its start as a farming center, Fort Worth grew up on the Chisholm Trail, route of the great cattle drives, and there were days when as many as 200,000 buffalo skins were swapped for gold and silver. And even today, while Dallas men are more likely to sport Brooks Brothers suits than cowboy boots, Fort Worth remains at heart a cow town, with almost daily cattle auctions and weekly rodeos.

A Museum Devoted to Art of the Old West
No wonder then that Fort Worth takes immense pride in its Amon Carter Museum of Western Art, which houses more pictures and sculptures by Frederic Remington and Charles Russell than any other museum in the country, some 300 paintings and more than 100 bronze castings in all. For once, this is a mu-

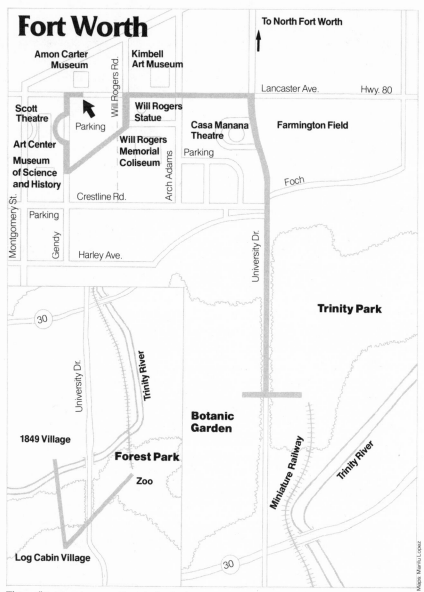

Fort Worth

Amon Carter Museum

Kimbell Art Museum

To North Fort Worth

Will Rogers Rd.

Scott Theatre

Will Rogers Statue

Lancaster Ave.

Hwy. 80

Parking

Art Center

Casa Manana Theatre

Farmington Field

Will Rogers Memorial Coliseum

Parking

Museum of Science and History

Arch Adams

Foch

Montgomery St.

Crestline Rd.

Parking

Gendy

University Dr.

Harley Ave.

30

Trinity Park

University Dr.

Trinity River

Botanic Garden

1849 Village

Miniature Railway

Trinity River

Forest Park

Zoo

Log Cabin Village

30

Maps: Marilu Lopez

This walking tour is approximately 4 miles long.

seum you can take your kids to without their starting to fret. They'll love to look at those Indian raids, roundups, buffalo hunts, chases cross the prairies, and of course the three most famous Remingtons of them all, which are on permanent display: the one of the lone cowboy running his horse down a steep hill (Lyndon Johnson hung it in the White House); the wall-size *Dash for Timber* of wranglers, one of them wounded and propped up in his saddle by his pal, being pursued by Indians; and that picture of Big Nose George holding up a stagecoach (a social error that resulted in his being strung up and skinned by vigilantes).

So don't worry about keeping your youngsters enthralled. In fact, this whole tour is tailor-made for families. You'll visit a great science museum; stroll through gardens that smell like a perfume factory the year round; rattle across trestles in an open-carriage, narrow-gauge train; explore a big zoo; and browse through an authentic log-cabin village, where you can observe the workings of a grist mill, a blacksmith's shop, and other frontier trades.

The Will Rogers Memorial Center

The Amon Carter Museum, starting point of the excursion, is part of the Will Rogers Memorial Center, an 85-acre complex devoted to recreational and cultural events, which calls itself the "Acropolis of the Southwest." However, the only deity worshiped here is Will, the late great folksy humorist, and he isn't a bad choice at that: like the old Greeks, he had a sense of the ridiculous. Besides, he always favored Fort Worth and loved to attend its rodeos. You'll pass his dynamic equestrian bronze statue, unveiled by President Eisenhower, along your route (see map). Meanwhile, you can park your car in the huge lot west of the Will Rogers Memorial Coliseum, or in the lot between the Coliseum and the Casa Manana Theater, a gleaming dome designed by Buckminster Fuller. For that matter, you might find a shady spot on the side street by the Carter Museum.

The sequence of the other museums you'll visit will depend mostly on where you are parked. There are, first of all, two more art museums, both entirely different, except that their hours are the same: 10 to 5 Tuesday through Saturday, and 1 to 5 on Sunday. If you go for modern, you'll want to concentrate on the Art Center. That's where you'll find the Feiningers, O'Keeffes, Ben Shahns and Andy Warhols—one anachronism:

Thomas Eakins' popular *Swimming Hole,* painted in 1883. If, on the whole, you prefer the traditional approach, however, the Kimbell Art Museum, just east of the Carter in a super-modern skylighted building, will be more to your liking. It's a fine place to introduce children to art, for the Kimbell has a bit of everything, and all of it top quality, the kind that takes Texas money to buy—Goyas, Rousseaus, Van Goghs, Braques, Gainsboroughs, et al., plus some extra-special stuff, like the Romanesque apse of a 12th-century chapel, picked up piece by piece in France and reassembled here.

The Museum of Science and History

Of universal interest is the Museum of Science and History, whose extensive collection ranges from dioramas of prehistoric skull operations to the moon suit worn by astronaut Alan Bean on the Apollo XII mission. Here again you'll have a hard time tearing the kids away, particularly from the "smell-touch-and-see" section that explains phenomena of basic science, and from the utterly incredible series of human embryo models (vastly enlarged, of course) that, step by step, depict the development of homo sapiens from what at first resembles nothing so much as a tadpole with learning disability. This museum is open daily from 9 to 6, Sunday from 2 to 5.

The Botanic Gardens

That ends the indoor part of your walking tour. Now hike south along University Drive to the Botanic Gardens, one of the showplaces of Fort Worth. You could spend several days just exploring those 114 acres where something is always in bloom: daffodils, daylilies, some 3,500 rose bushes, chrysanthemums, more than 100 varieties of flowering trees, from Mexican plum to redbud and hawthorn.

The gardens are always open and admission is free, except for their most special attraction, the Fort Worth Japanese Garden, which is exactly what its name implies—a small piece of Asia transplanted to the plains of Texas. Romantic pathways, lined by statuary and pagodas, undulate up hill and down dale, through a silent, fragrant paradise. On arched Japanese bridges, you cross lagoons flashing with goldfish and dotted with brilliant Mandarin ducks. If you're looking for an out-of-this-world experience, this is it. Admission costs $1; under 12, it's free. The hours are Tuesday through Friday 10 to 4, Saturday 10 to 5, and Sunday 1 to 5.

A Mini Rail Ride to the Fort Worth Zoo

After all this walking you deserve a ride. Cross University Drive into Trinity Park and board the fringe-on-top miniature railway that chugs south along and over to the Trinity River to Forest Park, yet another delightful preserve in this string of parklands. The trip takes about 12 minutes and costs 50 cents. You can catch a train every few minutes from 10 A.M. until well into the evening from the end of March to Labor Day, and from 10 to 6 on fair-weather weekends the rest of the year.

Your destination is the Fort Worth Zoo—provided you can get the kids past the amusement park at its gate. Among the best of the zoo's attractions is its African veldt, to the right just beyond the entrance. Lions prowl this domain along with elands, zebras, and ostrich, and you can't help but wonder how the weaker species survive. It takes some careful looking to discover that cleverly camouflaged moats separate predator and prey.

Another winner is the reptile house: cobras, king cobras, pythons, boas, rattlers, Gila monsters, monitor lizards, skinks. Feeding takes place usually on Tuesday afternoons and Wednesday mornings, and that's quite a show. Of course, the mice are served up dead; this is not a Roman circus. Also don't miss the aquarium, with its big seal tank and its outdoor pool of exotic carp in all colors. The zoo is open from 9 to 5:30 daily in winter, and until 6 in spring and summer. Admission costs $1; under 12, free.

Log Cabin Village

Directly across University Drive from the zoo, on a woodsy hillside above a tree-lined lane, you'll find the Log Cabin Village, a fine collection of pioneer structures dating back to the mid-1800s, and filled with authentic period furniture and furnishings—quilts, woven coverlets, old china, pie safes of pierced tin. Volunteers from the Tarrant County Historical Society demonstrate the old housekeeping skills, like early American cookery (try the slumgullion), candling, spinning, weaving, quilting, and there's a real grist mill where corn meal is ground the waterwheel way: you can take home a 2½-pound bag for $1. On weekends, you can also watch a blacksmith. Admission is nominal: 40 cents over age 12, and 25 cents under that. The hours, unfortunately, are limited, so you have to watch your timing. Monday through Friday, the gate opens at 8:30; Saturday at noon; and Sunday at 1, and it always closes at 4:30. Thus, if you're running late, you might want to come here first, and visit the zoo later—and leave the amusement park to the very last.

A Re-created 1849 Village

However, there's yet another way to round out the day. About half a mile north of the Log Cabin Village, on the other bank of the Trinity, is the 1849 Village, this one a commercial reconstruction (a venture of the "Bonanza" TV show people), whose brightly colored new-old buildings house some pleasant eateries, craft shops, and a theater. There's a gazebo on the village square, where outdoor music is offered in summer, and you can go for excursion boat rides on the calm river, or rent water bikes.

North Fort Worth

As an extension of your Fort Worth tour, you should certainly make a point to visit North Fort Worth, the part of town where cattle remains undisputed king. That's about 3½ miles north of downtown. To get there: proceed north on University; bear right on W. Northside Drive; take a left at North Main, follow North Main until it intersects with Exchange Avenue. Western store fronts, wooden sidewalks, and false-fronted buildings with overhanging roofs mark this crossroads. Here you can admire silver-trimmed, hand-tooled saddles at Ryon's Saddle & Ranch Supplies, shop for Western clothing and gear, and eat at the White Elephant Saloon with the wranglers who come for the cattle auctions (open to the public), which are held in the amphitheater of the Stockyards Exchange every Monday through Thursday morning. And, except in July and August, there's a rousing rodeo every Saturday night at 8 at the Cowtown Coliseum just down the street.

DOWNTOWN AND UNDERGROUND HOUSTON
G. S. Bush

There aren't many cities where you can amble back and forth between the centuries just by taking a few steps. That's possible, though, right in the heart of Houston, which in barely a decade has burgeoned into one of our biggest, busiest metropolitan centers, and is still gaining population at the rate of nearly 100,000 persons per year.

On the one hand, its opulent downtown, which suddenly sprouted skyward, is America's "most futuristic city" as Ada Louise Huxtable, architectural editor of the New York Times, called it. Yet, in the very shadows of Houston's adventurous, indeed far-out high-rises snuggles a meticulous preservation of what that little old Texas outpost was like 141 years ago. On the same walk, too, you can dip down into an underground network of glittering shopping arcades and "sidewalk" cafes whose umbrellas never feel sun or rain, and conversely you can peer up into the branches of a real hangman's tree that, not too long ago, quivered with the deaths of three frontier outlaws.

Midway in your tour, you can rest up by taking a free hour-long boat ride on a tranquil bayou, so well hidden between its steep banks you'd never guess it flowed right past downtown. And, finally, you can cap off your excursion with refreshments in a revolving restaurant, tall amid the glass and steel towers.

Sam Houston Park: Houston's Past
The houses that gave Houston its start also mark the start of your walk. They stand in Sam Houston Park, and a 12-minute slide show tells their history. There's no charge if you only want to stroll through the preserve, enjoying the old homes in their grassland setting, aglow with azaleas, Cherokee roses, and oleander. But if you want to see the interiors, there is a $2 charge; under 12, 35 cents.

"The Old Place" is the most fascinating of these structures. It was the first cabin in the county, hammered together in about 1824 of rough-hewn cedar logs, and you'll find it furnished in the manner of its day: a rope-strung bed with a mattress of moss, a separate pile of moss to bed down unexpected guests on the floor, a table that could be raised close to the ceiling—for animals shared their masters' sleeping quarters in those days.

Downtown Houston

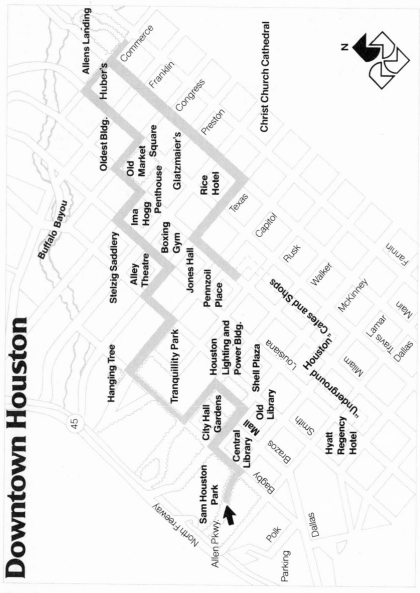

This walking tour is approximately 2½ miles long.

In contrast, there are later buildings, reflecting more prosperous times: Houston's first brick home, built in 1847; an elegant Greek Revival mansion of the 1850s (which once sold for $25, fancy horsehair furnishings and all); and most splendidly, an 1868 Victorian home with 14-foot ceilings, an indoor kitchen (unprecedented at that time), and an entry hall aglow with sunshine flowing through the angle-cut glass panes of the front door. You'll also want to look into "The Long Row," a reconstruction of Houston's first business buildings, with shops like they had in the mid-1800s: a store that sold chandeliers, ladies' fans, and other "fancy ware"; an old barbershop; even a library.

Sam Houston Park, operated by the Harris County Heritage Society, is open 10 to 4 Monday through Friday, 11 to 3 Saturday, and 2 to 5 Sunday. There's 2-hour parking in front of the house where you see the slide show, but this won't give you enough time for the whole downtown walking tour. So you'd better park in one of the nearby commercial lots around Allen and Bagby Streets; the maximum charge for all day is about $2.

Outdoor Concerts

If you leave Sam Houston Park shortly before noon, you'll be in time for the band concerts and troubadour serenades staged almost every summer weekday on the mall between the Old Library and the new Central Library, or across the street in the pleasant City Hall Gardens. Then you'll be passing the Shell Plaza, Houston's tallest structure to date, but soon to be dwarfed by an even higher high-rise.

An Exciting Architectural Area

Shell Plaza looks almost old-fashioned, although it was built only a few years ago. That's because it has regular windows. Many of Houston's newer buildings are towers of black glass—their windows are made of the same sun-reflecting material as the visors of astronaut helmets. In this exciting architectural area you'll see the Houston Lighting and Power Building next door to Shell. Take a quick look into the subterranean rock garden that fronts it on Walker Street, and then angle through Tranquility Park back to Bagby to see the "Hanging Tree," a giant old oak that was used as a neckstretcher when it graced the location of what was then the county jail.

Homes for the Performing Arts: Alley Theater, Jones Hall

Your next stop is the two-stage (one proscenium and one in the round) Alley Theater, which has been called "the most striking" theater in the country, even if it does resemble an atomic-age fortress more than a place of entertainment. Guided tours (weekdays only) take you deep into the bowels of this imposing structure, to the workshops where scenery is made and costume designers dream up dramatic wardrobes. You pay a nominal charge to see this unusual theater. To find out schedules contact the Greater Houston Convention and Visitors Council, 1006 Main; phone 658-9201.

Catercorner from the Alley Theater stands the Jones Hall for the Performing Arts, a $7.4-million palace that's home to Houston's Grand Opera, Ballet, and Symphony. If the lobby is open, you can see a breathtaking abstract sculpture, made of thousands of thin stainless-steel hexagonal rods, hanging from miles of shimmering gold-plated cables.

By way of contrast, as you walk up Louisiana Street, you'll soon pass an old red-brick building, which served as the gymnasium of the Texas Boxing Association. Joe Louis and George Forman, the latter a native Houstonian, were among the greats who trained there for their world-championship bouts.

Then quickly look up. On the roof of the next building you'll see the trees of a garden; it frames the penthouse of the late Miss Ima Hogg, whose millionaire-governor father had a whimsical if somewhat cruel approach to names. And just across the street you can peek into the windows of the Stelzig Saddlery Company, in business since 1870, whose artisans still handcraft ornate saddles and cowboy boots. Or walk in and browse.

Old Market Square Area

Now you are in Houston's oldest, and at one time most notorious, quarter. At the turn of the century, the buildings around Old Market Square housed some 50 gambling halls, fast-draw saloons, and parlors of free and easy ladies. The city's most venerable structure, on the north side of the square, on Congress Street, was once an Indian trading post and stagecoach stop; today it's a tavern whose walls are replete with nostalgic pictures and posters.

If your stomach's growling, as it should be by now, you couldn't find yourself in a more propitious location. Glatzmaier's

Seafood Market, Houston's oldest, sits just south of Old Market Square on Travis. You'd hardly call it elegant. You pick up your food at the counter, carry it to any empty spot you can find along the communal tables, and from then on it's a finger-picking, sauce-dripping feast, with paper napkins required by the dozen: gumbo, fresh crawfish and crabs, and huge New Orleans "poor boys"—buns stuffed with Gulf oysters and shrimp. No more pretentious, except that here you get waited on, is Huber's, in the block north of the square: same low prices, same briny fare, plus beer to go with it if you like, and newspapers for tablecloths.

Boat Ride on the Buffalo Bayou

To work off this luncheon, march briskly to Allen's Landing, the city's cradle. Two bayous converge here, the bigger one, Buffalo Bayou, continuing for some 50 miles down to the Gulf of Mexico. The Allen brothers, two real estate promoters from New York, bought the site figuring that it would make a great turnaround for coastal steamers—indeed a fine start for a town. Well, the Allens nearly lost their shirts when the turnaround was sited farther down the bayou, but Houston became a port city (now the nation's third largest) just the same. Allen's Landing, today, is all but deserted: there's only one small pier, which, however, serves a most pleasant purpose. It is here that you board a boat for a free trip to Buffalo Bayou, about 5 miles all told. What's so wondrous about this ride is that once you're cruising on the bayou, the city disappears completely behind its high banks. You chug along in a setting of weeping willows, philodendrons, chinaberry trees, and cane thickets, and the return leg offers a special thrill: you come around a bend, and suddenly, above the bank, rise the tips of Houston's stunning skyline.

A Street Wide Enough for a Cattle Drive

Next, walk south down Main to the corner of Texas, Houston's widest street, 100 feet across. The reason it's so spacious is that it used to be the route of cattle drives. Looking east on Texas, you'll see Christ Church Cathedral a couple of blocks down on the left: once a longhorn broke loose during a drive and smashed its way into the church's groundbreaking service. Ever since, the symbol of the Episcopal Diocese of Texas has included a longhorn logo.

At the northwest corner of Main and Texas is the Rice Hotel, which occupies the site of the capital of the Republic of Texas when it was briefly a nation. Your next stop is Pennzoil Place, Houston's most outstanding architectural extravaganza, designed by Philip Johnson and John Burgee—two slanting, glass-faced trapezoid high-rises, connected by glass arcades whose peaked roofs loom eight stories above indoor garden lobbies, green and fragrant with exotic trees and flowers.

Underground Houston

From there, you enter "Underground Houston" and follow its labyrinth of subterranean passages, as indicated on the map. There are shops of every kind, restaurants, and snack bars, all along these brightly decorated, ultra-modern catacombs. The most interesting underground stretch is just before you come back up again at the Hyatt Regency—it's on these southernmost and newest underground plazas that you'll find "outdoor" cafes, equipped with colorful umbrellas no less, presumably to protect you against neon-burn.

The Hyatt Regency

Then up the escalator into the 30-floor-high lobby of the Hyatt Regency (with a 56-foot-high golden free-form sculpture that gleams like a grubstaker's dream), and yet farther up in a glassed-in elevator to the revolving restaurant and bar up top. This scenic merry-go-round is called Spindletop after the first Texas gusher, and through its 360-degree panoramic window, you can see every place you've been to on this walk, and then some.

HOUSTON'S MUSEUM-GARDEN CIRCLE
G. S. Bush

Culture has always bloomed at its brightest in the radiance of great wealth, and the literally well-oiled Houston of today is no exception. Here, in this booming city that has yet to know a budget deficit, the showcase of what big money can provide for public pleasure and leisurely enlightenment is Hermann Park, a greensward of lawns and forests clad in Spanish moss. Within this sylvan preserve and ranged along its perimeter are splendid

museums, exquisite gardens, a stunningly modern outdoor the-
ater, and one of our country's finest zoos—and, with most of
the attractions having been donated by Houston's many multi-
millionaries, it's practically all for free, even the zoo.
Tuesday through Saturday are best for your visit. On
Sunday, the museums are open only in the afternoons, and on
Monday they are closed. Also check with the Greater Houston
Convention and Visitors Council, 1006 Main Street (phone
658-9201), for the schedule of the Miller Outdoor Theater.
Time your tour right, and you can round out the day with an
alfresco picnic supper on the grassy hill that overlooks the stage,
while enjoying an opera or Broadway musical, a ballet perfor-
mance or symphony concert, as dusk embraces the park.

The Houston Garden Center
Start your stroll at the Houston Garden Center, about a 3-
mile, 10-minute drive south of the downtown along Main
Street. Follow the drive route marked on the map, to the parking lot at the Garden Circle and you'll have no parking problem.
Camellias and azaleas usher in this garden's growing season in early March. They are soon followed by roses—some
3,000 varieties of every conceivable color, including the rare
peach-hued Tropicana and the lavender-petaled Angelface,
which smells especially sweet. The roses peak in April but last
well into summer, as late bloomers succeed earlier blossoms.
Adjoining the roses' realm is an unusual "Fragrant Garden," a
touch-me-gently nursery, which was originally planned as a
project for the blind. But you, too, may explore here, caressing
the plants, lifting their elusive scents on your fingertips for delightful sniffing.
The pavillion of the Garden Center often hosts special
events, ranging from flower shows (with lectures and green-
thumb demonstrations) to ethnic festivals that feature foods,
costumes, and customs. A recent Japanese fete, for instance, included a professional karate exhibition. Most such events are
free; for some, there's a nominal charge. Again, the Visitors
Council can advise you on the schedule.

The Museum of Natural Science
Your next stop, but a few steps away, is the Museum of
Natural Science. It's fronted by a bulky steam locomotive, a

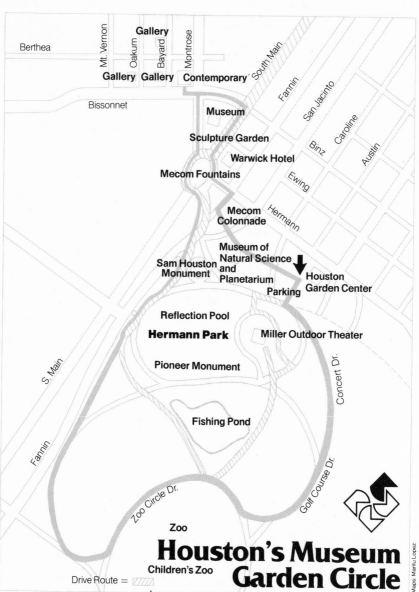

Berthea

Mt. Vernon
Gallery
Oakum
Bayard
Montrose

Gallery Gallery Contemporary

South Main
Fannin
San Jacinto
Caroline
Austin

Bissonnet

Museum

Sculpture Garden

Warwick Hotel

Binz

Mecom Fountains

Ewing

Mecom
Colonnade

Hermann

Museum of
Natural Science
and
Planetarium

Sam Houston
Monument

Parking

Houston
Garden Center

Reflection Pool

Hermann Park

Miller Outdoor Theater

Pioneer Monument

Concert Dr.

S. Main

Fishing Pond

Fannin

Golf Course Dr.

Zoo Circle Dr.

Zoo

Houston's Museum

Children's Zoo

Drive Route = ▨

Garden Circle

Maps: Marilu Lopez

This walking tour is approximately 2½ miles long.
The side trip to the Garden District adds another 1½ miles.

shiny black giant fancied up with red trim—a reminder of the
days when Houston was the hub of 17 railroads. The museum
itself houses a miscellany of esoteric treasures, among them pre-
Columbian art, wildlife exhibits, shrunken heads of Jivaro Indians, skeletons of prehistoric monsters, fossils, retablos (old
Hispanic religious paintings on tin plate), dioramas of Texas history, a glittering collection of minerals, a theater whose star is a
transparent anatomical manikin—her innards light up as she
slowly revolves on the stage while she explains the workings of
the human body in terms even children can understand.

But the museum's major attractions are its space exhibits,
including a chunk of moon rock and much of the equipment
carried on the lunar landings. And just as this unique collection
is appropriate for Houston, as the site of NASA, so is the museum's Hall of Petroleum: this city, after all, is the home of most
Western oil companies. You'll find it a very interesting exhibition, especially now that oil is always in the headlines. You'll see
an excellent diagrammatic light display of what happens to
crude oil in a refinery, a deep-diving submersible for oceanogra-
phic exploration, the model of an offshore rig, and juxtaposed
side-by-side, a modern oil-well pump and the very first one ever
used, a small hand-crank gadget that dates back to 1860 when
crude fetched $28 a barrel, more than twice its price today, as
dictated by the Arabs.

The museum also has a plush planetarium ($1.25; under
12, 50 cents; kids under 5 not admitted since they might get
scared in the dark). There are several shows daily in summer;
no shows Tuesday and Thursday the rest of the year.

Fine Greek Replicas and a Luxe Hotel
On your way over to the Museum of Fine Arts and its
Sculpture Garden (with a statue by Rodin), you'll be passing the
Mecom Colonnade, with its Corinthian columns, a fine replica
of the Greek fountain where the Oracle of Delphi was said to
hold court, and on another lawn island, a grouping of three-
tiered fountains (lit up at night), which also were given to the
city by mogul John W. Mecom. Across from the fountains, be
sure to stop in at the Warwick Hotel, reputed to be America's
most expensively appointed inn, with Greek statuary at its portals, priceless tapestries and wood adorning its public rooms,
and authentic Louis XIV furniture in its suites. You can ride the
outside glass elevator to the private club on the hotel's top floor,

and from its anteroom admire the view down tree-lined South Main, a prosaic name that belies this avenue's outstanding landscaping: visitors from Paris often compare it to the Champs Elysées.

Museums and Galleries

Then on, through the Sculpture Garden, to the Museum of Fine Arts, which epitomizes Houston's heritage of a tiny frontier cow town that matured into the Western world's petroleum metropolis: the museum's latest wing was designed by the late Mies van der Rohe, whose only other museum creation stands in Bonn, the German capital. And there are more contradictions that bridge time and cultures: on the museum's lower level, you'll find one of the most extensive collections of Western pioneer paintings and cast bronzes by Frederic Remington; on its upper level, Van Dyke and Rubens rub frames with Degas, Picasso, Matisse, and Lautrec. There are troves of golden jewelry, antique glass, sterling-silver tableware, and—believe it or not—an assemblage of Russian icons of such rarity that the Russians themselves borrowed it last year for a special showing at their famed Hermitage!

To see modern American paintings and sculpture, visit the Contemporary Arts Museum, a gleaming stainless-steel edifice catercorner across Bissonnet, and if you like to browse commercial galleries, several are located in the little streets behind this newest of Houston's museums.

Hermann Park

This ends the indoor portion of your tour. Now you walk past the Mecom Fountain, and cut across Hermann Park, the entrance of which is marked by an equestrian monument to Sam Houston, founder of the Republic of Texas, whose outnumbered ragtag troops defeated Mexican General Santa Anna in the Battle of San Jacinto, just east of the city, on April 18, 1836.

Down the park's mall stands the obelisk commemorating the area's pioneer settlers, and pretty soon you hear the shrieks of a steam whistle as a narrow-gauge train, loaded with youngsters, chugs through the greenery. The train's terminal (50 cents for the 15-minute ride) lies just beyond the stocked park pond, on whose banks you'll see kids fishing for croakers and mullets, casting their lines with expertise to miss the ducks and geese. Take the short trip if your children are along, or immediately walk into the Houston Zoological Garden, whose gate is right there, too.

The Houston Zoo

If you do the whole "43-acre" zoo, it'll add about 4 miles to your tour. But at the very least see its prime attractions, grouped around the reflection pool at the entrance. Foremost among these is the Small Mammals Pavilion, the first building on the left. It has a special room in which the day is turned upside down: after visiting hours, bright lights are turned on so that the nocturnal creatures think it's daytime, but during visiting hours (9:30 to 6; until 10 in summer) there's only infrared light, fooling the animals into believing it's night and keeping them active. A double-walled enclosure holds vampire bats—one of the zoo's real prides—and they are fed at 2:30 every afternoon.

The reptiles building next door houses snakes of all kinds from every part of the world, including rhinoceros vipers, cobras, and mambas, plus a unique collection of albino snakes, including an all-white diamondback rattler with pink eyes.

On the other side of the reflection pool is the tropical aviary, a beautiful reconstruction of jungle, with lush plants flourishing in the heavy, moist air. The primeval forest roars with the gush of artificial waterfalls and the very real cries of the most colorful birds you ever saw, flying free within the enclosure.

Farther on in the zoo is a special children's zoo, with a petting area, an animal nursery, and a hatchery with dated eggs, so you have an idea whether or not to stick around for a coming-out party.

Theater Alfresco

If you intend to take in a show at the Miller Outdoor Theater and want a regular seat, you've got to be at the box office for your free ticket between 11:30 and 1:30 (Monday–Friday) on day of performance. On Saturday at the same times, you may pick up Saturday and Sunday tickets. The limit is four tickets. But watching the show from the lawn is more fun. You can buy barbecue, pizzas, and hamburgers for your picnic at the theater—indeed, even cocktails, wine and beer—or if you want to create your own meal, pick up the fixings at the Jet Grocery, one block up from the Museum of Fine Arts, on Montrose Street.

SAN ANTONIO
G. S. Bush

Deep in the heart of San Antonio is where you'll find the true Texas: a blend of Latin past and lively present, of heroic history and futuristic vision, of small-town tranquility jealously maintained amidst explosive growth. On what is now a peaceful, sunny plaza, Davy Crockett and 187 other Texans died for the territory's independence in the hopeless Battle of the Alamo. In the Victorian bar of a hotel that fronts on the same plaza, Teddy Roosevelt later recruited his Rough Riders, plying them with hefty draughts of liquid fighting spirit. And, many years later still, a group of inspired citizens, seeing their Old San Antonio sink into decay as suburbs burgeoned, pushed through a most successful urban renewal project: the Paseo del Rio, or River Walk, a promenade that meanders for more than a mile through the most picturesque part of town—a parade of gardens, outdoor cafes, boutiques, and nighteries. Indeed, the Paseo's happy street life once again proves that people are much nicer to each other when they walk than when they drive.

Start at the Alamo

So get rid of your car in one of the lots behind the Alamo, and join the contented crowd on the Plaza. Stop first at the Visitors Information Center, directly across the Plaza from the Alamo Mission, or, more accurately, the Mission San Antonio de Valero, which dates back to the early 1700s. Pick up helpful brochures, then take in the Alamo Theater and Museum, three doors down (daily 9 to 5:30; admission $1.75; children 4–12, 75 cents).

Although a commercial attraction, this is well worth visiting. Its 30-minute wide-screen slide-and-sound presentation will put a lump in your throat while helping to orient you on the long-since paved and landscaped battlefield of 1836. There, near that flagpole on the lawn, is where Crockett was cut down. Jim

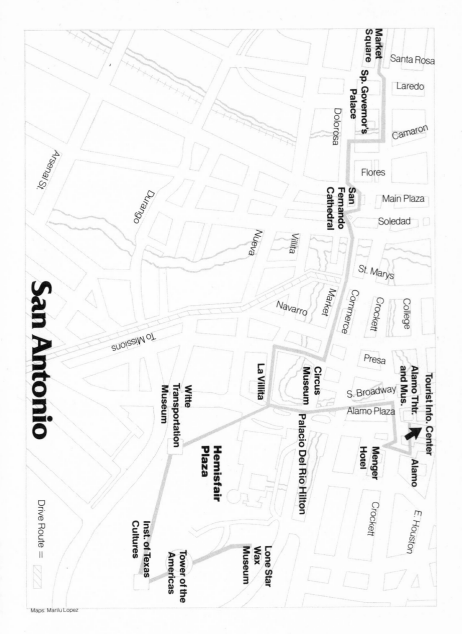

Maps: Marilu Lopez

This walking tour is approximately 4½ miles long.

Bowie, sick with tuberculosis, was killed on his cot where a Japanese yew now flowers, over to the right. Colonel William Travis, who commanded the garrison, took a Mexican bullet in his forehead when Santa Anna's troops breached the north wall—the Post Office now occupies this site, and droves of sightseers pass through the ghostly breach each day, oblivious of their intrusion into the spirit world; they're in a hurry to buy stamps for their picture cards.

Now step into the Mission, cool and dark when you enter it from the bright sunlight of the Plaza. Stroll through the gardens behind the chapel, and also see the exhibits in the Long Barracks, the only part of the fortification that still stands (weekdays, 9 to 5; Sunday, 10 to 5).

Your next stop, right beside the Alamo, is the Menger Hotel, with its Rough Riders Bar and exquisite patio. Read the menu posted on the wall. This must have been a gourmet's delight in Teddy's time; exotic soups, vension steak, even ice for drinks imported by steamer into the Gulf from colder climes, and then carted overland to early San Antonio.

The River Walk

From the Menger, continue west on Crockett Street, and down the stairs at the corner of Presa and Crockett to the liveliest stretch of the Paseo del Rio. There are pedestrian walkways on either side of this arm of the San Antonio River. In this secluded canyon, which loops through downtown some 20 feet below street level, you are removed from the fumes and clatter of the traffic. All you hear is talk and laughter, music from the cafes, the clinking of dishes from the restaurants, and the only smells are those of trees and flowers and good food.

Near the Market Street Bridge you can board a cruise boat that covers the complete Paseo del Rio circle in about 25 minutes ($1; under 12, 35 cents). Paddleboats, at $2 an hour, also are available.

Hemisfair Plaza—Museums and a Lookout Tower

Otherwise return to street level here, at the Palacio del Rio Hilton, and walk past the big, modern Convention Center to the brewery-sponsored Lone Star Wax Museum with its dioramas of Texas history, including a surprisingly realistic Comanche scalping that youngsters go wild over (daily 10 to 6, $1; under

12, 50 cents). Don't miss the unique mural in the beer and snack emporium from which you enter this museum: the picture is a mosaic of 10,001 rattler rattles.

Now head straight for the Tower of the Americas, which was built for the 1968 World's Fair, dubbed the "Hemisfair." An elevator in a glass shaft shoots you up to the 579-foot-high observation deck in 47 seconds—an adventure in itself, both coming and going ($1; ages 4 to 12, 50 cents). You have the choice of a discotheque and a restaurant up top as well. The disco is stationary; the restaurant slowly revolves, providing a 360-degree panorama of the Texas prairies.

Beyond the tower sits the huge, impressively modern Institute of Texan Cultures, a cornucopia of displays on the many ethnic groups, from Indians, Spaniards, and Britons, to Jews and Italians, that made this remarkable state what it is today. The Institute is open daily, except Monday, from 9 to 5 (free; donations invited). Try to show up in time for one of the exciting multi-media shows projected on 36 screens (at 11, 1:30, and 3:30). Your last stop on Hemisfair Plaza is the Witte Transportation Museum, where you'll find some interesting exhibits of stagecoaches and old automobiles (daily 10 to 6; donations invited).

La Villita—San Antonio's Nostalgia Corner

Your next destination, La Villita, offers a sharp contrast to the futuristic architecture and wide-open spaces of the fairgrounds. La Villita means "Little Village," and that's precisely what it is. This is where some of San Antonio's earliest settlers lived—Spaniards and Canary Islanders—long before the Texans holed up in the Alamo. La Villita was restored some years ago, and today it's the city's nostalgia corner, a maze of arts and crafts shops and studios, whose wares range from predictable junk jewelry to truly exquisite ceramics fashioned by experts. If you know something of crafts, you can find some interesting buys here. But even if you only windowshop, you'll enjoy the flea-market atmosphere of the area.

A Museum Devoted to Circus Memorabilia

Next on your agenda is what may well be the best public circus museum in the country—and because it's city-owned also the least publicized. That's the Hertzberg Circus Collection, which contains more than 20,000 items of big-top esoterica, including Tom Thumb's tiny carriage. It's open weekdays the year round, plus Sunday May to October, from 9 to 5:30.

A Return to the Past

After this detour into the realm of the absurd, you return to Old San Antonio, walking along Market and Dolorosa first to San Fernando Cathedral, an elegant French Gothic edifice of a style not often found on this side of the Atlantic, and a couple of blocks farther on, to the Spanish Governor's Palace, the residence of the rulers of New Spain in the 18th and 19th centuries. This city-owned restoration is filled with period furniture, and there's a luxuriant garden (weekdays 9 to 5, Sunday 10 to 5; admission is a nominal 35 cents).

A Mexican Market

Last, as you continue west on Dolorosa, you'll reach Market Square—several blocks of renovated buildings, including the newly built El Mercado, with its own labyrinth of sales stalls in a south-of-the-border Casbah style. Here you can buy almost anything from fresh vegetables to touristic curios, and eat one of the best Mexican meals ever: at the Mi Tierra on Market Square, very reasonably priced and, incidentally, open around the clock.

On weekdays, though unfortunately only until 6 p.m., there's a 10-cent bus, the "El Centro," which circles downtown, and, if you are tired from walking, it will take you back close to where you parked your car.

A Side Trip to the Missions and the Buckhorn Saloon

If you're trying to cover all of San Antonio in one day, you'll want to drive out to the Mission Trail in the afternoon before the famous old missions, shrines of the Conquistadores—churches that were also fortifications—close at 6. The nearest, 3 miles east of downtown via South St. Mary's, is Mission Conception, built in 1731 and the oldest unrestored church in the nation. Most popular is the next one, Mission San Jose, which is grander but not nearly so charming. Then there are two more, San Juan Capistrano and San Francisco de la Espada, a few miles farther on. Individual admissions cost 50 cents each; if you intend to visit two or more, buy a combination ticket for $1 at the first one.

On this side trip, also be sure to stop by at the Lone Star

Brewery, whose pride is San Antonio's old Buckhorn Saloon, which the brewery bought lock, stock, and barrel including the world's largest collection (and quite possibly the only one) of animal horns, stuffed heads, fish fins, and bird feathers, now all on display here. Free beer flows for adults, and the kids can cool off gratis with soft drinks after the long day of strolling in the Texas sun.

ARIZONA

PHOENIX
John Neary

Congratulations! You are about to join that hardy band of individualists who savor the joys of walking in Phoenix.

The secret to enjoying walking in Arizona's capital city lies in not being overwhelmed by the sheer size of the place and in picking out those fascinating havens of quiet that, here and there amid the bustle and the sprawl, await your exploration on foot.

Phoenix is gigantic, with a metropolitan population of 1.3 million living and working in 273.4 square miles of vast residential areas and business districts closely packed along boulevards whose blocks seem to stretch for hundreds of yards from corner to corner. It gets hot in Phoenix, too, sometimes well above 100 degrees Fahrenheit. For those reasons, many Phoenicians regard walking as a quaint pastime still pursued only in less mechanized, underdeveloped areas—or merely as a means of getting from the air-conditioned car parked as closely as possible to the air-conditioned home, office, or store.

Don't be deterred. Going for a walk in Phoenix may draw a stare or two, but it can mean coming face to face with some of the strangest wildlife, the most astonishing plants, beguiling artwork, and intriguing history anywhere.

Papago Park

Start when it's coolest outdoors, in the morning, at East Van Buren Street just east of Galvin Parkway at about 62nd Street. Here the Phoenix Zoo occupies 125 acres of sere desert in Papago Park. Around the zoo entrance are picnic tables with fireplaces, and canals wherein you may, if you are under 15, try for a fish. (Note: 14- and 15-year-olds must have an Arizona license.) Cross the canal, where ducks and geese vie with big turtles for the tidbits you toss them and you have begun a traverse of 2½ miles of roadway past the zoo's 1,200 animal exhibits. A safari train driven by a guide who gives a running narrative leaves the main gate every half-hour and costs 50 cents per passenger. The zoo is open every day of the year from 9 to 5 except Christmas, when it opens at noon. From May 25 to Labor Day, the gates stay open until 7 P.M. Wednesday through Sunday. Admission is $1.50 for those 15 and older; 50 cents for children 4 through 14 if accompanied by an adult and $1.50 if not; free for children 3 and younger. It takes about 2 hours to do the zoo, but that does not leave much time for lolling in the shade admiring the macaws on their special island or doing justice to the coatimundi.

The Desert Botanical Garden
Not far from the zoo—but too distant for comfortable walking—is the Desert Botanical Garden. It is best entered by car at 6400 East McDowell Road. The garden's 140 acres are graced with no fewer than 1,400 species of cacti, more than half of the total known in the world. They range from the tiny pebblelike lithops to the towering saguaro, which sometimes lives to be 200 years old, and the immense Mexican Cardon that weighs up to 10 tons, and include such botanical oddities as the hairy little "Old Man of the Desert," the sinuous "octopus" cactus, and the "Boojum Tree" from Baja, which looks like a big upside-down turnip. A gift shop offers plants, pictures, and a fine selection of reference books. The garden is open every day of the year from 9 to 5. Admission is by voluntary donation. Budget at least an hour for your visit, and if you go in the springtime, look closely at the deepest recesses of the spikiest cacti—that's where the doves like to sit on their nests, safe from everything except camera-carrying tourists.

Salt River Project Building
It is a short drive next to the headquarters of the Salt River Project, the big building on Project Drive (at 60th Street between Washington and East Van Buren Streets) where exhibits in the lobby and a small museum depict the history of the development of the Salt River Valley, a good introduction to the

Phoenix

N

27th Ave.

19th Ave.

7th Ave.

Broadway Rd.

Central Ave.

7th St.

16th St.

24th St.

32nd St.

40th St.

48th St.

Pima Frwy.

Priest Dr.

Mill Ave.

Black Canyon Frwy.

Thomas Rd.

Indian School Rd.

Camelback Rd.

East McDowell Rd.

East Van Buren

East Washington St.

East Washington St.

Buckeye Rd.

Maricopa Frwy.

Salt River

Drive Route =

Heard Museum

Art Museum
Museum of History

Pueblo Grande

Hall of Flame

Papago Park

Desert Botanical Garden

Salt River Project Bldg.

Zoo

Galvin Pkwy.

Invergordon Rd.

region surrounding Phoenix. Agriculture, the irrigation projects that have made life here possible, arts and crafts of the Indians, are all covered. Admission is free; the hours are from 9 to 5, weekdays.

The Hall of Flame

Across Project Drive from the Salt River Project office is the Hall of Flame, a diverting museum full of fire-fighting equipment from Phoenix and cities around the world. Twenty-seven fire-trucks are on display now; more will come out of storage as the museum expands; all belong to industrialist George F. Getz, who started his collection when he got a fire engine from his wife one birthday. The hall is open seven days a week, 9 to 5, closed Thanksgiving, Christmas and New Year's. Admission is $1.50 for adults, 50 cents for children 6 to 17.

The Pueblo Grande Museum

Drive next toward downtown Phoenix—west—to Pueblo Grande Museum, 4619 East Washington Street, where you may walk atop a prehistoric mound for a close look at the ways of some of the region's earliest inhabitants, the Hohokam In-dians, and see the remains of one of their villages and its cunn-ing irrigation systems, as well as a rare open-air ball court, last played upon some 500 years ago. Adjacent to the mound is a museum explaining the archaeology of the mound, with de-tailed exhibits of artifacts found during its excavation. Pueblo Grande takes about a half-hour to cover, although serious ar-chaeology buffs will want to stay longer; it is open from 9 to 4:45 Monday through Friday; from 1 to 4:45 on Sunday. The mound itself closes at 4:30; it is closed Saturday and major holidays. (Call 275-3452 or 275-9871 to check holiday hours.) Because of steps and ladders the mound might prove difficult for elderly or infirm visitors.

Some of the best walking in Phoenix happens to be in-doors, through the galleries of three museums in the heart of the city's downtown area, all within a few minutes stroll of each other. Park at the Phoenix Art Museum, 1625 North Central Avenue and you are roughly midway between the two others, the Phoenix Museum of History, four blocks south at 1242 North Central, and the Heard Museum of Anthropology and Primitive Art, which is four blocks north of the Phoenix Art Mu-seum and a half-block to the east, at 22 East Monte Vista Road.

The Phoenix Art Museum

Stroll around the plaza outside the Phoenix Art Museum and inspect the outdoor exhibits before going inside to the three floors and 20 galleries. They house a rich sampling of the world's fine art: Oriental, medieval, Renaissance, Baroque, 18th-century, Mexican, contemporary, and, of course, that regional favorite, Western art full of buckaroos and Indians. In addition to works by Dufy, Picasso, Braque, and other giants, it has a display of period costumes and an entire gallery of fascinating miniature rooms—tiny kitchens, drawing rooms and even a modern penthouse, all decorated and furnished with meticulous accuracy. The museum has a special audio treat for children, "Sounding Boards," an environmental work in which the kids plug headsets into a miniature forest to hear a surprisingly—and often hilariously—different sound each time they move from one tree to another.

A tour of the museum takes about an hour; galleries are open Tuesday through Saturday from 10 to 5, on Wednesday to 9; Sunday from 1 to 5; closed Monday and major holidays. Free tours start Sunday at 2, Wednesday at 7, and Friday at 1:15. Every Friday the museum holds what it calls "art breaks," 90 minutes of outdoor music in the courtyard starting at noon and, on alternate Fridays, hour-long tours of selected galleries starting at 12:15. Art breaks are free; so is admission to the museum—but a voluntary donation of $1 for adults and 50 cents for children is encouraged.

The Heard Museum—Devoted to Primitive Cultures

A six-minute walk north along Central brings you to East Monte Vista and the Heard, in whose cool and elegant galleries are some of the most beautiful relics of North American Indian and other primitive cultures to be found anywhere. Here, too, admission is voluntary, $1 suggested. The Heard can be rushed through in an hour or so, but if you can keep your visit that brief, you aren't really looking. One entire gallery, for example, is devoted to Indian silversmithing; another presents the relatively little-known arts and crafts of the Spanish colonial period in the Southwest, a trove of striking weavings and rough-hewn furniture from an era when this region was virtually an island, isolated from the fledgling nation to the east and from the rest of the world as well. Other galleries cover Pueblo Indian cultures, contemporary Indian art, baskets and pottery, and the science of anthropology itself. The seasonal rhythms of Hopi religious beliefs are vividly displayed in a gallery with some 450 kachina dolls, most of them from the collection of Arizona's U.S. Senator Barry Goldwater. A shop has fine jewelry, pottery, and a solid collection of books on Indian and anthropological lore for sale. The Heard is open from 10 to 5 Monday to Saturday and from 1 to 5 Sunday; closed holidays.

A Very Eclectic Museum of History
Visiting the Phoenix Museum of History, straight down North Central from the Heard, is a relaxing way to wind up your downtown walk, a bit like dropping into the home of a beloved but slightly daffy relative who never threw anything out. Among its displays are a replica of a 1930s Phoenix bedroom, a collection of toys from 1890 to 1930, stained glass from Phoenix movie houses, period gowns, a fine collection of old pharmacy items, a poignant display that chronicles the region's historic—and still ongoing—battles with flood and drought, and, in the backyard, one of the original generators from Roosevelt Dam. The museum is open from 10 to 4, Tuesday through Saturday.

SCOTTSDALE
John Neary

Scottsdale likes to call itself the West's most Western town—which can be confusing if that makes you think of *Old* West.
Don't let that cowboy-movie decor fool you.
Scottsdale is the *New* West, the Sunbelt right now, where you can glimpse some of the fanciest cars, prettiest women, most eye-dazzling shops and, also, where you can encounter some of the most mind-stretching ideas anywhere in the modern U.S.

Historical Perspectives
Historically, Scottsdale goes way back past the turn of the century, as does Phoenix, its sprawling next-door neighbor. Both cities, however, did not really begin to stretch out and boom until World War II. Scottsdale was still empty desert when

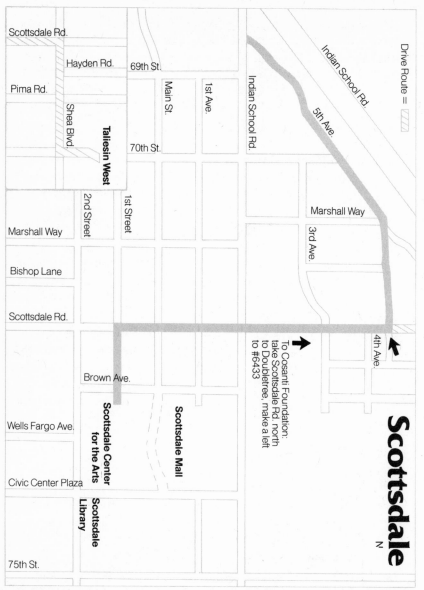

This walking tour is approximately 3 miles round trip. Taliesin and Cosanti add another ¼ mile.

a settler from Camp McDowell, in 1864, began cutting the hay that grew along the banks of the Salt River to fuel cavalry horses for skirmishes with the Apaches. From that hay camp, Phoenix began, a farm town for nearly the next century.

It was not until 1888 that an army chaplain, Winfield Scott (no relation to the famous general of the same name), happened to visit Phoenix while on a furlough and spotted some land that looked promising, just south of the Arizona irrigation canal in the desert outside Phoenix. Scott was transferred to Fort Huachuca in 1889 and, working on weekend passes and during leaves, undertook the task of transforming his 600-acre homestead 9 miles outside Phoenix into a citrus ranch. A most remarkable feat given that the fort is 180 miles away from the homestead site and there were no autos or planes then.

Bearded, slender, and intense, Scott had big ideas. He sent testimonials back East urging settlers to move out to join him, but response was less than electric. By 1897, just seven families called Scottsdale home. Scott died in 1910, his town still just a name on the map. Population was only 2,000 in 1951 but then Americans suddenly discovered it was more fun in the sun and Scottsdale's innkeepers hastened to oblige, turning their dude ranches into glittering resorts. By 1960 Scottsdale had grown to 10,000 and in the next 15 years spurted another tenfold until by 1975 it had some 95,000 residents living in its 89 square miles—all of them seeking the good life, Arizona-style.

Where once land on the rugged escarpments of Camelback Mountain literally could not be given away—an acre was yours just for the taking if you would only spend a night on it, but folks scoffed and said nothing would grow there but jackrabbits and rattlers—a room in a luxury resort on the mountain now can cost upwards of $65 a night for two during the peak winter season.

Scottsdale offers the full panorama of resort treats from golf to swimming to polo to just loafing in the sun, but even tourists who are just passing through can pause to enjoy one of the pastimes for which Scottsdale is best known: browsing among its countless shops.

A Modern Bazaar

Scottsdale is truly one of the world's most variegated bazaars, with gallery after gallery, boutique after boutique, all interspersed with antique shops, plain and fancy restaurants,

Western-wear places that sell peach-hued cowboy hats that would make an old-timer blush, and, around every corner, more galleries and shops.

As much fun as it might be to try, you cannot possibly even window-shop through all of Scottsdale in a single morning or afternoon, and the shops are not segregated into specialty districts, so pin-point assaults are out, too. Better just relax and enjoy some take-it-as-you-come serendipity afoot.

As good a place as any to start is at Scottsdale Road and Fifth Avenue; just pick a parking spot—they're free!—and start working your way down one side of Fifth and back up the other. Galleries abound here, with the emphasis on art depicting Western Americana, much of it the slickest of contemporary works. That does not mean, however, you won't come across candy shops, leather works, and traditional Indian jewelry, too.

Scottsdale Mall

Next you might want to move your car a few blocks south on Scottsdale Road, turning left on 1st or 2nd Street to enter the parking area for Scottsdale Mall, 20 acres of yet more shops and galleries—and close to even more stores back out on Scottsdale Road.

If you happen to arrive in the mall around noon, you just might chance upon a band concert; grab a sandwich in one of the handy restaurants and hurry back to sit on the grass and listen.

The Center for the Arts and the Library

The cavernous main floor of the Scottsdale Center for the Arts is a pleasant spot for a visit, with free concerts on Sunday and a changing display of paintings, drawings and sculpture that is open from noon to 5 p.m. throughout the week. Across Civic Center Plaza Street, just east of the arts center, is Scottsdale's large and modern public library, an ideal antidote for an overdose of shopping.

Taliesin West—Home and Studio of Frank Lloyd Wright

Scottsdale happens to have become home for two of America's—and the world's—most radical architects, men whose work and thinking have taken them beyond mere buildings into the realm of art and philosophy. The senior of the two, Frank Lloyd Wright, died in 1959, but his students still carry on in his spirit at Taliesin West, his home and studio in the foothills about a 20-minute drive northeast of Scottsdale, where visitors are welcome.

Wright's widow, Olgivanna Lloyd Wright, has quoted the master architect as saying, "Architects could learn from me to use the sun as a brush and the earth as a canvas. The pigment? Human nature." Indeed, architects and architects-to-be came from around the world to learn from Wright to meld their works with the very earth itself—and what better classroom for such an educational venture than the landscape around Scottsdale, where land and sky meet in a harsh and beautiful union?

Here at Taliesin West, working just as they did with Wright, "The Fellowship," as the students call themselves, learn design, drafting, construction, landscaping, gardening, cooking, interior decorating, and along with those skills and techniques that Wright felt were central to the art of architecture, they also work in poetry, sculpture, music, dance, and weaving. "All this, of course," Mrs. Wright once explained, "is to develop him as an architect, a builder, and a man with the knowledge of how to make use of his creative energy."

To reach Taliesin—which means "Shining Brow" in Welsh, evoking Wright's hillside emplacement of his home—go north on Scottsdale Road to Shea Boulevard and turn right (a bright-red metal sculpture points the way). Drive east on Shea to 108th Street and turn left (at another red sculpture). Follow the road without turning to the Taliesin parking lot. A slide show tracing the development of Wright's work is free, in the dining hall of the Wright School. A half-hour guided tour of the buildings, built by Wright and his students from 1938 to 1956, is mostly limited to exteriors and costs $3. Taliesin West, itself an embodiment of Wright's central notions of simplicity and the need for bonding buildings with their environment, is open from 10 a.m. to 4 p.m. every day from the end of September to May, but a phone call (948-6670) to be certain is advised.

Wright's magnetism as a creative giant—and the lure of the desert, too—brought Paolo Soleri to Taliesin as a student in the 1950s.

The Cosanti Foundation—Home of a Visionary Architect

On your way between Scottsdale's shopping areas and Taliesin West, you will pass Doubletree Road; turn west to number 6433 and there, on a perfectly conventional suburban street lined with quite ordinary ranch houses, you will find yourself confronted with some of the most unorthodox architecture on earth.

The mailbox says this is the Cosanti Foundation. A path from the parking lot leads you into a cool, shaded sanctuary of free-form concrete struts supporting concrete-shell roofs as delicate as seashells, pierced by stained-glass skylights. Music plays and bells chime in the breeze.

This is the home and studio of Paolo Soleri. Here on display is a huge model of Soleri's major project, Arcosanti, now under construction (and also open to the public, but only by guided tour, at 11 a.m. and 2 p.m.), 66 miles to the north at Cordes Junction. Arcosanti embodies Soleri's central belief that compression and miniaturization—in direct counterpoint to such sprawling urban areas as Scottsdale and Phoenix—are the way cities should develop in the future. Here at Cosanti, you can wander at will to study the distinctive designs of Soleri's shops and workrooms, listen to the bronze and ceramic windchimes he designs and sells, and ponder his blueprints for the future, which are on display everywhere around you. Cosanti Foundation is open to the public seven days a week from 9 to 5.

Don't be too surprised if, after walking around Cosanti, Taliesin West and Scottsdale, you are reluctant to go back to a world that seems a bit behind the times. It is not at all unusual to want to spend more time in Scottsdale. After all, you're in good company: Frank Lloyd Wright, Paolo Soleri, and even old founding-father Scott found it hard to leave.

Walking
the
Midwest

OHIO

DOWNTOWN CLEVELAND
Richard Wager

Local legend relates that Cleveland, Ohio's largest city, acquired its present spelling because the original "Cleaveland" was simply too long for the "banner" headline on a city newspaper. Inventive Clevelanders, anticipating the demands of progress, are an intrinsic part of this city's history—it was here that such "firsts" as outdoor electrical lighting and free mail delivery were introduced.

A walk through downtown Cleveland provides visitors with an opportunity to view many of the city's tributes to its sons' ingenuity and also to savor the historical roots in which Clevelanders take so much pride. This is, after all, the city in which Archibald M. Willard was inspired to paint his masterpiece, *Spirit of '76*.

Public Square: The Hub
What better place to begin our tour than Public Square, the very hub, which was staked out as a central park by General Moses Cleaveland, a Connecticut surveyor and lawyer, when he founded the city in 1796. (You can see a statue of the general in the southwest quadrant of the square.) The layout of the city is systematic—all main thoroughfares radiate from the square.

On the southwest corner, the 52-story Terminal Tower, built in 1928—the tallest building in America outside of New York until 1967—dominates the square. In the heydey of rail travel, the terminal brought passengers from subterranean tracks into the heart of the city. Now it is the downtown station for Cleveland's rapid-transit system, which connects with Cleve-

Downtown Cleveland

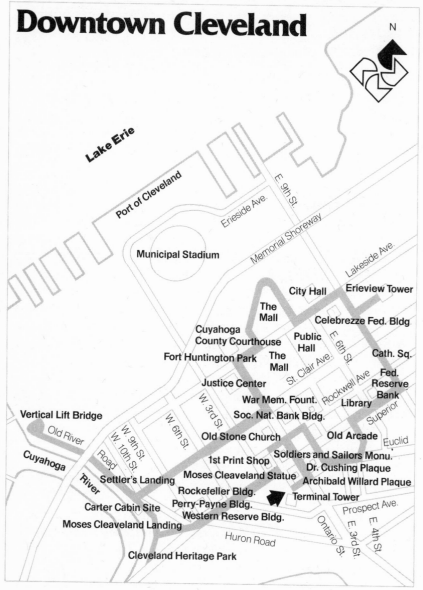

N

Lake Erie

Port of Cleveland

Erieside Ave.

E. 9th St.

Memorial Shoreway

Lakeside Ave.

Municipal Stadium

City Hall   Erieview Tower

The Mall   Celebrezze Fed. Bldg.

Cuyahoga County Courthouse   Public Hall   Cath. Sq.

Fort Huntington Park   The Mall

St. Clair Ave.   E. 6th St.

Justice Center   Rockwell Ave.   Fed. Reserve Bank

War Mem. Fount.   Library   Superior

Vertical Lift Bridge   Soc. Nat. Bank Bldg.

Old River   W. 3rd St.

Cuyahoga   W. 6th St.   Old Stone Church   Old Arcade   Euclid

River   W. 9th St.   W. 10th St.   Road   1st Print Shop   Soldiers and Sailors Monu.

Settler's Landing   Moses Cleaveland Statue   Dr. Cushing Plaque

Carter Cabin Site   Rockefeller Bldg.   Archibald Willard Plaque

Perry-Payne Bldg.   Terminal Tower   Prospect Ave.

Moses Cleaveland Landing   Western Reserve Bldg.

Huron Road   Ontario St.   E. 3rd St.   E. 4th St.

Cleveland Heritage Park

This walking tour is approximately 3-3/4 miles round trip.

land Hopkins International Airport among other points. You can see the classic grandeur of the terminal in the bronzed, vaulted-ceiling portico and the marble-walled ramps leading to lower-level shops, restaurants, food stands, and the rapid station, as Clevelanders call it.

Over the years the square has been a universally free podium for political candidates of many ranks as well as for anyone wishing to speak on any subject.

Abraham Lincoln, en route to his first inaugural in 1861, addressed a huge crowd here, and a little more than four years later, 100,000 persons filed somberly past his coffin as it lay in state near the center of the square.

Arc lamps invented by Clevelander Charles F. Brush illuminated the square as early as April 29, 1879, making it the first electric street lighting in the world. Two replica lamps, one at the corner of a restaurant off the northwest corner of the square, the other overhead at the northeast corner of Ontario Street and Rockwell Avenue, commemorate the achievement.

On the north side of the square, easily discernible by its ecclesiastical architecture, is Old Stone Church, founded in 1820. Many of the stained-glass windows were designed by Louis Tiffany. This, its second building, dates from 1855. Walking east on Rockwell Avenue across Ontario from the church, you'll see the ten-story Society National Bank Building, one of the highest weight-bearing-type structures in the world, depending on its walls for support. Continuing eastward a few steps, the northeast corner of the square opens onto the Mall, a park which extends three blocks north to the point where it overlooks Lake Erie. (Later on the tour, you will be passing through the far sector of the Mall.) Here, looking east from the square, is the War Memorial Fountain with its tall heroic figure symbolizing man's immortal spirit rising above the flames of war, dedicated to those who died in World War II and Korea. Extending your view eastward across the Mall you will see the Board of Education Building and in front, a statue of Lincoln erected in 1932 and paid for by pennies from Cleveland school children.

Continuing clockwise around the square you'll see the Federal Courts Building (immediately on your left), built around the turn of the century as Cleveland's Main Post Office. A tablet in the lobby honors Joseph W. Briggs, who, while working as a Cleveland postal clerk in 1863, conceived the idea of citywide free mail delivery and collection. He was later appointed by the

Postmaster General to install city free delivery throughout the United States.

Crossing Superior Avenue from the Old Federal Building to the southeast quadrant of the square, you'll find the imposing Soldiers and Sailors Monument, a towering column topped by a figure denoting the spirit of liberty, dedicated in 1894 to Civil War veterans. Their names are inscribed on inside walls, and there's a small museum. Admission is free.

Euclid Avenue

A few more steps and you're at Euclid Avenue, formerly considered one of the finest residential streets in the country. The stately homes which once graced "Millionaires Row" have been replaced by commercial establishments. Euclid is now Cleveland's main shopping thoroughfare. Walking south across Euclid Avenue, you'll see a plaque marking the birthplace (1869) of Dr. Harvey Cushing, a brain surgeon who pioneered in the use of the electric knife and also won a Pulitzer Prize in biography in 1925. Farther up Euclid a short distance, you'll find another plaque, in an alley marked E. 3rd Street, which commemorates the site where, in a fourth-floor studio, Archibald M. Willard painted his first version of the famous *Spirit of '76* in July 1876. You can see his finished masterpiece on the tour at City Hall.

Crossing Euclid Avenue at the next traffic light (E. 4th St.) brings you to the Old Arcade. Extending north to Superior Avenue, it was opened in 1890 as the largest structure of its kind in the world—400 feet long, its glass roof 100 feet high with room for 112 bazaar-like shops on five floors that stretch between office towers. The interior is in marble, brass, and wrought iron, replete in the Victorian style of the late 1800s.

Coming out of the Old Arcade onto Superior, you will see across the street the Cleveland Public Library in two buildings separated by the Eastman Reading Garden. It is the fifth-largest library in the United States. Treasures are displayed on each of the five floors of the main building. In Eastman Garden (entrance is through either library building) you can hear free noonday concerts of recorded music, May through October. Three other downtown parks—Hanna Fountains and Mall, Chester Commons and Huron Mall—have free live noontime concerts of popular music in summer.

Continue east on Superior across E. 6th Street to the Federal Reserve Bank, which will be on your left. Built in 1923, it was patterned after a Florentine fortress and had the world's largest vault at that time. Our walk turns north onto E. 9th Street at St. John's Cathedral Square, a complex of several buildings comprising the center of the Cleveland Catholic Diocese. The cathedral cornerstone was laid in 1849, and the complex was rebuilt and enlarged in 1948. If you continue north on E. 9th Street a little more than two short blocks, you'll see on your left the new Anthony J. Celebrezze Federal Building, one of Cleveland's tallest structures. It was named for the Cleveland mayor who became Secretary of HEW under President Kennedy, and later a federal judge. On your right is Erieview Plaza with a long, decorative pool, and the 40-story Erieview Tower. Stouffer's Top of the Town Restaurant affords an excellent view of the metropolitan area. The public is welcome. There is no obligation to purchase food or beverage. The best view is from the lounge, just off the elevator.

The Mall

From Erieview Tower, walk north to Lakeside Avenue and across E. 9th Street to City Hall, an imposing edifice with Grecian columns. This classic structure houses Willard's painting in its rotunda. Just across Lakeside Avenue from City Hall and a bit to the west is Public Hall, the main building of the Cleveland Convention Center—the rest is underground, with the exhibit areas beneath the Mall. Follow the sidewalk along the west side of City Hall north to the lookout and Pulaski Cannon at the north end of the Mall. There you can see Municipal Stadium, home of the Indians baseball and Browns football teams, one of the eight largest municipal stadiums in the world. Record crowds for each sport have exceeded 85,000.

In view from the lookout is the Port of Cleveland, where freighters dock from around the world. Permanently moored east of E. 9th Street is the U.S.S. *Cod*, a submarine that operated in the Pacific in World War II and the Korean War. Farther east you'll find Burke Lakefront Airport with scheduled commuter service to Detroit and Columbus. (Both the *Cod* and the Lakefront Airport are beyond comfortable walking distance of this lookout point.) The modest building across the railroad tracks just below the Mall is the new Amtrak station.

The Courthouse

If you are feeling energetic, you can visit Cuyahoga County Courthouse, west of the Mall, which houses several outstanding murals and a fine spiral marble staircase.

Fort Huntington Park, on the west side of the courthouse, is the site of Cleveland's only stockade, built in May 1813. It was here that General William Henry Harrison met Commodore Oliver Hazard Perry to plan strategy for the Battle of Lake Erie.

Turn south on Ontario Street and Cleveland's new $135,000,000 Justice Center will be on your right, easily noted by the controversial modern sculpture (its detractors call it a "twisted heating duct") in front. To complete the first segment of our walking tour, go south on Ontario Street, and you're back at Public Square.

Along the River

Another choice is to continue the walking tour west on St. Clair Avenue, or you may opt to drive the one-third mile to Old River Road and Settlers' Landing, a new development that combines history and commerce with the lore of the Cuyahoga River. Old River Road is a street of shops, restaurants and boutiques, ships' chandlers—buildings resurrected from the past and now a popular place to browse as you watch giant Great Lakes iron ore freighters, tugs, a city firefighting boat and pleasure craft passing on the river. The north end of the road offers a close-up view of a vertical-lift railroad bridge which is frequently in motion. If you look along the ground, you are likely to see some round taconite pellets (iron ore) brought from mines in the upper Great Lakes region for Cleveland steel mills.

Retracing your steps (walking or driving) on Old River Road brings you back to the foot of St. Clair Avenue, the site where Lorenzo Carter, Cleveland's first permanent settler, built a log cabin in 1797, and a short distance beyond, upriver, the place where Moses Cleaveland landed in 1796. About 200 yards still farther you can visit Cleveland Heritage Park with its replica of a log cabin. The park provides a view of the river (you can see why Indians named it the Cuyahoga, meaning "crooked") and many of its 29 bridges of various types—bascule, swing, truss, arch. Several of these move to accommodate surface and river traffic as needed. The Detroit-Superior span, virtually overhead, was the world's largest double-deck, reinforced-concrete bridge when built in 1917. The lower deck was used to carry streetcars, but with their passing was sealed over.

On the walk uphill to Superior Avenue and return to Public Square you'll pass several notable buildings constructed around the turn of the century. The eight-story Western Reserve Building with end and center bay windows was built for Samuel Mather, mining and shipping mogul. It has been renovated and has new tenants, among them United Airlines' regional headquarters. The Perry-Payne Building on the upper level of Superior was built to house the home offices of shipping and iron ore companies.

You'll also pass one of Cleveland's first skyscrapers, the 17-story Rockefeller Building—built by John D. Rockefeller Sr., one of Cleveland's most famous "sons" and at one time the world's richest man. A plaque in front of a Superior Avenue tavern near the Square marks the first print shop and newspaper office in Cleveland (built in 1818).

Another half-block and you're back at Public Square.

Some Eateries

Happily, there are benches for rest and relaxation at numerous points along our walking tour—in Public Square, the Mall, Erieview Plaza, at the side of City Hall, in front and back of the Anthony J. Celebrezze Federal Building, and in Fort Huntington Park.

Several good restaurants and snack bars at various price ranges are to be found along the tour.

Especially recommended are the Colonnade Cafeteria in the basement of the Leader Building (southwest corner of E. 6th Street and Superior Avenue) and the Cleaveland Crate & Truckin' Co., a former truck terminal, now a fun eatery, on Old River Road between the site of Moses Cleaveland's landing and Cleveland Heritage Park.

MICHIGAN

RENAISSANCE ON THE DETROIT RIVER
George Cantor

Detroit may be famous for its cars but it's still a river which makes this city run. The river brought the first French explorers, who came ashore in 1701 to establish a fort and farming settlement here. In the age of westward expansion, the river carried the settlers and the commerce which turned the little village into a city. And at the turn of the century, the river provided the cheap transport, the access to the iron mines of the north and to the markets of the east which made Detroit the logical focus of the infant automotive industry.

Now Detroit is counting on its river again, this time more than ever. Troubled more than any great American city by the social upheaval and racial conflict of the last decades, Detroit is moving toward a rebirth. The instrument of renewal is Renaissance Center, a massive riverside project that is the largest privately financed urban development in American history.

Water's Edge

So it is here along the river on Jefferson Avenue, on the eastern edge of the business district, that any walk through Detroit should begin. Actually, the Detroit River is not a river at all. It's really a strait connecting Lake Erie with Lake St. Clair. That's what the city's name means in French, "the strait."

It is an arresting sight—the busiest inland waterway in the world. Giant lake freighters bearing the flags of every seafaring nation on the globe pass by on their way from the St. Lawrence Seaway to the great ports of the Midwest, a thousand miles from the ocean.

The view in front of you is also very unusual. That city

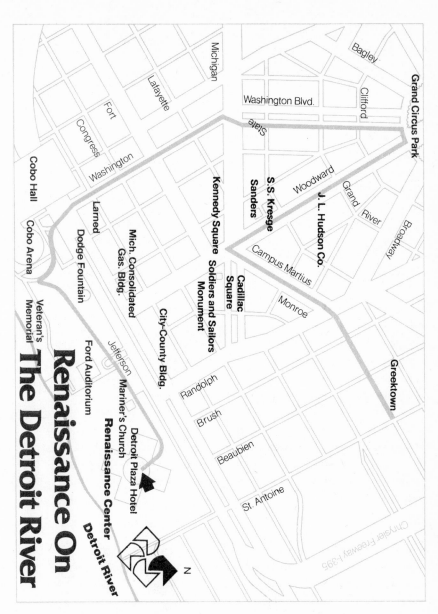

This walking tour is approximately 1¼ miles.

across the mile-wide stretch of water is Windsor, Ontario, and the direction you are facing is due south. It is the only place along the border from which you can look south into Canada.

Renaissance Center

Behind you rise the towers of RenCen, as it is abbreviated in Detroit. The huge structure at the center, a soaring cylinder of glass and steel, is the Detroit Plaza Hotel, at 740 feet the highest building in the state and one of the largest hotels in the world. The central tower is flanked by four smaller, broader office buildings and linked by shopping promenades which feature some of the most distinguished names in American fashion. The complex was designed by Atlanta architect John Portman.

Moving spirit behind the $350 million project was Henry Ford II, grandson of the man who remade the city 75 years ago with his gasoline buggy. Since its opening in March 1977, Ren-Cen has become a favorite tourist attraction for out-of-towners and Detroiters alike. They come to rubberneck at its vast, water-fall-laden lobby, browse in its shops, and eat at its huge selection of restaurants—everything from costly French cuisine to McDonald's.

A rooftop revolving restaurant, the Summit, opens out on views over a 50-mile chunk of scenery. The entire course of the Detroit River is visible from this vantage point, as well as the sweep of the Detroit metropolitan area, fifth-largest in the country. On clear days you can even make out the bubble of the Pontiac Silverdome, the domed sports stadium in the distant suburbs where football's Lions, basketball's Pistons, and soccer's Express frolic.

A Museum of Money

In the RenCen tower occupied by the National Bank of Detroit you'll find the Money Museum, a collection of ancient, unusual, historic, and beautiful legal tender assembled from around the world. Look at the exhibits on primitive money and Greek and Roman coins. Admission to the priceless collection is free. It is open during regular banking hours.

Just across the street from RenCen is a small reminder of an older Detroit which was obliterated by the automotive age. This is Mariner's Church, built in the 1840s as a place of worship for lake sailors who flocked to the old port. The church has been altered over the years and even moved a few blocks to make room for the adjacent Civic Center. But its nautical ties survive and its bell is still tolled for every sailor lost upon the Great Lakes.

Civic Center

West of the church is the Civic Center, the earlier phase of Detroit's waterfront redevelopment program. In the years following World War II, this district was a depressing warren of warehouses, docks and railroad tracks. In a tremendous burst of civic enthusiasm, spearheaded by then Mayor Albert E. Cobo, the area was cleaned out and three major riverfront facilities erected.

As you move away from the RenCen, you can see the Civic Center buildings—the Ford Auditorium, the Veterans Memorial, and Cobo Hall and Convention Arena. The auditorium is the home of the Detroit Symphony Orchestra and also the site of many concerts throughout the year. Cobo Arena also holds several big concerts in its 11,000-seat arena. The Veterans Memorial, completed in 1950, was the first of the group to open. It stands a few yards from the spot at which Antoine de la Mothe Cadillac led the founding party ashore in 1701—a date which preceded the settlement of either St. Louis or New Orleans.

The Philip A. Hart Memorial Plaza, a 10-acre landscaped park, runs the length of the Civic Center, between the river and Jefferson Avenue. The computerized fountain near its midpoint was a gift from the Dodges, another of Detroit's great automotive families.

Two other buildings face each other from opposite sides of Woodward Avenue, across the street. On the east is the City-County Building, fronted by a giant sculpted figure. Its official name is *The Spirit of Detroit* but because of its coating of patina everyone calls it "The Jolly Green Giant." Across Woodward, the Michigan Consolidated Gas Co. displays the Oriental influence of Minoru Yamasaki, an internationally known architect who lives and works in the Detroit area.

Take a Ride in a Portuguese Streetcar

Continue west along Jefferson to Washington Boulevard, then turn right away from the river. You now have a choice of either proceeding on foot or boarding a tiny streetcar for a ride on the rails up the boulevard. The streetcars were imported from Lisbon, Portugal, in 1976 and have proved to be one of the most popular attractions in the downtown area. Fare for the one-way ride is 25 cents.

Up Washington Boulevard

Some of the city's finest restaurants lie along Larned and Congress, the first two streets on the route, and at lunchtime they are jammed with members of the city's financial institutions, media personalities, and visiting celebrities. Fort Street is named for the northern boundary of the British fort which was built here in the 1760s and served as a base for raids on colonial settlements in the West. On Lafayette you'll find several of the city's fast-food institutions, the Coney Island restaurants clustered a block to the west. The restaurants are usually jammed at all hours of the day and night.

Past Lafayette, Washington Boulevard widens into a broad thoroughfare with statues and flowering gardens at each intersection. In former years, this was the most fashionable shopping street in the city. It has suffered some decay recently, but the newly renovated Radisson Cadillac Hotel, on the right, evidences a rebirth in this part of the downtown area too.

The Stores of Woodward

The boulevard comes to an end at Grand Circus Park, and a fast right turn will bring you back to Woodward. Many of the city's major retailers have outlets on this stretch of the street, which is being transformed into a pedestrian mall. J. L. Hudson Co., on your left a few blocks down, is the largest department store in the city. The ice-cream soda was invented at Sanders, on the opposite side of Woodward, and Detroiters regard the hot fudge sundaes served here as the best in the Midwest.

A Couple of Squares

One block farther down is Cadillac Square, the traditional heart of the city. Here you can see most vividly the results of the chaotic street plan that developed in this part of the city. Fire destroyed the city in 1805 and it was rebuilt along the model of the parks and squares of Washington, D.C. After a few years, however, that plan was scrapped and a grid pattern superimposed on it. The result is confusion for all, even lifelong residents.

The area on the right, known as Kennedy Square, is a favorite summer meeting ground for lunchers, who buy sandwiches to munch in the sunshine. Across Woodward is the Soldiers and Sailors Monument, a fixture here since the Civil War years. To its right is Cadillac Square, now defaced by a bus terminal. To the left is Campus Martius, which is the street you now want to follow.

Campus Martius eventually turns into Monroe Street and is lined by some of the oldest business facades in the city. Historians say they are an important architectural landmark and must be preserved; the city thinks they're an eyesore and would like to tear them down. Their eventual fate is still uncertain.

A Grecian Festival

Monroe soon narrows in width and after two more blocks you arrive in Greektown. It's only a block long, but this is downtown Detroit's liveliest after-dark corner. It is lined with Greek restaurants, coffeehouses, bakeries, boutiques, taverns, and even a theater. This is where the city comes together in all its diversity. College students enjoy a plate of moussaka seated next to uniformed policemen from police headquarters around the corner. Bearded musicians and suburbanites share a table and clap to the sound of the bouzouki together.

Stop in at one of the establishments for a cup of strong Greek coffee and a helping of sweet baklava. It's the perfect end for this walk through the changing scene that makes up the center of Detroit.

DETROIT'S NEW CENTER TO THE CULTURAL CENTER
George Cantor

Detroit's New Center hasn't actually been new for more than half a century. Its construction began in 1921, when the first rush of automotive big money was pouring into the city and men in the industry were dreaming big dreams. The New Center was one of the biggest—an alternate central business district located out of the traditional downtown area: offices, theaters, skyscrapers, all built far from the existing patterns of commerce.

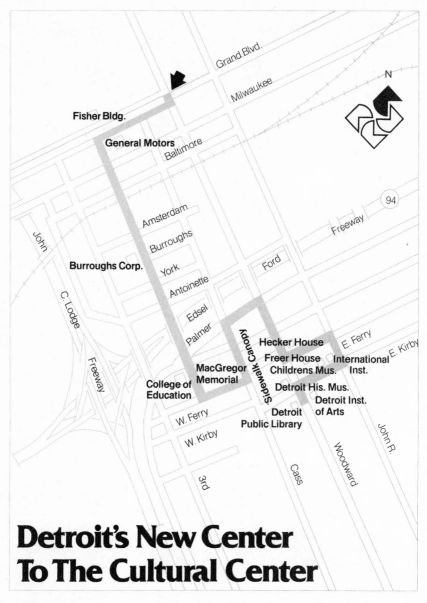

Detroit's New Center To The Cultural Center

This walking tour is approximately 1-3/4 miles.

It was a daring concept in its time—almost unheard-of in American cities. Yet the infant General Motors Corporation had grasped the idea that the expanding use of the automobile was making possible the construction of separate business districts. The GM Building and the New Center which rose around it were harbingers of the trend toward suburbanization which would follow several decades later.

Start this walk at the corner of Woodward and Grand Boulevard (known in Detroit simply as the Boulevard). It is a 10-minute cab ride from downtown, and the Woodward bus also runs to this intersection.

In the 1890s, the Boulevard represented the farthest limit of fashionable suburbia. It was laid out along the path of the city limits of the time, and wealthy Detroiters, who had made their money primarily in lumbering and small local industries, built imposing mansions along its route.

A Graceful Era Ends

In those years, Detroit was regarded as one of the most beautiful cities in the country. In the old photographs it presents a graceful, tree-lined vista with fine homes and shaded streets. But by 1921 that period was coming to an end because of the forces symbolized in the monolithic structure coming into view on your left, the GM Building.

This is world headquarters of the giant automotive corporation, the stunning creation of one of the city's greatest architects, Albert Kahn. He was closely allied with many of the pioneer automakers and practically invented the modern factory in his designs for Henry Ford. The New Center gave him a chance to display his genius on a grand scale. The GM Building is one of his showpieces. At its completion it was the second-largest office building in the country. It is a vast structure, occupying an entire city block. Shaped like a massive, hollow square, it looks almost like an impregnable fort. There is nothing beautiful about it. The building represents power, the forces which even then were remaking the face of Detroit and America. Look at its repeating rows of windows and columns, a form which is almost mechanical. They seem to allude to the products which were planned inside.

The main entrance had to be moved back several yards when the Boulevard was widened, but Kahn's total effect remains unspoiled. And the huge showrooms on the ground floor of the building are a handy place to check out the new lines in all GM divisions.

The Fisher and Its Shops

The skyscraper across the Boulevard from GM is the Fisher Building, another of Kahn's finest works. It was built in 1928. Although less than 30 stories high, it appears much taller because of the soaring central tower and the setbacks alongside it that make the tower seem to vault from the rest of the structure. The interior decoration along the shopping concourse is also worth a look. Notice the brilliant mosaics on the ceilings. The building houses Detroit's major legitimate playhouse, the Fisher Theatre, which previews many shows prior to their Broadway runs.

The New Center also anticipated another modern development, the underground urban shopping mall. The major buildings in the center are linked by well-lighted tunnels with attractive shopping concourses at their entrances, so one can stroll from one area to another without having to brave Detroit's unpredictable weather.

Second Boulevard is the street which runs due south from the Fisher Building. Cross the Boulevard in that direction and start walking toward the railroad viaduct.

The Wayne Campus

In a few blocks you'll pass the offices of the Burroughs Corporation, another of the machine makers that grew up along with the automobile industry. After you cross over the Edsel Ford Freeway, the street makes a sweeping curve to the right. Keep walking straight and you'll find yourself on the mall that runs through the heart of Wayne State University.

This urban institution, among the 20 largest campuses in the country, draws its enrollment overwhelmingly from the Detroit area. It is chiefly distinguished by the architecture of Minoru Yamasaki, an artist who has left as much of a mark on the city as did Kahn at an earlier time.

Yamasaki's most acclaimed work on the campus is the MacGregor Memorial Center, on the left side of the mall between Palmer and Ferry. There is such a sense of lightness and airiness to the architecture that this jewel-like building with its sunken gardens and spacious windows almost seems to float in air. Critics have compared it to a miniature Taj Mahal.

Across the mall is another of Yamasaki's Wayne State buildings, albeit one that met with far more controversy than the universally acclaimed MacGregor. This is the College of Education, a tiered construction which some critics complain resembles an inverted wedding cake. It is, nonetheless, a campus landmark.

After exploring the rest of this attractive central mall, start making your way east along Ferry. Cross Cass and on your left you'll see a concrete canopy over the sidewalk. Along this stretch of the campus lie some of its more interesting and amusing hangouts and shops. There is a sprinkling of eating places, galleries and bars. More popular with faculty members is the bar in the adjacent Belcrest Hotel, a holdover from the days when this was an attractive residential area. Now this part of the city, around the university and museums, is called the Cultural Center. But in its time, roughly 1875–1915, it was the most desirable address in town.

Victorian Echoes

For a look at a vestige of this era, turn right on Palmer and cross to the east side of Woodward. The miniature French Renaissance chateau at the corner of Ferry, now occupied by Smiley Brothers Music Company, was built in 1890 for the Hecker family and was one of the lavish mansions in the city.

Turn east on Ferry and there, surviving almost intact, is an entire block of mansions from the gilded age. The Victorians were decidedly not of the cookie-cutter school of architecture and these homes reflect the wide assortment of styles they favored. There are Italian chateaus, French chateaus, English castles. Notice in particular the craftsmanship in the stonework on the Freer House, now housing offices of the Merrill-Palmer Clinic. It was built as a rival to the Hecker house in 1890 and regarded as the city's showplace.

Turn right on John R and right again on the next block, Kirby. Now we are out of the Victorian fantasy and into the heart of the Cultural Center.

The Ethnic Mix

Detroit is noted for the diversity of its ethnic population and the building at the corner, the International Institute, is the embodiment of that cultural mix. The tight ethnic neighborhoods that once made up Detroit have nearly all disintegrated, but the city retains a lively interest in its roots. The institute, a liaison organization among the various groups, schedules activities over the year that reflect this interest. There are folk dances, art exhibits, picnics, all sorts of informal get-togethers. You may want to step inside and see if anything is going on during your stay. The staff will be happy to assist you.

A bit further along the block is the Children's Museum, run by the city's Board of Education and open to the general public. Most interesting are its African cultural exhibits and displays of animals native to Michigan. It's open 1–4 on weekdays and 9–4 on Saturday, October to May. Admission is free.

Historical Corners

Follow Kirby to Woodward and cross over to reach the Detroit Historical Museum. This building serves as a reminder of the city's colorful past in a place that too often has obliterated any physical evidence of its history. High points of a visit are the Streets of Old Detroit, a reconstruction of a typical city street over several eras in the city's past, and the hall of automobiles on the main floor. Open 9–5; closed Monday.

Across Kirby is the Detroit Public Library, believed to be the largest open-shelf facility in the country. It was designed by Cass Gilbert in the manner of a 16th-century Italian palace and opened in 1921. Its Burton Historical Collection is an invaluable source of documents on the old Northwest frontier. Of chief interest to visitors, though, is the series of murals on Michigan history rendered by local artists. It is on the second floor.

Institute of Arts

The other Italian palace that faces the library from across Woodward is the Detroit Institute of Arts, built as a companion piece in 1927. Appropriately enough, it houses one of the world's top collections of Italian Renaissance art. As you walk through the newly opened Italian wing of the museum, look in particular for Titian's *Man with a Flute* and the recently acquired *Conversion of the Magdalene* by Caravaggio.

The institute's most famous room, however, is the Garden Court, located directly behind the main entrance. The murals here are the work of Mexican artist Diego Rivera, who was commissioned to portray a sense of Detroit's industrial power on its walls. When his work was unveiled in 1933, however, it touched off the greatest artistic furor in the city's history.

His paintings of heroic workers and decadent bosses caused the furious wealthy patrons of the institute to accuse Rivera of indulging in Communist propaganda at their expense. Some seriously suggested that they be whitewashed away. But cooler heads prevailed and the murals remain as one of Detroit's best-loved treasures.

Make your way to the cavernous Kresge Court Cafeteria. If it reminds you of a medieval banqueting hall, that is precisely the intended effect. The institute, in fact, holds an annual medieval Christmas celebration here. It's the ideal place to end this walk through Detroit's past, sipping coffee and nibbling cake while the traffic on Woodward booms past unheard.

HILLS AND LAKES OF SUBURBAN DETROIT
George Cantor

Birmingham is one of the richest suburbs in the Detroit area. Its shady streets, spacious homes, and exclusive shops are a prime attraction for auto executives and professionals. It has managed to blend the ambience of an old-fashioned Midwestern small town with suburbia's most trendy ways.

None of this is what Birmingham's settlers had in mind at all. They chose to name the place after the famous industrial city in the United Kingdom because that's what they envisioned. They imagined a giant steel-manufacturing city sprawling across the hills of Oakland County, just north of Detroit.

Thankfully, that never happened. The town's iron foundry burned down in 1854 and was never rebuilt. And instead Birmingham and the adjoining community of Bloomfield Hills, home of the Cranbrook institutions, became the lovely places they are today.

The settlers weren't completely wrong, though. They were correct in assuming that the little river that ran through town was a good spot for industrial development. Farther downstream on the River Rouge is the site of the Ford Motor Company's mammoth automotive plant in Dearborn.

In these quiet green precincts in Birmingham, the Rouge languidly flows into beautiful Quarton Lake right in the middle of town. A walk from downtown Birmingham past the lake to

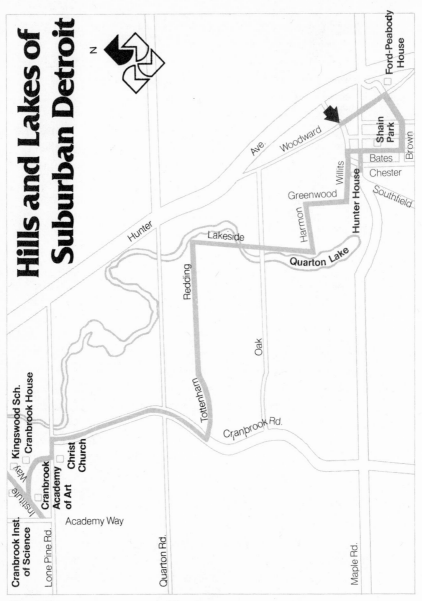

Hills and Lakes of Suburban Detroit

N

Ford-Peabody House

Woodward Ave.

Shain Park

Bates

Chester

Brown

Willits

Greenwood

Harmon

Hunter House

Southfield

Hunter

Lakeside

Quarton Lake

Redding

Oak

Tottenham

Cranbrook Rd.

Kingswood Sch.

Cranbrook House

Cranbrook Academy of Art

Christ Church

Cranbrook Inst. of Science

Institute Way

Lone Pine Rd.

Academy Way

Quarton Rd.

Maple Rd.

This walking tour is approximately 2¼ miles.

Cranbrook will take you to some of suburban Detroit's most compelling vistas and reveal some of the best living the motor city has to offer.

A Chic Country Town

Start the walk at the corner of Woodward and Maple, the center of the original country town of Birmingham. It's about 15 miles from downtown Detroit. For years the village was little more than a stagecoach stop and then a rail station on the long trek from Detroit to Saginaw. But in 1896 the electric interurban railroad arrived and Birmingham was slowly absorbed into the economic orbit of the great city to the south. At this corner you can see traces of the old facades that once made up the rural business district.

Walk south 2 blocks along Woodward past the fashionable shops that lend the town its tone. Here, and on the side streets on your right, are stores purveying merchandise ranging from chic to luxurious to esoteric—almost anything you've ever had an impulse to buy. There are outlets of nationally famous stores and imaginative local operations all employing, to the extent possible, the original turn-of-the-century storefronts. At the southeast corner of Woodward and Brown is the Ford-Peabody House, an Italian-style villa dating from 1879 and one of the last surviving Victorian mansions in the city.. Now it houses a collection of maternity clothes for modern ladies-in-waiting which is in keeping with Birmingham's present spirit.

Nostalgic Corners

Turn right on Brown and right again on Bates and you'll soon come upon more vestiges of the vanished country town. Here is Shain Park, the center of old Birmingham. In the traditional Midwestern fashion, the village square is flanked by the main public buildings—city hall, post office, and library. Band concerts are held here in the summer months. Summer and winter the square is a nostalgic reminder of the small-town life that has vanished forever from this part of Michigan.

Turn left at Maple and walk 3 short blocks to Southfield and the Hunter House. It is part of Birmingham Historic Park and is one of the oldest buildings in the area, dating from 1822. The Hunter brothers, John and Daniel, were the first permanent settlers in the area, arriving overland from Lake St. Clair; at that time swamps blocked the way from Detroit. This Greek Revival house was the second one they built here. Although it appears rather small and unimpressive to modern eyes, in the wilderness that was the Michigan Territory this white frame structure must have looked like a manor. The Birmingham Historical Society maintains the house and its antique furnishings. It is open on an irregular basis. Check in advance at City Hall.

Retrace your steps on Maple a block to Chester. Turn left, and then left again on Willits. Walk right a block to Greenwood, then left on Harmon to Quarton Lake, and finally right on Lakeside, along the park that borders the lake.

The old frame homes that line the streets you've walked down now give way to more expensive, contemporary houses. The green banks of the lake conceal equally lovely homes on the far side. The lake is actually an old mill pond, formed by an earthen dam that was built across the Rouge in 1830. The mill, one of the most important elements of the community's economic life in pioneer days, remained in operation until 1915. It had a capacity of 50 barrels of flour a day. Now the pond is a home for ducks and a haunt of strollers and picnickers.

At the head of the lake you have a choice. Either turn right on Oak, walk back to Woodward and drive the rest of the way; or continue the walk to Cranbrook, a distance of about 2 miles, and return by cab. It is a pleasant stroll through green suburban streets, past spacious homes with ample lawns, bedroom communities for some of Detroit's best-heeled sleepers.

If your decision is to walk to Cranbrook, continue on Lakeview to Redding, turn left, and follow the street until its name changes to Tottenham. At the intersection of Cranbrook Road, turn right. Cross Quarton Road and in another ½ mile you'll approach what appears to be a country town somewhere in England.

A medieval-looking church rises on your left. The road ahead narrows to the width of a lane, bordered by an old stone wall. Buildings constructed of the same gray limestone rise behind the wall. Across the lane, a parklike area stretches off into the distance. Those familiar with England might say it strongly resembled the rolling, green countryside of Kent, which is precisely the effect intended by George Booth, who put together the Cranbrook Educational Community.

Booth, who was born in Kent, became a wealthy man as publisher of the *Detroit News,* one of the first evening newspapers in the country. He built his country estate here after the turn of the century in a tract used first as a family picnic grove. Booth commissioned the great Detroit architect Albert Kahn to build a suitably impressive home here, Cranbrook House. By 1919, the Booths had expanded their plans a good deal. They saw their country estate becoming a great cultural complex, a self-contained community of artists and scholars.

For years, the Booths had sponsored an educational assembly for young children in the area. This evolved into Brookside Elementary School and Cranbrook, a secondary school. A meeting house for informal religious services grew into Christ Church Cranbrook.

As the Booths came to realize that their estate would outlive them, they formed the Cranbrook Foundation to ensure that their work would be completed. Out of this fund grew the Cranbrook Academy of Art and the Institute of Science. Today these institutions compose one of the most famous and widely respected educational centers in the country. And one of the loveliest.

Church and Mansion

As you approach the area on Cranbrook Road, the first of the buildings you'll come to is Christ Church Cranbrook. It's the very model of a medieval cathedral with its buttresses and soaring tower. The Episcopal church was actually completed in 1929 and most of the interior artwork is an adaptation of traditional liturgical art. But mixed among them are examples of ecclesiastical art from every century past the 12th.

The main gate to the Cranbrook grounds is just across Lone Pine Road from the church. The gardens are open May through October, from 1−5. Admission to the grounds is $1.

Follow the path back to Cranbrook House, the mansion that Kahn built for the Booths. It's on a hill surrounded by terraces, fountains, and formal gardens. Built as it was over several years, it does not have the unity of Kahn's more noteworthy achievements, but it is still an impressive and compelling place.

The house was occupied by Booth until his death in 1949, and it contains many personal family mementoes. In its early years the house was famed for its isolated location. Frequently dinner guests would be stranded by snowstorms for days at a time.

The house is open to the public every fourth Sunday of each month from 1−3. Make a circuit of the house, then stroll

232 WALKING THE MIDWEST

down to the lake behind it. Across the water are the buildings of
the Kingswood School, a secondary school for young women.
A family of swans lends the scene a European air. One can
sense the charm of the original picnic grounds of 70 years ago.

Cranbrook's Lively Fountains
Walk back toward the house, angling slightly to the western
end. At the foot of the terrace on that side you'll come upon a
tree-lined promenade called the Ramp of the Chinese Dog.
Follow its gentle slope to the adjoining hill. This rise was considered as a possible site for Cranbrook House but at the time was
regarded as impossibly remote. Now at its crest are the buildings
of Cranbrook School and Academy of Art, surrounded by the
fountains and sculpted figures of Carl Milles. An appealing mixture of heroic and playful figures, Milles' works here gave him a
national reputation. Linger especially around the long rectangular pool adorned by the sculpture of *Europa and the Bull,* with
the columns of the Academy of Art's porch forming the backdrop.

The academy is a showcase of changing exhibits by its
gifted graduate students. A few hundred yards away, along Institute Way, is the Institute of Science with a planetarium show
and outstanding exhibits on the geology and mineralogy of
Michigan. It is open 10–5 on weekdays, 1–9 on Saturdays,
and 1–5 on Sundays.

From here a short cab ride takes you back to Birmingham.
A call to the Birmingham Cab Company (644-0500) will bring
the taxi to Cranbrook. Fare to Birmingham is about $3.50.

INDIANA

COLUMBUS: AN ARCHITECTURAL SHOWPLACE
Karen Cure

In many ways, this small town of 30,000 is typical of a lot of others in the Midwest. Cornfields stretch on all sides as far as you can see. The residential neighborhoods are full of big trees and quaint frame houses whose porches have swings and rocking chairs. Like many other towns of its size, Columbus has shopping centers with ugly parking lots, new banks, new schools, a modern post office.

Here, though, the new buildings are not just boring boxes you've seen all over the U.S. They are really interesting structures. That they've been designed by some of the greatest American architects has been bringing the city accolades from town planners for years. That each and every one of them is as handsome to look at as it is famous—as handsome as a piece of fine sculpture—will make a walk through the town a decidedly pleasant way to pass a sunny afternoon.

Fixed-up Old Buildings

That's all the more true because not everything in Columbus is new. One of the big movements in architecture these days is to adapt old buildings to modern uses whenever possible.

That's been done all over Columbus—most notably in the Visitor Center at 5th and Franklin, where your walk begins.

The former townhouse of a wealthy Columbus family, this imposing old brick building has windows nearly as high as its 14-foot ceilings and a marvelous swooping staircase. Downstairs, a slide show will tell you a little about the modern buildings you'll see along your walk and will tell you how great archi-

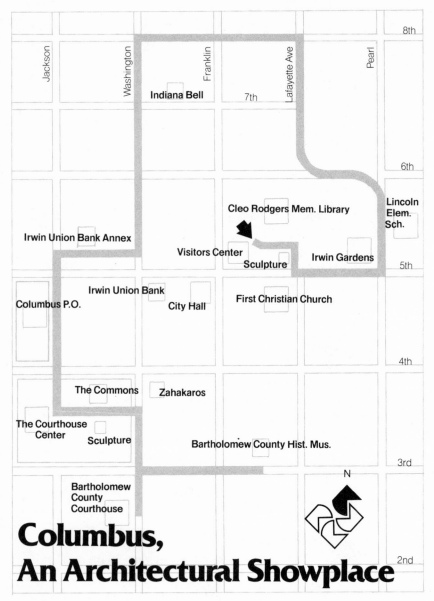

8th

Jackson

Washington

Franklin

Lafayette Ave

Pearl

Indiana Bell

7th

6th

Cleo Rodgers Mem. Library

Lincoln
Elem.
Sch.

Irwin Union Bank Annex

Visitors Center

Sculpture

Irwin Gardens

5th

Irwin Union Bank

Columbus P.O.

City Hall

First Christian Church

4th

The Commons

Zahakaros

The Courthouse
Center

Sculpture

Bartholomew County Hist. Mus.

3rd

N

Bartholomew
County
Courthouse

Columbus,
An Architectural Showplace

2nd

This walking tour is approximately 1-1/2 miles.

tects came to design for Columbus in the first place. A major force was the Cummins Engine Foundation, which in the 1950s offered a unique proposal to the local school board. The foundation agreed to pay architectural fees for school buildings with the stipulation that the school board choose the architect from a list of six or more first-rank American architects, submitted by a disinterested panel of two of the country's most distinguished architects.

The Visitor Center also serves the Columbus community as a branch of the Indianapolis Museum of Art. After the slide show, you can go upstairs and look at exhibitions of Japanese watercolors. It's open 10-4 Monday through Saturday. Sunday hours noon to 4, April through October.

Columbus' First Great Architecture
Walking around the building to 5th Street and looking across the pavement, you'll see the First Christian Church, a limestone structure designed by Eliel Saarinen in 1942. The sanctuary, painted white and furnished with bleached-oak pews designed by Charles Eames, is light and airy and, although stark, almost as exhilarating as the Gothic cathedrals of Europe.

Next to the Visitor Center and across from the church, the blocky brick Cleo Rogers Memorial Library is surrounded by a big plaza where you can take in art shows and outdoor concerts, including mini-festivals of the Cincinnati Symphony Orchestra. Standing in the center of the plaza, 100 feet from the library door, is Henry Moore's *Large Arch,* commissioned at the suggestion of I.M. Pei to complement the geometric shapes of the bricks and the building itself.

Italianate Gardens
The Irwin Gardens at 608 5th Street, designed by Henry Ayling Phillips in 1910, was the home of the Irwin family, a prominent Columbus family and founders of the Cummins Engine Company, which is still the city's largest employer and greatest benefactor. Don't miss the cozy arbor at the back of the gardens. (Weekends only; free.)

Down the street, the Lincoln Elementary School at 750 5th gives you an idea of the happy outcome of the Cummins Foundation school building project. When you peep through the doors—prior arrangements are necessary for visiting—you can see a huge multi-purpose birch-walled room. It's attractive, to be sure, but it's also an ingenious solution to the problem of the limited play space offered by the small downtown lot. Here, as elsewhere, the architects' contributions were not just buildings that look good, but buildings that *work*.

Trees and Old Houses

Just around the corner from all these modern buildings, up Pearl and Lafayette streets, you'll come to the tree-lined residential streets that are the other reason Columbus is such a pleasant place to live. Mainly what you see here are small frame houses with curlicues, spindles, and spokes and all the other wedding-cake ornamentation you might have found on old steamboats in the days when the houses were built. There's an endless procession of them—some painted gray and burgundy, some yellow, some striped and trimmed in shades of green. Small-town America gone spiffy, these houses continue to parade by like so many circus wagons far above 8th Street, where you'll turn and walk west to Franklin, then south on Franklin, passing, at 7th Street, the new Indiana Bell Telephone Building. The latter is a mass of mirrors which reflects the lacy trees planted on the other side of the street.

A Different Kind of Main Street

If you've seen one, you've seen them all—those narrow small-town main streets with traffic at a standstill as the result of too many cars parallel-parked or jockeying for places in front of ugly stores. These stores were renovated with what passed for taste a quarter of a century ago, their neon signs each trying to out-neon the neighbors.

Columbus isn't like that. That facades of all the old buildings are painted as colorfully as the houses on Lafayette—gold, blue, yellow, orange, and other colors that range from the cheerful to the nearly garish. Signs, however, are kept to a minimum and they're gradually being moved so that they hang flat against the buildings instead of sticking out into the street.

In the middle of all this, at 5th and Washington, is another reminder of how Columbus came to where it is today—the Irwin Union Bank and Trust Company Building. It's handsome but nothing special; the annex, added in back by Kevin Roche, John Dinkeloo and Associates in 1973, is far more striking. It's a veritable orchard of huge potted orange trees taking their light through walls and a ceiling of curiously striped glass. In 1954, when Eero Saarinen designed the main building, banks were supposed to be awe-inspiring places with fortresslike walls of brick or concrete. The walls of this new structure—inviting and open—are glass.

Even the Post Office Is Elegant

Walking through the annex and turning south onto Jackson will bring you to the big brown post office—designed by Kevin Roche, John Dinkeloo and Associates in 1970 and probably as elegant a structure as you'll find in the entire postal system— and to the Courthouse Center and Commons complex at 4th and Jackson.

The Courthouse Center section, a shopping mall named for the nearby Italianate courthouse, is a shopping mall with a difference. That's partly because of the wood floors, which are softer on the feet than hard tile and give the building the warmth of somebody's living room.

This shopping mall is also a community center because of the adjacent Commons Building, which, like the center, was designed by Cesar Pelli of Gruen Associates in 1973. In truth, you'd never know from appearances that they were separate buildings.

In the middle of the commons there's a wonderful piece of sculpture by Jean Tingueley, *Chaos #1*. It's a Rube Goldberg-type contraption with balls that roll down wire mesh chutes, then climb to the top on a rattling conveyor belt powered by a baker's dozen gears and chains, then buzz down the chute again.

There are occasional lectures, musical programs, plays presented from the nearby wooden stage. At Christmas, for instance, you're apt to catch the local grade-schoolers reenacting the nativity scene. Off at the other end of the commons there's a playground, and kids too young to sit still through the program can climb on bright-colored jungle gyms.

In the center, you'll find some interesting shops selling plants and gifts and fancy kitchen knick-knacks; in the back, toward the south side of the building, there's also what your youngsters will recognize as a fairly well equipped pinball-and-video-games parlor. You can get a meal in the cafeteria on the mezzanine, then pick up wonderful pastries and cream horns at the bakery near *Chaos #1*—or save dessert for Zahakaro's, across Washington Street from the Courthouse Center. Zahakaro's has one of those from-here-to-eternity marble-topped soda fountains that dispenses a rainbow of ice-cream specialties. South along Washington then eastward on 3rd is the Bartholomew County Historical Museum, set in another one of those Civil War—era brick buildings adapted to modern use a century later. Tuesday through Saturday from 1 to 4 you can stop in to learn about pioneer life in this part of the state. The Visitor Center is west on 3rd and then north on Franklin from the Historical Museum.

WISCONSIN

MILWAUKEE: HISTORIC JUNEAUTOWN
Bill Hibbard

Once known as the Athens of the Midwest, then as the Beer Capital of the World, always as a good place to live, Milwaukee has gained a reputation as a small friendly metropolis which has a lot to offer visitors.

A 3-mile walk in the Juneautown area of the city (downtown east of the Milwaukee River) captures the intriguing blend of Old World charm and New World vigor that's become something of the city's trademark.

Juneautown is named for Solomon Juneau, a fur trader who in 1830 became the city's first land developer and undisputed leader of this part of town.

A Museum and Arts Center
Begin your walk at the Milwaukee County Historical Society Museum at N. 3rd Street and W. Kilbourn Avenue, alongside the Milwaukee River. This is an appropriate place to start—local legend has it that Father Marquette (who along with Joliet explored the Mississippi River in 1673) landed here when he cruised the western shore of Lake Michigan in 1674, the first white man to visit the site. Pere Marquette Park memorializes the landing.

The free museum itself houses memorabilia of early Milwaukee, a community which dates its beginning in 1795 when Jacques Vieau, Juneau's father-in-law, opened a fur trading post here. (The museum is open 9 to 5 Monday through Saturday, 1 to 5 Sunday.)

Cross the Kilbourn Avenue bridge to the city's Performing Arts Center, commonly known by its initials, PAC. The center

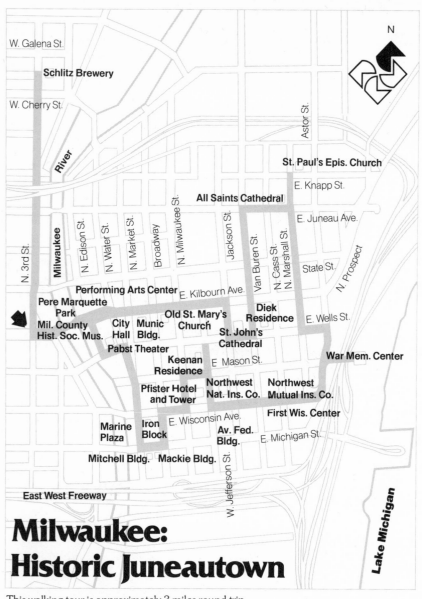

W. Galena St.

Schlitz Brewery

W. Cherry St.

River

N

Astor St.

St. Paul's Epis. Church

E. Knapp St.

Jackson St.

All Saints Cathedral

E. Juneau Ave.

N. 3rd St.

Milwaukee

N. Edison St.

N. Water St.

N. Market St.

Broadway

N. Milwaukee St.

Van Buren St.

N. Cass St.

N. Marshall St.

State St.

N. Prospect

Performing Arts Center E. Kilbourn Ave.

Pere Marquette Park

Diek Residence

E. Wells St.

Mil. County Hist. Soc. Mus.

City Hall

Munic Bldg.

Old St. Mary's Church

St. John's Cathedral

Pabst Theater

Keenan Residence

E. Mason St.

War Mem. Center

Pfister Hotel and Tower

Northwest Nat. Ins. Co.

Northwest Mutual Ins. Co.

Marine Plaza

Iron Block

E. Wisconsin Ave.

First Wis. Center

Av. Fed. Bldg.

E. Michigan St.

Mitchell Bldg.

Mackie Bldg.

W. Jefferson St.

East West Freeway

Lake Michigan

Milwaukee: Historic Juneautown

This walking tour is approximately 3 miles round trip.
The round trip to the Schlitz Brewery adds another mile.

boasts a wealth of ornate theaters and concert halls which lure many name companies and performers. It is home to the Milwaukee Symphony Orchestra, the Milwaukee Repertory Theater, the Milwaukee Ballet Company, and the Florentine Opera Company.

City Hall

Diagonally to the southeast stands one of Milwaukee's outstanding landmarks, the towering cathedral-like City Hall. This masterpiece of Flemish Renaissance architecture was finished in 1896. Flanking it, as you continue along Kilbourn, is the contemporary Municipal Building, which was added when the city government outgrew City Hall.

Across the street to the east is Old St. Mary's Catholic Church, the oldest church still in use in Milwaukee. This Federal-style edifice with a sharply pointed steeple dates back to 1846.

Continue walking east on Kilbourn Avenue, past the campus of the Milwaukee School of Engineering which extends to the north. Cut through Cathedral Square, a small plot of greenery which was the site of Milwaukee's first courthouse and which is the site of the city's famous *Immigrant Mother* statue, a tribute to all immigrant mothers. The statue was sculpted by Ivan Mestrovic.

Admire St. John Cathedral, central church of the Milwaukee Catholic Archdiocese. Completed in 1853, this edifice with its stepped tower ending in a domed cupola would look at home in Florence, Italy. The stately tower was erected in 1892 after its predecessor was found to be unsafe. The interior dates back only to the mid-1930s, when it was restored after being gutted by fire.

Turn east on Wells Street and walk a block and a half to view the Paul Louis Diek residence (718 E. Wells St.), an 1852 Italian villa–style house still used as a home.

Two Episcopal Churches

Stroll back west on Wells to Van Buren Street and head north, past the apartment buildings and shops of Juneau Village to the west. Turn east on Juneau Avenue for a few blocks. You'll pass the handsome Summerfield Methodist Church and All Saints Cathedral, seat of the Milwaukee Episcopal Diocese, noted for its beautiful interior art and woodcarving and its 16th-century Flemish triptych.

Just a block north, on the northeast corner of Knapp and Marshall, stands another noted Episcopal church, St. Paul's, which prides itself on its Tiffany stained-glass windows, a 1510 tapestry from Brussels, and a magnificent organ which blends medieval-style handcrafting with 20th-century electronics.

War Memorial Center

Head south on Marshall to Wells Street, taking note as you walk of the gracious old homes on what was an early Milwaukee Gold Coast, where Milwaukee's wealthy industrialists and businessmen once lived. Swing east on Wells and south on Prospect Avenue to E. Mason Street. Continue walking east across the pedestrian bridge to the War Memorial Center, easily identifiable by the huge mosaic mural on its facade.

The War Memorial Center, one of the last works of famed architect Eero Saarinen, is the home of the Milwaukee Art Center. The center offers changing exhibits as well as an increasingly sophisticated and valuable permanent collection—boasting seven Georgia O'Keeffes, several Lautrecs, and an outstanding collection of 19th-century decorative art. (Open 10 to 5 Tuesday through Sunday, closed Monday. Admission: $1 adults, 50 cents students and senior citizens, free for youngsters under 12.)

The center is a showplace of Milwaukee's "front yard"—its parklike lakefront—where residents and visitors swim, boat, fish, jog and bike. The annual Lakefront Festival of the Arts takes place just to the north of the center in mid-June, and Milwaukee's bubbling Summerfest, which draws an assemblage of top musical performers, is held a few blocks south of the center each summer, opening in late June for an 11-day run.

A Skyscraper and Two Greek Temples

Return across the bridge to Prospect Avenue and head south, then west where it curves into Wisconsin Avenue. Ahead stands Milwaukee's only skyscraper, the 42-story First Wisconsin Center. Magnificent panoramic views of the city and the lakefront may be seen from its 41st-floor observation deck. (Open 2 to 4 Monday through Friday.) Off to the south you can glimpse the port area where ships of many nations deliver and receive cargoes for much of the Midwest.

Across the street to the north you'll see an imposing building which resembles a Greek temple. It's the home office of the huge Northwestern Mutual Life Insurance Co. A block west of Northwestern Mutual lies another "Grecian temple," the home office of Northwestern National Insurance Co., which has been expanded into a striking contemporary tower. Both buildings illustrate the return to classicism prevalent in the architecture of the early part of this century.

To the south stands the castellated Federal Building. It is a carbon copy of many such buildings across the nation, reflecting an architectural style prevalent in the 1890s.

Northwest of the Federal Building stands the venerable Pfister Hotel. It exudes Old World ambience, with an ornate lobby and large, high-ceilinged rooms which have been brought up to 20th-century standards. A circular tower added a decade ago is topped by the Crown Room, a cabaret which offers more panoramic views of the city.

Wander north a block or so on Jefferson Street through the East Town area of fine shops, art galleries, and boutiques. Note the exquisite Mathew Keenan residence (777 Jefferson St.), an 1860 residence which would look right at home in Charleston, S.C., with its portico and double-curving entry stair. Check the side streets for interesting shops and restaurants and walk west on Mason back to Milwaukee and south to Wisconsin Avenue.

Continue west on Wisconsin to Broadway, then go south and turn west on Michigan Street. Across the way, you'll see the Mackie Building (225 E. Michigan St.) and the Mitchell Building (207 E. Michigan St.). Both illustrate the Victorian gingerbread style which was popular in the 1870s. For many years the Mackie Building housed the Milwaukee Grain Exchange and for a time the Mitchell Building was the home of the U.S. Signal Service, predecessor of the U.S. Weather Service.

Turn north on Water Street and you'll find yourself face-to-face with the Marine Plaza, a 22-story steel-and-glass slab which was the first step in Milwaukee riverfront redevelopment. A visit to its top-floor restaurant and cocktail lounge provides still another panoramic view of the city.

Wall Street

This area of the city is Milwaukee's "Wall Street," home of many banks and brokerage houses. Stroll a few blocks north to the Marshall and Ilsley Bank, the oldest bank in the Northwest Territory—now housed in one of the newest bank buildings. At the southeast corner of Water Street and Wisconsin Avenue stands one of the most unusual structures in the city, the Iron Block (205 E. Wisconsin Ave.). This 1860s building is faced with cast-iron pieces, which were designed like those on fashionable Eastern shops and shipped to Milwaukee by schooner.

Near the northwest corner of that same intersection is the site of Juneau's fur-trading cabin. And halfway up the block is the site where the first white child was born in Milwaukee. Plaques mark both spots.

From the front of City Hall, stroll west on Wells Street past the Pabst Theater, an 1890-vintage jewel recently reconditioned to its former luxury and beauty. Continue north on Edison Street toward the PAC and across the bridge back to the museum.

Slanted Bridges

Note as you cross the bridge that all the bridges in sight are slanted. That's because streets on opposite sides of the river don't line up. A young promoter named Byron Kilbourn developed the west side of the river in competition with Juneau and, to show his contempt for Juneau's settlement, deliberately planned his community so the streets wouldn't meet.

Eventually, bridges had to be built to link the growing communities, but the vendetta continued. One bridge was rammed by a Juneautown boat and another was chopped apart by the Kilbourntown crowd. The Juneautowners showed up with guns and a cannon and the Kilbourntowners responded in kind. Bloodshed was averted and, finally, tempers were cooled. The structures were rebuilt and peace prevailed, but the diagonal bridges remain as a legacy of this weird war.

If your feet still have some resilience left, walk a block or so north on 3rd Street to the area between State and Highland, where repainting and remodeling have reproduced the look of a century ago. You'll find a Germanic cluster that includes a cuckoo-clock shop, a sausage factory and shop, a cheese store, and one of the city's leading German restaurants. In addition, you'll discover an art gallery, an antique shop, and other businesses.

Schlitz Brewery

If you're still game to walk and want to visit one of Milwaukee's famed breweries, continue north on 3rd Street to Galena

Street, where the Schlitz Brewery offers tours topped with samples of the foaming brew which made Milwaukee famous. (Tours scheduled at 9, 10, and 11 and 12:30, 1:30, 2:30 and 3:30, Monday through Friday, September through May; 9, 10, 10:30, 11 and 11:30, 12:30, 1, 1:30, 2, 2:30, 3 and 3:30, Monday through Friday, June through August.) For additional information on daily activities in Milwaukee, call 799-1177.

ILLINOIS

CHICAGO'S ARCHITECTURE: THE LOOP AND OAK PARK
Karen Cure

Scarcely a city in the country has had more to do with what American towns look like today than Chicago. The skyscraper was born in the Loop and the modern ranch-style house a half-hour away in the suburb of Oak Park, where Frank Lloyd Wright spent nearly 20 of his most productive years. You can walk both—and have the equivalent of a short course in modern architecture—in a single day. Or you may want to dawdle in one area.

The Loop is crammed with interesting buildings, giant sculptures ("public art" they call it here), city scenes. Kids are out selling chocolate bars to raise money for their Sunday school or soliciting signatures for a radio-station contest. (The school that gets the most wins a prize.) Store windows beg you to browse. Leaflets want to tell you about a new Xerox place or a new religion. Political activists picket a store which trades with some oppressive government or other. Bells ring, horns honk, the El clatters and screeches overhead, and the wind that has Chicagoans holding onto their hats whips past your ears.

By contrast, Oak Park—accessible by Chicago Transit Authority trains direct from the Loop—is a desert island. Ernest Hemingway, who grew up there at 600 North Kenilworth, called it the city of broad streets and narrow minds. The narrow-minds part may not impress you—Oak Park was, after all, the scene of some of the most innovative home building the U.S. has ever seen—but the elm-shaded streets, often so wide you'd really want to call them boulevards, certainly will. Oak Park is sedate, full of big and architecturally noteworthy homes, a thoroughly comfortable place to live—and an interesting place to visit as well.

Architectural Innovation

The enormous museum of architecture which is Chicago is most enjoyable when you have a little background on the subject. Before you start walking, visit the Archi-Center at 310 South Michigan Avenue. Since this point is diagonally across the street from the Art Institute of Chicago, try to set aside time to see its important collections and marvelous shows.

The city's topography is decidedly flat and ideal for unseasoned walkers as it lends itself to easy strolling.

Begin your walk at the Monadnock Building on the southwest corner of Dearborn and Jackson. In the pre-skyscraper era, nearly all buildings had load-bearing walls like those of this handsome structure. To support its 16 stories, the walls had to be some 6 feet thick at the bottom; taller buildings would have required even more base. Few architects were willing to chance a new construction method in which a structural skeleton like a box made out of Tinkertoys held the whole thing up. Nobody thought it would work.

That was proved otherwise after the Great Fire of 1871, which left Chicago a ruin. Innovative young architects drawn to the razed city (and jobs) like flies to honey, told businessmen looking for cheap space that the new way was the practical way, and before anyone knew it, the city was filling up with "skyscrapers." Buildings like the three in Mies van der Rohe's Federal Center (1959–74) which occupies the entire block bounded by Jackson, Clark, Adams, and Dearborn (across from the Monadnock Building), and the 110-story Sears Tower (1974) at Jackson and Franklin, are merely taller, more sophisticated versions of the handsome structures put up around 1890.

The World's Tallest Building

From the observation deck of the Sears Tower, all the other skyscrapers look like toys. (The "Skydeck" is open 9 A.M. to midnight daily; there's a $1.50 admission fee for adults, $1 for children.) In the lobby downstairs, look for Alexander Calder's mobile Universe—a wall full of big bright yellow, red, blue, and black circles, pennants, and corkscrews.

Leaving the Sears Tower by the same door you entered,

Chicago Architecture:

CTA To Oak Park

Lake

Randolph

Franklin

Wells

La Salle

Clark

Dearborn

State

Wabash

Michigan

Washington

Marshall Field & Co.

Reliance Bldg.

Madison

1st. Nat. Bank Bldg.

Monroe

Marquette Bldg.

Adams

Sears Tower

The Rookery   Fed. Center

Jackson

Monadnock Bldg.

The Loop

Van Buren

Augusta St.

Marion St.

Bellefort

Forest Ave.

Woodbine Ave.

Kenilworth Ave.

Grove Ave.

Oak Park Ave.

Harry S. Adams House

East

Elmwood Ave.

Ridgeland Ave.

Iowa St.

Petersens Ice Cream

Chicago Ave. Store

Euclid

Linden

515 Fair Oaks Ave.

Wright Home & Stuido

Heurtley House

Fair Oaks

Superior St.

Edward Hills House

Mrs. Thomas Gale House

Erie St.

Ontario St.

Frank W. Thomas House

N

Austin Gardens Park

Village Mall

Lake St.

North Blvd.

Unity Temple

South Blvd.

CTA

Oak Park

This walking tour is approximately 2¾ miles.
The tour of Oak Park adds another 2 miles.

turn left onto Franklin, take a right onto Adams, then walk east. The Rookery (1885–1888) at 209 South LaSalle Street and Adams is one of the city's oldest skyscrapers. Through the handsome arching entranceways, ornamented with birds and other shapes from nature, you can see the white-and-gold lobby designed by Frank Lloyd Wright during a 1905 remodeling. Continuing east on Adams, you'll pass Mies van der Rohe's Federal Center once again. Be sure to notice the Alexander Calder stabile, *Flamingo*, a sort of mammoth three-pronged archway painted tomato red.

Plazas, Statues, Mosaics

In Chicago, you learn to notice buildings which in other cities you'd pass by without a glance. Turn left on Dearborn and stop at the Marquette Building (1893), for instance. Look inside and you'll see a lobby full of lovely Louis Tiffany mosaics of explorers and Indians.

Along Dearborn, many of the buildings have pedestrian plazas where you'll find more works of public art like the Calder pieces you've just seen, or Marc Chagall's mosaic *The Four Seasons*, at the First National Bank Building plaza on Dearborn between Monroe and Madison. Arrive about noon in the summer and you can enjoy a concert or dramatic performance along with the throngs of office workers who lunch there alfresco. You'll see the controversial Picasso sculpture—one of the city's first pieces of public art—down the street at the Richard Daley Center; the fact that there's not even a place to sit down in the huge, flat open space makes the red construction seem even bigger than its 15 stories and 162 tons.

Ice Cream and Another Mosaic

When Marshall Field and Company was built in 1892, electric lighting wasn't widespread, and so the building was provided with huge windows (the Tinkertoy construction method made this possible) and was built in sections with each section's shopping areas arranged on balconies overlooking a skylit central courtyard. Later, when electricity became commonplace, the skylights were covered over—one of them by a Louis Tiffany mosaic in the bright blues and gold of a madonna's cloak. To find it, enter the store at the first Randolph Street door east of State and walk southward through the store to Washington.

In the pink-and-white Crystal Palace Ice Cream Parlor on

Field's third floor, don't miss the store's specialty, Frango mint ice cream, served here and only here in some of the most exotic meal-sized ice-cream sundaes anywhere.

The Most Famous Old Skyscraper

You may not recognize the Reliance Building at the southwest corner of Washington and State for what it is; it's badly maintained and full of seedy-looking businesses. But look carefully and you'll see the clean lines, finely wrought detailing, and delightful proportions which make it the most elegant building in Chicago with the exception, perhaps, of Louis Sullivan's Carson Pirie Scott Store (1899) at 1 South State nearby. The ground-floor facade is completely covered with scrollworked cast-iron work as delicate as Italian filigree. Inspecting the area around the windows as you walk south on State, you can see how successive enlargements in 1904, 1906, and 1960 became progressively less ornate as the cost of hiring the skilled artisans needed to duplicate the original skyrocketed.

When you've walked the length of the store, retrace your steps back to Madison. To catch the CTA elevated to Oak Park, walk east a block.

Ranch Houses

Of all the American architects generally acknowledged to be among the world's greats, only Frank Lloyd Wright focused on the family home, and it was in Oak Park that he did some of his most important work. Here he perfected the low-lying Prairie Style homes with wide eaves and simple contours; the absence of attic and basement and the simplified floor plan (more economical to build, heat, and clean) were eventually incorporated into modern ranch houses. In addition, you'll see the work of Wright's contemporaries; the common denominator is a clarity of form and a near-absence of the shingles and scrollwork you'll see toward the beginning of your walk in the impressive Queen Anne—style houses of Forest Avenue.

There are about 130 buildings in Oak Park in the Prairie Style. The Frank Lloyd Prairie School of Architecture District was made a National Historic District in 1974.

To get to the beginning of your Oak Park walk, exit the El by the Marion Street door and walk north through the Village Mall. Turn right where you see the "Heart of the Mall" sign, walk straight to Forest Avenue, and then turn left. Between the turn and the first house is the Oak Park Visitors Center (open April to October), where you can watch a slide show and see photo exhibits about architecture.

The first Wright house on your walk, the Frank W. Thomas House (1901) at 210 Forest, was also the first Prairie Style house in Oak Park; its hidden entranceway (not the big archway on the ground level, as you'd expect, but a smaller inconspicuous door hidden under the eaves) and the simple unornamented shape of the house are Wright trademarks you'll see again and again—first at the Mrs. Thomas Gale House, just off Forest at 6 Elizabeth Court (which actually looks something like a pile of well-placed interlocking blocks), and later at the Heurtley House at 318 Forest, one of Wright's most famous homes. Between the Heurtley House and the Mrs. Thomas Gale House are a couple of less typical Wright buildings—the Edward Hills House at 313 Forest Avenue, one of a number of dwellings that Frank Lloyd Wright remodeled, and the house next door at 333 Forest, an exotic half-timbered mix of Tudor, Gothic, and Mayan styles originally designed by Wright in 1895 and remodeled by him in 1923.

Wright's Own House and Studio

So far, all of the houses you've seen have been privately owned, and are not open to the public, and in a way that's too bad, because the interiors are part of what's so interesting about Wright's work. The architect's own home at 951 Chicago Avenue is, however, under restoration and open for viewing from 1–2:30 Tuesday and Thursday and 1–4 Saturday and Sunday (July and August, additional hours). Admission is $2; discounts for children and senior citizens. The porch, produced by protruding rectangles like those you saw at the Gale House, is so small and dark that you feel as if you're in a cave—so that when you go through the door, the spaciousness of the interior seems all the more striking.

Afterward, turn and walk west on Chicago Avenue until you get to Petersen's Ice Cream Store—an Oak Park institution known for its huge, rich 50-cent cones—at 1100 Chicago on the corner of Marion Street.

The rest of your walk takes you past dozens of Prairie Style homes designed by Wright's contemporaries. The Harry S. Adams House (1913) at 710 Augusta is the last of Wright's Prairie Style houses in Oak Park. And one of his earliest is at

515 Fair Oaks Avenue. Certainly the most famous is the Unity Temple on the corner of Lake and Kenilworth—which looks strangely familiar by the time you get to it; here are all the interlocking rectilinear shapes you've seen on the other houses, the interior walls divided up into panels by wood stripping as in Wright's own home. Wright elevated the status of concrete, formerly thought suitable only for subways and grain silos, to a higher aesthetic plane when he chose it for this church.

The Temple is open to the public, but the hours vary, so check first with the Visitors Center at 158 Forest. A tour is given on Saturday and Sunday at 2 the year round. Admission to the Temple is $2; $1 for senior citizens and children.

CHICAGO'S LAKEFRONT, LINCOLN PARK, AND NEW TOWN
Karen Cure

Nothing distinguishes Chicago from most other major American cities so much as its glorious windswept lakefront—unless it's the green ribbon of parklands that edge the water on either side of Lake Shore Drive. This walk takes in some of both, then sends you prowling through the shops of New Town, which has replaced Old Town of late as the liveliest store-hounding, eating, and drinking area of the city.

Begin at the Waterfront
Walk north under the underpass just slightly north of the intersection of Oak Street and Michigan Avenue. As soon as you come out into the sunlight, you'll know you're at the shore. On a windy day—and in Chicago they come often—there will be huge waves crashing on the sand at the Oak Street Beach. On your way up to the North Avenue beach, you'll pass bicyclists, joggers, and assorted other takers-of-constitutionals. Chicagoans don't take their lakeshore for granted.

Nor do they ignore Lincoln Park, the largest of the 430 parks in the city system. Designed by Frederick Law Olmsted, the same landscape architect who gave New York City its Central Park, this one has playing fields, an assortment of statues of famous people—Lincoln, Hans Christian Andersen, and Shakespeare among them—plus two museums, a conservatory, and a first-rate zoo.

When you come out of the underpass from the North Avenue Beach, you can see the Chicago Historical Society—certainly one of the most interesting attractions in the park—a couple of blocks away and straight ahead. Follow the pathways underneath the trees. At North Avenue and Clark Street, turn south on Clark to get to the museum entrance.

Inside you'll see antique autos, old-time costumes, carriages, pioneer knick-knacks, Civil War memorabilia. In the exhibit of Lincolniana, one of the best in the country, you'll see pages from Lincoln's grade-school notebooks and letters (including one in which he reports on his marriage: "Nothing new here, except my marriage, which to me is a source of profound wonder"). Period photographs of Civil War soldiers and battlefields remind you of the horror of the war Lincoln had to cope with.

Three new galleries explore 19th-century American life through the original furniture and decorative accessories. The new Chicago Galleries (scheduled to open in the spring of 1979) will tell about the city's beginnings, its early commerce and transportation, and the Columbian Exposition and 1934 World's Fair.

The Historical Society is open Monday through Saturday from 9:30 to 4:30, from noon to 5 on Sunday. Admission is $1; 50 cents for children 6 through 17; 25 cents for senior citizens. Free to all on Monday.

The Farm in the Zoo
Leaving the Historical Society, turn right, then follow Clark Street and LaSalle to the short pedestrian walkway under La-Salle. You'll emerge at the end of a long wide alleyway arched over by enormous trees with lawns on either side. Straight ahead you can see the duck pond and, next to it, the barns and sheds that are part of the Farm in the Zoo. When you get to the pond, follow the path counterclockwise around the pond and take in the scenery—an island full of willows which nearly touch the water out in the middle, and willows that fringe your path. Olmsted was always aiming to landscape his parks so that they looked like nature, only better, and he almost always succeeded.

Cross the bridge, where there may be some kids out fish-

Lincoln Park and the Lakefront

Belmont

Belmont Harbor

Clark

Broadway

New Town

Diversey Pkwy.

Lincoln Park

N

North Pond

Lake Michigan

Fullerton Pkwy

Conservatory

Stockton Dr.

Lake Shore Dr.

Zoo

Armitage

Farm in the Zoo

South Pond

North Ave. Beach

North

LaSalle Dr.

Chicago Hist. Society

Division

Oak St. Beach

Oak

LaSalle

State

Michigan

This walking tour is approximately 4¾ miles.

ing, and follow the barnyard smells into the farm, where you can watch chicks in incubators pecking their way out of their shells and see cows being milked in milking parlors as fancy as any on a Wisconsin farm. Afterward, in other buildings, you can pet the goats, pigs, and sheep which are baaing, grunting, snorting, and munching at the straw. You don't have to be a kid to enjoy it all.

Looking across Stockton Drive, the narrow street which curves north and south through the park, you can see the Chicago Academy of Sciences, whose lively exhibits are devoted to the ecology and the natural history of the Midwest. It's open from 10 to 5 daily. Admission is free. There are frequent special programs; to find out what's on, call 549-0606.

Monkey Business at the Zoo

From the front door of the Academy of Sciences on North Clark Street, walk around to the back of the building and follow Stockton Drive to the Lincoln Park Zoo. It's actually the smaller of the city's two zoological parks—the other is out in the suburbs—but don't let that put you off because this is quite a big zoo indeed. All the usual lions, tigers, birds, and hartebeests are here, plus turtles, lizards, snakes, crocodiles, and gila monsters, and a lot of other weird-looking reptiles you wouldn't want to meet in a dark alley.

There are sea lions and birds of all sorts, including bald eagles, loons, albatrosses, petrels, and penguins. Some are in cages; some are in the free-flight bird house. In one particularly interesting exhibit, nocturnal animals are displayed under red light. Since their eyes don't perceive red, they think it's night outside and they're actively feeding, burrowing, climbing, sniffing. They sleep at night, when all the room lights are switched on.

Probably the most amusing of all the exhibits is the brand-new Great Ape House near the monkey and reptile houses on the east side of the park. The new Great Ape House—home to one of the largest groups of great apes in captivity—is a windowless, cylindrical building partially buried underground. At the center of the three-story structure, there's a slightly smaller cylinder with glass walls (this also about three stories high) which is split up into pie-shaped areas, each home to a different kind of large monkey—great apes, chimps, and such.

What's unique about this ape house is that when you look

at the monkeys you don't have to stand 10 feet away behind barricades and restraining bars, but instead you're on a ramp that winds upward right next to the glass. Because quite a few of the ropes and platforms where the monkeys play are right next to the glass, you stand so close that you can inspect them right down to their fingernails, their eyelashes, and even their freckles. It may be the closest you'll ever get to a monkey.

Jungles, Deserts, and Some New Town Stores
    North of the zoo is the conservatory—worth visiting especially if you keep house plants, for here you'll see dozens of different kinds of all the old standbys, everything from ivy and dieffenbachia to cacti and orchids. There are special shows of mums in the fall, poinsettias at Christmastime, azaleas and camellias in February and March, and lilies at Easter. The conservatory is open from 9 to 5 daily, and usually until 9 during major shows. To find out what's on, phone 294-4770. Admission is free.

    Lincoln Park continues north for another 4 miles, and takes in the Chicago Yacht Club at Belmont Harbor (wonderful to visit for the dozens of boats you can see gleaming white against the water), a golf course, tennis courts, and another harbor, Montrose. And there are places to walk all the way up.

    But it's pleasant and convenient at this point to visit New Town, which begins about Diversey at Broadway and Clark a couple of blocks west of the lake, and continues up North Broadway above Diversey to Belmont. There are literally dozens of shops to visit between Diversey and Addison: you can buy rattan furniture, dresses, plants, health foods, Indian imports, and more.

    One particularly interesting establishment is on North Clark just above its intersection with North Broadway. The Century, a theater-turned-shopping-center, has shops selling women's clothing, plants, cards, kitchenware, gifts, and the like, set around the edges of the various levels. You ride a glassed-in elevator to the top and walk down browsing as you go. When you get to the bottom, you can have a meal or a snack in the ground-floor cafe or pick up anything from gyro sandwiches to goulash to Chinese food along North Broadway.

PULLMAN VILLAGE
Karen Cure

From the windows of trains that whiz along the west edge of this historic south Chicago neighborhood, all you can see is a blur of close-together houses that nearly blend into the urban landscape. It's another story entirely when you explore the neighborhood on foot.

The Hotel Florence
Certainly the Hotel Florence, where your tour begins, is your first clue to that. Ten years ago it was a flophouse. The roof was as holey as a sieve and the clientele consisted of drunks and old men in undershirts. Now undergoing restoration, thanks to its new owner, the Historic Pullman Foundation, it will be nearly as splendid as it was when George Pullman built it to house foreign dignitaries visiting Chicago's World's Columbian Exposition of 1893. The 12-foot-high mirrors in the ladies' sitting parlor downstairs have been polished, along with the solid cherry woodwork. The original shutters for the floor-to-ceiling windows have been repaired. Upstairs in George Pullman's own private suite, there's a splendid mahogany four-poster adorned with carved pineapples and a suite of elegant Victorian chairs and settees. Ask the clerks behind the desk to take you up.

A Planned Community
The hotel was the centerpiece for a whole community—one of the first of America's planned communities. The driving force behind this enterprise was George Pullman of the Pullman Palace Car Company. He believed that pleasant surroundings made for happier workers and that happier workers were more productive. Accordingly, he and architect Solon Beman installed flush toilets, hot and cold running water, central gas lighting, and so many other then-newfangled conveniences that one young bride fresh from a farm in Poland thought her worker-husband the richest man in the world. The community had an arcade with 50 shops, an 8,000-volume public library, and the most elaborate theater west of the Alleghenies. Garbage was collected daily, can and all, and a clean can deposited in place of the full one. The company had a nursery, a greenhouse, and landscape and maintenance crews to keep the area polished.

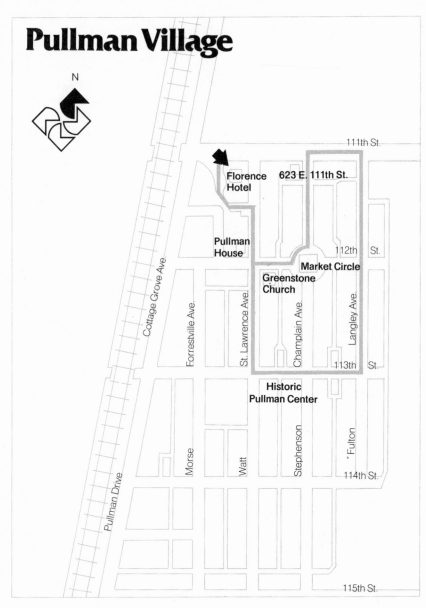

Pullman Village

N

111th St.

Florence
Hotel

623 E. 111th St.

Pullman
House

112th St.

Market Circle

Greenstone
Church

Cottage Grove Ave.

Forrestville Ave.

St. Lawrence Ave.

Champlain Ave.

Langley Ave.

113th St.

Historic
Pullman Center

Morse

Watt

Stephenson

Fulton

114th St.

Pullman Drive

115th St.

This walking tour is approximately 1 mile.

Withal, the rents were low—about $14 a month, just a quarter of the average worker's monthly take-home pay.

Drinking was not allowed, of course; Pullman was a moralist as well as a practical philanthropist. But a shrewd Joseph Schlitz had established two blocks of saloons and stables (and apartments and homes for his own personnel), just across the tracks from Pullman, and Pullman's drinkers had only to walk a block for a beer. So there was a waiting list for Pullman housing.

The entire town stayed under the Pullman corporation ownership until after Pullman's death in 1897, when most of the houses were sold to residents.

Unlike most other south Chicago areas, the property owners continued to live in the homes they owned, and while other neighborhoods in this part of the city deteriorated, Pullman stayed clean and stable. In the last ten years, as real estate prices rose in other areas equally convenient to the downtown Chicago business district, young professionals started joining the longtime blue-collar residents. Today it's the kind of real live utopia where neighbors trade baby-sitting time and even swap cars and run errands for each other.

Except for the church and the hotel, many of the public buildings have been torn down. But there are still plenty of houses to see, all immaculately kept with pots of geraniums on the stoops or marigolds edging the gardens.

Row Housing
From the Hotel Florence walk diagonally across the new park—also recently renovated—to 112th Street.

One of the hallmarks of Pullman housing was that each level of management lived in a distinct style of building. Ceilings rose, rooms became more numerous and doors more ornate, moldings grew increasingly fancy as you went from unskilled workers' quarters to skilled workers' flats on up to executive housing. Built for Edward Pullman (George Pullman's nephew), number 602 112th Street was one of the fanciest. It didn't stay his home for long, however, because his wife decided that living there was beneath her and moved the family to Hyde Park, near what is now the University of Chicago, a little to the north.

Nearly all the buildings in Pullman have a story of their own. The Market Circle at the intersection of 112th Street and Champlain Avenue had originally been constructed to break up the monotony of the regular grid system along which Pullman streets had been built. The original Market burned down and was reconstructed in 1893. The Market House in the center was the only place in Pullman where George Pullman—ever hygienically minded—would allow meat, vegetables, and other perishables to be sold. The vegetables, incidentally, had been raised on the town's outskirts at "Sewage Farm," so called because the fertilizer used there had been taken from the company-owned sewage plant. Incidentally, the baker-father of Eliot Ness, one of the Untouchables of Chicago gangland fame, rented space in the Market for $40 a month.

Some of the apartments in the colonnaded structures around the square were originally used to house Exposition visitors for whom there was no room at the Florence; after the Exposition was over, they were home to company inventors.

More executive housing was provided on 111th Street. Most of the buildings have tall windows and elegant moldings, doorways, and windows. Inside there are fireplaces and elegant parlors. The house at 623 East 111th belonged to the company surgeon, who reportedly saw some 10,000 patients in his offices adjoining the house.

Going south on Langley, between 11100 and 11200, you can see the bottom end of the housing hierarchy on one side— the two-, three-, and four-room tenements where newly arrived foreigners lived and shared baths while waiting until they could afford to bring brides or families to this country. On the west side of the street in that block and the next one south are the single-family dwellings—the ones for which everybody was saving up—plus small apartments. From the outside, they have the look of housing in Dublin or England, though on a smaller scale.

Along 113th Street, you find a couple of boarding houses and a big old school between Forrestville and St. Lawrence; and between 112th and 113th on St. Lawrence there are red-brick houses for skilled, rather than unskilled, workers.

Greenstone Church

Not far away is the Greenstone Church, still by far the most impressive of the town's buildings with its Romanesque arches, its columns, and its huge stained-glass windows. Built of green serpentine stone, it turns almost emerald after a rain. For a long time—though it had only 600 seats for the 12,000 members of the community—it was the only religious structure that Pullman allowed in his town. Visit on Sunday and you can hear the organ which, along with the splendid oak interior, has been recently restored.

Inside the Houses
With the exception of the Hotel Florence, open daily, and the Greenstone Church, open on Sundays, the structures you'll see on your walk are not open to the public. However, once a year in October, selected householders open their doors as part of a fund-raising tour sponsored by the Historic Pullman Foundation. For dates and information, write the Historic Pullman Center at 614 East 113th, Chicago, or call 785-8181.

TURN-OF-THE-CENTURY WOODSTOCK
Karen Cure

Woodstock, Illinois
Though you're only 90 minutes by train from Chicago's Loop—about 60 miles northwest—you feel light-years away when you stand in the Woodstock town square in the shade of the curlicued Victorian-style springhouse. Looking across the lawns and flower gardens of the square, you'll spot a couple of Civil War monuments; above the trees are the slanted roofs of the turn-of-the-century courthouse and the opera house.

Should the local policeman notice you studying a map, he'll be quick to offer directions. You can inspect the creases in his shirt, fresh from the laundry, while he wishes you happy walking. What you hear, otherwise, are birds, car doors slamming, and engines starting (but no honking here) as people go about business as usual—unless, that is, you've been lucky enough to arrive on a summer weekday, when the square will be full of the oom-pahs of a local band.

Main Street
Clearly, Woodstock is no ordinary Midwestern town. Imperious brick and stone buildings like the courthouse and the opera house crowd sidewalks and county seats all over the Midwest, but in Woodstock these handsome edifices have a

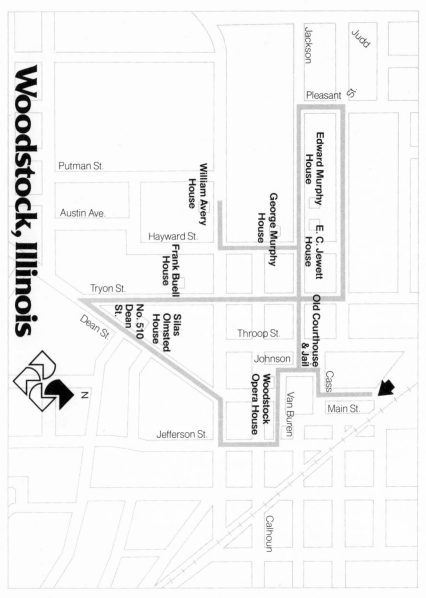

Woodstock, Illinois

Judd St.

Jackson

Pleasant

Putman St.

Austin Ave.

Hayward St.

Tryon St.

Dean St.

Jefferson St.

Throop St.

Johnson

Main St.

Calhoun

William Avery House

George Murphy House

Edward Murphy House

E. C. Jewett House

Frank Buell House

Silas Olmsted House

No. 510 Dean St.

Old Courthouse & Jail

Cass

Woodstock Opera House

Van Buren

N

This walking tour is approximately 2¾ miles.

sparkle and shine that tell you that somebody cares. The decorative wrought ironwork and the moldings and the lintels all have the prosperous look that only a first-rate new paint job will give—as do nearly all the other structures in this neat village of 10,000.

Your walking tour will bear out your first impressions. For the most part, the shops on Main Street between the train station and the town square don't display the kind of ugly plastic signs that usually scar small-town main streets. Instead there are old-fashioned sign boards painted with quaint motifs like the antique bicycle that points out the bike store.

In addition to the usual farm-equipment stores and stationery stores and clothing stores, there's a nifty pottery shop and a huge antiques bazaar.

The Opera House

The town's most celebrated structure—and the spot where you'll begin your walk—is Woodstock's opera house, at the corner of Johnson and Van Buren. To see it now, you'd never guess that it was down at the heels and scheduled for demolition only a few years ago. In fact, when you hear its history, you'll find it hard to believe that anyone would ever have let it decay in the first place. Orson Welles, who attended Woodstock's now-defunct Todd School for Boys, called it "a real, old honest-to-horsehair opera house." He appeared on its stage, as did Eugene Debs, Count Leo Tolstoy, and Jane Addams in earlier days; Betsy Palmer, Paul Newman, Tom Bosley, Geraldine Page, Shelly Berman, and Lois Nettleton were members of the Woodstock Players at one time or another in the '40s and '50s.

The theater's recent restoration has left the auditorium in better shape than it was back then. The downstairs room, a community center used for meetings and some pretty good art exhibitions by local professionals, has the shiniest wood floor outside of a basketball court. The tiny hall over it is full of old-fashioned chairs—no longer horsehair, to be sure, but elegant all the same; the ceiling is gilded and painted with stars and geometric shapes. Crystal-and-brass gaslight fixtures gleam on the walls. In the evenings, year-round, you can watch musicals and plays—classics like *The Music Man, Guys and Dolls, Annie Get Your Gun, The Sound of Music.* For information about tickets, call 815-338-4821, or stop in at the box office in the opera house.

Old Courthouse and Jail

The old courthouse and jail on the other side of the square—the next stop on your walk—had also seen its glorious heyday—Bugsy Malone and Al Capone and company put in appearances here when Chicago's jails were overflowing with other bootleggers during Prohibition days. The courthouse had, nonetheless, also been targeted by the town's tear-it-down forces, and had, like the opera house, to be rescued at the 11th hour and restored in the spiffiest possible way—black-and-white awnings matching the black wrought-iron trim and the white-limestone window frames.

What you'll see inside are shops—a little one called the Seasoned Chef; another, Witherspoon's, purveying fine ladies' and men's clothing; greenery at the Greenery; and a remarkable selection of cards and prints and ethnic and designer jewelry at the Courthouse Gallery. The Old Courthouse Inn, which has a separate entrance downstairs to your left as you leave the building, serves soups, sandwiches, salads, and hot plates for lunch, except Sunday (when a splendid brunch, country-style, is the order of the day), and steaks, chops, lobsters, and the like for dinner. Some of the tables are installed in the original cells.

Upstairs, as if that menu weren't enough to have you checking your watch in the hope that it's mealtime, there's Madeleine's, a charming Victorian tea room installed in the original sheriff's quarters. The marble-topped soda fountain is stacked with plates of croissants, tiny cakes, and linzer tortes; the menu lists sacher torte—the famous Viennese semi-sweet chocolate cake with apricot filling—and fanciful ice-cream sundaes (burgundy cherry, chocolate Arabian raspberry, rootbeer). You can go in immediately or schedule a stop there at the end of the walk when you feel virtuous from your exercise. Woodstock is certainly small enough that Madeleine's won't be out of your way.

The Residential District

The people who settled Woodstock in the mid-1800s, originally from Woodstock, Vermont, and before that from Woodstock, England, had carefully planned the town. They aimed, no doubt, to avoid the haphazard growth and the torturous streets of the big Eastern cities of the day. The streets, now mostly lined with huge trees, are broad and laid out at right angles to each other so that, as you walk onward into the residential districts that surround the town square, you never end up wondering whether you're going north or south.

The same care that went into the planning of the town went into the building of its houses. Some of them have been maintained over the years. The Woodstock Landmarks and Bicentennial Commissions' 1975–76 project to present special plaques to families who restored their houses in a historically authentic fashion has put many of them into the condition in which you'd have found them had you walked under the maples here a century ago.

Following the map, you'll see many of these dwellings. As you're walking down Jackson after leaving Madeleine's keep your eye peeled for the imposing Steamboat Gothic on the southwest corner of Tryon and Jackson and down the road on the north side, the E. C. Jewett House at 310 Jackson—all cupolas and vines. Next door is the dark-green clapboard Edward Murphy House, its white trim looking as bright as it might have when it was put up in the mid-1870s. The George Murphy House, a pilastered blinding-white Greek Revival at 128 Hayward, the next street you'll stroll, is a standout.

Each few hundred feet gives you a different perspective on the houses you've just passed. Retracing your steps on Hayward, for example, after you've walked South Street far enough to inspect the circa-1883 William Avery House at number 415, you'll notice the ornate woodwork under the eaves of the Edward Murphy House and the fancy balustrade around the peak of its roof.

Detailing is what these homes are all about, and each one is different. The Frank Buell House at 336 Tryon has a big curving veranda on one side; on the other is a portico that looks as if a carriage might drive up at any moment. The windows are leaded in diamond and teardrop shapes. The walls are covered with rectangular and scalloped shingles and with clapboards that run diagonally as well as horizontally.

At number 362, an immense weeping willow droops over a front yard so crowded with spruce and other evergreens that you can scarcely see the house for the plantings.

Number 510 on the west side of Dean Street, which angles northeast from its intersection with Tryon, has a beautiful oak door and leaded-and-beveled-glass windowpanes. The Silas Olmsted house at number 410 on the same street is striking for its beautiful big oriel window.

These are small things, of course, but the wealth of small things in Woodstock is what makes such a big difference.

Back to the Square
When you head back to the square along South, Jefferson, and Van Buren streets, perhaps you'll be following the strains of a local band playing in the lacy bandstand; perhaps you'll be listening to the promptings of your stomach, urging you on to Madeleine's; perhaps you're dying to get back to the antiques bazaar. The local policeman may appear and inquire as to how you enjoyed your walk and maybe invite you back to the evening's performance in the "real honest-to-horsehair" opera house. The friendliness—you've seen it all over town—is just another little thing that makes you glad you came.

MISSOURI

A SAMPLE OF KANSAS CITY
Harry and Phyl Dark

Kansas City is no longer the rip-roaring cattle town which it managed to remain until late in the last century. But as one of our youngest great cities, it offers the constant change and improvement, the freshness and virility, the modern good looks and the excitement of many things to see and do that keep it high on the list of America's best places to be.

No one can cover Kansas City in a day or two—not even in a week or two—but on this walk you can get a good enough sample of this up-to-date metropolis to direct your thinking toward another visit here—and perhaps another.

Spanish Architecture at the Plaza
Let's start our walking tour where most Kansas Citians would—at the Plaza—Country Club Plaza, that is—in the high 40s between Main Street and Southwest Expressway. Frequently billed as the nation's first suburban shopping district, Country Club Plaza was originated in the 1920s by J. C. Nichols, a prominent builder who wanted to provide a buffer between his elite residential development to the southwest and the city's rapidly encroaching urbanization.

The Plaza's architectural theme is imported entirely from Spain, specifically Seville, KC's "sister city." A visit here is truly a journey into Old Spain. The Moorish buildings and fine works of genuine Iberian art along all the walkways are complemented by many fountains. The latter have been foremost in establishing KC as America's "City of Fountains," with more water displays than any other city in the world except Rome.

Some of the city's finest jewelers, portrait photographers,

haberdashers, couturiers, and gourmet dining spots are here in the Plaza. Toward its western edge between 47th Street and Nichols Parkway is Seville Square, a four-level shopping mall with restaurants, specialty foods, theaters, and dozens of stores.

A series of multilevel parcades offering free parking, plus ample metered street parking, make it easy to leave your car and proceed afoot. Wander up and down the many short blocks at will throughout this windowshopper's delight, but don't overlook the numerous outstanding architectural and historical features. By all means, bring your camera to capture the gorgeous fountains and statuary.

Fountains Honoring Myth and Fantasy

Stop by the Nichols Memorial Fountain on 47th between Nichols and Main and admire its circa-1910 French sculpture. At 47th and Nichols you can't miss the tall, graceful Giralda Tower and adjacent Seville Light, replicas of monuments adjoining the great cathedral of Seville. Pan, the Arcadian god of prophecy, woodlands, and sensual pleasure, is honored with his own fountain in Chandler Court, 47th and Wyandotte. In another water display at 47th and Wornall Road, Neptune rises from the sea in a sculpture cast in lead by the Bromsgrove Guild of Worcestershire, England, in 1911.

Next to Neptune is *The Wild Boar of Florence,* created by the Italian sculptor Benelli in 1857, one of the area's unique works of art. Sweet innocence portrayed in white Carrara marble is the theme of *Sleeping Child* by Ferdinando Andreini. You'll see it at 47th and Broadway. A rare all-year-round running fountain is that of Pomona, the strikingly beautiful goddess of vineyards and orchards, whom you can visit in her own courtyard at Broadway and Ward Parkway. At 47th and Central, you'll enjoy the Spanish Murals, depicting a bullfight in hand-painted tiles from Seville. All of these artistic triumphs are gathered together in a central area of the Plaza covering only a 6-block walk.

Buy, Sell, and Trade the Staff of Life

The Board of Trade, incorporating the nation's largest winter-wheat market, recently moved to its own building at the south side of the Plaza, 4800 Main. An interesting spectacle of frantic verbal bidding amid flurries of note paper, it operates the

A Sample of Kansas City

This walking tour is approximately 4 miles. The tour of Crown Center adds 1½ miles and the tour of Swope Park adds another 3 miles. (Map is not drawn to scale.)

year round during regular market hours. A must for the uninitiated.

Nelson Gallery

The Nelson Gallery of Art, a few blocks east of the Plaza on 47th Street (go to Oak and a block north), is one of the world's great galleries and art museums, a gift of the founder of the *Kansas City Star.* The gallery is world-renowned for its collection of Oriental treasures. Open daily except Mondays, 25 cents for adults and 10 cents for children under 12; free on Saturdays and Sundays.

Westport—the Oldest New Town in the Area

The oldest part of Kansas City is now the "newest" in terms of development and renewed commercial interest. Westport, the several-block-square section around Broadway (Nichols Parkway) and 39th Street, was the area's first organized town. It was established in the 1830s by entrepreneur John McCoy to become a rival of nearby Independence, Mo., as the major outfitting post for the thousands of wagon trains headed west on the Santa Fe Trail. Within a decade Westport had taken most of the business from Independence, only to find itself being encroached upon, and later actually absorbed by, its immediate neighbor to the north, the Town of Kansas, as KC was first known. Westport almost lost its identity as a community as urban growth engulfed it. Yet today's Kelly's Westport Inn, 500 Westport Road, one of Kansas City's most picturesque and best-known taverns, owes much of its attractiveness and strong customer appeal to the fact that it occupies Kansas City's oldest commercial building. The masonry edifice counts its age from before 1854, when Albert Boone (grandson of Daniel) first opened an outfitting station there, providing the early residents with salted meat, skillets, pans, knives, beads, shot, and lead, along with trade goods they would need when they arrived at Santa Fe. Today modern tourists see a refurbished Westport. With Westwood Square as its center, this is a tiny town-within-the-city mainly around Westport Road and a block or so to either side from Baltimore to Pennsylvania, a distance of 4 blocks.

Shoehorned into this small section are no less than a baker's dozen restaurants and taverns, including some of the city's most interesting, such as Stanford & Sons and the Happy Buzzard.

There is also a score of specialty shops with a wide variety of clothing and shoes, lamps, imports, exotic rocks and minerals, games, and other intriguing goods and services. Westport is for browsing and an occasional stop for a drink, a meal, or a purchase of something you might not be able to find elsewhere. To reach the next stop on our KC tour, return to Main Street and walk or drive 1½ miles north to Crown Center.

Crown Center

Until recent years, the high limestone-bluff section that ranges southeast from the intersection of Main and Pershing was a blighted eyesore dubbed "Signboard Hill." Its only function was to serve as a blatant and poorly maintained form of advertising. If that's your impression of the site, you're in for a pleasant shock. With basic financing from Hallmark Cards, Inc., the famous greeting-card company with headquarters in Kansas City, this 85-acre area is now a $200-million fully integrated commercial and entertainment complex, the nationally famous Crown Center (named for the Hallmark logo).

Crown Center is almost a city itself. It boasts a 750-room luxury hotel that is noted for having a stunning five-story-high *natural* waterfall in its main lobby. Also there are miles and miles of specialty shops—more than 85—devoted to folk art, metal sculpture, wines and foods, fine woolens, Western wear—including many of Kansas City's top retail names. The restaurants here—International Cafe, West Village and American Restaurant—offer everything from gourmet fare to hamburgers and hot dogs.

Crown Center Square, 10 acres of terraced parkway, offers a program of the performing arts and festivals during the summer months and major holidays and ice skating all winter long.

A Landmark with a View

Across Main, beginning at the southwest corner of the Pershing intersection, stands Liberty War Memorial, Kansas City's outstanding landmark. The 217-foot-high monument of light gray limestone was erected in memory of Kansas Citians who died in World War I. An elevator takes visitors to the observation deck at the top, affording the best possible view of Kansas City and its environs in all directions.

Looking north from the promontory on which the memorial is built, you have an eagle-eye view of Union Station, the handsome facility that has kept Kansas City the third-largest rail center in the nation.

On a low knoll immediately to the southwest of the memorial grounds is *Pioneer Mother,* a sculpture that pays tribute to the grueling hardships of pioneer life endured by the early families of the area.

Kansas City boasts an innovation you should look over if you have time for a more extensive look at the city's downtown shopping areas. It's called Dime Town, where all the city buses, from the river to 25th Street, cost a dime. You can ride from the Crown Center Hotel on Pershing through the downtown area all the way to 3rd Street, near the Missouri River, getting off and on as you wish at "a dime a time." Stop at City Market for the city's best produce shopping (it's especially lively on Saturdays, when it's chiefly a "farmer's market") and return through downtown to Crown Center.

Swope Park

From the south side of the Plaza it's 1½ miles on Main to 63rd Street and another 1½ miles east, just past Paseo, to the nearest corner of Kansas City's great Swope Park, the home of Starlight Theatre, where popular Broadway musicals and variety shows are enjoyed by thousands of visitors and residents on summer evenings. You can drive or take the eastbound No. 47 bus and ask the driver for transfer directions to Swope Park.

The park's 1,772 acres make it one of the largest municipally owned parks in the United States. It contains two 18-hole golf courses, several good fishing lakes, picnic areas, many interesting hiking trails, and the Kansas City Zoo, open the year round and among the nation's best.

The Kansas City Zoo, 75 cents for adults, accompanied children 15 and under free, is open every day 9–5 except Christmas and New Year's Day. Free parking. A narrow-gauge railroad, optional at 50 cents a person, tours the entire zoo. A walking tour covering the complete zoo totals 3½ miles, and you can easily spend an entire day here. Some of the sights to see are the Great Cat Walk, Great Ape House, Wolf Pack Woods, and the African Veldt. There are milking demonstrations daily at 10, 12, and 2 in the Dairy Barn, and you mustn't miss the new Tropical Habitat Building, where fauna and flora of the hot humid climates, from crocodiles to banana trees, dwell in more or less peaceful harmony. Of special interest is the brand-new exotic animal nursery operated with dedication and skill by Jan Armstrong, the zoo's curator of animal health.

A Side Trip to "Worlds of Fun"

Worlds of Fun is a mandatory side trip if you're traveling with children. One of the newest of the super theme parks, WOF is open weekends in spring and fall, daily June through August. One price, $8.95 (under 3, free), covers everything except food, drink, and souvenirs.

As a last-minute check on things to do and see in Kansas City, dial the KC Fun Phone as soon as you arrive. The number, 474-9600, is a 24-hour "entertainment hot line." You may wish to write in advance for printed information on Greater Kansas City from the Convention and Visitors Bureau, 1221 Baltimore, Kansas City, Mo. 64105.

MINNESOTA

MINNEAPOLIS: "FROM MINNEHAHA FALLS . . . TO THE MALL"
Ron D. Johnson

Minneapolis—the city of 22 lakes and 160 parks—is one of the world's most beautiful and livable cities. It boasts a strikingly beautiful downtown area with a tree-lined mall, a unique skyway system, a mixture of modern and historic buildings and a natural beauty rarely matched anywhere.

"Ladies and gentlemen, you are about to take a tour of the most beautiful city in the world," says Bob Bourne, veteran tour guide, before he starts his Gray Line tour of the city. Although many people smile skeptically at his statement at the beginning of the bus tour, at tour's end the majority agree.

Come with me, then, on a walking tour of Minneapolis. First to Minnehaha Park, site of Minnehaha Falls; then downtown to the Nicollet Mall and a stroll through Loring Park; and, finally, to a circuit of one of Minneapolis' scenic lakes.

Minnehaha Falls
Drive or take a bus or taxi to Minnehaha Park in south Minneapolis. This is where you'll find Minnehaha Falls, immortalized in Henry Wadsworth Longfellow's famous *Song of Hiawatha*. (Longfellow never saw the falls; when he wrote about it, he drew upon the logs of explorers, missionaries, and early Minnesota fur traders.)

The 53-foot cataract is the chief attraction of 144-acre Minnehaha Park. On Sundays and holidays, thousands of visitors flock to the park to see the falls, picnic, or walk from the falls along a tree- and shrub-shrouded pathway to the Mississippi River.

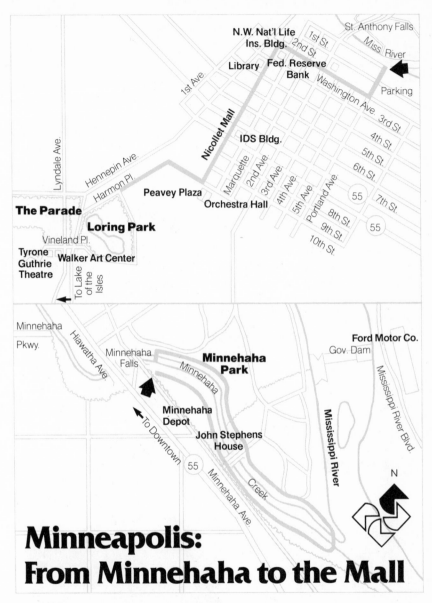

Minneapolis:
From Minnehaha to the Mall

This walking tour is approximately 4½ miles.
The walk along Lake Calhoun and Lake Harriet adds another 2½ miles.

There are wildflowers, squirrels, chipmunks, and all types of birds to be seen and enjoyed during your ½-mile hike from the falls to the river. You can sit on one of the huge boulders at the end of the path and watch the river traffic—towboats, fishing boats, canoes, pleasure craft. There's a view of the Ford Motor Company plant across the river, and a lock and dam (one of 30 on the Mississippi used for navigation and flood-control purposes) directly across the river from the Ford plant. Bring a lunch and picnic at this scenic spot on the Mississippi.

When you're ready to return to the falls, cross the bridge at the end of the creek. You'll pass the deer pen, where deer used to cavort a few decades ago. Now, it's a place for picnicking and a new sport called "disc golf," played with a Frisbee.

Tall elms, oaks, and evergreens arch over the path. The gurgle of Minnehaha Creek is omnipresent as you walk the ½ mile back to the falls. In the spring and summer months, especially when the water is high, you'll probably meet several canoeists, paddling on the creek to the river below.

Back at the falls, you can follow a path which takes you so close to the falls you'll feel the mist on your face and hear the roar of the rushing water in your ears. A stairway takes you back to the park proper where there is a variety of views of the falls and snapshot possibilities.

Statue Built by Pennies

Walk the short distance upstream from the falls to the statue of Hiawatha carrying Minnehaha across the creek. This beautiful statue was sculpted nearly 50 years ago and was paid for by pennies donated by Minneapolis schoolchildren.

Cross the footbridge just above the falls and walk to the refurbished old Minnehaha Depot, resplendent in its maroon and gold paint (Minnesota Gopher colors) and gingerbread trim. Built in the 1870s as a stop on the Milwaukee Railroad's Chicago-Minneapolis run, the depot once served heavy commuter traffic to and from downtown Minneapolis.

Nearby, you'll find the John Stevens House, the first wood-frame house built in Minneapolis. It was moved to Minnehaha Park several years ago. Like Minnehaha Depot it is a Minnesota historic site, maintained by the Minnesota Historical Society.

A Mall and Skyways

From Minnehaha Park, you can catch a city bus downtown, grab a taxi, or drive your car to Hiawatha Avenue (Highway 55) and head for the Minneapolis loop and the next leg of your walking tour—the Nicollet Mall and Skyway system. Begin your walk at St. Anthony Falls, discovered by Father Hennepin in 1763 when he was exploring the Northwest Territory.

There is ample parking at the Lock and Dam Observatory near Portland Avenue and 2nd Street. From the observation building you can view St. Anthony Falls (largest falls on the Mississippi) and the lock and dam. Across the river, you can see the old Pillsbury "A" mill, one of Minneapolis' first flour mills. The city was once the flour-milling capital of the United States; it even had the nickname "Flour City." You'll also see an excellent restaurant, Pracha-on-Main, in a restored warehouse. It features great steak and seafood. This famous eatery is in the heart of the riverfront restoration area, and you can reach it by walking or driving over the nearby Third Avenue Bridge.

After you've viewed the locks, walk south 2 blocks to Washington Avenue, turn right, and stroll past the old Milwaukee Road Depot to the beautiful Northwestern National Life Insurance Co. Building. This modern, white-columned Greek-style building was designed by Japanese-American architect Yamasaki and has fountains outside and Bertoia's beautiful *Sunlit Straw* sculpture in the lobby.

Across Washington Avenue stands the Federal Reserve Bank, an unusual structure with 12 floors strung up in the air by cables, similar to the Golden Gate Bridge. Outside, there are round bench seats, where you can rest and perhaps watch kids skateboarding down the sloping concrete around the bank.

Now, you begin your stroll down the 8-block Nicollet Mall. Stop by the Minneapolis downtown public library—the library's gold dome houses a planetarium. There are daily shows, lectures, movies, and educational productions in the library's theater.

The mall is a walker's paradise. Mini-buses and taxies are available, but no autos are allowed. It has heated bus shelters, heated sidewalks (keeping them free of snow in the winter), trees, flowers, fountains, and music. There are band concerts and other entertainment on the mall, sidewalk cafes, and shopping of all kinds.

The IDS Building

Focal point for activity is the immense 57-story Investors Diversified Services Building. Its crystal court, unique mirrorlike exterior, many fine restaurants, the deluxe Marquette Inn, movie theater, and more shops make for an exciting downtown adventure. Take the elevator to the top of the IDS for a magnificent look at Minneapolis, its lakes, and its tree-lined boulevards. On a clear day you can see past St. Paul into Wisconsin. There's a museum on the top floor which houses an excellent Minnesota and Minneapolis history exhibit.

Some of the things you shouldn't miss on your mall trip, if you have time to linger, include the huge clock on 8th Street, the weather barometer on 7th Street, the fountains, and, only a block south of 10th Street (the mall's end), famed Orchestra Hall and lovely Peavey Plaza.

From the IDS Building you can branch off and tour the downtown area by using the unique skyway system—20 glass-enclosed bridges which connect all major downtown buildings, department stores, and hotels. They will eventually total 76 and you'll be able to walk just about anywhere you want in downtown Minneapolis without worrying about the cold, snow, rain, or heat.

After you've toured the skyways, you might want to try one of several good restaurants in downtown Minneapolis—the Rosewood Room, Wine Cellar (French menu), Haberdashery in the Radisson Hotel (great hamburgers), Magic Pan (crepes), and Charlie's Cafe Exceptionale on 7th Street.

Loring: The Downtown Park

You can extend your trip from the mall to Loring Park, only ½ mile south of the mall. Loring Park has a lake filled with ducks and geese, tennis courts, horseshoe courts, flower gardens, the ever-present elm trees, and plenty of benches for the weary. You can also see a statue of Ole Bull, the great Norwegian violinist who performed in this city a century ago, and the lovely Berger Fountain, a replica of the famous fountain in Sydney, Australia.

Then just across Lyndale Avenue from Loring Park, you can tour the Tyrone Guthrie Theatre, one of the greatest repertory theaters in the world. The adjacent Walker Art Center has excellent changing exhibits of modern art, sculpture, and photography.

Lake of the Isles

The last leg of our Minneapolis tour is a stroll around Lake of the Isles, 2 miles south of the Loring Park-Guthrie Theatre area. If you're energetic, you can walk to it, traveling south on Hennepin or Lyndale, then turning west on Franklin or 24th Street to the lake.

Lake of the Isles is just one of the city's beautiful lakes and lagoons—all 22 offer some type of fishing. Many have excellent beaches for swimming, as well as boating, sailing, and canoeing.

On Lake of the Isles you'll see ducks and geese, canoeists, fishermen, and people out walking, jogging, and bicycling. There are separate paths for hikers and cyclists.

Lake of the Isles is tranquil, beautiful, and brimming with zestful human activity. A walk around it perks you up, makes you feel alive, no matter how bad your day has been. Hike around the lake (about 1½ miles) and if you're energetic, continue your walk south across Lake Street to Lake Calhoun, and then on to Lake Harriet, one of the city's most beautiful. Lake Harriet has band concerts in the summer—every night at 8. Both it and Lake Calhoun see much sailing action in the summer months. In the winter the skaters take over.

Parks for People

There are many more fine walking tours in Minneapolis. There are paths for hikers and usually another for bicyclists, around the city's other lakes. The fine parks in the city are for people, and they're safe day and night and much used.

The Eloise Butler Wild Flower Gardens in Theodore Wirth Park feature wild Minnesota plants, a magnificent garden, and rewarding bird-watching. You might also want to visit Fort Snelling State Park and the University of Minnesota campus or Butler Square, in the artists' warehouse and gallery district, and St. Anthony Main, two renovated old warehouses filled with a variety of shops and restaurants and many more walking adventures. All of these await you in Minneapolis, consistent winner of Quality of Life awards. A great place to visit and a wonderful place to live.

ST. PAUL: HISTORIC SUMMIT AVENUE
Ron D. Johnson

St. Paul, capital of Minnesota, is a friendly city of 310,000 persons and is much like a small version of Boston. Streets angle

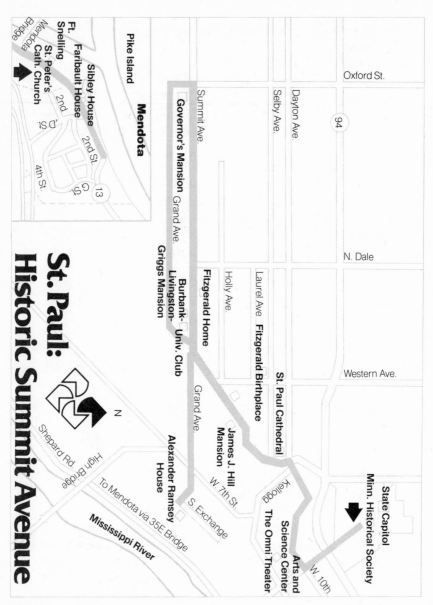

This walking tour is approximately 4½ miles.
The walk to the Ramsey House and through Old Mendota adds another 2 miles.

out of its bustling downtown area and away from the Mississippi River like spokes on a wheel.

Originally settled by the French, who developed Minnesota's early fur trade, the city gradually grew into a large manufacturing and transportation center. St. Paul attracted many Irish immigrants, who built the city's great Catholic churches. Next came Western Europeans, Yankees from the East, and finally Scandinavians. Today, St. Paul, like Boston, is known as an Irish Catholic city. It also is where the East ends. Across the river, in Minneapolis, the West begins.

Popular opinion to the contrary, St. Paul and Minneapolis are in reality the "un-Twin Cities." They're delightfully different. St. Paul is historic, quaint, friendly, smaller, and Irish. Minneapolis is Western, modern, more sophisticated, Scandinavian—also friendly.

Remnants of the affluence of the days of James J. Hill, Frank B. Kellogg, and, later, F. Scott Fitzgerald remain in the magnificent mansions along St. Paul's Summit Avenue. And that's where we'll go on this walking tour.

We'll also visit Old Mendota, Minnesota's first town, a village adjacent to St. Paul—a distinctive and charming little river town.

The State Capitol

Our tour begins at the magnificent State Capitol just off Interstate Highways 94 and 35E and only a few minutes' drive from downtown.

Parking is available in lots and at parking meters close to the Capitol. On weekdays during the legislative session (mid-January through mid-May) it's much tougher to find a spot, and you may have to park a few blocks away and walk or take a bus to the Capitol.

The State Capitol, one of the finest in the nation, was completed in 1904. It was designed by architect Cass Gilbert, a St. Paul native, who also designed the U.S. Supreme Court building in Washington, D.C., and the George Washington Bridge, which links New York and New Jersey.

The Capitol is constructed of several different types of Minnesota stone and 20 varieties of imported marble. Inside, visitors can view paintings (including all the Minnesota governors), murals, and sculpture relating to the state's history. You can take a free tour of the Capitol—narrated by an expert guide.

Tours are held throughout the year; schedules are available at the St. Paul Convention and Visitors Bureau.

History, Art, and Science

Exit from the main door, turn left, and walk a short distance to the Minnesota Historical Society Building. This huge gray structure houses the oldest institution in the state, created by the territorial legislature in 1849. The society maintains a vast collection of materials on the state's history (excellent resources for genealogy buffs), Scandinavian-American history, Indian culture and artifacts, and American history.

You may also want to visit the St. Paul Arts and Science Center, 30 East 10th Street—only a few blocks from the Capitol. The center has several scientific and archeological exhibits, fine arts displays, and a science museum and is home of the noted Chimera Theatre, which features top theatrical productions like *Fiddler on the Roof* and Shakespearean plays.

From the Arts and Science Center continue west on 10th Street for a block to the William L. McKnight 3M Omni-Theater. The Omni-Theater is not only a theater, but a showcase for scientific displays highlighting astronomy and history, space sciences, earth sciences, oceanography, climatology, and anthropology. The theater opened in the summer of 1978, and you may want to check times and admission prices with the St. Paul Convention and Visitors Bureau at 222-5561.

Continue your stroll west along 10th Street for a block and turn left on Main Street for another 2 blocks. Make a right onto 6th Street and follow the hill to Summit Avenue. Turn left onto Summit.

Summit Avenue

Now you're heading for the heart of your St. Paul walking tour, which begins at the St. Paul Cathedral, an imposing structure dominating the city's central district. You can take a guided tour of the cathedral at no charge. The cathedral, begun in 1905, was designed by Emmanual L. Masqueray in classic Renaissance style. Its interior is Neo-Baroque, and walking inside it is akin to stepping inside Notre Dame in Paris. The Cathedral seats 4,000 for a mass and often fills up for Easter and Christmas services.

When you leave the Cathedral, stroll down Summit, keeping to the left, and you'll come to the James J. Hill mansion at

240 Summit, which now houses offices of the St. Paul Archdiocese. This is where the one-eyed railroad baron lived while
he constructed his railroad empire. Called the "Empire
Builder," Hill founded the Great Northern Railroad and was the
first railroad magnate to reach the West Coast along the northern route.
    The Hill mansion is a gigantic and elaborate red-sandstone
structure. Now open for tours, it is operated by the Minnesota
Historical Society.
    If you'd like to see the apartment building where F. Scott
Fitzgerald was born and spent the first 2½ years of his life, walk
north on Western Avenue (a block off Summit) to Laurel and
take a left to 481 Laurel, a row house now subdivided into
apartments.
    Afterward, continue walking along Summit Avenue. This
grand residential avenue, shaded by stately elms, oaks, and an
assortment of other trees, is like a tunnel of natural beauty.
Make a stop at the University Club. It's a private club, and
Fitzgerald was a member. In the basement barroom his name is
carved on the old wooden bar, along with hundreds of others.

An Imposing Mansion
    Right next door to the University Club stands the imposing
Burbank-Livingston-Griggs Mansion. This lavish villa was built
by St. Paul shipping millionaire James C. Burbank in 1863. In
the 1920s, Mrs. Theodore Griggs remodeled the home's Victorian interior into ten European period rooms, with 17th- and
18th-century Italian, French, and English paneling, furniture,
and art. You can tour the mansion for a small fee.
    As you leave the villa, continue along the right side of
Summit, past a variety of mansions—once homes of St. Paul's
affluent, now subdivided into apartments. You'll pass Victorian
mansions, Elizabethan-style homes, Queen Anne cottage-design
houses, and Cass Gilbert-designed row houses. The row house
at 599 Summit is where Scott Fitzgerald lived in his young
manhood. Local legend reports that Fitzgerald ran out of his
home down Summit Avenue (on a chilly November day) and
yelled to everyone, "It's finished . . . it's finished!" He was
talking about *This Side of Paradise,* his first novel. The book became a best seller when the author was in his early 20s and established him as one of the nation's rising young writers.
    After your stop at 599 Summit, the rest of the avenue may

seem anticlimactic. But the beauty of the homes with their well-tended gardens and the fantastic churches along Summit combine to make for a pleasant walk down to the Governor's Mansion at 1006 Summit, an impressive, large mansion with a fence around it.

The Alexander Ramsey House

Take a left off Summit to Oxford and walk a block to Grand Avenue. You can either walk to our last St. Paul stop or take a bus; the latter is recommended. If you take the bus, be sure to get off at Ramsey and Grand, then turn right (south) and walk to Exchange Street and continue left a block to the Alexander Ramsey House.

President Zachary Taylor appointed Ramsey as the first territorial governor of Minnesota. The 15-room French Renaissance–style mansion which he had built in 1872 is solid Victorian—from the carved walnut woodwork and marble fireplaces to the crystal chandeliers and Brussels carpeting. The wooden carriage house serves as a visitor center and Victorian gift shop. A tour, at a reasonable charge, is a must for any St. Paul visitor.

Across the street from the Ramsey House is restored Forepaugh's Restaurant. A lunch or dinner at Forepaugh's, a mid-Victorian mansion, is an unforgettable experience—something you should save until the end of your St. Paul walking tour. The food is excellent, atmosphere unique, and service very good. In the evening, there is entertainment in the piano bar.

Although this ends your Summit Avenue walking tour, I strongly recommend you get into your car, drive down to Shepard Road, which hugs the Mississippi, and cross the bridge over the Mississippi on Highway 35E. Turn right on Highway 13, and head into Old Mendota, only a mile away.

Mendota: Minnesota's Birthplace

Mendota, a village of 320 people, 60 dogs, and as many cats, is the birthplace of Minnesota. It was the home of Minnesota's first pioneer farmer—fur trader Jean-Baptiste Faribault, and Minnesota's first governor, Henry Hastings Sibley. Perched on a bluff above the Minnesota River—just above the point where it flows into the Mississippi—Mendota, which means "meeting of the waters," is a scenic, historic, and swinging town. It swings because it has been the hub of traditional jazz music for years.

Our walking tour of Old Mendota is just a mile. Start your walk at the top of the hill on Highway 13 at St. Peter's Catholic Church, the state's oldest church in continuous use. This site offers an expansive view of Fort Snelling across the Minnesota River. You can also see the confluence of the Mississippi and Minnesota to your right as you stand on the church grounds.

Walk down Highway 13, past the auction house, to the Sibley Tea House, once the home of Hypolite DePuis, General Sibley's private secretary. The tea house is maintained by the Nathan Hale Chapter of the St. Paul Daughters of the American Revolution and at times opens and serves great meals.

Right across D Street from the Sibley Tea House sits a hugh white building, the Emporium of Jazz—Mariner Restaurant complex. The restaurant has excellent seafood, and jazz music is played on weekends by the Hall Bros. New Orleans jazz band or other well-known jazz artists such as Ralph Sutton, Wild Bill Davison, and the World's Greatest Jazz Band. The late Bobby Hackett, the cornetist, played his last out-of-town concert here.

Bypass the Jazz Emporium, temporarily, and walk down a winding road to the Sibley House, a limestone structure built by Minnesota's first governor in 1835. Tours of the Sibley House are conducted during the summer by the DAR. Next door stands the Faribault House, a similar structure built a few years after Sibley's. Tours are offered from May to October by the DAR.

You can walk back up the hill, and dine at the Mariner Restaurant or have a beverage in the Jazz Emporium lounge. If it's a weekend, you may want to stop back in the evening to hear some great New Orleans jazz.

This ends our tour of St. Paul and historic Old Mendota. There are many other walking tours of the city. You can obtain booklets and information on them from the St. Paul Convention and Visitors Bureau in the Osborn Building in downtown St. Paul. Downtown St. Paul, like Minneapolis, has a skyway system connecting downtown buildings, which makes walking comfortable and enjoyable the year round. Happy walking to you!

Walking the Northwest

WASHINGTON

SEATTLE'S WATERFRONT
Janice Krenmayr

Seattle's waterfront is more than piers, buildings, and boats.

It is the city's lifeline, past and present, throbbing with the stirring events of history, constantly changing present, and exciting prospects of the future.

The waterfront is the dramatic take-off point of the Alaska gold rush, the scene of Chief Seattle's most momentous speech, of the hustle and bustle of dock scenes, of windjammers and sailing schooners unloading window sashes, molasses, grindstones, calico, and loading lumber for ports elsewhere.

It is a fleet of steamboats and ferryboats, faithfully carrying passengers and goods regularly to Puget Sound islands and ports, aging then being replaced by newer models.

It is Henry Yesler's sawmill perched onshore, with logs shooting downhill to the water on "Skid Road"—a chute of short logs laid crosswise. (The rugged working phrase has since been adapted and corrupted both in meaning and form to "Skid Row.")

It is mud and tide flats, later filled in with tons of dirt, sliced from a steep, nearby hill. So where else can one walk over what once was salt water?

It is a sailing ship, too dilapidated to bother hauling out, buried forever under the new, paved street in the filling process. So where else can one walk over a buried ship?

It is the warship *Decatur*, anchored offshore in 1856, during the Battle of Seattle, when a couple of salvos from its deck guns helped to turn the tide of attacking Indians.

It is seafood restaurants, curio shops, huge dockside warehouses, an imposing ferry terminal.

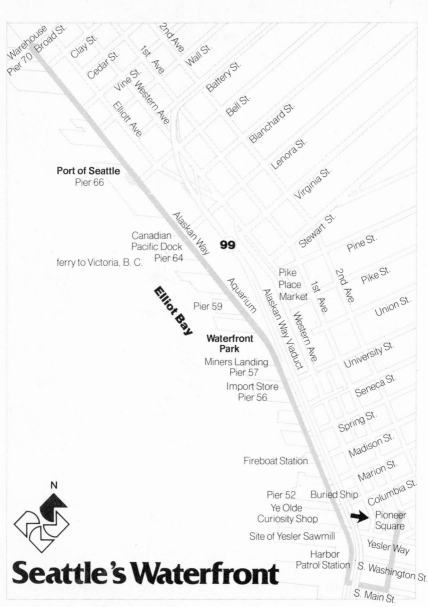

Port of Seattle
Pier 66

Canadian
Pacific Dock
ferry to Victoria, B. C.   Pier 64

Pier 59

Waterfront Park
Miners Landing
Pier 57
Import Store
Pier 56

Warehouse
Pier 70   Broad St.
Clay St.
Cedar St.
Vine St.
Elliott Ave.
Western Ave.
1st Ave.
2nd Ave.
Wall St.
Battery St.
Bell St.
Blanchard St.
Lenora St.
Virginia St.
Alaskan Way
99
Aquarium
Elliot Bay
Stewart St.
Pine St.
2nd Ave.
1st Ave.
Western Ave.
Alaskan Way Viaduct
Pike St.
Union St.
University St.
Pike
Place
Market
Seneca St.
Spring St.
Madison St.
Marion St.
Columbia St.

Fireboat Station

Pier 52   Buried Ship
Ye Olde
Curiosity Shop   Pioneer
Square
Site of Yesler Sawmill

N

Harbor
Patrol Station   S. Washington St.
Yesler Way
S. Main St.

Seattle's Waterfront

This walking tour is approximately 3⅓ miles round trip.

It is a fireboat station, to reach and rescue a blazing ship out on the water; and seaside hotels, where you can fish right out of your room window.

And, as of recent days, it is a spanking new Waterfront Park and Aquarium.

Most of all, it is an area that never loses its enchantment, where you can walk 2 blocks or 2 miles, whatever your mood, under balmy blue skies or in brisk, windy gusts or misting rain, feeling an air of expectancy, of change, of discovery. You're never disappointed.

Pioneer Square

Since Seattle's history began at Pioneer Square, First Avenue and Yesler, so should your walk. For many years, this area and its buildings were neglected as commerce moved north. But in the past decade, noble action by "those who care" brought a renaissance: dingy old buildings restored to former dignity, old-fashioned paving brick creating pleasant malls, outdoor cafes, restaurants, and souvenir and antique shops blossoming along the streets.

Then Bill Spiedel, Seattle's eminent historian, discovered "Seattle's Underground"—buildings and streets that were covered over in a major fill-in years ago to level out steep streets. Shops and stores still sleep under the present bustle. Now visitors by the thousands come to tour the fascinating underground city.

"The Point"

When and if you can tear yourself away (come back another day!) walk south on First Avenue 2 blocks to Main Street, "The Point," as it was called before the fill-in. Here, early white settlers slashed a clearing from the forest, erected a sawmill, a store, a blacksmith shop, to build the new city. Turn right and walk toward the water, to Alaskan Way.

Once, the bay swarmed with canoes of the tillicums (Indian friends), a pioneer wrote, "and the shores were filled with a mass of their dusky humanity," when Chief Seattle, head of the Duwampsh Confederation of Western tribes, began a speech near here. His "trumpet-toned voice rolled over the multitude like the startling reveille of a bass drum, and the silence was as instantaneous and perfect as that which follows a clap of thunder from a clear sky."

The old chief's speech, given at a demonstrative reception staged for Governor Isaac I. Stevens, first governor of Washington Territory, in December 1854, on his first visit to the new village of Seattle, has since been considered one of the finest, most eloquent of any given by an American Indian.

A Walk Through History

Now walk north along the waterfront. At Washington Street, the tide once lapped up to First Avenue, where pioneers crossed the street on a little wooden bridge. Now, a historic plaque at the old Harbor Patrol Station and public boat dock marks a relic underneath—the wreck of an old side-wheeler that served as a mission hospital to seafarers early in the century.

At Yesler Way, the next street north, Henry Yesler ran his sawmill, Seattle's first big industry. Like Boeing Airplane Company today, it put a lot of citizens on a payroll. Sailing vessels at Yesler's Wharf unloaded their goods here on the dock and took on lumber for San Francisco. A bronze plaque recalls the mill, while another beside it commemorates the Battle of Seattle. Indians attacked two small forts from thick woods uphill, and the warship *Decatur,* anchored offshore, helped repel the attackers with its booming shells.

Four steamboats made regular calls here at Yesler's Wharf, too, beginning in 1864. One was a mail boat, the *Major Tomkins,* on a weekly run from Olympia to Victoria, B.C.

Ye Olde Curiosity Shop

Just north of Yesler is Ye Olde Curiosity Shop, one of Seattle's oldest waterfront stores. Patterned after an Indian longhouse, the new home for this venerable institution was built during the 1962 Seattle World's Fair. The tall colored poles which marked the entrance to the fair were preserved and used as columns for the new shop. Browse inside if you like, but fair warning: there are fascinating oddities crammed to the roof— "Sylvester's Mummy," shrunken heads, totem poles, ad infinitum. Time flies, and much more lies up the avenue.

At Columbia Street, look right. Under the ground at the far-left (northeast) corner of the next intersection at Western Avenue lies the wrecked sailing vessel *Windward.* It was beached to salvage the metal, used as a diving platform by young boys for a while, then came the railroad. To avoid moving expenses, the wreck was left where it was and covered over.

Washington State Ferry Terminal

Across the same waters the wrecked *Windward* sailed now can be seen cross-Sound gleaming white ferryboats, their full bodies loaded with cars and trucks. Their haven on this side is the Washington State Ferry Terminal on Colman Dock, Pier 52, just north of Columbia Street. An overhead walkway on Marion Street, the next block, allows quick access for ferry passengers to First Avenue. The dock has been rebuilt through the years. Once, in 1912, soon after a new one went in, the steel-prowed *Alameda*, out of control, rammed straight through it and into a stern-wheeler on the other side.

North of the Terminal at Madison Street is a fireboat station. Another historical plaque there tells of the beginning of the vast Puget Sound Ferry system in 1888.

Snacks and Shops

Ivar's famed Acres of Clams restaurant provides an inviting alcove next, for a rest and seafood snack, either from an outdoor bar or inside.

An import store, offering exotic furniture and items from all over the world, appears at Pier 56 in the next block above Seneca Street, and in between, more snack stands and a ticket booth for a harbor cruise well worth the price, if you've time.

Another seafood restaurant, the Galley, huddles with the mercantile shop Pirate's Plunder in the old warehouse boldly labeled "Miner's Landing," which relates to the next attraction.

"Miner's Landing"

At the foot of Union Street, the next block, a plaque describes the most exciting and profitable period in Seattle's history, when newspaper headlines screamed "Gold! Stacks of Yellow Metal" to herald the arrival in 1897 of the "Ton of Gold" ship, the *Portland*, bearing newly rich miners and their gold nuggets. It was the beginning of the Alaska gold rush.

The New Waterfront Park

Here begins the delightful new Waterfront Park, with extended piers, walkways, rustic picnic tables, benches, and decorative tub plantings well out over the water for marvelous views of ships and ferries. Far across the Sound are the snow-capped Olympic Mountains.

Bordering the north side of the Park, between Pike and

Pine Street, is an interesting, large aquarium. And across the avenue, a combination of stairway plus elevator takes visitors up and down the hill from downtown First Avenue.

Pike Place Market

At the top, the elevator will deposit you inside the Pike Place Market. This gem of an old-fashioned commercial enterprise began in 1907 when the mayor proclaimed August 1 "Market Day," inviting nearby farmers to use the facilities of this locale to sell their produce directly to the city folk. City dwellers, anxious for a bargain, then as now, came in droves; the farmers were seemingly more skeptical of the mayor's arrangement and only a few responded to the call. These budding entrepreneurs sold out in a flash and rapidly spread the word about this bonanza. Within three months there were 120 farmers selling from their wagons. By 1927 the market expanded to its present four buildings with more than 400 farmers providing the daily cornucopia of goods. Today this market boasts every kind of the freshest fruits, flowers, vegetables, meats, poultry, and dairy products, and such mouth-watering specialties as pastries, spices, herbs, teas, and coffees. All of this diversity with each ethnic group contributing its own special style.

For Eager Walkers—Another 10 Blocks

If you still have oomph left, your walk need not end here. Return to the waterfront by the elevator-stairway. Four blocks farther north, past a succession of piers, is Pier 66, the port of Seattle Dock, Bell Street Terminal. Another 4 blocks along is the British Columbia Ferry Corporation's Pier 69, from which the lovely cruise ship *Princess Margarita* carries hundreds of passengers to sightsee Victoria and Vancouver, B.C., daily in summer.

On that dock's far side, on Pier 70, a huge old warehouse has been delightfully renovated. You can spend an entire afternoon among tiny shops with goods ranging from imported coffee, cheese and sausages, leather clothing, bric-a-brac, to furniture not only on the street level but also in the upper loft, where beautifully crafted hobby items are found in a senior citizens' gift shop.

Finish the day with steak and lobster dinner in a restaurant on the same dock while you watch the ships go by. If you're looking for a home for the night, retrace your steps 4 blocks to the Edgewater Inn, Pier 67. Snooze in a room overlooking the water; and in the morning, stick a fishing pole out the window to catch your breakfast!

TACOMA'S POINT DEFIANCE PARK
Janice Krenmayr

When Fort Nisqually was erected with its blockhouse and commercial buildings, the thought of going for nature strolls outside its stockade probably would have amused its hardworking occupants.

Now, the fort is merely an interesting peacetime historical attraction, and the peninsula to which it was moved as a permanent restoration is one of the Northwest's finest park areas for walks, as well as other diversions.

Tacoma residents are grateful for the foresight of their forebears of 1888, who set aside the peninsula's 640 acres, a former military reservation, as a public park. The City of Tacoma obtained a license to occupy and improve it, subject to possible repossession by the federal government if deemed necessary. In 1905, the city acquired firm title to the land as a park. The years since have seen many improvements and added attractions.

A Park with a Wide Variety of Different Walks
Few locations offer such environmental variety for walking pleasure all to your own choice: from a few steps to many miles; through virgin woods filled with wildlife; on open beaches facing blue water and sky; on high, scenic bluffs or through the paths of history. For many years, a senior citizen and nearby resident hiked 7 miles daily as his private constitutional and pleasure. And every day, rain or shine, he discovered something different—a squirrel's fir-cone cache, a bald eagle's nest, nature in all its variety.

How to Get There
Point Defiance Park forms the northern point of the city. To get there from Interstate 5 Freeway or from South Center

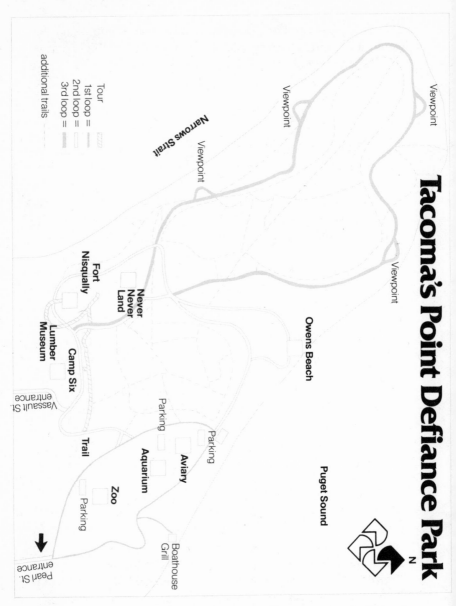

Tacoma's Point Defiance Park

Narrows Strait

Puget Sound

Viewpoint

Viewpoint

Viewpoint

Viewpoint

Owens Beach

Fort Nisqually

Never Never Land

Lumber Museum

Camp Six

Trail

Vassault St. entrance

Parking

Aquarium

Aviary

Parking

Zoo

Parking

Boathouse Grill

Pearl St. entrance

N

Tour
1st loop =
2nd loop =
3rd loop =
additional trails ----

This walking tour is approximately 2 miles round trip. There are miles of additional trails within the park.

Mall, head west to Bantz Boulevard, then follow signs north to the park. From downtown Tacoma, go west on Sixth Avenue and turn right on Pearl Street to the park.

When you enter the park, you are on a one-way road with many options. There are three loop roads, each extending outward from the other. So you must complete entirely either the first, which encircles the zoo and aquarium; the second, leading to Fort Nisqually, Never Never Land, and Camp Six; or the third, a 5-mile walk around the outer edge of the peninsula. There is no turning back to pick up one of the other loops. The third loop doubles back on the same route as the second, so the same sights are included.

The first loop also allows a dip down to shoreline and its Boathouse Grill, a year-round seafood restaurant. The second loop has a branch to Owen Beach, with saltwater swimming and picnic area, and on the third loop are scenic views of Puget Sound, Commencement Bay, and the Narrows. Somewhere on these shores the first white men camped—part of the crew who surveyed the Puget Sound for Captain George Vancouver's expedition in 1782. Breathtaking views are here—the Olympic Mountains to the northwest, the Cascade range to the east, and always the "Mountain That Was God"—Mount Rainier, to the southeast.

The Aviary, the Aquarium, and the Zoo

Since most of the main attractions are within a 2-mile radius, we'll group them into a short walk for orientation. With any time remaining, or on return visits, you can explore the other trails.

For your first walk, follow signs to the aquarium or zoo parking lots. (On weekends and holidays, when these are full, you may have to park in the two large overflow lots marked "Aviary Parking," flanking the main road just before turning off on the aquarium loop.)

Visit the aviary, aquarium, and zoo first. They hold delights for every age. In the aquarium you'll see a friendly octopus taking a tidbit from its keeper; in the zoo are a rare echidna and platypus.

To begin your 2-mile round-trip walk, follow either of the two paved roads that lead into the loop road above the aquarium or zoo. They are the one-way return routes for traffic on the outer loop roads. You will face oncoming cars.

To the Fort

Better still, find one of the trails that take off at several points above the aquarium and zoo; keep bearing left, and walk the wide, moss-bordered path through deep woods among huge cedars and Douglas firs. (For the most direct trail, continue on the loop road uphill as it swings left above the zoo about ¼ mile, facing traffic. Here the forest path is easily distinguished. Follow it until it crosses the paved road. The fort is dead ahead.)

Just past the fort is Never Never Land, featuring storybook characters in natural forest setting. If it is late, catch this "show" before it closes at dusk.

Then treat yourself and the kiddies to a sure-enough historic Northwest fort, built in 1833 by the Hudson's Bay Company for a trading post, the first permanent white settlement in the Puget Sound country.

Inside its stockade enclosure one easily walks backward in time. You can almost hear the blacksmith's anvil ringing, the Indians crowding and bargaining in the fur-trading store, the soldiers dashing to the lookout tower at a sudden call for survey of surrounding woods. The small museum will hold you for long minutes with its fascinating collection of household relics of that age.

The fort boasted many other firsts: first commercial enterprise on Puget Sound; first steamship operating from it; first cattle, sheep, and chickens raised on Puget Sound; first white couple married there; and the first white child born on Puget Sound.

The fort actually is a reconstruction in fine detail. The original Fort Nisqually was located 17 miles south, near the mouth of the Nisqually River. The United States purchased the company holdings in 1867, ending British rule of the fort. By 1934 only two buildings, the granary (oldest building in Washington State) and the Factor's House, remained. The Young Men's Business Club of Tacoma moved them to this splendid promontory overlooking the Narrows Strait, and added the other buildings to conform to originals, using construction materials of pioneer days: hand-adzed uprights, split-cedar shakes, hand-forged hardware, and wooden pegs.

A Glimpse of the Old Logging Industry

From your sojourn into the past, walk back down the road to Camp Six for a visit in the more recent past—this one in a period following pioneer settlement, when logging became the number-one industry. Here is a 20-acre lumber museum, with original bunk cars on railroad wheels—the "hotel" for loggers—a caboose, yarders, loaders and other logging equipment, a 110-foot Spar tree and 300-ton Lidgerwood skidder. Now and then a demonstration is given of the old-time ways of hooking up a fallen tree and hauling it to the railroad. You may even be on time to purchase tickets for a train ride on tracks that disappear into the deep forest below.

Follow the paved road or the trail, seen across the road, back to the zoo or aquarium parking area. If there is no time left, you will want to return again and again to find your own favorite combination on the network of trails that thread the park. A clear, inexpensive map showing park roads and trails may be purchased at the museum in the fort.

OREGON

PORTLAND'S OLDTOWN
Terence O'Donnell

Here on the river, the city began—on an autumn afternoon in
1843 when William Overton and Asa Lovejoy, canoeing on the
Willamette from Fort Vancouver to Oregon City, stopped on the
riverbank to rest. Intrigued by the site, they decided to file a
"tomahawk" claim and slashed firs to outline a rectangle of 320
acres. It was a good place to start a town. A few years later the
fir forest was platted into 16 city-size blocks, a location on a
river deep enough for oceangoing ships with fertile valleys
nearby. Soon after they settled in, the early townsfolk carved
out a road so that the farmers could bring their produce to the
river—and revenue to the town.

As the gold rushes and Indian wars of the 1840s brought
profit to the West, Portland grew. By the 1870s it was no longer
a straggle of little wooden buildings along the river, but a grid of
streets lined with "commercial palaces"—some of them the
finest examples of cast-iron architecture in the country. However, in the '90s decline began. Population increases and
frequent river floods pushed the town inland, while the coming
of the railroad further encouraged people to abandon the river
streets. South of Burnside, Oldtown's north-south dividing line,
the "palaces" survived as warehouses until the 1940s, when the
wrecking ball that preceded an expressway destroyed many of
these classics. The north side of Burnside, however, which we
will tour, remained alive and rowdy as it became the turf for loggers and sailors in town for a bash.

Such were the city's river neighborhoods until the late
1950s when rebuilding began. Today, many of the cast-iron
buildings have been restored and adapted to current needs,

creating a living monument on the historic riverbank spot where Portland was born.

The Skidmore Fountain

Our walk starts at the crossroads of S.W. Ankenny and 1st Street, location of the Skidmore Fountain. The chief glory of Oldtown in its prime, this fountain was donated by a local druggist for the benefit of the "horses, men, and dogs, of Portland." Well-known sculptor Olin Warner—he created the bronze entry doors of the Library of Congress—was brought all the way from the East Coast to design it. The location was originally chosen because at that time it was a six-sided plaza, cobbled in Belgian block and surrounded with grand buildings in the Baroque and Florentine style. Today, the rich backdrop has almost vanished, but because of its illustrious past, this fountain—completed almost 100 years ago—continues to be the city's pride.

Opposite and to the west stands the New Market Theatre, built in 1872 as both a market and a theater. Sopranos sang arias on the second floor while merchants sold cabbages on the first. The Poppleton Building next to it invites memories of the somber yet graceful structures which once surrounded the fountain.

Tunneling beneath the Burnside Bridge (site of an outdoor Saturday market held weekly from mid-spring to Christmas), we come to the Blagen Building, perhaps the best remaining example of a "commercial palace." The ground floor supports a cast-iron colonnade along with cast-iron lions and ladies which ornament the whole facade. In the past, long streets were lined with buildings like this.

Second Avenue—the Main Drag

Reaching Second Avenue, we arrive at Oldtown's main drag. No place in Portland contains such a mix of people: smart matrons walking side by side with beggars, boys hefting in warehouses, attractive young women in charge of boutiques, mod architects, gypsies and sailors. One of the street's most charming buildings is the former Merchants Hotel. Built in 1885, it has served variously as a dance hall, cracker factory, billiard hall, and, after World War I, a Japanese business complex. The Davis Street side of the building is the most interesting—it

Portland's Old Town

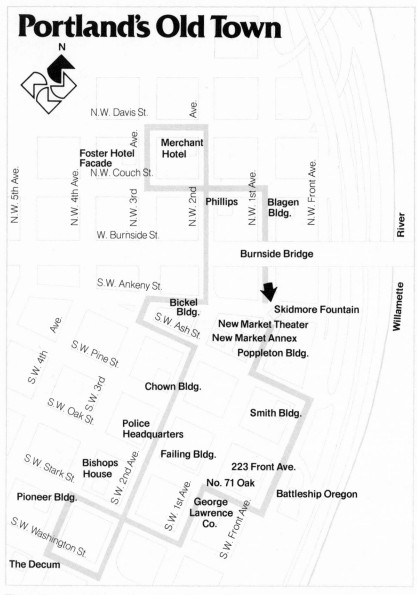

N

N.W. Davis St.

Ave.

Foster Hotel
Facade
N.W. Couch St.

N.W. 5th Ave.

N.W. 4th Ave.

N.W. 3rd

N.W. 2nd

Ave.

Merchant
Hotel

Phillips

N.W. 1st Ave.

Blagen
Bldg.

N.W. Front Ave.

River

W. Burnside St.

Burnside Bridge

S.W. Ankeny St.

Bickel
Bldg.

Skidmore Fountain

Willamette

S.W. Ash St.

New Market Theater
New Market Annex
Poppleton Bldg.

Ave.

S.W. Pine St.

Chown Bldg.

S.W. 4th

S.W. 3rd

S.W. Oak St.

Police
Headquarters

Smith Bldg.

S.W. Stark St.

Bishops
House

S.W. 2nd Ave.

Failing Bldg.

223 Front Ave.

No. 71 Oak

Pioneer Bldg.

S.W. 1st Ave.

George
Lawrence
Co.

S.W. Front Ave.

Battleship Oregon

S.W. Washington St.

The Decum

This walking tour is approximately 1 mile round trip.

boasts a fine three-storied screen of pilasters and arches, with an alley in the middle leading to a fountained courtyard.

Innovative Ways of Preserving the Past

Around the corner on Third Avenue we see an interesting example of preservation. While the hotel which once stood here has been replaced by a parking lot, the facade of the hotel has been kept as a portal to the lot.

Preservation of another kind can be found in the Philips Building at Second and Couch. Here is the Portland Police Museum as well as the Architectural Preservation Gallery of Portland.

These interesting museums are free and open from 10–3 Tues. through Thurs. and 12–4 Fri. and Sat.

A Five-Sided Building

Cross Burnside and you will see below one of Portland's more unusual townscapes—a plaza surrounded by oblique facades. Abutting it is the Bickel Building (also known as the Wachsmuth Building), a five-sided wonder crowned with four gables. On the Second Avenue side is the face of a tiny mustached king who looks down on the people below. On the north side, the building fronts Ankenny, one of the few streets in town which goes off at a tangent. The reason is that here the town's first plat, aligned with the river, joins a later plat aligned to the compass.

As we complete our circuit of the Bickel, we see ahead the New Market Theatre Annex. Despite its imposing bulk, it has some graceful details—wall ties in the shapes of crosses and starfish, and splendid wrough-iron fire escapes.

Ash Street's Past

You are now at the intersection of Second and Ash. It was once one of Oldtown's principal crossroads. At the river end of Ash there were important docks which served passengers going to and from Portland in the 1880s. A steady stream of visitors from Salem and Singapore and other far-off cities would walk up Ash to visit family boarding houses, Turkish baths, a Chinese laundry, three churches, some theaters, a number of saloons, and what were often called "cotes of soiled doves"—the brothels. This was not simply a business district, but home for many people who worked, worshiped, and wiled away the hours here.

On from Ash

Continue south on Second Avenue and you will come to the Chown Building. Built in 1889, it is interesting for a variety of reasons. Note the Romanesque second story. Across the street is the Hazeltine Building, which boasts a plaque showing the water level of several early Portland floods. These floods were so high that boat races were held on them, the spectators quenching their thirst at floating bars set up on the water.

The Police Headquarters has been located at the corner of S.W. Oak Street and Second Avenue since 1872. Among its first prisoners were five temperance ladies who were arrested for disturbing the peace because they persisted in singing hymns in Portland saloons.

Turning right on Stark, we come to Bishop's House. Originally an annex to the Catholic cathedral, which once stood there, it has had a succession of colorful tenants, including a Chinese tong, a speakeasy, and the American Institute of Architects. In the foyers of the Pioneer Building at Third and Stark, there is a photo exhibit which illustrates this area at the turn of the century.

Finally, on the corner of Third and Washington, there is an ornate old bastion built in 1892 by Frank Decum, a Bavarian confectioner who also founded the Portland Songbird Society. The decoration on the building reflects his interest in pastry and plumage. Note in particular the carved entrances.

River-Ward

Turning east, we are on Washington Street, walking toward the river. Follow the map until you reach the corner of S.W. Oak and First. Here stands the Flailing Building, a prime example of restoration, while catercornered from it is the George Lawrence Co., a prime example of a well-preserved building. Number 71 on the next block is another good example of recent restoration. This little building may be the oldest in town, possibly constructed in the 1850s before the era of elaborate cast-iron fronts. A stunning example of cast-iron architecture is found around the corner at 223 Front Avenue. The plaque of the local foundry which cast the iron is mounted on the building's lower right corner.

Front Avenue also houses the Battleship *Oregon* Monument. Called the "Bulldog of the Navy," the *Oregon* served valiantly in the Spanish-American War. During World War II the hull was abandoned in a Guam lagoon, but sailors brought the mast back to honor it.

Back to the Beginnings

Returning along the riverbank to the Skidmore Fountain where our tour began, we cross an area that was edged with maple, fir, and cottonwood when Overton and Lovejoy beached their canoe nearby. In time the trees were replaced with warehouses and docks, shipping offices, emporiums, hotels, saloons, and oyster houses. Then, almost imperceptibly, that activity began to slacken. Shop after shop moved inland and the buildings themselves were vacated. Finally, the emptiness resounded with the crash of wrecking balls. But not all buildings were lost. Here, for example, on the corner of Front Avenue and Ash Street, stands a remnant of the Smith Building, restored to its former elegance. Throughout the area other old buildings are being rescued and restored, reminding residents that Oldtown is again a vital center.

PORTLAND: DOWNTOWN AND NEWTOWN
Terence O'Donnell

Portland has been called a "dreamworld urbanism; a city blessed by nature and man" by Ada Louise Huxtable, architectural critic for the *New York Times*. Walking through Portland you experience the excitement of a vital urban center and the quiet refreshment of natural splendors as elegant parks and pounding waterfalls interlace with handsomely restored historic buildings and towering skyscrapers.

The Park Blocks

Our tour begins at the intersection of S.W. Park Avenue and Jefferson Street and takes you along the historic blocks which stretch from the hills to the Willamette River. This ribbon of a green mall was dedicated in 1852 as the first city park. At that time young bucks would gather here on the weekend to brag and challenge each other to horse races along what was a dirt track. During the week, sober, hardworking farmers, their wagons laden with goods, passed across this intersection bringing their produce from the rich Tualatin Valley to the oceangoing ships at the dock.

In time the dirt track was planted with elms and grass. Gradually churches, schools, rows of town houses, a gentleman's club, fountains, and statues—Roosevelt on a prancing charger, Lincoln during the Civil War—were added so that what was once a nondescript dirt road became an elegant and graceful mall which today celebrates the historic spirit of Portland.

The Portland Art Museum

Facing the park on the west is the Portland Art Museum (hours noon to 5 P.M. daily; noon to 10 P.M. Fridays; closed Monday). Designed by the world-famous architect Pietro Beluschi, the museum was deemed by the American Institute of Architects to be one of the 100 best-designed American buildings built between 1920 and 1940. Inside, it houses outstanding examples of European and American painting and sculpture, English silver, Northwest Coast Indian art, and much more.

Alongside the museum the beautifully designed sculpture mall, also the work of Belluschi, occupies what was once a street. An example of recent urban planning at its best, it gives you an opportunity to examine the art works in a peaceful setting, set apart from the hum of city traffic.

Now, look across the mall to its western end to see the magnificent canopy of the town's oldest elm. Then walk down into the sunken court, look up, and see the cream-and-brick-red tracery of a church tower. It will be the next stop on our tour.

First Congregational Church

The tower you glimpsed from the mall is an example of Venetian Gothic architecture. Built in the 1890s, the First Congregational Church is today a cherished city landmark, a regal tribute to the past. It's beauty sets it apart from the taller but less distinguished towers of the newer buildings.

In the Park

Return to the park and walk north. You will come upon a graceful fountain settled inside a glade of elms, donated to the city by grateful immigrant Joseph Shemanski and named after

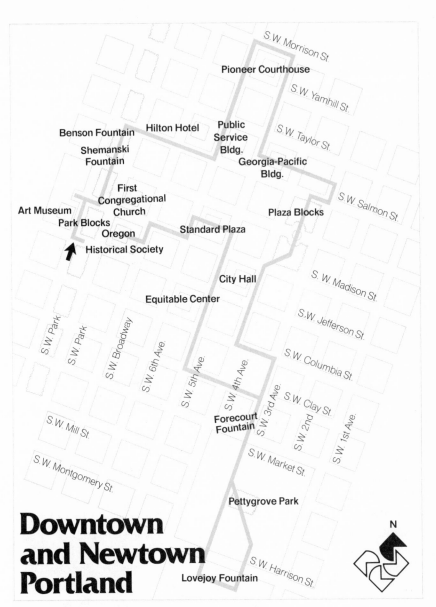

S.W. Morrison St.

Pioneer Courthouse

S.W. Yamhill St.

Benson Fountain   Hilton Hotel   Public Service Bldg.

S.W. Taylor St.

Shemanski Fountain

Georgia-Pacific Bldg.

First Congregational Church

S.W. Salmon St.

Art Museum

Plaza Blocks

Park Blocks

Oregon Historical Society

Standard Plaza

City Hall

S.W. Madison St.

Equitable Center

S.W. Jefferson St.

S.W. Park

S.W. Park

S.W. Broadway

S.W. 6th Ave.

S.W. 5th Ave.

S.W. 4th Ave.

S.W. Columbia St.

S.W. 3rd Ave.

S.W. Clay St.

S.W. 2nd

S.W. 1st Ave.

Forecourt Fountain

S.W. Mill St.

S.W. Market St.

S.W. Montgomery St.

Pettygrove Park

Downtown and Newtown Portland

N

S.W. Harrison St.

Lovejoy Fountain

This walking tour is approximately 1¼ miles round trip.

him. Continue your walk north and you will find another interesting drinking fountain situated in the half-moon plaza. It is one
of a number of identical fountains given by the wealthy lumber
merchant Simon Benson, who gave them to the city in order to
dissuade Portland loggers from drinking stronger potables.

Broadway and Salmon

After tasting the refreshing waters, walk east on Salmon
Street and you will come to Broadway. True to its name, Portland's version of "The Great White Way" was in the mid-'20s
the center of city nightlife, replete with elaborate movie palaces
and cafes. Jackson Tower, which stands 2 blocks north, evokes
memories of the '20s style with its pagoda-like clock tower
trimmed with flags and light bulbs. In marked contrast to the old
theaters is the modern Hilton Hotel. While we may admire its
tall pedestal base and hanging gardens, the building alarmed
merchants when it was first constructed. They feared it would
start a trend and the streets would be lined with walls rather
than shops.

Another contrasting structure, the handsome Public Service
Building, stands at the corner of S.W. Salmon Street and Sixth
Avenue.

The Town Center

Walking on to the intersection of Sixth and Morrison, you will
find yourself in the center of town. Imagine, if you can, an elegant hotel where the large asphalt parking lot now spreads. There
are now plans to turn this lot into the town's main square.

Most of the present buildings were constructed in the early
1900s, and many were designed by A. E. Doyle, who dominated Portland architecture for 20 years. Opposite the parking
lot is the Pioneer Courthouse. Begun in 1869, this courthouse
was one of the first major public buildings in the Northwest. For
years its cupola was the highest vantage point in the area, and
hearty townspeople would climb the stairway to enjoy a bird's-
eye view of the town. In 1903, the building was embellished
with two additional wings. However, in 1933 a new Federal
Courthouse was built and the building fell into decline. After a
long struggle by preservationists, it was restored and became
the headquarters of the 9th Circuit Court. Inside, there is a small
gallery on the street level with a pictorial history of the building;

on the second floor is the courtroom, a handsome chamber done in Oregon oak and Baroque plaster. The furnishings in the building came from various western courthouses whose judges wished to participate in the preservation of this, the oldest functioning courthouse in the West. The restored cupola is open to the public.

Georgia-Pacific Building

For a change of pace we turn south on Fifth Avenue and come to the Georgia-Pacific Building—a 30-story modern structure, replete with a sculpture on the plaza. It is the international headquarters of the world's largest manufacturer of plywood. Cross the entry plaza and walk through the foyer. You will find yourself on a terrace looking down on some of the 30 gracious London plane trees that surround the building. If you have the time, take the escalator below to explore a small but important logging museum. (Hours 10 to 3 Tuesday through Friday; admission free.)

The Plaza Blocks

Leave the museum by walking through the tunnel which opens onto Third Avenue. You come onto the spacious Plaza Blocks which were dedicated as courthouse squares in 1852. The elk standing between the blocks evokes memories of the time when this site was used as a grazing ground by a bull elk which lived in the hills to the west. Look beyond and you will see a pink-pillared palazzo. It is City Hall, built in 1895, a distinguished structure with fine architectural details. Note the pilasters on the east facade, the balustraded roof, its corners topped by urns, and the imposing entrances.

Portland's Newtown

Ada Louise Huxtable has called Portland's urban renewal area a "remarkable exercise in art and environment." It contains an impressive spectacle of thundering waterfalls, terraced rock formations, and secluded parks. It was begun in 1963; more than 1,500 people and 200 businesses were relocated and 400 structures demolished in order to make room for this eminently successful project.

Our view of this renewal begins on Fourth Avenue at the magnificent Forecourt Fountain designed by Lawrence Halprin, a distinguished landscape architect. One of the most impressive urban spaces in the United States, the fountain takes the form of a series of waterfalls in order to evoke the magnificent cascades along the Columbia River and in the Sierras. The water begins on the top as quiet rivulets flowing in a maze of concrete slabs. As the rivulets increase in volume, 13,000 gallons of water per minute cascade down an 18-foot-high concrete cliff to a sunken pool 10 feet below street level. Around the pool's "floating" concrete platforms, amphitheater-type steps rise, creating terraced platforms where one can climb, walk, crawl, or meditate, enveloped by the soothing rhythms of the falling water. Opposite the fountain on the east is the Civic Auditorium, a site which has housed various entertainment centers for over 100 years.

Pettygrove Park

After leaving the fountain, we enter a mall which is the continuation of S.W. Third Avenue and make a left just beyond the reflecting black building to enter Pettygrove Park, covering a city block, 200 feet by 200 feet. One can escape the bustle of the city here. Also the work of the Lawrence Halprin firm, the park became a hippie haven several years back and it even became the site for a hippie wedding. Both hippies and nonhippies now enjoy its quiet seclusion of contoured mounds and graceful paths.

At the end of the park mall stands the Lovejoy Fountain, also designed to evoke the waterfalls of the High Sierras. The plaza surrounding it is a lively, peopled place and is often the scene of art exhibits and fashion shows; street musicians, craftsmen, and strollers enjoy their walk and each other.

Walk north on Third to S.W. Clay, west on S.W. Clay to Fifth, and then north along Fifth. After several blocks, stop by the Equitable Center and see two of Portland's newer "towers" —the Portland Plaza condominium and the First National Bank.

Walking 2 blocks farther on Fifth, you will come upon Standard Plaza on your left. Take the outside escalator, look down at the shifting cityscape, pass through the foyer, and, as you cross the bridge to Sixth Avenue, be sure to look down at the garden with its box-bordered, raised parterres, and playing fountains.

The Oregon Historical Society—the Past in Harmony with the Present

On reaching Broadway, turn left to enter the Oregon Historical Society. The building, an imposing structure of slotted aggregate, is situated on the very land where farmers used to pass with lumber and grain. Inside the society building, there is a museum, a library (with information on all the historic structures and monuments noted in this tour), a gift shop, bookstore, and numerous exhibits. Perhaps it is fitting that our tour concludes here, for the society records the changing nature of Portland which we have experienced on this walk—its rustic past, splendid parks and fountains, and ambitious renewal programs.

Walking the West

COLORADO

DOWNTOWN DENVER
George S. Bush

It's only fitting that you begin this tour at the U.S. Mint. After all, that's what built Denver; first the gold, and later also silver, which were then the country's coinage. Indeed, the city itself was founded on a jumped claim, back in 1859, and although it soon ceased to be a mining town and grew into an assaying and trading center, most everything you'll see on your walk—the lavish homes, museums, public buildings—came from the wealth dug out of Colorado's innards by intrepid (and lucky) prospectors. Not surprisingly, even the State Capitol's dome twinkles with real gold, if not quite as much as you might think. Only 253 ounces went into its plating, less than $40,000 worth at gold's current value.

The Denver Mint
You'll see considerably more gold, around $2 million worth, on your guided and carefully guarded 20-minute tour through the Denver Mint. But the knee-high pile of bars on display is only a fraction of what's kept in the vaults. This elegant Italian Renaissance building, patterned after the Medici Bank in Florence, remains the largest American bullion depository outside Fort Knox.

The fact that the coins stamped on the mint's presses these days are no longer of precious metal takes some of the glamour out of the proceedings, but you'll be hypnotized just the same by the sight of all those coins, from pennies to dollars, tumbling into bins, and by their clinking through automatic counters, at the rate of 20 million shiny new pieces a day.

The Denven Mint, which you enter on Delaware Street be-

Downtown Denver

N

Blake St.

Market St.

Larimer St.

Lawrence St.

Larimer Square

18th St.

17th St.

Arapahoe St.

16th St.

Curtis St.

Champa St.

14th St.

Stout St.

13th St.

California St.

12th St.

Welton St.

Eisenhower Chapel

Glenarm St.

Brown Palace

E. 18th Ave.

E. 17th Ave.

Tremont St.

Court Pl.

Cleveland Pl.

E. 16th Ave.

Visitors Info. Center

W. Colfax Ave.

U.S. Mint

Civic Center

E. Colfax Ave.

State Capitol

Galapago St.

Fox St.

W. 14th Ave.

New Court House

E. 14th Ave.

Molly Brown House

Denver Art Museum

Colorado Heritage Center

Elati St.

W. 13th Ave.

E. 13th Ave.

District of Victorian Homes

Spee Blvd.

W. 12th Ave.

E. 12th Ave.

Delaware St.

Cherokee St.

Bannock St.

Acoma St.

Broadway

Lincoln St.

Sherman St.

Grant St.

Logan St.

Pennsylvania St.

This walking tour is approximately 1½ miles round trip.

tween Colfax and 14th, is open Monday through Friday from 8 to 3 in summer, i.e., Memorial Day to Labor Day, and from 9 to 11 and 1 to 2:30 the rest of the year. There's no admission charge, of course; you pay for this show every April 15. (As you can see from the map, you'll be passing Denver's Hospitality Center after you leave the mint; you might want to stop in there for maps and brochures, and to get specific questions answered.)

A Super-Modern Art Museum

The Denver Art Museum is your next stop, and again, like the mint, it's of Italian design, only this time super-modern, a bizarre futuristic version of a medieval fortress. As a piece of art, it's no less interesting than its contents; architect Gio Ponti covered its high, nearly windowless walls with prismatic tile that sparkles in Denver's crisp sunshine, and each of the windows (you have to step into the stairwell to find most of them) is placed in such a way that it frames a particular view, like the frame of a painting. There's one, for instance, that looks across 14th Street, down into the neoclassic outdoor amphitheater of the Civic Center, and another that frames the Capitol to its best advantage.

Within this walk-in sculpture of a building, you'll find rich selections of art, from ancient to modern. Most interesting of all is the second floor, devoted to American Indian cultures. The deities carved into tall totem poles lord it over the main hall, while in the adjoining galleries you'll find an incredible variety of beadwork, costumes, masks, basketry, artfully decorated skins, Navajo rugs, Kachina dolls, papoose backpacks, and pottery.

The museum (free) is open daily except Monday. The hours are usually 9 to 5, but on Sunday it's open only in the afternoon. There's a restaurant with a small terrace; in summer you can lunch outside.

The State Capitol

Then onward, past the Civic Center, to the State Capitol, every molecule of whose impressive bulk, except the steel framing, is of Colorado origin. It is, for instance, the only building anywhere whose interior walls are paneled with Colorado onyx, a pink, richly veined stone in whose texture you can imagine all kinds of faces and figures when you look at it long enough. The reason it's the only edifice adorned with this rare rock is that there was none left when they finished the building in 1908.

Buffalo Bill Cody lay in state on the first landing of its grand staircase in 1917, bathed in the light from the cupola windows of the 150-foot-high dome. Walk on (or take the elevator) to the third floor, whence you reach the 93 iron steps, deep in the walls of the building, that take you to the gallery around the dome. The view is stunning; the mountain metropolis lies at your feet, the Rockies rim the western horizon, and the Great Plains stretch endlessly toward the east.

As you exit the Capitol building on its west side, note that the 13th step is marked—you are now precisely 1 mile above sea level. No decision has been made about what to do with the sign when we shift to metric.

The Colorado Heritage Center

The state historical museum, the Colorado Heritage Center, a terraced edifice behind the new white-limestone state courthouse, is located on W. 13th between Broadway and Lincoln.

The center is open from 9 to 5 on weekdays, 10 to 5 on weekends. Its contents include excellent dioramas from the history of the area—mining scenes, covered-wagon treks, mule trains, Indians slaughtering buffalo, the Mesa Verde cliff dwellings; altogether an amazing and delightful potpourri. All the machinery of the original Denver Mint is here, too, as is a room-size miniature of Denver of 1960. There's also the Tabor collection, which includes several of famed Baby Doe's dresses, the original rags-to-riches playgirl from Missouri who married H. A. W. Tabor, the silver king, and then, impoverished after the silver crash of 1882, was found one morning, frozen to death, guarding her last possession, the Matchless Mine in Leadville, with a shotgun.

Home of the Unsinkable Molly Brown

You'll now visit the home of yet another glamorous lady of the Colorado frontier, Molly Brown, who flirtatiously told reporters when she was picked up from a *Titanic* lifeboat in 1912, "I guess I'm just unsinkable." Her house on Pennsylvania Street was known as the "House of Lions" because of the sculptures of beasts and sphinxes that adorn its entrance. The house, a Victorian extravaganza with horsehair sofas, platform rockers, and leaded-glass windows, and with pictures of good-looking Molly on the walls (like so many women of those days, she changed from lovely to lordly), is open from 10 to 4 Tuesday through Saturday, in summer also Monday; and on Sunday from noon to 4. Admission is $1; under 12, 50 cents.

Some Victorian Palaces

Continue south on Pennsylvania to browse among other turn-of-the-century architectural adventures. The area where you'll find these precocious palaces is roughly bordered by Seventh Avenue to the south, Pennsylvania to the east, and Logan to the west. At 12th and Pennsylvania, for instance, three of the corners are occupied by classic Victorian structures, and at 11th and Pennsylvania, you'll see a fantastic Victorian mishmash nightmare that must have cost a fortune. The Governor's Mansion (open to tours on Tuesday afternoon in summer) is at Eighth Avenue and Pennsylvania, and in the same block, over on Logan, you can gaze at Sayre's "Alhambra," a Moorish palace (now a school for girls) whose original owner decorated his living room with an Indian scalp he'd taken in the massacre at Sam Creek.

The Brown Palace Hotel

Now you'll be able to stretch your legs with long strides. Follow the map to the Brown Palace, Denver's most famous hotel, one of the many buildings financed by Tabor before he and Baby Doe lost their shirts. Step into the lobby of the original building; it was the first lobby that went all the way to the roof, with galleries for every floor.

The Financial District

A couple more blocks up 17th Street is the Eisenhower Chapel, located on the second floor of the Denver Club Building. It contains a fine stained-glass window and is open to the public. This area is Denver's financial district; if you happen to be passing here during the noon hour in summer, you can listen to outdoor concerts and strolling musicians most days in the plazas of the United Bank Center (17th and Broadway) and the First of Denver (17th and California).

Larimer Square

Your next destination is Larimer Street, one of the oldest in town. The block between 14th and 15th is now called Larimer

Square, one of those urban-revival areas that specialize in craft shops, restaurants, wine tasting, and nostalgia for "the good old days" when everybody was looking forward to the future. The Italianate tower you'll see looming over 17th Street is all that remains of one of the old department stores, Daniels & Fisher, now merged with the May Company. The tower is a somewhat enlarged replica of the Campanile in Venice.

Return Trip: A Street Lined with Shops
Turn around and retrace your way along Larimer until you get to W. 16th Street. Make a right to walk west on W. 16th Street. That's where the big stores are, including the original Denver Dry Goods Company, now simply called "The Denver."

CENTRAL CITY
G. S. Bush

You can be pretty sure there's a fortune underfoot almost every time you take a step in Central City, 28 miles west of Denver in the front range of the Rockies. Gold veins still run through them thar hills, once acclaimed as the "richest square mile on earth," and the only reason these lodes aren't being mined today is the high cost of labor. But with the price of gold going up, who knows? Maybe there'll be yet another Central City boom.

Meanwhile, the little town that launched the Colorado gold rush in 1859 and once had a population of 40,000 lives quietly on its past—a magic turn-of-the-century mood it somehow has managed to maintain without exaggerated artifice.

In your explorations here, you'll enter the tunnels of old mines and visit the plush Opera House, where common miners were first relegated to the balcony but got even by spitting their tobacco wads at the nabobs below. You'll see the haunting, albeit slightly faded "Face on the Barroom Floor" of the famed song—and its not quite x-rated obverse on the ceiling of yet another tavern. You'll ride a narrow-gauge mining railroad, and drool over gold-nugget jewelry; with a 13-cent stamp you might mail about $300 worth, but no more.

Not that you'll see pure gold like this in the mines. Nuggets are rare finds. That's why they are worth so much more than poured ingot. Some Central City residents, adept at swirling a pan, still make their living washing gold dust from the mud of the creeks that rush through the gulches of this region, and once in a while they'll turn up a real nugget. But, for the most part, gold is mixed with other minerals, maybe 7 ounces to the ton if you're in luck. The veins you'll see look about as valuable as clay. Anything that glitters is fool's gold—pyrite, which is mostly iron and sulfur.

Chances are you'll be huffing and puffing on this walking tour.

Central City sits at 8,497 feet, and Eureka Street, one of the two main drags, climbs a fairly steep slope. So it's best to start the tour from the top. By the time you head back uphill to your car, you should be used to the elevation. The place to park is the lot of the Opera House, on the left side of Eureka above A Street. This way, too, you'll be all set if you want to attend an opera performance in the evening.

The Lost Gold Mine

If you want to see a mine first thing, there's one about a block up on the other side of Eureka. It's the "Lost Gold Mine," with reputedly the richest vein in the area. The reason all that ore is still there where you can see it is that, for several decades, people had apparently forgotten about this particular claim. It was rediscovered by accident only a few years ago. You can visit the mine from 10 until dusk. Admission is $2; ages 5 to 11, $1. Not a bad way to make a living, and it's easier than digging.

Teller House and Opera

Now walk down Eureka (Greek for "I found it!") to the Teller House, the establishment where all the rich folk stayed when they came to inspect their holdings. The Teller's rooms fairly drip with overstuffed Victorian splendor. Note the mirrors, which have a lot more three-dimensional depth than ordinary ones. That's because their glass is backed with tiny diamond disks, creating an effect few of us could afford these days. The hotel's special pride is the room once reserved for President Ulysses Grant. The owners were so anxious to please the old general, they wrote to Washington for his measurements, and had a chamber pot made especially for him. But Grant never spent the night: he arrived inebriated, and stayed that way (which was easy to do in Central City and still is), and departed without ever bothering to go upstairs.

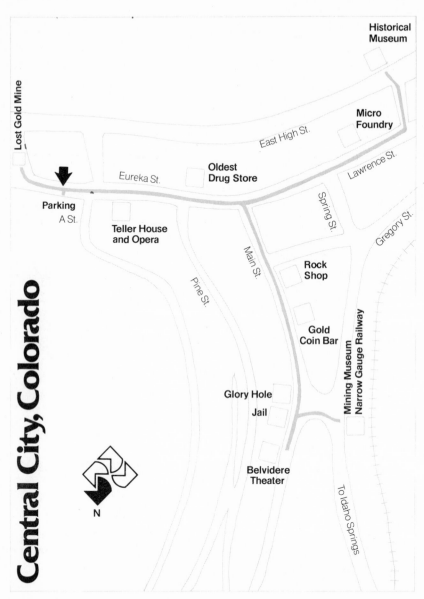

Central City, Colorado

- Historical Museum
- Micro Foundry
- Lost Gold Mine
- East High St.
- Lawrence St.
- Oldest Drug Store
- Eureka St.
- Parking
- A St.
- Spring St.
- Gregory St.
- Teller House and Opera
- Main St.
- Rock Shop
- Pine St.
- Gold Coin Bar
- Mining Museum
- Narrow Gauge Railway
- Glory Hole
- Jail
- Belvidere Theater
- To Idaho Springs
- N

This walking tour is approximately 1 mile round trip.

The bar where he imbibed is where you buy the tickets to tour the hotel and the Opera House, which are separated by a delightful little garden with tables where you can sit in the crisp mountain sunshine. The combined admission costs $1.75; children under 12, 50 cents. Hours are 10 to 5 daily except Monday; Sundays from 11 to 4.

Main Street
Down the hill and turning right, you'll be on Main Street, which, like Eureka, is practically all of 1870s construction; a fire destroyed Central City in 1874, whereupon it was immediately rebuilt, and it hasn't changed much since. You'll want to stop in at the Glory Hole; that's where you'll find the girl on the barroom ceiling, an innocent-enough painting by today's standards, and all the more charming for it. Amazing what people used to think of as risqué.

If you have kids along take them next door to the jail where animated figures à la Disneyland are presented in slapstick-humor tableaus. One more building over is the Belvidere Theater, with stage productions in summer, and in the same building a restaurant you'll want to keep in mind for dinner: you can eat a good meal here while watching a movie. For lunch, though, go to the Duration just across the square, which offers truly superb hamburgers.

Mining and Historical Museum
It's only a few steps from there to the Mining and Historical Museum (open May into October; admission $1; under 12, 50 cents), and the mine tour that goes with it. Now, a mine is a mine, but you don't want to miss this one. The museum tour will give you a really good idea of how the miners dug all that yellow wealth out of the ground. Hand-carved wooden figures depict the various activities, and there are displays of mining machinery and other tools of the olden days, from rifles to apple peelers and button hooks.

A Short Rail Ride
The railroad ride also starts right here. The Colorado & Southern used to chug up from Golden, but now only the last ½ mile still has tracks, and although it's a short ride, only a shuttle really, it's worth the $1.75 ticket for the view of Central

City's valley from the mountainside, a perspective you don't get from the highway.

The Gold Coin Saloon

On the east side of Main you'll find the Gold Coin Saloon, which has been in business since 1878. Of its several music machines, only one player piano, the one in the back, still works; feed it a coin and hear it tinkle old-time tunes. In the same block is the excellent Rock Shop, which specializes in nugget jewelry plus all sorts of other rockhound dreams, from amethysts to petrified wood. If you want to see jewelry made, visit the Micro Foundry on Lawrence Street, which is what the lower part of Eureka is called. On Eureka/Lawrence, too, are several art galleries, as well as Colorado's Oldest Drug Store, started in 1874 and still in business; it's now equipped with a Roaring Twenties-type marble-topped soda fountain.

Old High School—Now Historical Museum

Of course, you don't have to follow the exact itinerary cited here. Central City is for browsing; you'll be passing the same places time and again on Main Street and where it tees into Eureka and Lawrence. But before you go back up the hill, be sure to visit the old high school (see map). It's now the city's official historical museum, and a veritable treasure trove of memorabilia. There are hand-crafted tools, assaying scales, Victorian hats and gowns, family pictures, storefronts, old jewelry, priceless silk curtains—it's like a musty old attic stuffed with good things, a real voyage of discovery. It's open daily, except Mondays, from 11 to 5. You could spend hours in there, and it costs only 50 cents.

How to Get There—Other Spots to Visit

Note: The fastest way from Denver to Central City is to take Highways 6 and 119 to Black Hawk, then follow signs. For exciting mountain scenery on the way back, drive the Virginia Canyon road between Central City and Idaho Springs, where you hook up with I-70/US-40. En route, about 1 mile outside Central City, you can visit the Glory Hole Mine.

Beyond the Glory Hole, however, this route is recommended only for experienced mountain drivers. It's narrow and twisty, with precipitous drop-offs and no guard rail. Morning light is best for the views from this road. If you want to stay overnight in Central City, reserve at the small, old-fashioned Chain O'Mines Hotel, at the corner of Main and Eureka. Rates are very reasonable, starting at around $10; you may have to make do without a private bathroom, though.

NORTHERN CALIFORNIA

SACRAMENTO
Margot Patterson Doss

Sacramento, California's capital, surges to the thrust of government. Its heartbeat is the pulse of a state that would be the tenth-largest country in the world if it were to "run up the Bear Flag" and declare its independence.

Half-strangled though the city may be in a tangle of freeways, its gracious old downtown seems like a Southern grand dame, determined to be valiant come lull or low water. For walkers, this silken-gloved resolve makes for pleasant strolling indeed.

At One Time Travelers Came by Riverboat
If it were still possible to reach Sacramento via riverboat, this would be the way to come. During the California Gold Rush of 1849, in which Sacramento grew up overnight, half the world made its way "to the diggin's" from San Francisco via the Sacramento River. For nearly 100 years thereafter, San Franciscans went upriver via such steam-driven stern-wheelers as the *Delta Queen,* which now plies the Mississippi. Traditionally, a riverboat's bar would open only after passing Red Rock in San Francisco Bay. More than one law has changed its wording en route between the seaside city and the capital.

Today most Californians approach Sacramento by car. They miss the fun, the romance, and the dramatic impact of arriving at the riverfront. Especially they miss the growing sense of destiny one gains walking from Tower Bridge up Capitol Mall to the imposing domed and colonnaded Capitol building itself, surely one of the most beautiful in the nation, set like a pearl in 40 acres of grounds whose lawns are graced, coincidentally, by a vast arboretum of rare trees.

To Arrive by Train

The next best thing to taking the nightboat to Sacramento was to arrive by train. Fortunately this is still possible. Amtrak's Zephyr and Coast Starlight trains both pull into the big old vaulted Southern Pacific depot, whose tremendous mural of the first Transcontinental ground-breaking ceremony, classical architecture, and steamheated benches make it a candidate for historical landmark status. The station is across I Street from Chinatown, recently redeveloped with great Oriental elegance.

Old Sacramento

One block farther lies Old Sacramento, a 28-acre riverfront state park, a *tour de force* of historic preservation which has been compared to Disneyland. There are significant differences: Old Sacramento's theme is itself, the real thing, history as it was lived here. It is full-scale, fully authentic, and probably the most imaginatively recycled architecture this side of the Taj Mahal.

Mansion Inn

Unless you arrive by train (in which case you can do this walk in reverse) pretend for kicks that you are any of 13 governors and begin instead at what was once the Governor's Mansion. The stunning old white Victorian confection at 16th and H streets is now a state park. For a sweet contrasting taste of contemporary California comfort, elsewhereans may want to step into the Mansion Inn, across H Street, to see the lushly planted interior garden courts and fountains, a blend of the tropics and the Orient, before walking west on H to 15th. At 15th, bear left or south 4 blocks to L Street, passing the Italian-Romanesque Memorial Auditorium en route. Come along this way about sundown and the rooftop chimes, which normally strike the quarter hours, will surprise you by playing "The Star Spangled Banner."

Capitol Park

You will know when you reach Capitol Park by the impressive bordering rows of 100-foot-tall feather dusters, the only native California palm, *Washingtonia filifera*. Trees from every part of the world thrive in Capitol Park. Among them, to name a few, are the kumquat, the bunya bunya, the jacaranda, the deodar, the stiff bottlebrush, the weeping myall, the golden raintree, the saucer magnolia, orange, tangelo, tangerine, carob,

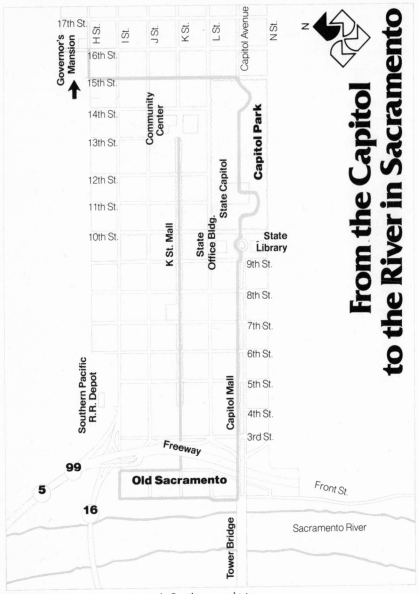

From the Capitol to the River in Sacramento

N

17th St.

Governor's Mansion

16th St.

15th St.

14th St.

13th St.

12th St.

11th St.

10th St.

H St.

I St.

J St.

K St.

L St.

Capitol Avenue

N St.

Community Center

K St. Mall

State Office Bldg.

State Capitol

Capitol Park

State Library

9th St.

8th St.

7th St.

6th St.

5th St.

4th St.

3rd St.

Southern Pacific R.R. Depot

Capitol Mall

Freeway

99

5

16

Old Sacramento

Front St.

Tower Bridge

Sacramento River

This walking tour is approximately 2 miles round trip.

camphor, cork oaks, and monkey-puzzle trees. Tempting as it is to walk among the stately trees instantly, forbear. Especially if you are an Easterner and it is winter, continue along 15th one block to Capitol Avenue at the center of the park to see roses in December. The 800 varieties in the rose garden usually include last year's prizewinners and sometimes next year's. Gather your rosebud impressions while ye may before stepping out into the old straight road to the Capitol, now closed to cars, to view its golden dome down the main *allée* of topiary-cut yew trees.

The Cactus Garden

Facing the dome, bear half-left along a meandering path to reach the Cactus Garden, a circle on the site of the original state fairgrounds. In 1914 schoolchildren sent the boldly sculptural plants to Governor Hiram Johnson so the desert could be represented here. When you have examined the leaping cholla, marveled at the massive beavertails, and winced at the golden barrel cactus, swing back to the *allée* and approach the Capitol.

A class may go by, botanizing with the help of tree labels and the tree guide which is handed out free in Capitol information booths. A Seville orange may drop at your feet. One taste will tell you why these are preferred for marmalade.

Camellia Grove

Wander to the north side to discover a grove of 300 tree-sized camellias honoring Fray Junipero Serra, founder of the chain of Spanish missions which first colonized California. "Lest we forget. Lest we forget," the church chimes nearby remind us in classic Big Ben meters as one nears the modules where the Senate and Assembly sat during the Capitol reconstruction, reminders also of the Liberty Bell reproduction and the bell of the battleship S.S. *California* if you happen to be passing near the trout pond when they sound.

The Senate and Assembly

Go into the building for a look at the 58 county displays behind showcase windows lining this umbilical corridor. You can also pick up free literature, get information on every pending legislative bill, tag onto a guided tour, or listen awhile to the gears of government grinding in the Senate or the Assembly.

The Tower Bridge

Go out the south wing between some impressive coastal redwood trees and bear right, skirting the building through pine trees until you reach 10th Street. Standing immediately in front of the Capitol, look through the circle of lawn flanked by the twin neoclassic State Library and State Office Building number one, toward Tower Bridge, visible dead ahead.

Once past the Sacramento Union Building, whose sunken grassy lawns at the original flood-plane level remind us that the Sacramento River has rampaged occasionally, cross the freeway via viaduct, bearing ever on Tower Bridge. With luck, you may see it drawn for a passing pleasure craft.

A Tour of Old Sacramento

Cross the traintrack and suddenly, Madre de Dios! Sacramento! You are at the river! Hard by is Old Sacramento, with all its charm, its several museums, its wooden sidewalks and cobbled streets, its one-room schoolhouse, its Eagle Theatre, its great old diamond-stack locomotives, its monuments to Judah, who conceived spanning the nation by rail, and to the Pony Express, which got the mail from coast to coast remarkably well compared to subsequent systems, and its many shops and restaurants. Don't miss Hammon's Archives and Artifacts if you are a bibliophile, nor Gaylord's Mercantile if vintage calendars are your turn-on. Follow the tracks to reach them all.

The Tramride from K Street Mall to 14th Street

When you have reached the fatigue point, look for the little open trams. This is the shopper's delight which will return you to your wheels via the K Street Mall, reserved for pedestrians only. The tram goes under the freeway to emerge beside Macy's, then threads its way through the shops, trees, and fountains to end at the Community Center at 14th Street. Cost: one thin dime.

By the time you have completed this loop, you'll know what many civil servants of Sacramento have yet to learn: That their lovely city is infinitely easier to get about on foot than by car. And twice as pleasant.

THE OLD PUEBLO OF SONOMA
Margot Patterson Doss

Old Sonoma lies on the land like a song whose melody is unending. A subtle ambience hovers over its sunny heart. Bees buzz. Summer seekers drowse in the shade on park benches. A few fat ducks waddle lazily into the pond. Lovers picnic on wine and cheese, then stretch out on the grass for a snooze. In the air, the promise of the grape harvest hovers like a kiss.

Old Sonoma Plaza
Shady Old Sonoma Plaza is a national historic landmark, an 8-acre patch of public land surrounded by a dozen or more historical buildings that have witnessed the unbelievable transition of California from wilderness to bewilderedness. Stroll it once, some uneventful day when time has her way with you, and you will find yourself beguiled, like a youth newly in love, and possibly determined, as many thoughtful visitors have been, that not another stick nor stone of this sleepy pueblo should change.

Old Chief Sem Yet Ho, Mighty Arm of the Suisun tribe, has stridden bare-armed around this square. The undisciplined John Frémont, the pathfinder; genial General Mariano Vallejo; winegrower Agoston Haraszthy, father of California viniculture; the raw Bearflaggers; voodoo queen Mammy Pleasant, onetime slave and Western financier of the Underground Railway; author Jack London; and General "Fighting Joe" Hooker—all have passed this way.

Begin This Walk at the Mission
They came in the wake of Fray Jose Altamira, who founded Mission San Francisco Solano de Sonoma, the last and northernmost of California's 21 missions, here on July 4, 1823. The mission, restored and open as a museum of the state park system, is the logical place to begin this walk for historical perspective.

To reach it, Highways 101, 37, and 12-121 are the key.

Park where you can around Sonoma Plaza and seek out the northeast corner of 1st Street East and East Spain Street. When General Vallejo laid out the Pueblo of Sonoma, oldest Northern California town north of San Francisco Bay, measuring the land with his walking stick and siting it with a pocket compass, he created a geographical joke: half of 1st Street is on one side of the plaza, the other half on the opposite side. Significantly Vallejo also deeded the mile-square pueblo to the people of Sonoma. This doesn't necessarily mean to its government, as city fathers have found out, sometimes to their dismay.

Ranged around the plaza are the Blue Wing Inn, once a hotel; Sonoma Barracks, headquarters of that *opéra bouffe* insurrection known as the Bear Flag Rebellion; servants' quarters of Casa Grande, General Vallejo's first adobe home here; the Swiss Hotel, built by his brother Salvador and still operating as a restaurant; Salvador's home; Ray House, officers' mess for the Stevenson Regiment in 1847; Fitch house, built by Jacob Leese, a second settler of San Francisco; a Bear Flag monument; a children's playground; and in the center of the square, a city hall built in 1908. To know more of each building, pick up a landmark leaflet in any shop that is open.

Lachryma Montis

After you have visited the low, plain tile-roofed building that is the mission (and learned that it was used as a wine storehouse after secularization until purchased by the state in 1903), circle the plaza completely to enjoy its ambience and the crape myrtle trees. Then return to West Spain Street and walk west 2 blocks to 3rd Street. Bear right into the lane of trees that lead to Lachryma Montis, Spanish for "Tears of the Mountain," General Vallejo's home from 1851 on. First-time visitors to this state park (there is a modest fee) find the airy carpenter's lace on its early prefabricated Victorian manse as great a surprise as the nearby Chalet, now a museum. Look near the arbor to find the spring for which Lachryma Montis is named.

Adobe Landmarks

When you have vicariously lived the life of the Don long enough, retrace your steps to the plaza and browse among the country stores sandwiched between adobe landmarks. Farmers still flock in on Saturdays to do their shopping in buildings as venerable and historic as their well-marked neighbors. The El Dorado, for example, is reputed to be the home of "malfatti," a chef's mistake that became a delicious success, while the Swiss Hotel boasts a rare $3 bill.

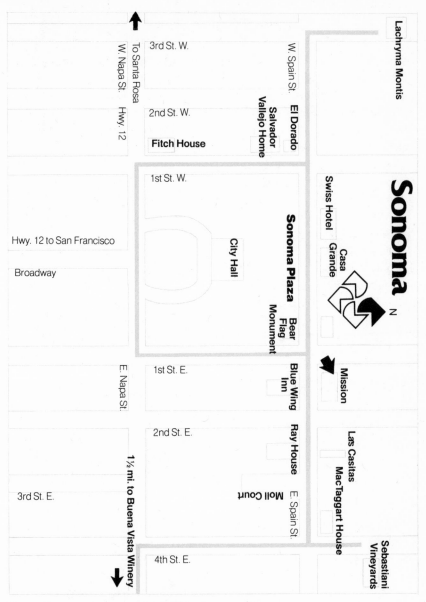

This walking tour is approximately 2½ miles round trip.

The Best of the Old and New

When your circumambulation brings you to the Mission corner again, continue east on East Spain Street to 4th Street East. Lovely old houses with gracious gardens interspersed with Las Casitas, a community that has tried, with surprisingly good results, to incorporate the best of old and new. Farther along, Trinity Episcopal Church, handsome as it is, will never have the character of Sonoma's mission, but it boasts a tree-enclosed outdoor circle. Grapevines twine over doorways and fences. Hollyhocks sprout near Moll Court. Here and there a vegetable garden is visible.

Sebastiani Winery

On 4th Street East, bear left at the house that says Mac-Taggart. In a trice you are at Sebastiani Winery, a welcome rest stop with a tasting room and an informal museum of Indian artifacts picked up by plowmen in the vineyards. Children will enjoy crossing the street from the tasting room to see the large collection of stone metates, used by the Indians to grind pinole, or acorn mush.

The First Vineyard in Sonoma

To find the first vineyard planted in Sonoma, cross the railroad track and walk toward Schocken's Hill. The grapes planted in 1825 were the coarse Mission vines. Today Sebastiani's grapes are prized varietals. Some of them are Zinfandel, first brought here in 1861 to nearby Buena Vista Winery.

Buena Vista Winery

Wine buffs and cross-country walkers will find Buena Vista, 18 blocks east on old Winery Road, worth the visit if only to see its hand-hewn caves. Haraszthy, first owner of Buena Vista, is famous, not only for his introductions of good *Vitis vinifera* varieties, but a true gentleman of fortune for having been eaten by an alligator while building a Nicaraguan railway.

Moon Vintage Festival

Once each year, sleepy Sonoma wakes to play, parade, and pray. The occasion is the Valley of the Moon Vintage Festival, annually held late in September. Then the grapes are blessed, queens are crowned and kissed, big and little folk dance, wine is tasted, and the harvest celebrated with tribal rites. Like the land which has the same sweet use today for grapes as it did a century and a half ago, the pattern hasn't changed much.

Oh summer, you old Indian summer . . . .

OAKLAND'S LAKE MERRITT
Margot Patterson Doss

Gertrude Stein didn't mean to, but she probably did Oakland a favor when she said she left her native city because "there is no there there." Even after, Oakland has been improving itself in its efforts to live down Miss Stein's literary remark.

Today there is plenty of "there" in Oakland. Some of it is spectacular. Much of it can be enjoyed on a walk around Oakland's lovely Lake Merritt, a 150-acre natural saltwater lagoon in the heart of the city. Formed by damming the north arm of San Antonio Creek, as the Oakland Estuary was originally known, Lake Merritt has been a state game refuge since 1870, the first of its kind on the North American continent. Annually at least 4,000 of our fine feathered friends, flocks representing more than 75 species, drop into this resort on the Pacific Flyway during their annual migrations.

Diverting as they are, the buffleheads, greenheads, and baldpates, the helldivers, greater and lesser scaups, double-crested cormorants, marbled godwits, coots, loons, spoonbills, ruddy ducks, and the common tern are only a scintilla of the action around Lake Merritt. Little El Toro sailboats tack back and forth. Ladies of the Oakland Women's Rowing Club may labor past in their whaleboat. Crews of the Lake Merritt Rowing Club or the University of California team may scoot by in their sculls like waterbugs. The pride of the lake is the *Merritt Queen,* a model Mississippi riverboat that would have tickled Mark Twain. Waterlife notwithstanding, the shoreline walk is elegantly urbane. Street furniture, pergolas, civic buildings, and other amenities largely take their grander plan from the "City Beautiful" architectural movement, circa 1910. The exceptions are the stately Lady of the Lake, a mansion built 100 years ago that was Oakland's museum for nearly 60 years, and the impressive new museum, its replacement. Alameda County Courthouse, Oakland's Main Library, Oakland Auditorium, and the Laney

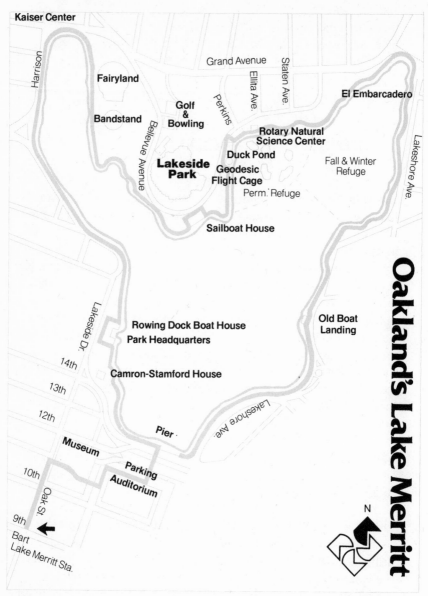

Kaiser Center

Harrison

Grand Avenue

Ellita Ave.

Staten Ave.

Fairyland

El Embarcadero

Perkins

Golf & Bowling

Bandstand

Bellevue Avenue

Rotary Natural Science Center

Duck Pond

Lakeside Park

Geodesic Flight Cage

Fall & Winter Refuge

Lakeshore Ave.

Perm. Refuge

Sailboat House

Lakeside Dr.

Rowing Dock Boat House

Park Headquarters

Old Boat Landing

14th

Camron-Stamford House

13th

12th

Lakeshore Ave.

Pier

10th

Museum

Parking

Oak St.

Auditorium

9th

Bart
Lake Merritt Sta.

N

Oakland's Lake Merritt

This walking tour is approximately 4 miles round trip.

College campus all stand within a block of the lake. Kaiser Center, a striking office building noted for its roof garden, uses Lake Merritt for a reflecting pool.

BART to Oakland

The great surprise for most first-time visitors is to find that Oakland is a place of Mediterranean climate, character, charm and beauty. BART, as local citizens have nicknamed the Bay Area Rapid Transit trains which slide underneath San Francisco Bay, is the magic carpet to transport one to Oakland. From any San Francisco station (four are scattered downtown along Market Street), board one of those luxurious BART coaches bound for Fremont, the green line on station maps. DisemBART at the Lake Merritt Station. Walk a block north on Oak to the new Oakland Museum.

The Oakland Museum

The museum, designed by Kevin Roche, from without seems to be a forbidding fortress. Inside, it is half Mayan temple, half Hanging Gardens of Babylon.

Continue on Oak to midblock to enter on its uppermost level (there is a modest fee for nonmembers), see the top galleries devoted to California artists, and go out into the interior court gardens for your first glimpse of Lake Merritt, cradled in the East Bay hills of the Coast Range.

Next level downhill within the museum is a walk through California history. Below it is a level devoted to an ecological walk across California. Go through it to see California terrain in miniature. Then seek out *The Planet,* a tremendous redwood-burl sculpture near the bookstore. From it, walk out on the lowest level and bear left at the long square pond and walk through the arches. At the end of the building, cross the street toward Oakland Auditorium, scene of many annual events, among them the circus. Skirt the building toward the left through the magnolia-shaded parking lot. When you are abreast of the carved word *Intellectual* over the auditorium side doors, look opposite the doors. Fifty paces ahead of you is a ramp that leads down to the lake through a gleaming white tunnel sunlit through the interstices in roadways overhead.

When you emerge from this pedestrian underpass, bear right at first to discern Oakland's very own watergate at the 12th Street bridge. Local papers referred to it as a "Merrittorius project" when it was created by Dr. Samuel Merritt, mayor of Oakland in 1906. The dam's hydraulic gate controls the water level of the lake.

Lake Merritt Walk

Step off the ramp and look underfoot. You are on an unexpected hard-sand beach near a small fishing pier. On weekends the waterfront trail is reserved in the early mornings for bicyclists. Walkers have exclusive use of the 4-mile loop around the lake after 11 A.M. Start around the water's edge to the west (left as you face the water), using the fine old Victorian Camron-Stanford mansion as a landmark. The last of many such homes which once ringed the lake, one of its many distinctions is that "Lemonade Lucy" and her husband, President Rutherford B. Hayes, were guests here. Lucy won the nickname because she permitted no alcohol in the White House.

Next landmark along the waterside is a rowing dock and boathouse, which also serves as park headquarters. Swerve around it, then return to the shore to continue past apartment buildings and hotels whose water views are prized. Joggers that pass as you walk may be ballplayers from the Oakland A's, the Golden Staters, or the Raiders. If you come along on a summer Sunday afternoon around 2:30, music will be issuing from the colonnaded bandstand visible on the Lakeside Park peninsula across the west arm of the lake.

Skirt the water and soon you are at Children's Fairyland, where nursery rhymes and children's tales come to life in vignette with guinea pigs, geese, rabbits and such. (There is a fee. Adults must be accompanied by a child to enter.) Championship lawn bowling greens and the Lakeside Garden Center lie beyond, hidden in the trees of 88-acre Lakeside Park. A Japanese tea garden, a cactus garden, tropical conservatory, and show gardens for Oakland's famous cascading chrysanthemums, a triumph of the gardeners' skills, are nearby.

Round Turkey Knoll and you come upon the Sailboat House, where rentals and lake excursions on the stern-wheeler can be arranged. The floating log bumpers visible from here delineate a bird refuge which boats may not pass. Feeding time, daily at 3:30. You can also take a duck to dinner for a quarter at the slot machine near Lakeside Inn. The Inn, which has an outdoor dining patio overlooking the lake, is a great place for the hungry walker to rest his calves and enjoy the dabblers and divers below.

The big flight aviary visible nearby was the first of Buckminster Fuller's geodesic domes to be installed in the United States. Architectural students who had fabricated the dome at the University of California, Berkeley, installed it in less than a day. Large birds nest in the standing globes. The brown building beyond the duck pond is the Rotary Natural Science Center, the aerie of a flock of naturalists. Five man-made islands offshore, which look like giant Easter baskets, offer sanctuary to nesting waterfowl.

Hew to the shoreline and after you pass the Kiwanis Kiddy Korner, where swings are seahorses, you reach El Embarcadero, a romantic pergola so like a Greek pavilion, Maxfield Parrish could people it with nymphs and naiads. Before the *gringo* came, when Oakland was still the oak-studded plain on Rancho San Antonio, boats could come in here from the Pacific Ocean. This was a shipping center on the Spanish land grant of Don Luis Peralta.

Swing on along the eastern lakeshore and you soon reach sculptor Gerry Walburg's *Pipe Dream,* purchased from an exhibit called "Public Sculpture: Urban Environment." Nearby, the unused boat-dock steps make a great place to rest awhile in the sun before crossing 12th Street Dam, where fishermen gather, to complete this loop back at the underpass to Oakland's marvelous museum. Gertrude should have lived to see the day!

GOLDEN GATE PROMENADE IN SAN FRANCISCO
Margot Patterson Doss

"The Frenchy'd give his chapeau and the Cockney'd give his whip for a sight of San Francisco from the Hyde Street grip." This was true in 1901 when Gilett ("I Never Saw a Purple Cow") Burgess wrote it, and if anything, today the view is even better.

The Hyde Street Cable Car
No other walk in the world can compare with the new Golden Gate Promenade which leads one along the northern

San Francisco's Golden Gate Promenade

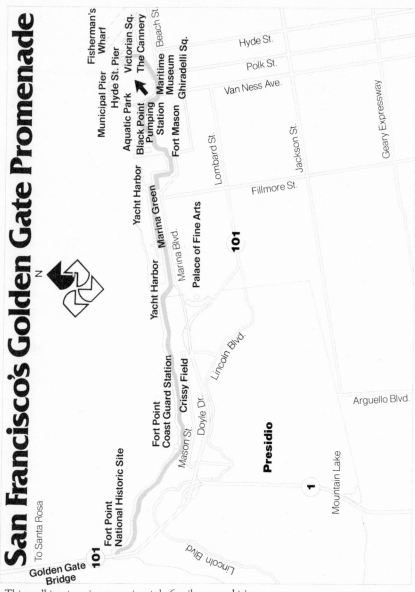

This walking tour is approximately 6 miles round trip.

waterfront from Hyde Street to the bridge. For one thing, you reach its trailhead via the most spectacular urban ride in any American city. The Hyde Street grip, or cable-car line, begins at Powell and Market streets, passes Union Square, swings up over Nob Hill, skirts the fringes of Chinatown, and slides down Russian Hill in a tantalizing succession of changing glimpses.

The ride ends in Victorian Square, now part of the Golden Gate National Recreation Area, a 34,000-acre park established in 1972. Within half a block of the cable car turntable are seven delightful places to visit. If it is your first time in "The City," as Californians call San Francisco, take them in any order that suits your fancy:

• Hyde Street Pier at the foot of the street is a historic park itself, with four museum ships to clamber on: the lumber schooner *C.A. Thayer;* the steam schooner *Wapama;* the scow schooner *Alma;* and the ferry boat *Eureka,* which has vintage vehicles and a working sail loft aboard.

• Fisherman's Wharf, which more travelers to California come to see than anywhere but Disneyland, is one block east.

• The Cannery, hard by, is an entrancing rabbit warren of boutiques and restaurants around an olive-tree-shaded central court where street mimes and musicians entertain (and pass the hat).

• Across Beach Street from it, The Wine Museum offers free, changing shows from all over the world and a remarkable permanent collection related to Dionysius' classic libation.

• Ghirardelli Square, once a woolen mill and later a chocolate factory, is now a complex of the chic and the showy, jumping night and day at what all Americans do best—eat and shop.

• The Maritime Museum is the building that looks like a landlocked concrete ship, stranded near the beach. Inside, one can see soul-stirring seagoing artifacts, such as the figurehead of Lord Clive or the anchor of the *Constitution.*

• Municipal Pier (locally shortened to Muni Pier) is the curving walkway over the water where fishermen and small boys indulge their daydreams, sometimes effectively. Bass, crabs, and leopard sharks are the commonest catch. The view back at the city from the end of the free pier is as good as a boatride on the bay.

Golden Gate Promenade

Beguiling as these diversions may be, they are only the foreground. To find the even more exhilarating San Francisco its citizens love, when you dismount from the cable car, walk resolutely away from the obvious eye-catchers toward the water. There you will find a broad half-moon of a walk that outlines the beach. It leads past bleachers (Columbus annually comes ashore here around October 12 and through the alchemy of pageantry discovers San Francisco) toward the lush green trees of Fort Mason, headquarters of the Golden Gate National Recreation Area. Take this trail as far as you can, past the venerable rowing clubs whose members scull and swim all year round however cold the water, past the *boccie* ball courts, where old Italian gentlemen play in the sun, past the Sea Scout home base, around the periphery of Aquatic Park to the old Black Point Pumping Station at the foot of Van Ness Avenue. Here, beside the pier where prisoners once went fearfully to Alcatraz, look for the blue-and-gold sign that marks the Golden Gate Promenade.

It will lead you safely up a little rise past unexpected rocky sea stacks, as eroding rocky points of land are called, through an old cypress windbreak in Fort Mason to emerge at San Francisco's front lawn—indeed, the western front door of the continent. A yacht harbor snuggles into Gas House Cove in the lea of Fort Mason (the brick gas house, worth a look for its remarkable coffered ceiling, now houses Merryvale antiques, and the neighboring Safeway is reknowned for its tremendous mural). Following the water the next delight is the totally uncommercial Marina Green, a block-long grassy mall where kite flyers, joggers, sunbathers, sea gulls, strollers, and sightseers walk beside an old cobbled sea wall, mossy, barnacled, and rich in the combination of grace, taste, and age that the Japanese call *shibui.*

Palace of Fine Arts—Presidio

Good as the green is, the best is yet to come. Keep walking past yet another yacht harbor and when you are parallel to the Palace of Fine Arts, a grand old Beaux-Arts building built during the Pan Pacific Exhibition of 1915 complete with its own mirroring lagoon, you have also reached the Presidio, a Spanish military post dating to 1776, still in use by the U.S. Army. Take in the Exploratorium, a free science museum inside the Palace of

Fine Arts, if you wish. Then veer once again toward the water along a lane of clipped eucalyptus trees planted 100 years ago by pioneer Rudolph Herman, who once had a private swimming club, the Harbor View Baths, here. Exactly at the water's edge, bear left, or west again, through the broad stone plaza of the pump house that is almost concealed in greenery. There beside its sea stair, the Golden Gate Promenade continues.

Nearing the Golden Gate Bridge

Here the Promenade's ambience changes sharply. Instead of the Old World urbanity of yacht harbor and green, this is an unpaved, though well-beaten, and wilder shore. Beside the red-rock trail, random riprap of old brick and stone walls hold back the lapping water. Crabs and small sea creatures scuttle among them, but you may not notice them, for that great scene stealer, the Golden Gate Bridge, soars across the horizon, ever closer as you walk. Soon you are beside Crissy Field, where the first China Clippers took the mail to the Orient, now a heliport. Alongside it, the trail passes an unexpectedly broad sandy beach, sometimes populated with fishermen, rockhounds, beachcombers, picnickers, resting cyclists, and other citizens at play. Pass the Fort Point Coast Guard Station, easily identified by its palm trees, red roofs, and neat white buildings, via the ramp especially built to take the walker on the Promenade up over two docks. Soon you emerge at another, the historic Mine Dock, used by the army in two wars to protect the harbor. Now the L-shaped pier has its own coterie of poke-pole fishermen.

Fort Point

The Golden Gate Promenade ends at Fort Point, the only Civil War fort on the West Coast, and in its day an engineering feat so admired by Joseph B. Strauss, engineer of the Golden Gate Bridge, that he created a frame for it within his own re-markable creation. Before you arrive at the fort, however, you will walk over the earliest Spanish embarcadero of San Francisco outlined by a massive anchor chain. Alongside it, surf slaps in at certain tides like a restless wall of water. There is drama in every resounding wave. Surfers in wetsuits ride offshore (but you needn't get wet as you walk). There is the fun of riding with them vicariously on the swift eddies and current where old Papa Sacramento River reaches its narrowest funnel, the Golden

Gate Straits, which lie between the bridge and the Sundown
Sea, as native Costanoan Indians called the Pacific Ocean.

Fort Point is open to visitors at no charge. Inside, National
Park Rangers dressed in Civil War uniforms give free guided
tours, and there are signed certificates for young visitors who
participate in the cannon drill.

Public Transportation Back to Union Square

At the fort, the total distance you will have walked from
Hyde Street is 3 miles. For tenderfeet who want wheels to take
them back to Union Square, there is public transportation up
the cliff at the Golden Gate Bridge Toll Plaza, an easy 6-minute
climb worth making for the view alone.

Across the Bridge and Beyond

Gung-ho walkers in the great tradition of John Muir can
keep on trekking north across the Golden Gate Bridge. Distance:
2 miles. From the north side of the bridge, foot trails removed
from automotive traffic follow the ridges and shoreline for 60
miles to the tip of Tomales Point. They are within park land all
the way.

Return Via the Golden Gate Promenade

For the less ambitious but still eager walker, the return to
Hyde Street via the Golden Gate Promenade is just as sensational as the westering way. With the city skyline as a backdrop,
you will see a thousand things you didn't notice the first time
over the trail. You may discern the functioning factorylike building under the grass of the Marina Green. It is larger than an
ocean liner, well hidden in plain sight. You may discover the
Par-Course of exercise pillions and posts. Or find the last stone
placed by the craftsmen who built the cobblestone sea wall.
And best of all, the fun and freedom of walking that gives you
back your own soul.

A REDWOOD GROVE NEAR SANTA CRUZ
Margot Patterson Doss

As tall as the Coast redwood grows—and it is the tallest evergreen tree of all—one would hardly think it could hide. Yet hide

A Redwood Grove Near Santa Cruz

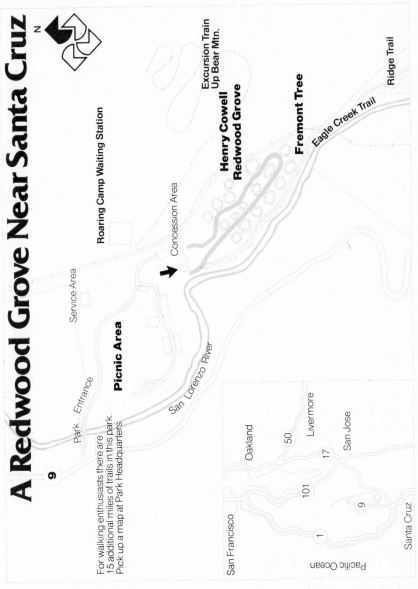

N

Roaring Camp Waiting Station

Excursion Train Up Bear Mtn.

Henry Cowell Redwood Grove

Fremont Tree

Eagle Creek Trail

Ridge Trail

Concession Area

Service Area

For walking enthusiasts there are 15 additional miles of trails in this park. Pick up a map at Park Headquarters.

Picnic Area

Park Entrance

San Lorenzo River

9

San Francisco

Oakland

Livermore

San Jose

50

17

101

9

Santa Cruz

1

Pacific Ocean

This walking tour is approximately 1 mile round trip. There are 15 additional miles of trails within the park.

this shy tree does. To get some idea of the immensity of redwoods, imagine hiding thousands of buildings, each one room
in circumference and 30 stories tall, which is about the height
and girth of *Sequoia sempervirens,* to use the botanists' name.
It is in the steep sheltered valleys of California, snug behind the
cliffy ridges of the Coast Range of mountains, that the redwood
hides. Catching the evening dews and damps in its feathery
needle sprays, it drops the water gently down, down, down 300
feet to its sensitive roots in the loam below.

   It hides so well that for 200 years after California had been
discovered by white men (for the resident Zayante Indians knew
all along it was there) it went unnoticed. Juan Rodriguez Cabrillo, the Portuguese explorer for whom a length of the coast
highway is named, sailed right by the redwoods in 1542. How
Sir Francis Drake missed them in 1579, landing as close as he
did to many great forests, we'll never know. But miss them he
did. So did Viscaino, although redwoods surrounded his party
of explorers in 1602 when his ship's padres built an altar and
said mass "under a tall oak" near Monterey.

First Redwoods Sighted by Walkers in 1769

   Not surprisingly, the credit for finally seeing a redwood, really seeing it, trunk, bark, and needle, goes to walkers. They
were members of the Portola expedition of 1769, which is also
credited with the first sighting of San Francisco Bay. One who
recorded his impressions was Fray Juan Crespi, Portola's scribe.
He described the terrain he saw as "well forested with very high
trees of a red cedar, not known to us. They have a very different leaf from cedars, and although the wood resembles cedar
somewhat in color, it is very different and has not the same
odor; moreover the wood of the trees that we have found is
very brittle. In this region there is a great abundance of these
trees and because none of the expedition recognizes them, they
are named redwood for their color."

   The surprising thing is that he didn't describe what it is like
to walk among redwoods. It is surely as serene and at once
awesome an experience as a walker can enjoy.

Henry Cowell Redwoods State Park

   Partly because it is so accessible to the casual visitor, and
partly because it is near the place Portola's party first saw the
redwoods, a favorite redwood grove is the Henry Cowell Red-

woods State Park. Many people think redwoods grow only to the north of San Francisco. The Cowell Redwoods, covering 1,737 acres, stretch for 2 miles along the San Lorenzo River, about halfway between San Jose and Monterey.

Directions to the State Park

To walk among them, transport yourself south from San Jose via the expressway, State 17, a fast short route to the coast from either Interstate 280 or U.S. 101. From the outskirts of Santa Cruz, take State 9 north 6 miles to the park, just shy of Felton, which has been a lumber town since logs were skidded out by oxen. It also boasts one of California's few remaining covered bridges. Vestiges of the still thriving lumber industry, which brought great wealth to this valley, are visible across a flat terrace, an old floodplain of the San Lorenzo River, as you approach the parking lot.

Stop at Park Headquarters

Shed your wheels, resist the local concessionaires, and follow the signs to park headquarters to pick up a leaflet for the self-guiding nature trail through the redwoods.

"You cannot sit still and expect the outdoors to come to you," admonishes a poster inside the headquarters building. "Walk and ramble, watch and listen, sense and feel. Only then will you truly find out what the world of nature is all about."

Andrew P. Hill's "Save the Redwoods" Campaign

"I will start immediately to make a public park of this place." With these thoughts, Andrew P. Hill, photographer and artist, began a campaign to save the "redwoods at Felton," says another wall poster, boasting a tintype-style photo of Hill and giving his lifespan as 1853–1922. What it doesn't tell the walker is that he is now standing on the site of a historic confrontation between a lumberman who refused to allow Hill to photograph a tremendous redwood tree unless he paid $100, a fortune at the time, for the privilege of taking the tree's picture. Nor, that Hill, a founder of the Semper-virens Club, believed that 2,000-year-old redwoods were not merely standing inventories of timber to be exploited for private gain, but a legacy to be treasured and shared by all mankind, two points of view that have yet to be resolved in California. Ironically, now that it is a park, commercial photographers may have to pay as much as $500 a day to photograph here.

The Walk
"Take nothing but pictures, leave nothing but footprints," the trail guide cautions as it starts you off at the exhibit shelter on a .8-mile walk. There are 15 miles of hiking trails in the park, but as short as this trail is, it leaves most walkers feeling as refreshed as a long weekend. So cleverly is it routed among the great trees, it also gives one the feeling he has been a time traveler back through many centuries.

Thoughtfully placed hand-hewn benches are located in forest niches off the main path. Pause awhile on one to look and wonder at the forest, watching motes float in the filtered sunlight, listening for birds or the unexpected crack of a shifting tree limb. Linger awhile by tree number 7 and a passerby, depending on his expertise, is sure to remark on either its club-foot or elephantiasis, which is a burl rich with potential for a new tree.

Halfway around you will discover the hollow tree in which pathfinder John C. Frémont, a government surveyor who figured prominently in the Bear Flag Rebellion in 1848, is supposed to have camped in 1846. "It's a good story. Let it stand," Frémont said when asked about it later.

Train tracks discernible through trees beyond the split-rail fencing are still used by the Southern Pacific Railroad for hauling logs. Once visitors came from Santa Cruz by steam to walk among redwoods at the whistlestop here called Big Trees, a name more generally accorded the *Sequoiadendron gigantea,* or Sierra redwood, a shorter, fatter cousin of the Coast redwood. Other contenders for greatness are the Kauri trees of New Zealand and one of the many eucalyptus species of Australia.

From the pointer near the rest-stop water fountain, one can see the Giant's top, one of the few places a visitor can see a tree for the woods. As you stand, the toot of a train whistle may draw your attention to the little yellow excursion train pulled by *Kahuku,* a narrow-gauge steam locomotive that used to pull sugar cane on Oahu. Now it pulls tourists on a winding 5-mile trip up Bear Mountain. Part of the fun of the last half of this redwood walk is to see it reappear at ever higher elevations through the great trees on the east side of the park.

In the fashion of the late 1800s, the largest trees on the nature trail were named for presidents and generals. McKinley, Harrison, Teddy Roosevelt, Ulysses S. Grant, and William Tecumsah (War Is Hell) Sherman were honored when public men seemed monumental as the trees.

The Jeter Tree

Frailing on the banjo, intrusive when it is amplified, enticing when it is not, may be audible through the forest near the little Dawn redwood, a deciduous tree thought to be extinct until rediscovered in China in 1944. It was planted here for comparison. Before you respond to the banjo's lure to seek out the Roaring Camp waiting station, next-door neighbor to the park, pause for a moment by the Jeter Tree. It was William T. Jeter who helped make possible the preservation of this grove as a county park before it came into the state system in 1954. Without his efforts and those of Hill, these great trees, and countless other groves nearby, might well have gone the way of the vast Mediterranean forests, logged off long since and forgotten before we or our great, great, great, great grandchildren ever had a chance to walk within the natural cathedrals they create.

SOUTHERN CALIFORNIA

A WALK THROUGH SANTA BARBARA'S HISTORY
David Clark

"Santa Barbara is finely situated with a bay in front and an amphitheatre of hills behind."
Richard Henry Dana, *Two Years Before the Mast*

The Santa Barbara which you will see today is quite different from the simple adobes and run-down mission which Richard Henry Dana saw in 1836. It is an affluent community of 79,000 inhabitants, and its principal industries are aerospace research and tourism. Despite these modern developments, Santa Barbara still boasts of architecture and culture which celebrate its historic past and recall the Mexican California that Dana visited. On our tour we will try to explain the differences between the romantic image suggested by these buildings and the stark realities of life in early California.

Ortega Street
Take Highway 101 to the State Street exit. Turn right (north) and take State one-third mile to Ortega Street. Our walk will begin on Ortega Street, named for Sgt. Jose Ortega, who in 1769 guided the Portola expedition which marked the beginning of Spain's colonization effort in California. In the 17th century the Spaniards had thought that California was an island inhabited by Amazons. In 1782 Ortega returned to establish the Santa Barbara Presidio, the last military outpost built by Spain in California.

The first Spaniards to arrive reported that about 10,000 Chumash Indians lived in the area. The Indians originally welcomed the Spanish, but after suffering from mistreatment and European diseases they sometimes rose in revolt. By the time of the U.S. conquest in 1846, many Indians had formed strong territorial bands under war chieftains. The Mexicans, who numbered only 7,500 in California, were restricted to a narrow strip of coast.

State Street

State Street from Ortega north 6 blocks to Victoria is marked by Spanish architecture and broad red-tile sidewalks. The street's Spanish appearance came about quite recently, and through a "convenient" natural disaster. Simple one-story adobe structures, totally unlike the present buildings on State, had characterized the Spanish and Mexican eras. After the U.S. conquest, State was filled with Victorian structures. By the 1920s Southern California had begun to draw millions of tourists with promotional literature describing the area as a paradise on earth (or even as "Italy without the Italians"). Communities competed for adornments and features which would draw tourists. In Santa Barbara, plans were laid to remake the downtown section in Spanish Colonial and Mission Revival, but businessmen were reluctant to tear down their serviceable, though ugly, Victorian structures. Then came unexpected help. On June 28, 1925, an earthquake destroyed 14 blocks of State Street. The planning committee required that all rebuilding be done in a Mediterranean style. State Street now boasts a host of newly constructed Spanish-like buildings.

Casa de la Guerra

Continue north along State Street, past de la Guerra Street, until you come to an archway with shops, just before the Joseph Magnin store. Turn right (east) into the Paseo and follow it around to the right into the courtyard of the Casa de la Guerra.

The Casa de la Guerra, home of Jose de la Guerra, commandant of the Santa Barbara Presidio from 1815 to 1839, has been the setting for at least two early California romances. It was here that in 1836 Dana attended the wedding of de la Guerra's daughter to Alfred Robinson, an American trader. And in 1806 in San Francisco, Concepcion Arguello, the daughter of the commander of the garrison, and Count Nikolai Rezanov met and fell in love when Rezanov stopped at the mission to

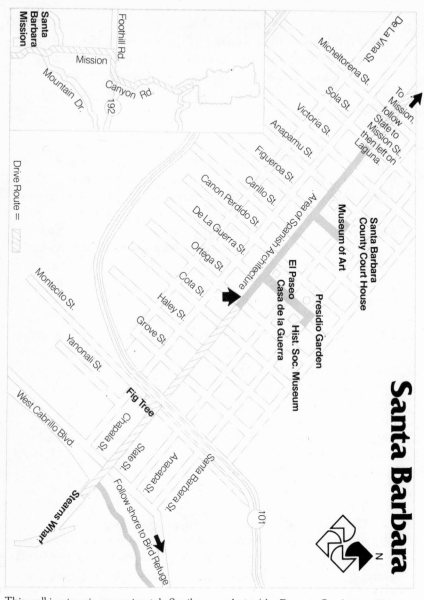

Santa Barbara

Santa Barbara Mission

Foothill Rd.

Mission

Mountain Dr.

Canyon Rd.

192

De La Vina St.

Micheltorena St.

Sola St.

Victoria St.

Anapamu St.

Figueroa St.

Carillo St.

Canon Perdido St.

De La Guerra St.

Ortega St.

Cota St.

Haley St.

Grove St.

Montecito St.

Yanonali St.

West Cabrillo Blvd.

Chapala St.

State St.

Anacapa St.

Santa Barbara St.

Fig Tree

Stearns Wharf

Follow shore to Bird Refuge

101

To Mission, follow State to Mission St. then left on Laguna.

Museum of Art

Santa Barbara County Court House

El Paseo Casa de la Guerra

Hist. Soc. Museum

Presidio Garden

Area of Spanish Architecture

Drive Route =

N

This walking tour is approximately 3 miles round trip. (the Botanic Gardens walk is not included in this figure) obtain supplies for the starving Russian garrison stationed south of the Russian colony in Alaska. They became engaged and Rezanov left for Russia to obtain the Czar's permission to marry the Spanish Californian. Concepcion waited for him for 36 years, until she heard one day from a passing traveler at the Casa de la Guerra that Rezanov had died while crossing Siberia.

Presidio Gardens

From the courtyard of the Casa de la Guerra, turn left (east) on de la Guerra Street, and walk about 100 feet to the stone-paved walkway—called "Street in Spain"—which is filled with specialty and import shops. Then continue on de la Guerra Street, half a block past Anacapa Street, to the Presidio Gardens, on the north side of the street.

After the Mexican War of Independence against Spain began in 1810, Spanish ships no longer came to the Presidio and the military payroll fell as much as 20 years in arrears. Trade with the United States then became an important source of revenue. Californians sent hides and tallow to the shoe and candle factories of Boston in ships like Dana's, in exchange for manufactured goods.

Historical Society Museum

Continue east on de la Guerra Street to Santa Barbara Street. Cross to the south side of the street to the Historical Society Museum.

The museum is filled with reminders of Santa Barbara's Spanish and Mexican past. Inside, for example, you will see the signature of Manuel Dominguez, in 1849 one of the signers of California's first constitution. In 1857 Dominguez was denied the right to testify in court because he was part Indian. The early California settlers were predominantly of a mixed ethnic background. Most came from the Mexican province of Sinaloa, where approximately 40% of the population was of African descent. Pio Pico, the last governor of Mexican California, was a mulatto. As Bill Mason, curator of the Los Angeles Museum of Natural History and an expert on this period, points out, "It is regrettable that this fascinating mixed heritage is not acknowledged."

The Covarrubias Adobe, which stands across the back courtyard from the Historical Society Museum, was once the home of Governor Pico's sister.

Canon Perdido Street

From the Historical Society Museum, return on de la
Guerra Street to State Street. Proceed north a block on State to
Canon Perdido Street. You will pass the Joseph Magnin store, a
fashionable clothing store which occupies the site of the former
Wah Sing Chinese Laundry. This area became predominantly
Chinese in the late 19th century when many Chinese came to
California, driven by floods in southeast China in 1849 and the
Taiping Rebellion of 1851, in which perhaps 30 million people
were killed.

By 1910 the area had become Japanese. The original Presidio chapel, 1½ blocks east on Canon Perdido Street, had
become a Japanese Buddhist temple by that time.

The name Canon Perdido, "lost cannon," was decided
upon after a large cannon, left on the beach after the United
States conquest, was stolen by the inhabitants. The United
States commander panicked and warned Governor Mason of
an impending insurrection. The governor ordered the inhabitants of the town to pay a $500 fine for taking the cannon. The
sum was paid, but during the transaction the money was lost,
and in memory of these events, the city seal from 1851 to 1860
displayed a cannon and the inscription *Vale Quinientos Pesos*
("Good-bye Five Hundred Dollars").

The Courthouse

From Canon Perdido, continue north on State to Figueroa
Street. Turn right (east) on Figueroa, then left (north) on Anacapa and walk to the Santa Barbara County Courthouse. Pass
through the archway in the middle of the block to the Sunken
Gardens.

The Santa Barbara Courthouse shows the Spanish Revival
style at its most imaginative. The building was finished in October 1929, just before the Depression put an end to flamboyant
and nonfunctional public architecture.

From the four-story tower of the courthouse, the twin
towers of the Santa Barbara Mission are visible to the north.
Above the mission lies the Botanic Garden, a beautiful 75 acres
of wilderness with 5 miles of trails. The garden is devoted to native California plants and contains species, such as the Islands
Ironwood, that are indigenous only to the Channel Islands. In
addition to the Islands section, you will find meadows, forests,
redwoods, and many forms of chaparral and desert life. (If you

wish to visit the mission and garden later, or another day, take State Street north to Mission Street, turn right on Mission and left on Laguna, to arrive at the mission. The garden is 1½ miles farther up Mission Canyon Road, with a short right jog at Foothill.)

From the courthouse, return to State Street and Figueroa. Continue north on State to Victoria, where the red-tile sidewalk ends, then cross to the west side of State and take it back south to Ortega, where the tour began.

The remainder of State Street, north of Ortega, is filled with shops, arcades, art galleries, and, at Anapamu Street, the Santa Barbara Art Museum.

From Ortega, either walk or drive ½ mile farther south on State to Stearn's Wharf, where State Street meets the ocean.

At Montecito, just south of Highway 101, make a short detour half a block to the right (west) to the gigantic Moreton Bay Fig Tree, planted 100 years ago; it may be the largest of its kind in the world.

This fig tree marks the spot where Sergeant Ortega and the Portola expedition camped in 1769. The tree, and citizens' efforts to preserve it, are part of the reason that Highway 101 has not been expanded at this point.

Among the streets you will pass are Yanonali, named for the Chumash chief of the area, and Victoria, named for a Mexican governor whom the Californians ousted in one of the periodic rebellions that shook the state.

Santa Barbara's fondness for retaining Spanish street names has occasionally had humorous consequences. One street has long been called Salsipuedas, Spanish for "get out if you can," because of a muddy quagmire in which wagons often became stuck. In 1908, a hospital was built on this street and named the Salsipuedas Hospital. Once the Sacred Heart Sisters, founders of the hospital, became aware of the Spanish meaning, they quickly changed the name of the hospital to St. Francis.

Stearn's Wharf

To the west of Stearn's Wharf, above the yacht harbor, stands a high bluff which formerly included Castle Rock, site of the town's garrison for protection against pirates. The Bouchard raid of 1818, in which Monterrey and San Juan Capistrano were sacked and burned, showed that such fears were justified.

Three members of the Bouchard crew were captured near Santa Barbara, but when the pirateer moored his ships offshore and threatened to bombard the town, his men were quickly returned to him.

On Sunday along the beach east of Stearn's Wharf, artisans' wares are for sale. On a clear day you may be able to see the four Channel Islands, 25–30 miles from the coast. The islands are actually a submerged mountain range, rising slowly from the sea. On Santa Rosa Island the remains of a dwarf mammoth that was roasted by prehistoric men 30,000 years ago have been found. At that time the island was connected to the mainland.

Andree Clark Bird Refuge

The 50-acre Bird Refuge makes a pleasant and peaceful ending for your Santa Barbara walk. The refuge is a stopping point for many different species on migratory journeys. Mallard ducks, great blue herons, night herons, and sandpipers are among the birds that you may see here. If you have binoculars, closely inspect the island in the middle of the lagoon, where you will see herons sitting in the trees.

PASADENA: NEIGHBORHOODS OF THE PAST
Walter Houk

The most visible intersection in America every New Year's Day, where Orange Grove and Colorado boulevards meet, is the start and center of this tour. That is where the television cameras are placed that beam the Rose Parade to millions of television sets.

What those cameras do not see is what makes this walk fascinating. Two of the landmarks are recent, an art museum and the newest concert hall in town, but mostly it's an excursion backward in time.

You probe neighborhoods that convey a sense of continuity and permanence often thought to be lacking in the Los Angeles metropolis.

One neighborhood in Pasadena contains two kinds of

houses from the first 15 years of this century: millionaires' mansions and the more rustic (though often large) houses of the Arts and Crafts Movement. In revolt against rampant industrialization, the movement aimed at a handcrafted personal environment, and two of its nationally acclaimed leaders were Pasadena architect-designers Charles and Henry Greene. Our tour route passes an extraordinary collection of 15 of their houses, looks inside one of their masterpieces, and looks into two of the mansions.

You also go by a well-known bridge over the Arroyo Seco ("Dry Gulch" in Spanish), and get a view of that great canyon—the setting for the Rose Bowl.

The Starting Point

The starting point is the junction at Orange Grove and Colorado, and the walk branches out from this central intersection like two loops of a bow tie. You will walk the northern portion first, then return to the starting point to continue on the southern loop.

The Norton Simon Museum

Begin at the Norton Simon Museum of Art. An unexpected treasure house containing painting and sculpture of world stature, it is a sleek, tile-clad building dating from 1969. Rodin sculptures ornament the forecourt, which offers a panoramic view of Pasadena. The inner court is also a sculpture garden with works by Rodin, Renoir, Moore, and Maillol.

In early 1977, the museum almost doubled its collection, so that it now houses more treasures than most people can view in one visit. The outstanding European painting section includes a small roomful of Rembrandts worth $10 million. Also renowned is the Galka Scheyer collection of the Blue Four painters: Feininger, Jawlensky, Kandinsky, and Klee.

The museum is open Thursday through Sunday, noon to 6. Admission is $1.50 for adults, 50 cents for students and seniors.

Pasadena Historical Museum

Go west to Orange Grove, then north to Walnut and around the corner, to enter the Pasadena Historical Museum, surrounded by a garden that has become a forest covering the

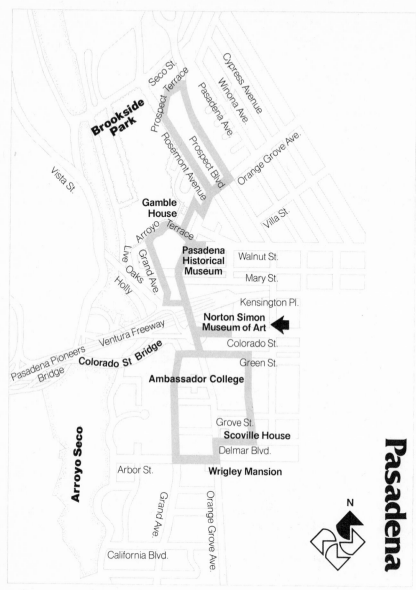

This walking tour is approximately 3 miles round trip.

4-acre premises. Tucked in among the leaves, a rustic low building is a sauna, reflecting the Finnish background of the family
who lived there.

The mansion's lower level contains displays of historical artifacts and photographs. Upper floors are much as they were
when the former occupants lived there; the rooms include a
romantic painting studio and a dramatic solarium.

The museum is open Tuesday, Thursday, and the last Sunday of the month, 1 to 4. A donation of $1 for adults, 50 cents
for students goes for upkeep.

The Gamble House

Returning to Orange Grove, you will see an impressive
array of big houses. Not all of these qualified as mansions even
though they were part of Millionaires' Row. Across the street
and half a block north of Arroyo Terrace is the 1908 Gamble
House, considered to be a masterpiece by architects Charles
and Henry Greene. It was the winter house for the Gamble
family of Procter and Gamble, a sort of large cottage.

This superb example of the rustic style of the Arts and
Crafts Movement of the early 20th century has been for more than
ten years the subject of well-researched restoration. The house is
owned now by the University of Southern California and the City
of Pasadena.

The front door has multiple panels of art glass. Inside, the
entry hall and all the living spaces are as meticulously finished
as fine furniture. It's a breathtaking production. Every detail was
designed by the architects, including light fixtures, stained-glass
panels, furniture, carpets, and landscaping—down to paving,
garden walls, planter boxes, and garden lights.

Gamble House is open for tours narrated by volunteers
Tuesday and Thursday, 10 to 3, and the first Sunday of the
month, noon to 3. A donation of $2 for adults helps support
the restoration (no charge for students).

A Noteworthy Residential Area

From here continue to walk northwest for a mile-long excursion through some interesting residential areas: north on
Orange Grove to Rosemont, left and down the hill, then right
onto Prospect Terrace, Prospect Boulevard, and Orange Grove.

Three-fourths of the way down Rosemont, look through

shrubbery on the right to see Frank Lloyd Wright's elegant and famous little Millard House. Prospect Terrace has a quaint mission-style house (No. 499) by Frederick Roehrig, designer of Pasadena's old Green Hotel. Prospect Boulevard is one of Pasadena's prettiest streets, with its arching camphor trees. At number 657 there is a restored residence by the Greenes, while the brick and stone portals at Orange Grove are also in their idiom.

On the other side of the Gamble House is another Greene house, now part of the Neighborhood Church complex there. At Arroyo Terrace turn right to walk past eight Greene houses. Some have been remodeled, but the style remains recognizable.

The most interesting in this unusual concentration are Charles Greene's own house, number 368, an accumulation of many additions, and the house at the corner of Grand. This is one of the Greenes' most unusual homes, with its great free-form parapets of rock and clinker brick, its pillars, pergolas and chimneys.

The View at the Arroyo

Both of these are on the brink of the Arroyo, and here you get a sweeping view of the canyon, the Rose Bowl, and the towering San Gabriel Mountains beyond.

Turn left on Grand and you pass two more Greene houses, at number 210 and at the corner of Holly Street. In this same block there are also other craftsman-period houses, and one in an intricate Victorian style.

At Holly, go left to Orange Grove. Then you can see the starting point close by and return to it.

Back at the well-known crossroads of Colorado and Orange Grove boulevards you begin the 1-mile southern loop of our walk.

The Colorado Street Bridge

To do this, cross Colorado on Orange Grove, past the elegant arched Colorado Street Bridge, from 1913. Curving from the west across the Arroyo 130 feet below, it became celebrated after the 1929 stock-market crash for the suicides it attracted until nearby homeowners—alarmed that this practice might have a bad effect on property values—urged the city to erect high fences along its sides. Next to it the Ventura Freeway has a straighter, newer bridge somewhat related in design.

At Green Street turn west and walk a block to its end at Grand. Along here are the former Vista del Arroyo resort hotel on the blufftop, much remodeled and now the property of the Army, two more Greene houses (numbers 195 and 215), and the delightful Italianate Shakespeare Club (unfortunately not open to the public).

Walking down Grand you are in a neighborhood of big houses, well aged and well kept, surrounded by tall half-century-old trees.

The Wrigley Mansion

At Arbor turn left to the Wrigley Mansion at Orange Grove. Headquarters of the Tournament of Roses, the house is a beehive of activity at year end, but then it quiets down. It is open for half-hour guided tours Wednesday afternoon from 2 to 4 (free).

Suitably opulent, it occupies a lawn as big as a park. Built in 1911, it was bought shortly after completion as a Western residence for chewing-gum tycoon William Wrigley; it affords another look behind the doors of a big Orange Grove establishment. The garden has tall palms and specimen trees and is well supplied with flowers—including roses.

Head back north on palm- and magnolia-lined Orange Grove. At Del Mar turn right. The 1909 Scoville house on the northeast corner is another Roehrig house in the Frank Lloyd Wright Prairie Style.

About halfway down the Del Mar hill, turn left on a broad walkway paved in stone. This takes you through some surprise gardens hidden from the street, along the central axis of Ambassador College's campus. Several Orange Grove houses, their styles ranging from Tudor to Mediterranean, were acquired by the college for use as dormitories. Newer campus buildings are at the foot of the hill to the east. On the right you pass the gleaming new Ambassador Auditorium, scene of concerts and other musical events, beyond a spectacular tall fountain of splashing bronze egrets.

To return, go left on Green, then right on Orange Grove.

DOWNTOWN LOS ANGELES
Walter Houk

You span nearly two centuries on this walk, from the venerable Plaza where Los Angeles began in 1781 to a 1977 space-age hotel. Much of it is unknown even to Los Angeles residents.

And you experience a walker's downtown that refutes the city's exclusively car-borne image. You walk through four pedestrian malls from the past half-century, and into an emerging new city where foot traffic moves from block to block on bridges high above the street.

The walk takes you inside splendors of Victorian and Roaring Twenties buildings, secret from the street. You discover new gardens concealed below street level and above, even gardens planted on roofs to improve the view for the new supertowers all around.

Almost none of this is visible from a car.

Weekdays and Saturdays are best for a visit; many of the most exciting spots are closed on Sundays.

Parking
Park either at the Main Street lot opposite the Plaza or at the Union Passenger Terminal, the last great depot built in America. Worthy of an exploration, its 1939 Art Deco–Spanish great halls now seem wistful for the glory days when crowds surged to and from 60 trains a day and this was the traveler's first sample of Los Angeles.

The Plaza
A more lively introduction today is the Plaza, a bit of Old Los Angeles. Facing it are the old Plaza Church, built 1818–20 with the skilled help of captured pirate Joseph Chapman (a Baptist) and partly financed by the sale of seven barrels of brandy donated by Mission San Gabriel, 7 miles away. The dim interior breathes a quiet antiquity today.

Facing it also are the Pico House hotel restoration project (built by Pio Pico, California's last Mexican governor), and the city's first firehouse, restored down to the turntable for a horse-drawn pumper.

Narrated Plaza walking tours are given several days a week; inquire about times at the Pueblo de los Angeles office on the Plaza, or telephone 628-1274.

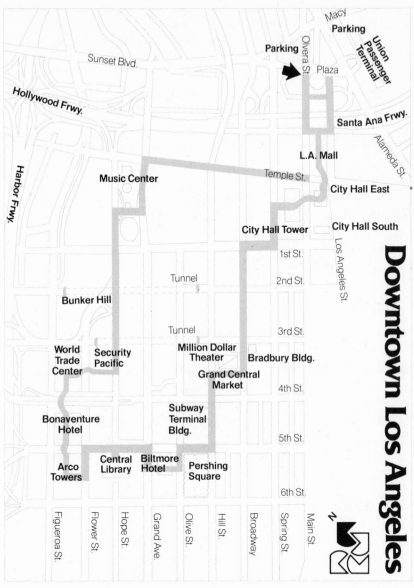

This walking tour is approximately 3¾ miles round trip.

Today's atmosphere is probably more colorful even than in the old days. It centers around the lacy wrought-iron *kiosko,* or Mexican-style bandstand, focal point for a fiesta at least once a month. Or it hovers about the pink, orange, yellow, and blue barrels of the Plaza fruit stand. As in Mexico, here you can buy a sliced mango or jicama doused with lime juice and sprinkled with salt and red-hot chile. Taste before you bite.

Olvera Street

And it fills Olvera Street, a pedestrian-way revived from an alley by citizen action 50 years ago as the first step in salvaging the historic heart of the city.

Starting at the north end of the Plaza, this block-long street is unusual: a tourist spot, but still a quality experience. English is only one of its languages, for the city's Spanish-speaking people like it, too.

Today the street is a cheerful mix of Mexican-inspired shops and stalls, pungent with the aroma of *carnitas* smoking on open-air grills, bright with the splashy colors of *piñatas* and paper flowers from Mexico, ringing with the song of strolling guitarists or the lilt of the hurdy-gurdy.

You can taste wines, have lunch or a snack, buy some excellent Mexican folk art (or some outright tourist trash), and just enjoy the lively street scene.

You can also visit the city's oldest house, the 1818 Avila adobe, and see the city's first brick house, now the Golondrina Restaurant. Its beams were salvaged from a shipwreck—a valuable source of lumber in this nearly timberless country.

Los Angeles Mall

By contrast, the Los Angeles Mall, south of the Santa Ana Freeway, is a quieter place, mostly hidden from the street. In its protected gardens tropical plants luxuriate among fountains and sculpture.

A notable first for city government, it has shops and restaurants on City Hall property. You can walk through the lower level, and cross under Temple Street, or choose city park up above and cross on a bridge. The curious tower bedecked with bright-colored Murano glass light fixtures is the Triforium; it puts on a light show computer-keyed to music—when it is in working order.

City Hall Tower: A Panoramic View from Downtown to the Sea

At City Hall East, near the south end of the mall, ride an elevator up to where you cross to the old City Hall in an enclosed pedestrian bridge above Main Street. Then take elevators up to the top for a panoramic view over downtown and from the distant San Gabriel Mountains south to the sea (open office hours, weekdays; afternoons only, weekends).

Two surprises await at Third and Broadway.

Bradbury Building

One surprise, on the southeast corner, is the Bradbury Building. Inside its drab exterior is one of the most electrifying sights in America, a soaring, skylit central court five stories high. Ride the slow openwork lift—oldest hydraulic elevator in the city—to the topmost balcony and walk down the ornate stairs for a stirring glimpse back into the last century.

The only major work of draftsman George Wyman, it is admired by architects the world over. Some have compared it with the Bibliothèque Sainte Geneviève in Paris, "only better." It was commissioned as a monument to himself by Colonel Louis Bradbury, who had made his fortune in Mexican mining, and whose mansion was nearby on Bunker Hill (now cleared for redevelopment).

Million Dollar Theatre

The other surprise, on the southwest corner, is the Million Dollar Theatre. Built in 1918, more than a decade before movies became talkies, it was promoter Sid Grauman's (Grauman's Chinese Theatre) first grand movie palace. Stop awhile to inspect its astonishing facade. A sculpture gallery of figures from performing arts in ages past, it includes bare feet dangling over 3rd Street.

Grand Central Public Market

Just south of the theater is the opening of the cavernous Grand Central Public Market. A block deep through to Hill Street, its aisles lead you through a bustling bazaar loaded with foods from around the world—with emphasis on the Mexican. This place, too, is almost bilingual, and many signs are in Spanish.

Tomatoes appear from Mexico in January and you see

such exotics as cooking bananas, papayas big as watermelons, cactus pads, and fruits, a dozen kinds of beans in bulk, and more kinds of chiles than you can imagine. Stalls are devoted to tortillas, sausages, cheeses, seafoods, coffees, teas, spices, wines, olive oils. It's an education and a temptation—as when you pass the burrito stand at lunchtime.

Biltmore Hotel

South on Hill, then over to Olive opposite Pershing Square is the Biltmore Hotel. Vintage 1923, its Renaissance-style grandeur has recently been restored.

Look in on its lobby, of cathedral-nave proportions, with a polychromed, ribbed, and vaulted ceiling, elaborate columns, and intricate balustrades. Then climb the stairs to the Galeria— a system of grand halls at the upper level opening on Grand Avenue. They are paneled in wood and colonnaded, with coffered and painted ceiling panels done by Giovanni Smeraldi, an artist brought from Palermo for the project.

Among the hotel's equally lavish public rooms, the Ballroom and the Biltmore Bowl—a supper club—were famous before World War II, and their social doings were broadcast during the golden age of radio. You may take a guided tour of the public spaces on weekdays by reservation. And you may attend a Sunday-afternoon musicale in spring or fall. For information, telephone 624-1011.

Central Library

In the next block west on 5th look inside the Central Library, one of the city's first "modern" buildings, built in 1926. Its second-floor rotunda is another interior space surprise, lofty under the pyramid-tipped tower, with high walls covered with California history murals by Dean Cornwell, popular illustrator of the period. Other murals are to be seen in the History and Children's rooms.

Again west on 5th, cross Flower Street to the looming black Arco Towers. Immediately below ground is a rarity in the Land of Sunshine, a subterranean shopping center.

Bonaventure Hotel

Cross 5th from Arco on a pedestrian bridge into the gleaming new Bonaventure Hotel, a cluster of one large and four smaller mirrored glass cylinders. The lobby is a space trip, six stories high, totally curvilinear, landscaped with lakes, enlivened by open air restaurants and bars and glass-capsule elevators that pass through the skylight ceiling.

Go to the eighth level, where you will find a pedestrian bridge high above 4th Street that takes you north into the World Trade Center. Covering a city block, the center houses an unsuspected two-story-high enclosed mall with shops devoted to imports and offices dealing with foreign trade.

From the mall still another bridge crosses Flower to the massive Security Pacific Bank headquarters, also a city block. You traverse the concourse level to come out in a circular hole-in-the-ground garden where sheets of water drop from high overhead into a pool shaded by weeping willows.

Then you ascend to street level atop Bunker Hill at the base of the 55-story building, with barren redevelopment area as neighbor. An immense red Calder steel stabile is the landmark, and the manicured grounds are a *de facto* public park—a genuine community contribution by the bank.

Go to the south end of this park and look across 4th to another roof garden. This one, planted by Arco, beautifies the top of a parking structure, another form of community service.

Music Center

Then go north on Hope to the Music Center. The three theaters and a charming plaza dominated by a Jacques Lipchitz bronze occupy an eminence that merits the term "acropolis." The great view is down the (nonpedestrian) County Mall to the landmark City Hall tower. You can buy tickets for performances, or to see the theaters, take a guided tour; call 972-7211 for information.

The return route is east, down 1st or Temple past Civic Center buildings to Main or Los Angeles, then north to the Plaza.

NEWPORT BEACH
Walter Houk

The climax of this walk through a reviving resort town is one of the most colorful native (and "authentic") minor spectacles in

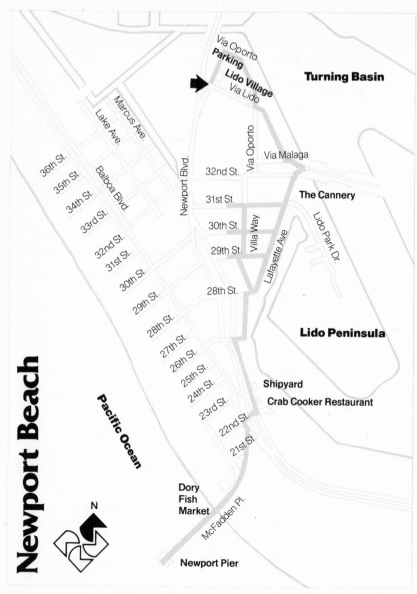

Newport Beach

Via Oporto

Parking

Lido Village

Via Lido

Turning Basin

Via Oporto

Via Malaga

Marcus Ave.

Lake Ave.

Balboa Blvd

36th St.

35th St.

34th St.

33rd St.

32nd St.

31st St.

30th St.

29th St.

28th St.

27th St.

26th St.

25th St.

24th St.

23rd St.

22nd St.

21st St.

Newport Blvd

32nd St.

31st St.

30th St.

29th St.

28th St.

Villa Way

Lafayette Ave

The Cannery

Lido Park Dr.

Lido Peninsula

Shipyard

Crab Cooker Restaurant

Pacific Ocean

N

Dory Fish Market

McFadden Pl.

Newport Pier

This walking tour is approximately 2 miles round trip.

Southern California, the Dory Fish Market, right on the beach. Both it and most of the territory you walk through are holdouts from the past.

Newport Beach got its start as the town at the end of the trolley line—the Big Red Cars of the old Pacific Electric system out of Los Angeles.

At first it was just a sandspit with tiny cottages on tiny lots plus fish canning and boat building on the channels of its small boat harbor. Then parts of it deteriorated, and cottages turned into shops or repair works, before the beach boom made the place fashionable.

Today the sandspit is definitely the high-rent district. Cottages now coexist with shops, the old beside the new or remodeled. Even factories, some of them imaginatively rehabilitated, now are prized for offices, boat lofts, and restaurants.

This transition from tacky to trendy (and all degrees in between) makes a walk here a voyage of discovery to find the gems amid the dross.

Parking

Start by parking—a problem on good summer beach days—in the parking structure on Via Lido, just off Newport Boulevard. Elsewhere parking is metered and limited to 2 hours.

Lido Village

You come out of the parking structure into an extraordinary private redevelopment project. Lido Village was converted from a row of two-story channel-front apartments into a complex of 75 shops around patios, off balconies, on the street and on the seawall. They sell everything from custom-ground coffees to yachts, from gourmet groceries to antique baby furniture.

Places to eat include a delicatessen and a bakery beside the seawall, and a new (but rusted) corrugated-iron warehouse with a garden dining area.

The unusual feature is the city street and sidewalks paved in brick. They are outfitted with elegant street lamps from which hang colorful flower baskets. Street furniture includes benches, bicycle racks, a tall clock, and fountains. It all comes together as an intimate, pedestrian-oriented village.

Cannery Village District

Proceeding east through a more conventional shopping area, at Lafayette Avenue go south to Lido Park Drive, at the end of a finger of a channel of Newport Harbor. Across the water is a seafood restaurant always crowded at noontime, with a dock where fishing-party boats load and debark. On the near corner is the Cannery, converted, complete with antique machinery, into a restaurant with a dark, lofty interior and a collection of old-time relics.

You are at a corner of the Cannery Village district, which extends from 32nd Street south to 28th Street and from Lafayette over to Newport Boulevard.

The best route through it is Villa Way, midway between Lafayette and Newport, going south and exploring such promising leads in either direction as strike your fancy.

You'll spot an ice house, a marine salvage store, a shop with about as complete a selection of fishing tackle as you'll find anywhere and a marine electronics store between two antique shops.

Three retail themes run through the area's miscellany: boats (you'll see sailboats, steam bilge cleaning, a parking lot for catamarans, yacht brokers, and ship building and repair); home-related wares (antiques, secondhand, and decorator and interior design places); and seafood (several shops, including a big new one, sell it fresh and one has it smoked).

There are also restaurants that range from the costly Ambrosia (dinner only) down to little sandwich places.

You come out on Newport Boulevard, headed south. On your left are two restaurants, one Mexican, one a boat-in place with a dock for customers, and yards full of boats for sale.

The Shipyard

Just beyond is the Shipyard. Head out to the seawall for a look at the colorful action on the channel, in the summertime the biggest boat traffic jam on the coast. A handsome office-building conversion from an actual shipbuilding factory, its marine railway is now a garden and a small beach, and it includes architects and an art gallery among its tenants. The complex also houses a supermarket of boats.

Crab Cooker Restaurant

You return to Newport Boulevard at the red Crab Cooker Restaurant (and seafood-restaurant market), a Newport Beach institution. Nearby the Old Spaghetti Factory inhabits a former movie theater.

Pick your way across the boulevard complex, a bit of traffic spaghetti left over from the old trolley right-of-way, to the colorful climax of the walk at the base of the Newport Pier.

Dory Fish Market

Here on the beach the Dory Fish Market operates every morning. The chief modern touch is that they have abandoned oars for outboard motors, but the operation still has overtones of antiquity. Dories set out to sea early, to return when they have a marketable catch.

Once on the beach, the fishermen set up umbrellas, get out their cutting boards, hone their knives, and are ready for business. You can buy rock cod, halibut, crabs, sea snails, and other seafood right out of the water—as fresh as can be found anywhere—and take it home wrapped in newspaper.

Knowing residents are there early. Visitors flock around with cameras to record the bright primary colors of the dory hulls. The action tapers off at midday (and prices may tend to weaken for the unsold remainder of the catch).

The Pier

The pier is worth a stroll out to the end. You can see what the relaxed fishermen are catching (if anything). And you get a good view back toward the beach and up and down the coast. Beyond the breaker line the sound of the surf is gone, and the quiet is surprising.

The landward end of the pier has nurtured a small cluster of shops and eateries, among them Alley West, a night spot with a certain local fame for its paintings of nudes and for its crab dinners.

The beachfront walk along here is also a bikeway. Beach cool among the kids includes two-wheeled trailers for surfboards towed behind bikes, or boards carried by the riders transported by skateboards.

Retrace your steps for the return trip. In the Cannery Village section you can return by Lafayette Street as an alternate to Villa Way.

LA JOLLA
David Clark

La Jolla is well known for its one-of-a-kind shops—the sort of places that celebrate the talents of the individual—the handmade—the rare. And yet, behind the beguiling facade of this affluent coastal town there exist lesser-known but no less fascinating nature-made spectacles.

Our tour begins with an exploration of one of these natural marvels, the Tidepool area that skirts the edge of the Pacific. Here you find a close view of a cross section of marine life and begin to understand just how delicately balanced our ecology is. Each creature in this microcosm (as in ours) is interdependent upon its neighbors and its environment for survival.

After pondering nature's incredible diversity, we return to walk among the little stores that front Girard Street. And, for a final change of pace, our tour ends with a visit to another one of nature's gifts—Torrey Pines Park.

Note: The Tidepool section of the La Jolla walk is best taken at low tide, when the pools are exposed and the marine life is visible. Check the newspaper for the time when low tide will occur. The lowest point of all in the 25-hour tide cycle occurs when the earth, moon, and sun are in line. This is called "minus" tide. In summer it occurs in the early morning, and in winter it takes place in the midafternoon.

How to Get There

La Jolla is 12½ miles north of San Diego. If you are coming from the north take Highway 5 to the La Jolla Village Road exit. Travel west on La Jolla Village Road, then turn left (south) on Torrey Pines Road, and right (west) on Prospect.

If you are coming from the south, take Highway 5 to the Ardath Road exit, opposite the turnoff for the Soledad Freeway. Travel west on Ardath until it turns into Torrey Pines Road. Continue west on Torrey Pines, then turn right onto Prospect.

At Prospect, turn right, sharply downhill, onto Coast Blvd., where a sign directs you to the La Jolla Cove. Park at the bottom of the hill, next to the Cove and Ellen Scripps Park.

The Tidepools

From La Jolla Cove the tidepools begin just beyond the rock formation known as Alligator Head, a rock headland

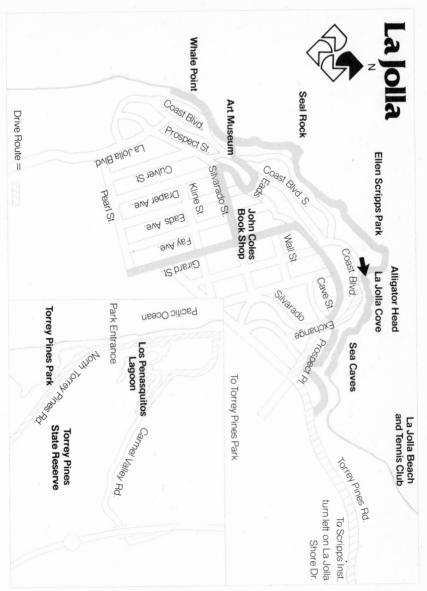

La Jolla

N

Seal Rock

Whale Point

Art Museum

Coast Blvd.

Prospect St.

La Jolla Blvd.

Culver St.

Silvarado St.

Kline St.

Draper Ave.

Eads Ave.

Pearl St.

Fay Ave.

Girard St.

Drive Route ≡

Ellen Scripps Park

Coast Blvd. S.

Eads

**John Coles
Book Shop**

Wall St.

Alligator Head
La Jolla Cove

Coast Blvd.

Cave St.

Silvarado

Exchange

Sea Caves

Prospect Pl.

**La Jolla Beach
and Tennis Club**

Torrey Pines Rd.

To Scripps Inst.
turn left on La Jolla
Shore Dr.

Pacific Ocean

Park Entrance

**Los Penasquitos
Lagoon**

North Torrey Pines Rd.

Carmel Valley Rd.

Torrey Pines Park

**Torrey Pines
State Reserve**

To Torrey Pines Park

This walking tour is approximately 3½ miles round trip.

pierced by a wave-cut arch. This cove beach is probably one of the most photographed sights in La Jolla. The rocks of the tidepool area can be very slippery, especially when they are wet or covered with algae, so be careful. Tennis shoes would probably be the best footwear.

The intertidal zone, the area on the beach between high and low tides, is perhaps the most densely populated place on earth. The rich mixture of nutrients in the pools creates a profusion of life forms which are fascinating to watch. It is not a peaceful world, however, for the different creatures are in constant competition. Each one is usually engaged in chewing on his neighbor's leg.

The tidepool creatures you will spot most easily are hermit crabs, starfish, mussels, and anemones. The hermit crab is the busiest inhabitant of the tidepools. With his vulnerable soft abdomen he finds protection by wearing a shell left behind by some other creature. Each inch he grows forces him out of his temporary abode to find a larger shell, so he is constantly house-hunting and fighting with other crabs over the best residences, much like any other prospective buyer in Southern California's real estate market.

Examine the rocks surrounding the tidepools and you will see tightly bunched clumps of shiny black mussels clinging there. Mussels live by filtering very small bits of food out of the water; a large one may sift through as much as 16 gallons in a day, and although it would seem that there would be safety in those bunches, mussels have enemies too.

The starfish is one. He uses the suction cups on his feet to pry open the mussel's shell, in a slow battle that may last for hours. And, if you notice neat, round holes in some of the shells scattered on the beach, these are caused by yet another enemy, the foot-long sea hare snail, which uses its filelike tongue to drill a hole in a mussel or clam shell.

It will be easy to identify the anemones because of their brilliant purple and green tentacles gracefully undulating in rhythm to the water. Their comely appearance belies their hungry goal. They sit in wait for an unwary fish to enter their ken; then they shoot out those tentacles to sting the creature and reel in the prey.

Look up and you will doubtlessly see numbers of seagulls gliding about the shore in wait for the right moment to sweep down and grab a meal. They dive into the pools to pick up an

edible tidbit as it becomes exposed by the receding tide, and
they carry the harder-to-eat shelled creatures into the air to
break the shells by dropping them. As you can see, having a
shell is no real protection in the tidepools. Someone is always
trying to pry your house open, drill through it, or drop you onto
a rock.

If you happen to be making this walk at dusk or dawn and
notice a shower of sparks whenever you kick the sand, this natural fireworks display is caused by a light-sensitive variety of
plankton that also causes "red tides" at the beach.

Sighting Whales at Whale Point

After Alligator Head, the shoreline curves increasingly to
the south. Head for Seal Rock. You will find it at the end of a
little cove opposite the only high-rise structure on the beach.

After Seal Rock you will notice another small cove, beyond
which a wall and lifeguard tower stand out from the coastline,
marking Whale Point. A little farther up the shore from the
cove, you'll see the gardens and building of the La Jolla Museum of Contemporary Art. Remember this spot between Seal
Rock and Whale Point, for this is where you will exit from the
beach toward the other loop of our tour that takes you to the
shops of La Jolla.

From Whale Point, in the months of December, January,
and February, look for gray whales making their southern migration. This gigantic ocean inhabitant journeys 7,000 miles between its breeding grounds in Baja, California, and the artic
waters where it feeds on billions of krill (tiny shrimplike fish that
eat plankton) in the summer.

Gray whales have been making this trip regularly for 8
million years. Cruising at about 4 knots per hour (their top
speed is 10 knots) they usually travel at a distance between ½
and 3 miles from the shore. Since whales are mammals, who
evolved from land back to the sea approximately 100 million
years ago, they must come to the surface to breathe air. You
can easily spot their geyserlike spouts when they stop to take a
breath.

Before whale hunting began as many as 1,000 gray whales
might be seen in a day from a spot such as Whale Point. San
Diego Bay occasionally became unsafe for small ships because
of the many whales passing through the harbor, but now the
numbers of the gray and other whales have been drastically

reduced by hunting. In the old days, when whaling was done in sailing vessels, the gray whale acquired the name "hard head" because when threatened it would turn to fight and ram the wooden boats with its head. Today, whales stand no such chance against the steel-hulled modern whaling fleets.

La Jolla Museum of Contemporary Art

When you reach the "No Trespassing" sign and the apartment complex at the end of Wipeout Beach, walk back the way you came to the cove where the La Jolla Museum of Contemporary Art stands. From the cove walk up the beach to the street. Turn left (north). At this point, Coast Blvd. South converges with Coast Blvd. Take Coast Blvd. South (the right fork) to Eads Avenue. Turn right (east) on Eads. Walk up the hill, then turn right (south) on Prospect to the entrance of the La Jolla Museum of Contemporary Art, where Prospect meets Silverado. Accurately described by its name, this museum presents a full range of exhibits and performances.

At the corner of Eads and Prospect, you will pass John Cole's Bookshop, in a rambling old house, the rooms of which are filled with an excellent collection. There is an especially good concentration of children's literature; and perhaps the large offering of Dr. Seuss books is attributable to the fact that their creator lives nearby.

Girard Street: For Browsing and Shopping

This main street of La Jolla is filled with a fascinating spread of little shops between Pearl and Prospect. You may proceed directly toward Prospect by turning left on Girard, or you can spend a longer amount of time wandering among the shops by turning right, walking as far as Pearl, and then coming back.

Like many other Southern California communities, La Jolla's roots are in the real estate boom of the 1880s, when the Sante Fe Railroad entered the region in competition with the Southern Pacific. Southern California was then promoted throughout the world for its beautiful climate, and the floods of tourists and health-seekers began. In only ten years, San Diego County's population increased fivefold. Real estate speculation boiled at a pace even more feverish than is the case today and among people newly arrived and unknown to each other. As one observer said, "It was a golden opportunity for the fakir and humbug and the man with a past he wished forgotten."

Land development in La Jolla began in 1887. Among the first activities of the La Jolla developers was the planting of 2,000 eucalyptus, cedar, and palm trees. Like most of the Southern California coast, in contrast to the once heavily wooded East Coast, the terrain was virtually barren until trees were planted on it.

From the shops, proceed north on Girard to Prospect. Turn right (east) on Prospect and continue to Exchange. From Prospect at Exchange, turn left to walk back toward the La Jolla Cove on Coast Blvd. Be careful of the traffic at this point.

The Sea Caves—A Coast Walk

At the Cave Curio Shop, which is on your right as you walk down Coast Blvd., you can descend through a tunnel to one of La Jolla's sea caves. Just beyond the shop, take the dirt path to the right, marked on the map as Coast Walk, for a walk along the cliff tops.

Seven caves in a row have been worn in the cliff face by the action of the waves, with many terraces created in the cliffs by erosion. Nesting seagulls and cormorants are ensconced on the terraces like tenants in an apartment building. The black shale which you see on the cliffs was formed there 70 million years ago, when instead of seagulls, giant flying reptiles, the pterosaurs, dove for fish in these waters.

Scripps Institution of Oceanography

Across the bay to the north, you will see the red-tile roofs of the La Jolla Beach and Tennis Club, formerly a favorite spot for smuggling opium and Chinese workers into the country. Beyond the club the 1,000-foot pier of the Scripps Institution of Oceanography is visible. One of the world's oldest and largest centers of marine study, the institution houses the Scripps Aquarium (open to the public 9 to 5, seven days a week). The Aquarium has some excellent exhibitions which might help you to further identify some of the tidepool creatures that you have seen today.

When you reach the end of Coast Walk, turn around and pick up your car at the La Jolla Cove. Return to Highway 5 the way that you came. If you wish to visit the Scripps Institution of

Oceanography, take Torrey Pines Road to the left. Make a left on La Jolla Shores Drive and follow La Jolla Shores until the Institution appears on your left.

Torrey Pines—Rare Survivors of a Moister Climate

If you have more time to spend in La Jolla, make a visit to Torrey Pines State Park. There is an admission fee of $1.50 per car for entrance to the park, and on weekends it is best to go in the morning. The number of people allowed to enter is limited to preserve both your feeling of space and the delicate ecological balance of the site. To reach the park continue on Torrey Pines Road until the entrance appears on your left.

The Torrey Pines which stand here, gnarled and twisted by the ocean breezes, are rare survivors of a time, approximately 11,000 years ago, when the climate of Southern California was more moist and Torrey Pine forests dotted the coast. The dramatic sandstone bluffs are washed with color—red coming from iron oxide deposits, and green from the fossils of sea life—and sculpted by erosion into trenches and gullies that take on new forms with a change in light, or the play of your imagination.

Los Penasquitos Lagoon

The island side of the park overlooks Los Pensaquitos Lagoon. It may be approached by continuing north on Torrey Pines Road and then by turning right (east) on Carmel Valley Road.

Los Penasquitos Lagoon is a favorite spot for large shorebirds, such as the blue heron, the night heron, and the egret. Here marsh plants have had to make unusual adaptations to the high salt level of the water, developing the ability to pump the salt out through their leaves. Look closely and you will see a light cover of salt on them. Mule deer must like these salty morsels since they may often be seen feeding on them at the south end of the lagoon.

To make your way back from the Lagoon, return to Highway 5 by continuing east on Carmel Valley Road.

AUTHORS' BIOGRAPHIES

WAYNE BARRETT is a free-lance writer who lives near Washington, D.C. He formerly worked for the National Geographic Society.

ROY BONGARTZ lives in Rhode Island and writes on travel and the outdoors for such publications as *Travel & Leisure*, the *New York Times*, and others.

GEORGE S. BUSH regularly writes on travel and recreation for a number of national magazines. His articles have appeared in *Better Homes & Gardens, Holiday, Vista USA, Skiing, Flying, Apartment Life,* and *Travel & Leisure.*

GEORGE N. CANTOR is travel writer for the *Detroit News* and the author of *The Great Lakes Guidebook,* published by the University of Michigan Press.

DAVID CLARK is a doctoral candidate in history at U.C.L.A. and the author of *L.A. on Foot.* He teaches history for U.C.L.A. Extension and California State University.

KAREN CURE has written articles on travel and recreation for *Travel & Leisure, Diversion, Vista USA, Better Homes & Gardens, Newsday, Family Circle,* and the *Chicago Tribune.* Her book *Mini Vacations USA* was published by Follett in 1976. *The Travel Catalogue,* her latest book, was published by Holt, Rinehart and Winston in the spring of 1978.

HARRY AND PHYL DARK are Missourians with many years of free-lance writing and photography experience in the travel, recreation, and family-life fields. Their words and pictures appear in several metropolitan newspapers and more than a score of the nation's magazines of multi-million circulation.

LYNN DETRICK, A professional writer, lives and walks in Pittsburgh.

MARGOT PATTERSON DOSS has been called the dean of contemporary walker-writers. Author, naturalist, and television personality on the prizewinning KPIX-TV Evening Show, Ms. Doss originated "San Francisco at Your Feet," the walking column she writes for the Sunday *San Francisco Chronicle.*

BILL HIBBARD has been travel writer, travel photographer, and travel editor of the *Milwaukee Journal* for 13 years. He is also Midwest Regional Editor for *Ski Magazine* and has written free-lance articles for *Better Homes & Gardens, Travel Magazine,* and airline in-flight magazines.

WALTER HOUK, formerly an editor of *Sunset Magazine,* is a writer-photographer who specializes in Southern California reporting.

RON D. JOHNSON is a free-lance travel writer for the *St. Paul Dispatch, Carte Blanche, Chicago Tribune,* and other magazines and newspapers. He is author of the book *Faces of Minnesota.*

MIKE KALINA is Travel Editor for the *Pittsburgh Post Gazette.* His travel articles have appeared in major papers throughout the country.

JANICE KRENMAYR is the author of *Footloose in Seattle,* Vols. I and II, and *Footloose Around Puget Sound.* For five years she wrote a weekly column on walking for the *Seattle Sunday Times Magazine.*

JOHN NEARY is a free-lance writer of books and magazines, and lives in Tesuque, New Mexico. His articles have appeared in *Life, People, Americana,* and *Smithsonian.*

TERENCE O'DONNELL is associated with the Oregon Historical Society and is co-author of *Portland, a Historical Sketch and Guide.*

EDWARDS PARK, a native Bostonian, was once a feature writer on the *Boston Globe.* He is now one of the Board of Editors at *Smithsonian Magazine.*

C. RAY SMITH is a critic of architecture and interiors and author of *Supermannerism,* a book about American architecture and design in the 1960s. He got his first interest in architecture by trying to date buildings as an insatiable walker and gawker in New York.

MARK A. STUART is an assistant editor of the *Bergen Record,* and has been writing about travel for 15 years, the last 12 for the *Record.*

DIANE C. THOMAS is a free-lance journalist who lives and works in Atlanta. She writes regularly for *Atlanta Magazine* and other national publications.

RICHARD WAGER has been a newspaperman 35 years, 14 of which have been as a travel writer and editor, and is author of *Golden Wheels,* a history of the 115 automobiles made in Cleveland and northeastern Ohio, 1892–1932.